# THE XINJIANG PROCEDURE

ISBN (paperback): 978-1-968919-20-7
ISBN (hardback): 978-1-968919-22-1
ISBN (ebook): 978-1-968919-23-8

ARMINLEAR

Armin Lear Press, Inc.
215 W Riverside Drive, #4362
Estes Park, CO 80517

# THE XINJIANG PROCEDURE

# ETHAN GUTMANN

ARMINLEAR

*To Bavi, who did it for his people*

**Author's note:** I have a "reader-first" policy. Despite the legitimate Uyghur preference for "East Turkestan," I use the better-known Chinese "Xinjiang" in the title and throughout most of this book. This is not a political statement. My intent is to make this book as accessible as possible for the casual reader. The same is true of my use of the term "Western"—which I use as a shorthand for both eastern and western democracies.

# CONTENTS

| | | |
|---|---|---|
| 1 | Don't Cry Rukiye | 1 |
| 2 | Postmortem | 49 |
| 3 | Inch by Bloody Inch | 105 |
| 4 | Over the Hills | 151 |
| 5 | The Perfect 28 | 213 |
| 6 | And Far Away | 283 |
| 7 | The Country of Lost Uyghurs | 301 |
| 8 | The Road to Slavery | 347 |
| 9 | Hearts and Lungs | 373 |
| | Afterword | 403 |
| | Acknowledgements | 413 |
| | About the Author | 421 |
| | Index | 423 |

# 1
# DON'T CRY RUKIYE

Once there was a little girl who played in the wild apricot trees with her brothers and always wore her headscarf. Rukiye—that's the little girl's name—was four years old. And the youngest of her brothers was four years older than Rukiye. And her middle brother was yet another four years older. And her eldest brother was four years older again—but the important part was that her brothers had a motorcycle.

Every day her brothers would talk about riding the motorcycle somewhere in the hills, not far from Ghulja. And every day, little Rukiye, like a hound dog seeing her master pick up the shotgun, would know that something was up. And Rukiye would beg them to take her along.

Sometimes, if they were just going to the village store or something like that, she would ride on the lap of her youngest brother. But most times her brothers made excuses, or they would even lie to her and say they had changed their minds about going anywhere. Then, just when Rukiye turned her back, they would disappear down the road in a cloud of dust.

Rukiye plotted her revenge. When the afternoon turned to twilight, she hid in the old shed and waited patiently until she heard the whining and popping of the motorcycle echoing on the hills and getting closer and closer. Only then, at just the right moment, she burst from the shed like a *Yalmavus*—a demon-witch—and they all fell off the bike.

One winter there was a great snow, and her brothers decided to take the motorcycle into town. But the wheels got stuck, so her brothers left the whining, popping motorcycle on the side of the road and made a deal with their friends. In the end, they all rode horses over the snow-covered hills, going from village to village and playing in the snow until it was dark. At the dinner table that night, her brothers solemnly kept a wooden switch on the table because Rukiye was a picky eater. Everyone knew they were a "tall and strong family." If Rukiye finished her food, the switch would stay on the table, and she would grow up to be like them.

Under the covers, at the end of that magical day, little Rukiye knew that she loved her brothers so much, more than anyone in the world, maybe even more than her mama and papa.

*  *  *

Twenty-three years later, when Rukiye recalled her brothers' stern expressions as she cleaned her plate, her voice began to shake, and the words came out in gasps, her face briefly contorting in an expression that somehow combined joy, love, and bottomless sorrow. Perhaps there was a hint of guilt playing on that face, too, but I'll get to that.

That buried sorrow, however suppressed, was significant: In three days of full-time interviews, Rukiye only fought against tears three or four times—always very briefly, and not even once from self-pity.

We were in my favorite interview spot in the world, a small breakfast room perched over the Hagia Sophia, Topkapi and the Bosphorus. And I was with one of the greatest Uyghur translators in the world: Rahima Mahmut, Uyghur activist and folk singer. We had come to Istanbul to interview Uyghur survivors of all stripes: a Uyghur engineer who had created the first facial recognition capable of racial profiling, a Uyghur rebel who had trained in the hidden corners of what he called occupied East Turkestan, and two Uyghur females who had experienced *something* while they were in Chinese captivity. If the Chinese Communist Party were selecting Uyghurs for organ harvesting, perhaps they had observed a lead or a clue, maybe in connection with a medical examination. Yet I also sensed that both women—Gulbahar Jelilova, middle-aged and recently sprung from the camps, and Rukiye Perhat, from an earlier vintage of the long-standing Uyghur persecution—had seen the demon *Yalmavus* up close.

Rahima informed me that Rukiye had already been interviewed by several camera crews from major television networks. Apparently, the interviews were, at best, ten-minute affairs where the correspondent simply pressured Rukiye to pull up her sleeves so they could photograph the scars (mostly from cigarette burns) that the prison staff had left on her body. As a former TV reporter back in the 1990s, I understood that this display was perceived as a time-effective approach of establishing witness credibility (although anyone with a grudge can give themselves scars if they are determined enough). Yet as the main point of a television interview, it verged on human rights porn, a circus freak show that demeans everyone who enters the tent. By contrast, when Rukiye walked into our tent, I was unprepared for her appearance, small, beautiful, and confident in her movements—and her eyes, watchful, guarded, and intelligent. I opened the interview by asking Rukiye to tell me about her childhood.

When Rahima translated this, Rukiye looked at me as if I were some sort of exotic species from another planet, or just a local half-wit. She started to answer, then stopped, and turned to Rahima:

"Is he serious? I've been in so many interviews. No one ever asked me about my childhood."

"Yes, he's serious. He wants to know about your family, your parents, your brothers. Everything. He's writing a book. You can speak freely, and you can take your time."

After a couple of hours talking about her childhood and adolescence—nothing was rushed—Rukiye suddenly addressed me directly: "These questions that you ask me. No one has ever asked me these questions before. So, I will not keep anything private. I will tell all. I want to give everything."

When faced with a young woman wearing a headscarf, one of the reflexive mistakes of Western media is to counterbalance our assumed "Islamophobia" by trying to make them harmless, to reduce them to passive victims. Rukiye's story is a little more interesting than that. So, I am profoundly grateful to Rukiye for giving "everything"—because without the imprints of Rukiye's childhood, we cannot make sense of the scars on her arms.

\* \* \*

Rukiye was eight years old when the Chinese guards came for her father. She admits that "she really didn't know him before then." Her father was tall, and his skin was deep brown, while Rukiye is small and fair, but "I have his nose and his eyebrows." She mainly remembers sitting with him while he drank tea and talked with his friends, her mother and father always had so many of them. He was an outgoing man—always joking, always finding ways to make people comfortable. In a word he was charismatic. And she still remembers the warm, secure feeling of sitting beside him.

When Rukiye had just turned five, in 1994, her father moved the family to Urumqi, the capital of the Xinjiang Uyghur Autonomous

Region. He set up a rug retail store, with a large enough space that he could hold classes for the children of the neighborhood in the back room—and perhaps some of their parents too—far from the eyes of the street.

It was only after his arrest in 1997—charged with the "illegal instruction" of children—and after her father's return from detention—perhaps a month, or six weeks—and after a lengthy recovery from—well, Rukiye didn't know what they had done to him, but he couldn't really walk right anymore. And it was only then that she began to really listen to what he was saying, as he sat and drank tea with his friends.

This was in the wake of the Ghulja massacre, where hundreds of Uyghurs were executed for a single demonstration at the town hall—anyway, her father didn't allow her to sit by his side anymore. Perhaps he wanted to distance Rukiye from the danger, from any hint of culpability. Yet his voice carried. So Rukiye, no longer interested in the motorcycle, would sit on the rugs in the showroom, and stay very still so she could focus on the sounds of her father constructing an argument: the rhythm of him laying the foundations, the staccato of the girders rising, and the booming climax, the lighting of the tower, her father's vision of what was to be done. Although she wouldn't have put it this way back then, Rukiye became aware that her father was an expert in Uyghur literature and history, and a committed Uyghur nationalist—although the "Chinese conquerors," her father said, would call him a "separatist" or a "terrorist."

"Was he a terrorist?" I asked.

"He was a businessman who cared about his people." Rukiye replied, looking me in the eye. I realized that my question was too stripped down, too close to the language she experienced in Chinese interrogation. I backed off, and approached it another way, asking Rukiye to tell me about her father's parents.

They were both dead. Little Rukiye had only been dimly aware of the circumstances. After her father's arrest that she learned—perhaps her brothers told her?—that her grandparents had been declared "black class," that is, wealthy by the standards of the time—the Great Cultural Revolution, and a relatively impoverished place, Ghulja. Yet like a black man who owned a larger house than a poor white man in the antebellum South, the outcome was predictable. Chinese forces—officials or perhaps Red Guards—murdered Rukiye's grandparents. Her father had shielded Rukiye, perhaps hoping that ignorance of this crime might allow Rukiye to avoid a similar fate.

Rukiye knew her father was passionate about Uyghur survival but tormented by anxiety over his inability to protect his family. After his arrest, everyone in the family, particularly her brothers, had a sense that surveillance was everywhere. Her brothers stopped telling Rukiye about where they went with the motorcycle, explaining: "Our homeland is the most important thing that we have now, Rukiye. We must fight for it, and you must learn to be independent." Her father would only speak about his wife when she had left the house, and he was safely alone with his friends. She had never heard her father cry before, but when he briefly allowed himself to imagine what might happen to her, he began sobbing uncontrollably. It frightened Rukiye a little, but she wasn't sure that she fully understood.

Her father's "ignorance plan" for Rukiye might even have worked, but Rukiye had already fallen in love with the tower he had constructed. She had not realized "how strong, how much integrity he had. How much he cared. How great were his responsibilities." Rukiye knew her father did not want political power. He simply believed with all his heart that "education is the key to Uyghur survival." She vowed to live by those words.

Yet there were dark issues that Rukiye did not really understand.

Her father spoke about how the Chinese had devised "a plan for the Uyghurs." Rukiye recalled overhearing her father talk about a specific incident in a particular prison where "Ten men were taken away for medical exams. Then they died. It's a mystery. But it's always the healthy men that end up missing." And then, Rukiye thought she heard her father talking about "hearts," and then "kidneys" and at one point he said, "the liver." But she knew that, whatever it was that he was talking about, he would somehow protect her from this too.

Rukiye was twelve years old in the early morning when six cars full of black-uniformed Chinese police came for her family. The police handcuffed everyone, but Rukiye was still little, so she wasn't shackled. A policeman acting as an interpreter announced that their father was accused of "terrorism" and "instigating anti-government activities." Then the family was forcibly separated and driven to the local prison in separate cars. Rukiye was placed in her own cell, just like the rest of the family.

The next day the Chinese armed police interrogated her: Who came to your house? Who came to the store? What did they talk about? It was easy for Rukiye, just twelve years old, to feign ignorance, particularly when her accusers seemed to already have all the answers. She didn't know about her brothers, but the real point of the Perhat detention seemed to have something to do with medical testing.

It began with an elaborate blood test, an x-ray, and an ultrasound. Then it was four consecutive days of testing, each spent in a different clinic at the hospital with a specific specialty: the kidneys, the liver, the lungs and breathing, and finally, the heart. Rukiye does not remember a specific clinic for the eyes, but she remembers a lengthy and comprehensive vision test.

Finally, on the fifth day, the guards escorted her into a room with a strange-looking machine that looked like a *girde nan*, a sort of Uyghur bagel that Rukiye had seen in the markets. From her description of the device, it appears that the Chinese authorities had decided to CT-scan Rukiye's brain. As the assistants prepared her, a woman finished with the machine was just on her way out. Seeing Rukiye, she stopped, and looked at Rukiye with wide eyes, that seemed to say: *You are so young. What are they doing to you? Why are they looking at your head?* A Uyghur doctor quickly intervened and repeated the same thing that Rukiye had heard for four days running: "Don't worry about it Rukiye. It's just orders from above."

"Why are you doing this? I'm healthy."

"We're just doing you a favor," the doctor said. "Ordinary people don't get this level of care."

There was a final hurdle. Rukiye had never had a full gynecological exam, so she was uncomfortable that a Chinese doctor, even a female, could have such access to her genitals. The doctor administered a cervical swab. Perhaps because the entire atmosphere of a prison hospital is so severe, Rukiye bled and spotted "for weeks." Rukiye suspected that the injury was intentional, and when she had brief access to her younger brother in a chance meeting, she whispered to him about it. He wept at the thought of what had been done to her.

After sixteen days, the entire family was released. While it was confirmed early in the testing process that the family had no blood disorders, no birth defects, no congenital anomalies—the Chinese guards had even commented on the blood tests ("Wow. So healthy."), yet Rukiye's mother was forcibly sterilized during the sixteen days—or shortly afterwards, Rukiye was not sure about the exact timing. Either way, the medical explanation given was "inflammation." Ten years later, mass sterilization of Uyghur women would be recognized as an established fact.[1]

Returning home, her father connected all this medical attention to his family to "organ harvesting"—a phrase that was unfamiliar to Rukiye. Her mother chimed in, saying that she had witnessed the aftermath of a 22-year-old getting a kidney extraction while they were in detention.

Rukiye had faith that her father would reveal the real situation over time, in his own way. When her father was back with his friends, and Rukiye was sitting quietly in the showroom, her father revealed follow-up "health checks" for everyone in the family but Rukiye and himself. His friends kept remarking on the high rate of cancer among Uyghurs, and that kidney failure seemed to be on the rise, but her father dismissed these as distractions, saying: "This situation is beyond the ignorant Uyghur imagination. The risk is extreme. The majority are still not aware of the Chinese government plans."

The final time her father was arrested, Rukiye was 13 years old. This time, it was over before it started. All she remembers is that it was cold that afternoon (probably late Autumn 2002), and the courtyard of her house had been occupied by ten armed men in plain clothes. Her mother was standing by what appeared to be a wrapped body on some sort of makeshift pallet. The men's rifles, and above all, her mother's eyes, made it clear that Rukiye shouldn't come any closer. She watched as the men presented her mother with a document, although they made it equally clear that she had no right to read it. She signed it anyway. With the CCP's execution and burial procedures legally sorted, her father's body was quickly carted out of the courtyard into a van and driven away under the weak afternoon sun.

---

1    Adrian Zenz, "Sterilizations, IUDs, and Mandatory Birth Control: The CCP's Campaign to Suppress Uyghur Birthrates in Xinjiang," Jamestown Foundation China Brief, July 21, 2020.

\* \* \*

For Rukiye's father, Islam was about action, not words. You make a promise to God, you commit to fulfilling it. If your words and actions are in harmony, God will respond. *Insha'Allah*, if Allah wills it, the phrase of the fatalist, passive Uyghur, did not exist in her father's personal vocabulary.

After her father's death, Rukiye studied the Koran with great intensity. Through word of mouth, she offered herself as a Muslim teacher for young people in the district. She would exploit any makeshift space as a classroom, so long as it was hidden. Yet the CCP has always regarded adherence to Islam in Xinjiang as little more than a hiding place for Uyghur separatism. I asked Rukiye: "Given the repression and surveillance, why did you decide to teach Koran?"

She replied without artifice: "The CCP had made the decision to wipe out the Uyghurs. We had to fight—and my father always said that education was our weapon. It's important to die fighting."

\* \* \*

Rukiye recalls that "we all wore thick coats," so it was probably a cold day in early November 2008. Usually, Rukiye taught the Koran (almost exclusively reciting the Koran from memory) to her young students on Saturday afternoons. This time they would make a weekend of it, starting at 10 am, and the Saturday night sleepover was a special treat, as if they were sleeping over at the mosque itself. There were sixteen children and teenagers in all, ranging from nine- or ten-year-olds to a boy who, at 18, was a year older than Rukiye. Of course, they could not do this openly, so Rukiye had arranged to use a friend's basement not far from the train station. It was clean and nice, and they had all brought food and refreshments. Late in the evening, everyone changed into their nighties and pajamas and slippers. With a curtain hung through the middle to separate the boys and girls, they settled down to sleep.

At 2am the basement door was kicked in, and a unit of State Security police, guns drawn, surrounded them from all sides of the room. The only words was a single barked command in the Uyghur language—"Face the wall!" Everyone stayed silent while they listened to the policeman stomping through the house, searching for religious texts and paraphernalia. Then the police pulled out cattle prods, slipped black hoods over the children's heads, and, with two policemen flanking each child, guided them to the vans and police cars idling in the cold night. Within minutes, they found themselves in a basement cell, somewhere near the center of Urumqi. They were left, as if for dead, for three days with no food and water.

It's difficult to survive without water for two, let alone three days, so when the cell door opened and they were told, "Prepare yourselves for questioning," it was almost a relief. The black hoods returned, and ten police escorted them to a glass room, a sort of viewing deck with bench seating, inside a much larger and brightly lit room. The big room was bare but filthy, the floor peeling, the walls smeared from some sort of repetitive handling, like a monkey house at a zoo. Seven people, both males and females, were being herded in. Because they were naked, they stood awkwardly covering their genitals. They are Uyghur, Rukiye thought, and they are all somewhere around the age of 35—and that was her last bit of rational observation for the night. In fewer than 60 seconds, a group of armed police in full uniform, clearly professionals, strode briskly into the room, wooden sticks in hand, and the show began. After chasing down the Uyghurs who tried to lunge for the door, the police cornered them all and then systematically beat them—"so hard, so severely"—for perhaps 30 minutes (it was difficult for Rukiye to make time estimates for us; she admitted that time probably slowed down under the dual conditions of shock and dehydration). As the children screamed—it seemed impossible not to react to watching the assault by at least moaning or rocking back and forth—one of the police guards responded almost gently to the children, in a sort of whisper:

"Be quiet. These people are religious extremists. They refused to confess. If you follow the same path, the consequences for you will be even worse. If you cooperate, if you admit that you are following the path of religious extremism, you will be released rather quickly."

Outside the glass, the police were dragging the naked, bleeding Uyghurs through the doorway by their feet—as if they were already dead, Rukiye thought.

About an hour later they were taken to a new room. This time it had three walls made of glass. But Rukiye had trouble identifying much more about the physical plant as two of the children—the two youngest, Hadachan, whom she believed was 9 or 10, and Imam, 11 or 12—were taken away from the group and forced to stand against the wall on the far side of the room.

Rukiye often used to ask the two of them, "You are both so young. Why aren't you out playing and having fun?" Both agreed this was more important. Hadachan told Rukiye that his older brother had been beaten to death, so he wanted to grow up to be a policeman.

Then six policemen came into the room and beat them to death.

"How did you know they were dead?"

"They put them into bags."

It didn't happen all at once. Three of the policemen—the killers, it was clearly their job—had ear attachments. All six just stood there initially and waited for about five minutes. The boy was fidgeting, so one of the three policemen struck the boy a couple of times on the shoulders. Another minute passed, then suddenly the three men began raining blows on both children. There was a camera in the room, and Rukiye suspects that the policemen had just received an external kill order.

The children made a dash towards Rukiye the same way that children, faced with a wild animal, instinctively run towards an adult. The police tackled them before they got close to her, dragging them back to the center of the room as they called out for their mothers. Then one policeman took turns holding their arms behind the child while the other policeman inflicted the most severe damage that they could on the child's skull, face, and ribs, until the child went limp.

Rukiye was screaming too: "What is their crime? Why are you doing this? I'm older. I'm responsible. Take me. Beat me. Beat me instead."

The policemen flanking Rukiye were very relaxed—as if it were a routine on-Tuesdays-we-kill-kids operation. Rukiye turned to the Uyghur officer: "Why can't you just stop them? They're your children too." The officer replied evenly, almost politely, in Uyghur, "You should think about your own life. Your turn is coming." The other guard, a Han Chinese policeman was clearly annoyed by Rukiye's shouting in Uyghur, so he simply hit her as hard as he could, gouging her flesh with some metal object. (Rukiye still has the scar. I didn't take a photograph.)

As she told the story to Rahima and me—"The boy was in his pajamas and the girl was in her nightgown and there was blood everywhere."—Rukiye was breathing heavily, having trouble, gasping that she did not want to see the panic or the horror or the faces of the killers again, "These people were born human. But they had no human emotion. They were passionate, but like Devils. Or monsters. The beating was designed to be fatal."

Rukiye noticed two policemen bringing in a stretcher and some black body bags. "They ended up using the bags. The stretcher just sat there. . . ."

There was no time to grieve. The black hoods were shoved on

again, and the police marched the depleted group back to their original room where a policeman addressed them: "If you cooperate with us, you will have incentives. Otherwise, the results will be even worse than what you have witnessed."

They were given steamed buns, but no water. So Rukiye kicked the cell-door like a maniac until the guards brought some. Of course, the water was not enough for them all, and she found herself handing down her ration to the younger children. The police broke up the group, dispersing them to new cells and Rukiye found herself alone and dreadfully thirsty. She also found a sort of clarity, the same feeling that many people get when things finally go to the dogs, when they hit rock bottom, the same feeling a soldier gets when he finally enters combat. No more waiting. No more fear. Here is the Yalmavus. "Even though I was quite young, I was mature in my thoughts." Rukiye said to me. "I prepared myself. And I knew what happened to those children is going to happen to me very soon."

\* \* \*

Rahima Mahmut, Rukiye Perhat, and the author in Istanbul. Photo courtesy of Hotel Valide Sultan.

*   *   *

A personal word here. Perhaps it would help the reader if I told you that Rahima and I couldn't get the children out of our minds for several days.

But I would also like to take you backstage for a moment, because Rukiye is an interesting witness, and a challenge. We say she was arrested in 2008 when she was eighteen. Yet she remembered her arrest as taking place when she was seventeen. She didn't really know, so we are going on the word of Rukiye's aunt. But her aunt's estimate of her birth—on February 14, 1989—came later in Rukiye's life, was part and parcel of a false identity, and may have been a legal device to get her out of China.

So Rukiye is not good with years. She's not particularly good with describing her physical surroundings either; her account of what was—probably—one-way glass where she observed the seven naked Uyghurs being beaten sounded as if she were trying to walk us through an alien spaceship. Rukiye-time is always a little elastic too. I doubt that it took 20 minutes to kill two children. And I wonder if there was any glass separating her from the children—why else would they have tried to run to her when the first blows started raining down?

Yet Rukiye's ability to notice certain details—particularly when operating on three days of starvation, awed me: There was a camera. Three policemen wore ear attachments. As if it were a choreographed dance, they suddenly murdered two children. Did they receive a remote command to kill? That feels plausible. And there is little question in my mind that the Uyghur policeman said: "Don't shout, your turn will come," or words very close to that.

The death of children as they screamed "Oh mommy!" may haunt you too for a few days. But that will pass. In a conversation, a few weeks on, you might recall that Gutmann's book had some disturbing moments. Ten years on, you will recall that some bad things happened to the Uyghurs back in the day. Well, that distancing, that act of forgetting, is exactly what happened to Rukiye.

Rukiye's occasional tendency to tell stories backwards wasn't that different from other survivors, particularly Falun Gong, whom I've interviewed. It's a trauma effect. Part of moving on with one's life involves active amnesia. And when some people like Rahima and I come along, for Rukiye, it must have been like digging through old letters in the attic—the final correspondence is usually the one on top, the first one retrieves from the box. To go further, to remember a specific day or incident, Rukiye had to cross contaminated, forbidden zones. Or at the very least, Rukiye had to flip the switches on memory banks that needed to warm up before she could access them. Yet the memories are no longer quite linear. They form a spider's web, and to reach the center requires climbing over dead husks that have been sucked dry.

At any rate, specific incidents—the slaying of two children— might stand out to Rukiye, and to us, as clearly as brightly-lit signs on a highway, but the mileage, the GPS position of where we were, was never fully clear. At times, her description of prison life felt like an oval racetrack: Warning shot. Interrogation. Public degradation. Threats. Torture. Rest and repeat. The stations of Rukiye's cross are marked by a toenail ripped out, or a spasm on an electric chair.

There are many Rukiyes who didn't make it, so it was excruciating at times to condense the events from hours of interview files, but Rukiye needs a story, not a legal brief. And this account is as close as we will probably come to that story, at least in this lifetime.

\* \* \*

For all the psychic release of finally facing combat, Rukiye found that she couldn't sleep, so she kicked the door until the guards arrived. She told the guards that she was ready to talk. They pulled the black hood over her face, and Rukiye was guided down three flights of stairs. The black hood was pulled off, and she found herself standing in a darkened room with a sturdy metal bar, stationed at crotch-level.

Rukiye sized up her interrogators: one Uyghur, four Chinese males, and one Chinese female. The Uyghur began:

"You should know why you are here by now."

"No, I don't know."

"You will know soon then. What is your name?"

"Why did you bring me here?"

"Just answer my questions."

"You need to tell me why you brought me here. Then I will answer your questions."

"There is no bargaining here. You cannot ask me for anything. Your job is to answer any questions I might have, otherwise you will be 'chopping off your own feet.' You've seen what happened. There is no point in shouting or screaming. Just answer, or the consequences will be even worse."

"In front of my eyes there are two children. You can smell the mother's milk. Another seven Uyghurs are possibly dead. I need to know why—if you can tell me that, I can give you all the answers. But I didn't commit any crime. There is nothing for me to confess."

Before the sentence was fully out, the Chinese woman slapped Rukiye's face, and one of the Chinese policemen impulsively began punching Rukiye's upper body. Growing up with three brothers, Rukiye's instinct was to hit back, always. She kicked the policeman fast and hard, aiming for the testicles. The officials immediately surrounded her, forcing Rukiye into a prone position against the metal rail, then pulling her neck up to tie the black hood over her head. Rukiye was dragged back to her cell and tied to a chair.

Rukiye only allowed herself iron rations of pride, but it after hearing this story, Rahima began to use the phrase "the Iron Lady" whenever she referred to Rukiye in the third person. The phrase stuck.

* * *

Following the performative murder of her students, Rukiye's initial resistance to answering a single question gave her a kind of VIP status in the collective police mind. A mythology sprung up overnight, as revealed in subsequent interrogation sessions: "Did you study literature?"

"Did you study law?"

*"Who trained you?"*

Yet Rukiye's resistance was simple; she understood the game. First, the shock treatment (the children). Second, the offer of an incentive, an option (Rukiye instinctively grasped that the first interrogation was supposed to lead to this outcome). Third, she would give people up (although the police probably knew their names already). Fourth, even if she gave them up, the Chinese wouldn't free her, and the shock treatment had already proved that they had no inhibitions about killing her. No matter how she played the game, or didn't play the game, Rukiye accepted that death was inevitable. Perhaps—this is conjecture—this realization was a kind of liberation for Rukiye: it meant that any pain was bearable because it was temporary. And because there were no more decisions to make, there was no self-doubt.

Leaving Rukiye's humanity aside for a moment, it needs to be stated that resistance, if the individual can survive long enough to tell their story, is a precious jewel. The struggle becomes a test, not just of their own character, but of the character of their enemies. Resistance can become a probe, like a gamma knife, that pierces surgically through the the layers of oppression, revealing the techniques—pain, sexual humiliation, slaughter of loved ones, even self-loathing—long established to break the individual down, and, like a table game in poker, anticipating the order they will turn up. With a nod to George Orwell, resistance can open the door to the secrets of Room 101.

*　*　*

Two days passed. On the third day, the guards shackled Rukiye and took her to the question room in the middle of the night. It was a good cop routine: two men on both sides asked her questions, all variants of the "Who trained you?" theme. She gave the same response: "I broke no laws." Strangely, as if there was confusion on how to handle her at the highest levels, there was no beating, just three hours of solemn threats occasionally delivered with wistful crocodile sighs and the shaking of heads.

The next day Rukiye was moved to a new interrogation room, very narrow, no windows, and brightly lit. The police made her assume different positions: the airplane, the motorcycle, anything that involved holding out one's arms or arching one's back in an unnatural position that was impossible to hold for any length of time, particularly if they added weights. (Perhaps therapeutically, Rukiye acted the positions out for us, and I accommodated her by taking photos, which I haven't reproduced here). The game remained the same: if you don't hold the position, you get beaten. "Was the anticipation of the beatings the worst thing?" I asked.

"If one can die from the beatings, I would have died. Sometimes you just don't die." Rukiye said, shrugging off my mental-pain hypothesis.

This form of almost childish discipline went on for four days; every session lasted four hours. Then she was left alone for a week. The cycle of torture and interrogation that did not bear fruit, essentially *maintenance torture*, lasted "about a year," according to Rukiye.

She knew it could be much worse; during the quiet times in her cell, tied up or not, Rukiye could often hear women screaming. It travelled through the walls. Sometimes, as the noises reached a crescendo, she could clearly hear women scream "Please kill me!" Muslim women don't say that. It's *haram*, forbidden. So Rukiye assumed they were being raped. And she assumed it would happen to her someday, but nothing prepared her for the late afternoon when she and a small horde of other prisoners were escorted into a sort of classroom with scores of policemen looking on.

The lights were turned down theatrically, and on the makeshift stage, four Chinese policemen in uniform were standing around. Then four, "very beautiful"—and stark naked—Uyghur women entered the stage, chose a Chinese partner, and serviced the policemen in a graphic pornographic display. Rukiye didn't really want to fill in any details, just that the sexual positions always went on "for about an hour," and that everyone was forced to watch the whole thing in silence.

When the demonstration was over, Rukiye was rushed to a room—"a rape room." The strange furniture, the clothing and the wrappers on the floor told Rukiye that this was a 24-hour facility. Today, two young men and two young women were handcuffed against a large bed, prison uniforms pulled down, "in the rape position."

There was an unfamiliar tension in Rukiye's voice, as she avoided looking at me, only making eye contact with Rahima to check if she really understood what she was saying.

Five naked Chinese policemen—Rukiye suspected they had been in the classroom a few minutes ago—entered from a hidden door and then systematically raped the young Uyghurs "from behind." One of the girls was a former student of Rukiye's.

Rukiye reported that the rapes took about 30 minutes and there were covers underneath the metal bar to catch any blood or "slimy stuff." I asked where Rukiye was in the room. Her answer was that her mouth was taped, she was shackled, her uniform pulled down, and two naked men sexually violated her in a "disgusting way," but did not have actual sexual intercourse with her.

Two new security officers appeared two days later.

"What are your thoughts now? Have you thought about confessing? Did you think about what you witnessed and that it can happen to you? Do you want to avoid that, or do you want to continue?"

"To me, you are not human," Rukiye said. "Less than a dog. There is nothing for me to confess, no reason for me to say anything."

"So, nothing has made any impact on you."

Perhaps to punish her for this latest resistance, the police made the sex into a routine. Every two days she was forced to witness the pornographic performance, followed by a session at the rape room. The victims were always new, and mostly female. She was the regular, the witness, and she was molested too, yet the naked policemen were clearly still under orders to avoid actual sexual intercourse with her.

At the same time, her forced "medicine"—Rukiye didn't remember exactly what euphemism they used—went from one pill each day and one injection per week to twice the dosage. Rukiye noticed that her periods stopped, so she assumed the first effect of the "medicine" was "sterilization." The second effect, although she had no direct evidence for this, was that it "weakened the nervous system."

At this point in the interview process, it became difficult for Rukiye to estimate time. She simply remembers that one morning very early, the guards came in through the door and told her "to go for a wash." Rukiye was surprised. After the shower, a cream was applied to her face. Rukiye was taken to a car waiting outside in the cold dawn, and the police put the hood on. They drove a long way, then they pulled the black hood off—and there was her home, four Uyghurs standing in the courtyard. Once again, there was a body on the pallet. "Take the cover off. Take it off." Rukiye said, as the police restrained Rukiye from coming any closer. They unfurled the cover, revealing her mother's face, her purple-blue lips torn open from a severe cut on the mouth. Rukiye had heard that her mother had been tortured before. Now Rukiye was certain that her mother had been beaten to death.

"Let me kiss her. Let me kiss my mother at least once." Rukiye begged the four Uighurs standing there.

They shook their heads and looked at the emptiness of the stone deck.

This was "cruelty beyond imagination," but Rukiye did not cry or shout. She would not show tears. "I had seen too much," she told us.

A death warrant was produced. Rukiye would not sign it without reading it, and no one would agree to read it to her. The police, perhaps to avoid an incident, drove her back to the prison. For two days they left her alone in her cell, no interrogation, and no rape displays.

Then, she was given the soft approach in the question room with the two policemen: "What have you seen Rukiye? Any impact? Are you going to confess?"

It was now clear to Rukiye that her mother was the final act. They wanted her not just to fear, but to despair. So Rukiye said to herself: I am not going to give them what they want. I must be even stronger than I was. I need greater courage.

So, as they told her to sign her mother's death warrant, Rukiye simply shook her head. "Okay," they said, at the next meeting, "you will have your fingernails pulled."

The new meeting came quickly. Now there were three Chinese policeman and one Uyghur. He spoke softly to Rukiye: "You are young.

You have so much life ahead of you. So much to enjoy." Then he asked her to sign her mother's death certificate. It was in Chinese.

"No," Rukiye said.

They pulled out two nails. She had previously had this done, but this time the bleeding did not stop, and it took five days for the infection to stabilize. Some sort of white powder was applied twice a day, but other than that she was left alone to lie on the cement floor, with a blanket for warmth. Then the police took Rukiye back to the question room. The Uyghur policeman spoke softly and almost wistfully:

"This is the end of this style of questioning. We gave you all the opportunities. Prepare yourself for new police officers. Or, just confess now."

"I'm prepared. I'm innocent. You don't need to give me these warnings."

"You'll see," the Uyghur policeman replied.

Five days later, Rukiye was taken to the rape room, but, to her surprise, she was still a "spectator." Nothing had changed. And then, like a false war, there were fourteen days without any questions.

On the fifteenth day, the police took Rukiye to the real torture room, the one which she had never seen. "It was wired for electric shock" Rukiye said. "There were eight metal chairs and all these wires." Rukiye described what is often called a *tiger chair* by Falun Gong practitioners, with metal bracelets and a neck lock. Rukiye's clothes were stripped off, she was fastened to the chair, and then her bare breasts were fitted with a bra-shaped sleeve that apparently contained full voltage. Behind her stood a man who operated the controls with clearly delineated do-not-cross lines for the staff.

It is impossible to describe the pain, Rukiye said. It centers around the breasts, but so unbearable that your body panics and must move.

"And so impossible to stop the spasms, that I tore my wrist ligament on the metal brace. You can still see it."

Rukiye passed out and woke in the treatment room, her hand dangling off her wrist. "The doctors cut the skin and reattached the tendon, and they left me."

A few days later, the policemen walked into Rukiye's cell with her youngest brother and her middle brother. In an obviously prepared statement, they asked her to sign their mother's death certificate. Rukiye was overjoyed to see them, but she refused to sign and they were quickly taken away. "So, none of that had an impact on you." The policeman remarked, as he closed the cell door.

Then it was early morning. The car was waiting. You could hear the birds singing just before the morning prayer. Then the shackles, the black hood, and Rukiye knew that something terrible was going to happen, probably to her brothers. As they drove on, she could hear planes, and Chinese voices, and then the car stopped.

She was in a vast military parade ground, surrounded by police, troops, tanks and other vehicles. Clearly the space doubled as an execution ground. Fifty yards away, there stood five convicts, including her two brothers. Facing them, 20 masked soldiers. Standing next to Rukiye, two policemen were saying: "Rukiye, you need to confess now. You really need to confess," but to Rukiye, they were just traffic noise. As the soldiers aimed their rifles at the five condemned men, a shout rang out: "Rukiye, do not cry!!"

It was her youngest brother. She knew his voice. Then the shots, then they fell, and to Rukiye's surprise, they were still alive. A fraction of a second of irrational hope, then the soldiers dragged the five men, still spasming, away by their feet.

Her brothers were gone. "Losing them, hurt me so much I can't compare it to any of the tortures that I suffered." For my part, when she told us the story, I finally understood her slightly haunted look of guilt when she cried as she recalled her brothers forcing her to clean her plate so many years ago. Don't cry—her brother's last command. Rukiye could not obey him even now.

The black hood was back. They drove her to her cell.

A few days later, a policeman told her that her eldest brother had received a life sentence but had tried to escape. They shot him, so, as the surviving member of the Perhat family, she had a financial commitment to pay the state for six bullets.

\*   \*   \*

*"Last night, I dreamed of my younger brother dressed very beautifully, wearing all white, in a dark room. He held a big knife and he looked very angry. My immediate reaction was: 'My God what if the police see him?' But he did not look worried. He cleaned the knife in the light, put it back on his side, and stepped away. Then my mother appeared: also beautifully dressed, and angry, yet slightly confused, looking around suspiciously.*

*Why does mama not come to me and embrace me? I'm right here. Perhaps she is scared of the police too, I thought. Then we were back in a room in my Urumqi primary schoolhouse. There were some people I recognized in the room, as if they had been waiting for us. Mama looked around slowly at everyone, but not at me. 'They damaged my daughter,' she said, her voice trembling with rage. 'They tested her. They broke her hymen.' She paused and hissed: 'We did not stand up for ourselves. You must stand up!' As she shouted at them, I woke up."*

I asked Rukiye about her brother and her mother's "anger." Was she angry with you? Was her anger, in some way malevolent, evil or frightening? No, Rukiye said. It was the anger of ghosts: "So much pain that they could not express. So much vengeance that they could not attain."

"Why do you think you would have this dream now, on the last day in Istanbul, near the end of our interviews?"

"My mother was sending me a message though that dream. To tell you that these things should not be forgotten. That I should reveal them in my own way."

The people in the classroom, Rukiye revealed, were ghosts too: five or six very young people who went to hospital for minor operations and never recovered.

"Maybe it is important to give you their names?" Rukiye asked: "Perizat, Hassan, Muhammad...", her voice trailed off. "All were young, all died early, all took at least a month to die. And of their deaths, my father said: 'You cannot just accept it. It is not God's will.'"

Rukiye's father claimed that the CCP had an eradication list of all the groups who they would kill over the next 100 years. There was talk of the health problems that had grown like mushrooms in the Uyghur population—birth defects, and disappearances, and physical troubles as if people were being slowly poisoned or were exposed to chemical weapons. Yet the more we discussed the medical history of the ghosts waiting in the classroom, it became clear that we were discussing kidney failure, something that resembled leukemia, and aggressive cancers that metastasize quickly.

Nothing about this description points directly to organ harvesting or even an intentional plan to get rid of a certain Uyghur demographic. Yet it might plausibly be traced to the CCP's policy of atmospheric nuclear testing at Lop Nor in the Tarim desert, about 300 miles south of Urumqi. The testing began in 1964 and continued until 1980, at which point the PLA moved the blasts underground. My colleague, Dr. Enver Tohti, was able to establish a 30 to 35% rise in cancer rates (hidden in a locked hospital filing cabinet) in Urumqi tracking from the onset of Chinese nuclear testing. The timing in Rukiye's dream fits: at least three, or possibly four of the ghost-victims of premature deaths in Rukiye's dream were born in the period between 1964 to 1973, when the first major tests, mainly ground bursts that produce far more radioactive dust and fallout, were conducted.[2]

\*   \*   \*

Rukiye was back in the rape room. This was following another classroom performance with a Uyghur male subbing in for a Chinese policeman. The female sexual partners were all Uyghur as usual.

This time, the rape room was occupied by six naked policemen, four Chinese, two Uyghur. Lined up against the bed, in the rape position, with their prison uniforms pulled down, were three Uyghur women. For the first time, one of them was Rukiye.

Rukiye gave no details.

A day later, in the question room, Rukiye received Chinese prison rape counseling: "Now maybe you can wake up and rethink what you should tell us."

\*   \*   \*

It's grotesque to analyze the prison rape of a virgin as if it were an ordinary event. Yet it may be useful to put it into context. Rukiye was incarcerated at age 18, or around 2007. Although establishing dates and the passage of time proved difficult for Rukiye, Rahima and I were able to estimate that Rukiye was in the prison for at least two years before she was finally physically raped, so we are speaking about 2009, or possibly 2010, approximately five years before the first camp construction in 2015, the genesis of the mass internment of Uyghurs

---

2    According to Dr. Tohti, an Urumqi schoolchild back in 1973: "There were three days that earth fell from the sky, without wind or any sort of storm." Personal conversation, July 2017.

and Kazakhs, reaching, at a minimum, one million by late 2016 or early 2017.[3]

Let's review the CCP techniques to break a tough resistance case like Rukiye's. The murder of Rukiye's youngest students took place on the fourth night of captivity. Although the police used various tortures on Rukiye—mainly holding positions, beating, and the pulling of fingernails—the first escalation to electric shock treatment came approximately a year in, and the execution of Rukiye's remaining family, after two years in the prison.

We can assume that rape was well-established as a tool when Rukiye entered the prison, but she was introduced to it gradually as a "regular" in the rape room but not stretched over the sex bench until she had been incarcerated for over two years. Rukiye's confession that she was physically raped, was delivered almost as an afterthought.

Why did the police take so long? Why the "humanity" in her case? I puzzled over this, while Rukiye hinted obliquely at the idea that the prison officials wanted to increase the anticipation, the fear. I wondered if the police had a touch of the male rape fantasy that exposure to explicit sex would eventually increase Rukiye's desire to have sexual intercourse with them. Or perhaps, somewhere near the top, the decision to make Rukiye witness rape on a regular basis, while forbidding the police from engaging in actual sexual intercourse, was not a message to Rukiye, but to the police. Consider Rukiye's responses during interrogation: she consistently told her tormentors: "If I say you are human, it is an insult to human beings. And if I say you are dogs, it is an insult to the dogs." Fine, but what is a dog?

The murder of children, the administration of torture, and the execution of Rukiye's family members—while these activities might

---

3    U.S. Department of State, ed., "International Religious Freedom Report for 2019, China (Includes Tibet, Xinjiang, Hong Kong, and Macau): Xinjiang," Executive Summary, 2019.

appeal to a few hardcore sadists in the police force most policemen don't want to do these things on a regular basis, and, at best, they consider these things as simply part of their job.

Yet rape is instinctual—dog-like even—and physically impossible to carry out without a measure of pleasure. Rape serves as a reward system for the rank-and-file policemen, much like fancy "execution meals" were used to incentivize the Urumqi Public Security Bureau to efficiently slay enemies of the state, back in the mid-1990s.[4] I am not suggesting that Rukiye was likely to be impressed by the policemen's restraint in the rape room. Yet what if the audience was not Rukiye, but the policemen? Perhaps the order not to engage in actual intercourse with Rukiye, yet to have her present at every sexual opportunity was a sort of top-down placement of a *memento mori* in the rape room, meant to be a constant reminder of the police failure to break Rukiye. And until the police broke her, they were not policemen, just dogs.

Yet there is a more coherent explanation for finally allowing the police to have sexual intercourse with Rukiye—an ominous one. It took Rukiye some time to lead us there. Not to be cute here, but I suspect that the process of how she revealed that is important for her credibility, so I'll take you on that journey. At this point in the narrative, Rukiye's story also begins to diverge from the "routine." In other words, similar, less-detailed accounts have emerged from the Uyghur and Kazakh refugees from the Xinjiang camps, but also from the numerous Falun Gong refugee accounts of sexual abuse that I came across while researching my previous book, *The Slaughter*.[5]

Most of the sexual practices that Rukiye has described so far make an appearance in more recent refugee accounts of the Xinjiang camps—covered in detail unusual by BBC standards, particularly the

---

4    Ethan Gutmann, *The Slaughter: Mass Killings, Organ Harvesting, and China's Secret Solution to Its Dissident Problem* (Prometheus Books, 2014), 20

5    Gutmann, *The Slaughter*, 16, 144-45, 176, 209, 236, 298-99

testimony of Tursunay Ziawudun and Sayragul Sauytbay. How the BBC got those accounts is an interesting story, but, at least from my personal perspective, there is little reason to doubt that Tursunay and Sayragul were telling the truth.[6]

There are several common themes from Rukiye's time, the pre-camp-era, to Tursunay and Sayragul, the camp-era.

The first similarity is defined by public displays of explicit sex within the confines of the carceral environment. These performances were clearly more pagan, uninhibited, and exploited as a sexual stimulant in Rukiye's time, than the sort of punitive, embarrassing, sex-as-punishment, fear/dominance displays, as described by Sayragul and Tursunay. But the net shock effect—we can do anything we want—is the same.

The second similarity to the camp era is just outright rape by policemen. However, there may have been an evolution over time from gang rape to a more personal approach. Rukiye was never subjected to one-on-one sexual intercourse. Recent camp refugees describe a more personal approach to rape which occurred in small, confined spaces, mimicking the exploitation of women as prostitutes. There may

---

6     Shortly before my interviews with Rukiye in Istanbul, I wanted to interview Sayragul Sauytbay, a Kazakh veteran of the Xinjiang camps in Sweden. Based on a tip from a legitimate Kazakh source, I strongly suspected that she had been raped in the camps. When I came to visit, Sayragul was sitting in the kitchen with her husband——a passionate man, overflowing with powerful stories. I knew his entire family had been through hell and I did not have the heart to ask Sayragul about rape in front of her husband. The need for privacy and maintaining appearances goes beyond Muslim culture. I was not there to cause serious harm or death, and that includes the death of a marriage. It's also germane that one of the first women whom I interviewed in Kazakhstan was a Uyghur camp refugee named Tursunay Ziawudun. She appeared at my safe house several days in a row with her physician husband. Once again, I knew that she had been raped, but, similarly, I respected her marriage. Ultimately, I tipped off my friend David Campanale at the BBC. As luck would have it, when the BBC interviewed them, their husbands were not there, and the BBC did an excellent story. They didn't credit me. I expect the BBC likes to keep up the appearance that it has journalists all over the world just like the good old days. Yet, in defense of the BBC, the story featured a lot more than women showing their scars and was a genuine human rights contribution at a critical moment in time.

even be an economic incentive involved—mass incarceration presents all sorts of entrepreneurial possibilities—but the main difference may come down to density. The facilities that Rukiye describes were relatively underpopulated: she had her own cell. Interrogations and electric torture sessions were intimate "curated experiences" in first-world jargon. The only activity where Rukiye saw other prisoners was usually in sexual situations. One theory—purely speculative—is that the prison administrators enforced a gang rape policy for security and unit cohesion, but also to prevent the growth of any sexual or romantic attachments, even of the Night Porter variety, within the police ranks.

The third similarity to the camp era is homosexual rape. While Rukiye describes a police preference for women at approximately two to one, both men and women were exploited as rape targets in Rukiye's account. While it is shameful to be the victim of rape in any human culture, I suspect it's a cross-cultural phenomenon that it is considered particularly shameful to be the victim of male-on-male rape. It's hard to acquire first-hand data. Although neither Sayragul or Tursunay spoke explicitly on this point, I have had contact with at least one Uyghur male who was a victim of homosexual rape in the camps.[7]

The fourth commonality with the camp system is underage rape. Rukiye mentioned that one of her students was in the rape room group sessions. While we neglected to ask her age, she was younger than Rukiye, and, based on her informal descriptions of her sixteen students, I suspect that she was no more than 15 or 16 years old. The practice seems to have continued into the Xinjiang camp era; in my interview with Sayragul, she observed that when she was teaching Chinese, some of the younger female students would come into class, faces flushed, and hair curiously stirred. Sayragul, intelligent and highly observant,

---

7    Abduweli Ayup, witness statement, UK Tribunal to Investigate China's Alleged Genocide and Crimes against Humanity against Uyghur, Kazakh and Other Turkic Muslim Populations, 2021, hereafter "Uyghur Tribunal".

surmised that these young women had been sexually violated by Chinese policemen throughout the night.

The final practice, and the final commonality with the camp system, is the use of rape to defile the Uyghur racial and ethnic identity. It's also the key to understanding this chapter.

Islamophobia, in Rukiye's experience, was the dog that did not bark. The police had only a glancing interest in defiling Islam— through rape or rhetoric or any other means. The question room was not aimed at Rukiye renouncing Islam; rather it was obsessively focused on Rukiye implicating members of the Uyghur community as "separatists" or "terrorists." The pattern in Uyghur and Kazakh camp refugee testimony is much the same. Other than as an excuse for the original arrest, Islam rarely comes up.

Finally, let's consider the Hui Muslims of China. Hui are stricter followers of Islamic practice than the Uyghurs and nearly equivalent to Uyghurs in population size, but they speak Mandarin and look Chinese. Only a small portion of the camp refugees that I interviewed reported seeing a Hui individual in the camps at all. Yet half the camp refugees brought up Chinese racism without my asking.

Rukiye never mentions that she was forced to eat pork in prison. While the forced consumption of pork and the command to eat during Ramadan has become a more common feature of Chinese rule during the camps era, sex, while it is uncomfortable for everyone to talk about, still occupies a much larger place in the human psyche. And Han Chinese sexual attitudes towards Uyghurs are larger than life. When I worked in Beijing back in the early 2000s, my Chinese business counterparts knew that a good time meant a Uyghur club. The fun was daring each other to eat boiled donkey penis while you watched alleged Uyghur women in Kismet garb twist and turn. Great music. The best in Beijing. But it all felt transgressive, segregated, and exploitative—like being transported into a black jazz club during the Roaring Twenties, a distinct feeling of Han Chinese superiority, combined with a tinge of envy at the Hun's sensual nature.

Rukiye believed that nearly all the Uyghur women, and about half of the men, were raped in the prison at one point or another. That doesn't mean that universal rape was carried into the Xinjiang camp system (and it's difficult to make numerical estimates of sexual abuse because victims are highly resistant to speaking about it). According to Sayragul, the Chinese guards preyed nearly exclusively on the young women. But there is some evidence that the Chinese lack of sexual inhibition extended beyond young and attractive Uyghurs into pure power scenarios.

As I mentioned, while we were in Istanbul, Rahima and I interviewed Gulbahar Jelilova, an ethnic Uyghur from Kazakhstan, born in 1964. Gulbahar had been detained in 2017 in an Urumqi-based camp, which she referred to as a "woman's prison." Gulbahar told us that for several hours, a male interrogator had been trying to get her to sign a document confessing that she had financially supported Uyghur terrorist activities using WeChat transfer. Gulbahar didn't even understand how WeChat worked, so she kept saying: "No, I can't sign this."

Finally, the interrogator's frustration peaked. He pulled out his penis and said: "I should stuff this into your mouth."

"How can you say that to me? Don't you have a mother? Don't you have a sister?"

"How dare you compare yourself to my mother! Or my sister?" The interrogator reached over and poked Gulbahar in the face: "Look at yourself!"

There was a mirror on the side of the room, and Gulbahar got a glimpse of a woman she did not recognize. The face was filthy.

Unwashed. Aged. Sagging. Grotesque. When Gulbahar had entered the woman's prison, the police forced her to stick her head in a hole in the wall where unseen hands used a hair clipper on her. Now she had a ridiculous bald head, like a clown, mottled with skin ulcers.

My God, he's right, Gulbahar thought, and began to weep. I shouldn't have made the comparison to normal people. I shouldn't have said anything at all.

*　*　*

My first thought was that they were mimicking a scene from George Orwell's dystopian novel, *1984*, specifically O'Brien interrogating Winston Smith in the Ministry of Truth:

*'You have thought sometimes,' said O'Brien, 'that my face—the face of a member of the Inner Party—looks old and worn. What do you think of your own face?'... 'You are rotting away,' he said; 'you are falling to pieces. What are you? A bag of filth. Now turn around and look into that mirror again. Do you see that thing facing you? That is the last man.*[8]

Gulbahar's interrogator exposed his penis as a symbol of his power and simultaneous disdain. If Gulbahar had been a young woman, the story might have had a different ending. When Gulbahar tried to shame him by invoking his mother, he was able to imply that she was too ugly to be a whore, too pathetic to be a Madonna, or even a member of the human race. And, like Winston Smith, Gulbahar broke down like a child.

Was this interrogator "Islamophobic"? Is this the CCP version of the Spanish inquisition? Not really. Rejection of Islam and conversion to Party loyalty is mainly a pretext. Persecution of any religion, the sort of interrogation of Falun Gong that I was familiar with, exploits humiliation, torture, and displays of power. Occasionally a particularly

---

8    Nineteen Eighty-Four. London: Secker & Warburg, 1949.

resistant Falun Gong woman was thrown into a Chinese male cell to be gang-raped. But the interrogator, not a surrogate, as an active sexual predator suggests that something more elemental is involved. In scenario after scenario, it revolves around a Chinese man penetrating a Uyghur woman, an act squarely aimed at the Uyghur male psyche.

And yet the rape culture exposed by Rukiye in her account goes beyond that: the captive women, and even the men, are nothing more than the warm holes found in animals.

For the rapist, bestiality is initially transgressive, but ultimately it can feel profoundly liberating. The exuberant phase is acted out in public rape, pornographic displays, and group sex. The latent shame phase is marked by sterilization, sexual mutilation, and murder.

\* \* \*

Rukiye doesn't know how many months passed after her first rape. After refusing to sign the death certificate again, it was back to the electric shock room, then interrogation and cigarette burns, then rape, and then recovery. Although the police pulled out her toenails, Rukiye's resistance stayed constant.

One night the police came to Rukiye's cell in a state of strange excitement. They blindfolded her and she was taken seven or eight floors down. Deep in the ground, there was a kind of lounge, with comfortable sofas. There, presented on the central sofa, spread-eagle in the unforgiving light, was a naked woman.

"One breast had been cut off."

"The woman was alive?" I asked, rather stupidly.

"The woman was dead." Rukiye replied. Then she started struggling with her words.

"Below that. . . words can't. . . can't describe her state. It was below, on her body, below the waist?"

"Her genitals had been mutilated?"

For the first time in several days of interviews, Rukiye looked upset with me: "Please do not ask such questions. I can only tell you what I can tell you. I am trying my best."

"Sorry Rukiye."

"They said to me, 'If you do not cooperate, your state will be worse than hers.' Even in that state, I saw the woman—she was a very beautiful woman. . . . It affected me so. . . so badly. That image. The memory of that flesh. That flesh in my mind."

The police brought Rukiye back to her cell. The image was burned in.

*　*　*

Rukiye had a problem: Whatever torture they threw at her—two more visits to the electric torture room and, at one point, they even allowed dogs to attack her legs—she healed quickly. Perhaps too quickly. "With the dogs, I had also had a thought in my mind. We have a saying that 'if a mad dog bites you, you become mad too.' Well, if I become mad, I thought, then maybe I can beat these bastards. And yet even those wounds healed so quickly, although I still have the scars. But my determination to resist was fading and was not as strong as the past."

The prison's determination to make her cooperate appeared to be changing as well, and this was revealed in the Question Room.

Both sides went through the motions, like a chess opening that both had played many times, the one that always leads to stalemate. But the policeman in charge of the interrogation unexpectedly pushed the board aside: "You have been here for three years now. You've experienced a lot. I cannot understand what you are made of. Are you not sorry for your own body? Or yourself? Are you human—or what?"

"None of the torture really had an impact on me. Because I cannot consider you to be human."

"We *are* human, just like you. But you don't cooperate. You do not make confession. All you had to do was to cooperate. . . to give us the names."

The policeman was making a point that anyone familiar with Mainland Chinese culture would surely understand: *All you had to do was make a deal. That's all we really wanted. Just enough to cover our ass. We could have saved you.* Rukiye also understood the subtext: *But we can't do that anymore.*

Something about the way Rukiye told us the story indicated that she knew that the policeman was expressing a kind of sincerity, however wheedling and self-justifying. Yet she chose to ignore this in favor of what she thought might be her final words:

"You cannot become the Masters of this world. You cannot destroy the Uyghur race. . . . If one Rukiye dies, 1000 will be reborn. So do not feel so proud that you have so much power over our people. Whenever you want to kill, you kill us. Whenever you want to torture, you torture us. But in Uyghur language, we have a saying: 'Even if the truth lies buried beneath the seven layers of earth, it will still be revealed one day.'"

*   *   *

The prison authorities moved Rukiye to a prison in Aksu for eight months. There she was essentially left alone, save for a daily two-hour commitment in the "water prison."

The water prison was located down in the basement. It comprised a square wooden box, with a depth of seven or eight feet, with water running through it. The prisoner would be fixed onto a chain above the center of the box, lowered in, and would have to fight to keep their head above the waterline. The water was very cold. It was also filthy, brimming with chemicals, and pathogens from human waste.

I had run across water prisons before; when I was researching

Falun Gong, several female practitioners referred to their experience with "water torture." I confess the torture description sounded unnecessarily baroque, until I understood the function of dirty water.

It's a slow-acting poison. Over time, the victim's body will become weak from the daily fight against the cold, the struggle to keep breathing, and the constant exposure to bacteria. Then the entire body will become "puffy and swollen" (both Falun Gong practitioners speaking in Mandarin, and Rukiye speaking in Uyghur, used similar phrases to describe this). At a certain point of physical deterioration, recovery is impossible. The victim would then be released from prison or die in their cell, depending on whether the Chinese State preferred to make a public example of the prisoner, or wanted the prisoner to die "of natural causes" in the controlled carceral environment. Either way, the water prison has induced a gradual, low-impact death that leaves no scars.

Rukiye was given this treatment for eight months until the lights went out.

She was lying in a bed. A nurse was in the room.[9] The nurse said: You are here, because you have a good Aunt.

Soon after the person who was said to be Rukiye's aunt came to her room and sat in the chair next to her bed. She called her "Amina."

Aunt said that when you were taken out of prison, you appeared to be dead. But you were still breathing. It took a month before you came out of your coma, and another month before your eyes began to see things. Now go to sleep Amina. I'll be back soon.

\* \* \*

Rukiye's aunt had purchased Rukiye's freedom for 70,000 RMB (roughly 10K). She transported Rukiye from Aksu to Urumqi, and

9     I have chosen to withhold the clinic's name and location to protect the medical staff from the Public Security Bureau of China. Rukiye's aunt's words here are a reconstruction from Rukiye's account of conversations with her aunt, months later, which established the pattern of recovery.

Rukiye was in a clinic for eight months. The first months, she was awake but seemingly had zero recognition. In six months, she began recovering. By eight months, as her health advanced quickly, there was genuine fear that the Chinese Communist Party would take her back, so Rukiye's aunt moved her to a new clinic, and then another. After 18 months of treatment in clinics, Rukiye began to recognize people again.

Rukiye's aunt raised about one million RMB (approximately 150K) to buy Amina a new *hukou*, a residence permit, with a new identity and a new passport that officially swapped 'Rukiye' for 'Amina.' At the end of 2012, or 2013, Amina left China.

\* \* \*

We interviewed Rukiye during her final days in Istanbul, as she, finally, had been granted asylum in Germany. Her plane was leaving in less than 12 hours, so, at Rahima's suggestion, I pressed two fifty Euro notes into Rukiye's hand. She resisted as I closed her fingers around them.

"This is not a payment, not a gift." I said. "You will need this where you are going, that's all. And we will not forget you."

It was the only time that I touched Rukiye.

\* \* \*

From the moment that Rukiye had walked into the breakfast room, Rahima and I sensed she was a remarkable witness. Yet as the explosive material accumulated during the interviews, we were both concerned that there would be attacks on her credibility, both from the Chinese Communist Party, but also, potentially, from competitive Western journalists. We couldn't second-source Rukiye's account. Even if one could go into Xinjiang or establish a remote connection with someone who had been in the same prison, there was simply no secure method to ask questions without the risk of getting someone else imprisoned or killed.

Yet neither of us were concerned that we were dealing with intentional deception or fantasy.[10] Rahima is a highly skilled judge of character and had developed an unusual level of trust with Rukiye from the very beginning. I also instinctively believed Rukiye: once, during a relaxed meal at a Uyghur restaurant, I asked Rukiye a question along the lines of what she really thought of the Chinese. She replied "They are animals, lower than animals," but it wasn't the content that rang true— Rukiye had said nearly the same thing in her interrogations—but the venomous way that she spat out the words, like a blast furnace opening for a fraction of a second. Because of my background interviewing Falun Gong refugees, I knew that it was easy enough for someone to exaggerate an account. The problem was the energy required to sustain the story over hours and hours, and we had three full days with Rukiye.

Thinking about it now, Rahima and I were probably more worried about the exclusive nature of the content: infanticide, public sex, group rape. We didn't know that we would be partially supported by the BBC report on rape in the Xinjiang camps a year or two later, which, by necessity, also rested on three unconnected single witness accounts.

Yet I still had questions. Once Rahima had started speaking of Rukiye as the Iron Lady, we were unconsciously encouraging her to talk about her steadfast resistance—and just as subtly discouraging Rukiye from talking about her own fragility.

I didn't want Rukiye to have to stand naked before the world,

---

10   From the beginning, Rahima had been troubled by what I called the "resume issue." Rukiye's dates – really, just getting the years straight – were scattershot, starting with questions over her birthdate. We eventually learned that Rukiye's aunt claimed it was Valentine's Day, 1989, but I argued that date was for "Amina" not Rukiye, so it was possible that this specific date was fictional to begin with. While Rahima found it incredible that someone would have forgotten their own birthday, I pointed out that my own mother-in-law had reported her daughter's birthday off by a full year, throughout her entire childhood, and the discrepancy between my wife's passport and her driver's license and her actual birth date had dogged her for years. Yet my mother-in-law hadn't gone through years of trauma, followed by water prison; she just was kind of hazy about timelines. Rahima was able to resolve this by sitting down with Rukiye over lunch and coming to agreement over an informal timeline, which held together in a plausible way.

but I also understood that she had avoided giving us an account of the sexual abuse she received. Without it, there was no way to answer that original question: Why did the rapes start two years in? Just another pressure technique to make Rukiye confess? Or was it a sign that the authorities had given up on her? I didn't want to pry. I wasn't looking for scars on her arms, and I certainly wasn't looking for tears. But no matter how embarrassing or shameful, we needed, or more correctly, her critics needed, to know exactly what happened to Rukiye Perhat. And the more I thought about it, the more I sensed that I was the main impediment to that occurring. One year after the Istanbul interviews, I called Rahima in London, asking if she could contact Rukiye and drive to Germany with me.

To give Rukiye her privacy, I won't mention the name of the town. It's small by German standards, a market town in some gently rolling hills, an hour's drive from Frankfurt. Rukiye's new home, a sort of generic euro-dorm for immigrants, had been constructed on a hilltop on the edge of a farmer's fields, and beyond that, dense pine woods. I mention this because the placement of the housing seemed to match Rukiye's mood: lonely, but at peace. Rukiye said that she had been studying the Koran. She was, I think, pleased to see us, so we picked up where we had left off, with her escape from China, and the first two hours were dominated by Rahima's clarification questions. I've incorporated some of those answers into Rukiye's original story. But then the shadows in the small conference room I'd rented started to creep up the walls, so I turned the recording off and said directly:

"Rukiye, you are a devout Muslim woman and I'm a Jewish-American male. I know that you have tried your best to tell us everything. But sometimes it's difficult to do that when I'm sitting here, particularly when it comes to rape and sexual abuse. And if Rahima translates for me, it will just slow things down. I've never been to this area of Germany before, so I'm going to take a long walk. And while I'm out, please tell Rahima everything that happened to you. Everyone who raped you. In detail. For example, if you have a name, please share it. It may lead to justice someday. I know this will be very uncomfortable, and I'm sorry about that. But if you don't do this, there will be people out there who will never believe your story."

Rukiye nodded slowly. After 90 minutes, I came back, we made our goodbyes in the dark of the parking lot, and Rahima and I got in the car to drive back to Frankfurt, as we had an early flight the next morning. Rahima stayed silent on the drive, only saying a polite "good night" to me at the hotel in Frankfurt. The next morning at breakfast, back to her bubbly old self, but keeping her voice low, Rahima confirmed that the interview was very disturbing. She would translate it for me down the road. Though Rahima and I remain close friends and colleagues, she never got around to translating the interview, and I didn't have the heart to pressure her.

Several years later, my long-term fixer-translator, Bavi, came up to my house in Vermont, and I asked him to spend a weekend translating the interview. I've edited his version, as Rahima spent a lot of time on technical issues such as the architecture of the rape room and how many rapes Rukiye witnessed. Yet the interview also sheds a very clear light on how inexperienced Rukiye was when she was raped, and why the corpse of the murdered woman had such an impact on her. The explicit nature of the interview also explains Rahima's silence on the drive back to Frankfurt.

\* \* \*

"Talking about these things is a very difficult issue for me. But I wasn't alone in prison, and truly, by the power of the Almighty, I was saved and became a living martyr (*shaheed*). Apparently, he has entrusted me with the duty to tell these things. . . . So, I have nothing to hide.. . ."

"You can talk. . . about how you were repeatedly scared and treated horribly—the moments when you were raped. You can tell it like it's being told by someone else, not like it happened to you."

In the room, silence fell. The women remained silent for a long time, then, taking a deep breath, Rukiye began to speak.

"The process is as follows: they remove our clothes and lay us on the bed, untie our hands and tie them to the bed, then our legs, and tape our mouth shut. After that, these men enter. . . All these men are completely naked. . . The first time, due to shock, I didn't see and didn't try to see who was assaulting me. . . I won't talk about others, but when they did it to me for the first time, they did it from behind. . . When they do it from behind, you are lying on your stomach and cannot see who is assaulting you. When I was raped for the first time, I screamed and cried.

"But when your mouth is closed [taped], how can you scream?"

"My voice may not be loud, but it still comes out and you don't have to shout too much. Since the mouth is fixed, you can yell in a lowing voice."

"Were there times when you showed insubordination?.... You have your mouth taped shut. . . But you can fall right?"

"Yes, but when I fall, several men who are there immediately put me back on my feet. But for the most part they stand in the back all the time. . . . The first time it happened, I screamed and cried. Next time, I didn't cry or scream. Since they are capable of these things, why should I insist on screaming and crying?. . . I thought about suicide, but I also thought about how my father raised me and this stopped me from thinking this way."

"What happened to other women and men? You said that they were raped at the same time? Did they also show disobedience?"

"Many tried to scream and cry even if their mouths were taped, both women and men. A lot of them. . . . Yes, there are times when we scream and try to free ourselves, in those cases they act as if they want to take revenge on us. They rape us harder with blows. They beat us with electric batons if we strongly resist. These are also people who rape us but are simply waiting for their turn or behind us."

"Does this always happen in the same place?"

"Yes."

"And there are other women victims, you are not alone?"

"Yes, I'm not alone."

"Does each victim have two to three rapists?"

"Yes, everyone has their own rapists."

"Are all of these rapists Chinese? Were there Uyghurs among them?"

"I was not raped by Uyghurs, but some were raped by Uyghurs. Since we are all in one place I can see it."

Rukiye estimated that she saw somewhere between 600 to 1000 rapes every year.

"Do they wash you before raping, maybe for themselves? Or do they put on these things [condoms]? For example, to prevent pregnancy. . . ? The plastic thing, do they rape you wearing it?"

Her voice low and surprised, Rukiye said: "I don't even know. . . ."

Then, talking to herself, Rukiye said: "Ah, so that thing is for that."

"Yes, because if they don't do that, and they ejaculate inside you, you'll feel it. . . ."

"Yes, like some slimy substance comes out. . . ."

"Yes, to hold that slimy stuff back, they wear it. Many young couples wear it if they don't want to have children or before their wedding, if they have had other sexual contact. Do they wear it? Do you understand? I personally suspect they don't want women to get pregnant there. That's why they use such things."

"Is this thing in a box?"

"Yes, it's in a box. It's like the thing doctors wear on their hands. They take it out of the box and put it on, correct?"

"Yes, yes, there is such a thing. Yes, they had some boxes when they came in."

Speaking to herself again, Rukiye said quietly: "So that's what they use it for. That's it."

"Because if they spill that dirt outside, you'll feel it on your body."

"The first time they raped me, they didn't wear such a thing."

"But they raped you from behind, right?"

"When they did it for the very first time, they did it from behind but to the front of me [the vagina]. But they didn't wear such a thing.... It turns out something comes out after they do it, I learned about it.... In general, at the moment when they wanted to rape me, many times they didn't wear such a thing. But I noticed that when they raped others, I remember they wore such things. I saw that."

"Can you tell me about the moment when you were detained and taken down to the basement to be interrogated, and you saw a dead woman. Can you talk about this again?"

"These are topics that I would not like to talk about and my tongue does not dare to say."

"You mentioned that she had a pretty face despite her hair being horribly disheveled, her breast being cut... and her vagina being in such a state that you can't describe it?"

There was a beat, then Rahima continued:

"We want to expose China's crimes against us, and these topics affect me very deeply as well, sometimes even haunting me in nightmares. We're discussing this now because. . . we want to tell the truth to the whole world. I don't want to force you either; when I ask such awful questions, I see how your demeanor changes, and I feel awkward. But you know our purpose."

"This is a problem."

There was a pause before Rukiye continued:

"In prison, I haven't spoken about this before, but they also rape from the front and from behind simultaneously."

Rukiye paused again.

"When I saw our [dead] sister. . . in that room, I immediately understood what had happened to her. I experienced it myself. That is, when they rape both from the front and from behind simultaneously, they don't tie you to the bed, they make you stand. For example, several rapists did this to me from both the front and the back. Not even a week or several days later, it happened again. So, when it happens non-stop, like what happened to this woman, she had a terrible hemorrhoid. Her anus looked like a piece of meat."

"What position was she in? Were you able to see her face and intimate areas?"

"They showed her to me completely, so I saw it. She had her legs spread apart. . . I saw her hemorrhoid protruding. I had the same issue. It turns out it's very difficult to treat. I was treated for a long time with traditional medicine."

"Did you have surgery?"

"No, I wasn't operated on. One very experienced traditional medicine doctor decided that I could manage with traditional medicine. But initially, they wanted to treat me with surgery. So, this girl was raped non-stop. And from her vagina, there was also a very large piece of flesh protruding—probably the uterus."

"So they showed you to say that if you don't obey, the same thing will happen to you?"

"Yes, they said that."

"Did you scream when you saw this?"

"No, I didn't scream. . . . I was deeply upset by what I saw that time, but I didn't scream."

"What traces did she have on her body? You said she. . . ."

"Besides her organs protruding from both the rectum and the front, she had a lot of bruises, and marks from electric shocks. She was shocked in the chest area for sure. Her whole body had traces of electric burns. There was some blood and bruises from baton strikes."

"I think all the details have been provided, what we wanted to know. We can finish here today."

We have finished here too. Ultimately this is not a book about rape, but about forced organ harvesting. Yet Rukiye has done the world a *mitzvah*, a good work. Her almost superhuman resistance created the conditions for the Chinese Communist Party, not Rukiye, to stand naked before the world. Her recovery appears to have been an act of pure will. And finally, while it was profoundly painful for Rukiye to speak about what had been done to her, Rukiye has spoken to readers across the Western world, sitting in comfort, that yes, the things that you consider *impossible and unthinkable*, are actually quite real. Perhaps Rukiye proves an important negative too: the difference between forced organ harvesting and rape is that rape can—for better or worse—be a survivable crime for the victim. Rukiye cheated death in both cases.

Perhaps with this account, however imperfect, Rukiye's obligation as a living *shaheed* is paid in full. It is my prayer—I have thought about this so many times—whether or not there are apricot trees, motorcycles, or men in her future, that Rukiye will be happy just to be alive.

# 2

# POSTMORTEM

In the late 1990s, a Taiwanese doctor began independently experimenting with live organ harvesting. He knew that, like a flower cut under running water, organs extracted from a living human being are far less likely to be rejected by the new host's body. Faced with a long-term comatose or a terminal patient, the doctor would look for a decline in body temperature and pulse rate to begin the procedure.

The doctor didn't have a surgeon's hands, but he didn't really need them, for he was a man of notable intelligence who inspired protectiveness and deep loyalty among students and young surgeons, especially those second to none in steadiness of hand and temperament. Casting aside the "Dead Donor Rule" the doctor would order the extraction of the precious organs, fast-tracking the demise of incurable patients, while giving years of new life to others.

Through trial and error, the doctor recognized that everything came down to a few critical moments of extraction. The patient's heart still pumping blood to the last second should theoretically ensure oxygenation of the kidneys, the liver, and even the lungs at the point of removal. Yet, with light or local anesthesia, a scalpel blade cutting into a living being with intact spinal reflexes could still resemble the emergency lowering of control rods in a nuclear reactor, creating unpredictable spikes and dips in the donor metabolism, sometimes even accompanied by reflexive physical motion that turned surgery into temporary chaos. Yet heavy anesthesia would place a sluggish organ in the new host, also problematic. Even if the anesthesia balance could be solved, and the donor and the new host were physically side by side, there was still a pause—effectively a period of oxygen death—before the organ was securely transplanted.

But what if you could bypass the donor's circulation? A machine gently forcing oxygenated blood directly into the organs in question through the final surgical cuts, and beyond, had been briefly tried in the past. Beginning in the 1970s, extracorporeal membrane oxygenation (ECMO) machines had been used to successfully support dysfunctional hearts and lungs. Live organ harvesting without family consent was technically illegal. Exploiting an ECMO device to carry it out was merely off-label use.

Back in the mid-1990s, the doctor, as a researcher at the University of Minnesota, had become familiar with Medtronic, a local medical company that produced ECMO machines. The doctor found that Medtronic's machines produced dramatic results, not just with the organ's viability in the new host, but with longevity, as many organs had four hours of artificial life at best. With ECMO, it was more like eight or even twelve hours. All the routine delays that led to organ failure in the new host—missed planes, the hand-off to a new surgical team, late nights where the transplant surgeon desperately needed a couple of hours sleep before starting fresh—suddenly had breathing room.

The doctor quietly spread the gospel of live extraction, ECMO, and Medtronic, including how to handle non-believers. The doctor included instructions on which medications to administer to terminal organ donors to transform them into thoroughly dead donors should the medical examiner happen to be making the rounds.

The doctor was Ko Wen-je. He would go on to be the mayor of Taipei, the founder of the Taiwan People's Party (TPP), and a competitive Taiwan presidential candidate in 2024.

All that would come later. Back then, Taiwan perhaps felt a little small for Dr. Ko. With the Mainland transplant industry in the throes of explosive growth and the People's Liberation Army (PLA) hospitals leading the way, Dr. Ko published his ECMO technique in a PLA medical journal. The Mainland transplant industry responded, welcoming Ko as an honored guest. In late 2004, as Dr. Ko negotiated organ prices for elderly Taiwanese organ tourists in a mainland hospital, the Chinese surgeons revealed the secret behind their apparently inexhaustible supply of healthy kidneys, livers, lungs, and hearts: "All the organs will come from Falun Gong."[11]

Dr. Ko kept a straight face. He went on with his business. And he never really spoke of what he had learned until July 2008, the day that a bald, middle-aged American and his young assistant who never seemed to blink came to his Taipei office.

*   *   *

The most valuable evidence is usually the hardest. Even a patient who was partially harvested and somehow lived to speak about it has far

---

11    This is a composite portrait of Dr. Ko Wen-je based on interviews with several sources: Dr. Vincent Sue, the key whistleblower behind the Taiwanese allegations, recordings of the Control Yuan's confidential session with then-Mayor Ko (where Ko confirmed the Taiwan extractions), a member of the Control Yuan (name withheld by request), a long-term medical associate of Dr. Ko (name withheld by request), Ko's ECMO guides, and my interview with Dr. Ko in July 2008 (Gutmann, *The Slaughter*, 253-258). One disclaimer: This chapter is not intended as an attempt at psychoanalysis, or as an attack on the use of ECMO in transplantation. Rather it's an educated guess; it's impossible to know Ko Wen-je's exact frame of mind when he was experimenting with ECMO. I wasn't there, and any account from Dr. Ko since he became a full-time politician must be treated as provisional at best. Regarding ECMO, two transplant surgeons have examined my impressionistic text to confirm that my layman's understanding is, at least, ballpark.

less credibility in the collective human mind than the most trusted professionals in the world.[12] The testimony of a doctor who either performed transplant surgery in China or was inside the Chinese transplant industry *is the gold standard of this investigation*. The snag is that if the Hippocratic oath embodies the principle "First, do no harm," the Chinese state puts greater weight on an unspoken codicil: "Preserve face."

This is not a textbook on organ harvesting. The China Tribunal provided a textbook in 2020. *The China Tribunal Judgement* is a doorstop—over 600 pages, written by ten authors, with original testimony from experts and witnesses alike. This book makes no claim to be the "definitive work." My goal is to introduce new or little-known evidence, victims, and investigative methods—not the final word, but critical evidence to build a platform for the investigation going forward. Yet as the first page of this chapter suggests, this can be a technically challenging subject, and it might require some background for you to understand what happened in Dr. Ko's office that day.

There are always exceptions that prove the rule–that's what footnotes are for–but I respect your time, so my approach is to answer three questions for you in a cutthroat fashion:

First: What are *the basic facts* of Chinese forced organ harvesting?

Second: What is *the basic timeline* (to 2016)?

Third: What was *the basic evidence* that persuaded the US House of Representatives and the China Tribunal that the Chinese Communist Party is exploiting political, ethnic, or prisoners of conscience for their organs?

---

12    Tasnim Nazeer, "First Known Survivor of China's Forced Organ Harvesting Speaks Out," *Diplomat*, August 19, 2024. I suspect that Cheng Pei Ming was being used as a transplant teaching prop or perhaps the equivalent of a "parts car" for a specific Party member.

# THE BASIC FACTS

1. Live organ harvesting is China's default method because it creates ideal conditions for the recipient.[13]

2. The "donor" does not survive.[14]

3. China is the only nation that performs state-sponsored organ harvesting on a mass scale.[15]

4. The extraction, the transplant, and the recovery of the recipient takes place in Mainland China.[16]

5. Harvesting is profitable.[17] The retail organs from a single human being, including corneal tissues, and assuming distribution to foreign organ tourists at the going rate, are worth approximately 600K to 700K in current USD.[18]

---

13   Matthew P. Robertson and Jacob Lavee, "Execution by organ procurement: Breaching the dead donor rule in China," *American Journal of Transplantation* 7 July 2022. See also Gutmann, *The Slaughter*, Chapter 1.

14   A single kidney extraction, survivable because we all carry a spare, barely appears in Chinese medical records by 2008. In 2015, China created a state-sponsored voluntary donation program of very limited utility, and even then, a family member kidney donation was statistically rare. M. P. Robertson, , R. L. Hinde, and J. Lavee, "Analysis of official deceased organ donation data casts doubt on the credibility of China's organ transplant reform," *BMC Medical Ethics* 20(1), 2019.

15   The exceptions (that prove the rule) are the Islamic State or ISIS (proven), North Korea (alleged), Vietnam (possible), and Kazakhstan (unproven and likely non-systematic).

16   Rumors of organs transplanted in China and flown to Thailand or prisoner donors delivered by submarine to Japan are theoretically possible but have little evidential support. In general, the Chinese State prefers to monitor and control the transplant environment.

17   I interviewed a Chinese citizen (name and location withheld) who acquired a liver transplant for under 10K by shopping around and waiting over six months. A foreign organ tourist with expedited service would normally pay 60-90K at a minimum. The China International Transplantation Network Assistance Center price list as early as 2005 was stated as: Kidney 62K, Liver 98- 130K, Lung 150-170K, Heart 130-160K, Cornea 30K. David Matas, "Chinese Organ Transplant Website—CITNAC" PowerPoint (2019).

18   Garden-variety assumptions at 2005 prices: Kidney 62K + kidney 62K + liver 98K + lung 150K + lung 150K + heart 130K + corneas 30K = 682K.

6. It's essentially legal. Although foreign organ tourists are technically not eligible to receive organs, Chinese hospitals blatantly advertise transplant services in English and Arabic on the Internet, and photographic evidence of foreign organ tourists in specific transplant hospitals is indisputable.[19]

7. Twenty years ago, Chinese medical representatives said that China's primary organ source was legally executed prisoners.[20]

8. China's transplant volume is at least 60,000 per year.[21]

9. The routine, openly advertised, waiting time of two weeks for an organ cannot be sustained on voluntary donations. Beijing's published rate of voluntary donations is a fictional number based on an equation.[22]

10. The underlying argument in the West boils down to whether Beijing only harvests "death row" prisoners, or whether Beijing also exploits political, ethnic, and religious prisoners (often called *prisoners of conscience*) for organs.[23]

---

19    Gutmann, *The Slaughter*, 276, screenshot of "Omar Healthcare Service."

20    Gutmann, *The Slaughter*, 270.

21    David Kilgour, Ethan Gutmann, David Matas, Bloody Harvest/The Slaughter: *An Update*, June 22, 2016, 359-361, hereafter "Update".

22    Robertson, *et al.* "Analysis of official deceased organ donation data."

23    Ethan Gutmann, "Organ Harvesting: An Examination of a Brutal Practice," Subcommittee on Africa, Global Health, Global Human Rights, and International Organizations and the Subcommittee on Europe, Eurasia, and Emerging Threats, Committee on Foreign Affairs, House of Representatives, Serial No. 114-170, June 23, 2016, 12-14.

## THE BASIC TIMELINE

- Early 1990s: Chinese organ harvesting of executed prisoners becomes routine.[24]

- 1994: Local PSB units on Xinjiang execution grounds began shooting not to kill, but to send the prisoner's body into shock, with doctors ordered to remove the liver and kidneys as the victim died.[25]

- 1995: Dr. Enver Tohti, a Uyghur surgeon, is ordered to extract kidneys and a liver from a live prisoner in the Western Mountain Execution Ground.[26]

- 1997: In the wake of the Ghulja Incident, Uyghur medical staff were quarantined while the Public Security Bureau (PSB) purged Uyghurs from the police force, executed local Uyghur activists, wrapped and sealed their bodies, and patrolled cemeteries to prevent family members from examining the corpses.[27]

- 1998: Chinese Communist Party cadres began flying into Urumqi to receive transplanted organs extracted from Uyghur political prisoners.[28]

- 1999: Falun Gong persecution begins.

---

24    Gutmann, *The Slaughter*, 15-20.
25    Gutmann, *The Slaughter*, 15-20.
26    Gutmann, *The Slaughter*, 17-19.
27    Gutmann, *The Slaughter*, 21-27.
28    Gutmann, *The Slaughter*, 25-27.

- 2001: With approximately two million Falun Gong in China's *Laogai* detention system," Falun Gong prisoners are singled out for "retail organs only" examinations.

- 2002: Wait times for foreign organ tourists are reported to be two weeks or less.

- 2003: Incarcerated Tibetans and House Christians receive "retail organs only" examinations.

- 2007: The Chinese medical establishment claims that they are performing 10,000 transplants a year.

- 2012: Bo Xilai, a leading competitor to rule China, is quietly exposed as a potential accomplice in forced organ harvesting. Chinese medical authorities declare they will cease organ harvesting of death-row prisoners over the next five years.

- 2016: Individual Chinese hospital numbers reveal that China is performing a minimum of 60,000 transplants every year.[29]

- 2016: Mass health checks, including blood and DNA testing, of all Uyghurs above the age of 12 in Xinjiang province are completed.

---

29    Gutmann, "Organ Harvesting," 12-14.

## THE BASIC EVIDENCE

In the summer of 2015, the House of Representatives introduced House Resolution 343 (114th): "Expressing concern regarding persistent and credible reports of systematic, state-sanctioned organ harvesting from non-consenting prisoners of conscience in the People's Republic of China, including from large numbers of Falun Gong practitioners and members of other religious and ethnic minority groups." The resolution passed in 2016.

In 2018, a non-governmental "people's tribunal" (the China Tribunal), based in London, launched a major inquiry into forced organ harvesting in China, chaired by Sir Geoffrey Nice KC, formerly lead prosecutor in the International Criminal Tribunal of Slobodan Milošević. The China Tribunal received, by my count, 172 documents in the form of books, reports, testimony (official and witness interviews), news reports, and even several guides to interpreting this mound of evidence. The Kilgour-Gutmann-Matas 2016 report alone required several days to read in detail.[30] The seven Tribunal members[31] read these documents in preparation for cross-examination of the witnesses (55 witness and expert testimonies in two separate sessions, five days in all). This led the China Tribunal to issue an interim judgement in December 2018: "The Tribunal's members are certain—unanimously, and sure beyond reasonable doubt—that in China forced organ harvesting from

---

30  "The 2016 joint update [the Kilgour, Matas, and Gutmann Report] runs to almost seven hundred pages and almost 2,400 footnotes, each providing citations to verifiable supporting information. The China Tribunal judgment, with its appendices, runs to almost six hundred pages. The list of relevant academic articles is long. The problem that this accumulation presents is not too little evidence of the mass killing of Falun Gong for their organs but rather too much evidence." From David Matas, "Forced Organ Harvesting in China: The Facts and the Law," Remarks, East Asia Library, Harvard University, March 7, 2024.

31  Eight if one counts Hamid Sabi, China Tribunal legal counsel.

prisoners of conscience has been practiced for a substantial period of time involving a very substantial number of victims."[32]

What was the main evidence that persuaded the House and Representatives and the China Tribunal that the Chinese Communist Party is exploiting political, ethnic, or prisoners of conscience for their organs?

- **Wait-time.** In nearly all countries, the wait-time for an organ is one or two years. In China, the wait time was *two weeks*.[33] *Killing on demand* reached its peak in certain hospitals which specialized in "emergency liver transplants" with a wait-time of *four hours*.[34]

- **The Human Stable.** An emergency liver transplant is only possible with a *large stable of human tissue types*. It's difficult to sustain a human stable created from hardcore criminals and death row prisoners. 1) They are tracked in the Chinese legal system so disappearances must be accounted for, and 2) the majority have unusable organs stemming from widespread drug addiction and hepatitis. A human stable requires individuals who live healthy lives (or seen from a Muslim halal perspective, individuals who do not eat pork). It also requires secrecy, with little possibility of political, economic, legal, family intervention, early release, or escape.

---

32    Sir Geoffrey Nice, *Interim Judgement: Hearing before Independent Tribunal into Forced Organ Harvesting from Prisoners of Conscience in China* (China Tribunal), December 10, 2018.

33    David Kilgour and David Matas, "Report into Allegations of Organ Harvesting of Falun Gong Practitioners in China," July 6, 2006, 26-27.

34    Charles Lee, "Organ Harvesting: An Examination of a Brutal Practice," Subcommittee on Africa, Global Health, Global Human Rights, and International Organizations and The Subcommittee on Europe, Eurasia, and Emerging Threats, Committee on Foreign Affairs, House of Representatives, Serial No. 114-170, June 23, 2016.

- **Falun Gong vulnerability.** There are five advocacy groups–
  Beijing calls them the "five poisons"–that were eligible
  for the human stable: Tibetan independence, Xinjiang
  separatism, Falun Gong, the Chinese democracy movement,
  and Taiwanese independence. While organ harvesting of
  political prisoners began with "Xinjiang separatists" in the
  mid- to late 1990s, the ideal victim group beginning in
  2000/2001 was Falun Gong because they were 1) plentiful,
  with at least a million detained, and 2) Falun Gong arrests
  were carried out in a legal gray zone. Short-term detention
  centers and black jails meant that a trial was optional,
  there were few legal complications in extending sentences
  indefinitely, and no family interventions. The majority of
  Falun Gong withheld their names to avoid causing trouble
  for their families.

- **Transplant volume.** The meteoric growth of the transplant
  industry (2001 to 2012) mirrors the incarceration rate of
  Falun Gong. All Falun Gong adherents in detention after
  2001 were subject to organ scanning and blood tests for
  tissue typing (or "cross-matching") with potential organ
  recipients.[35] From 2001 to 2016, I estimate that between
  125,000 to 250,000 in Falun Gong were harvested,[36] with
  an estimated 1,000,000 to 450,000 in detention at any given
  time.[37] Chinese transplant volume quickly went from the
  low thousands to the global leader in transplant volume.

---

35    New victim groups were exploited for organs: House Christians in 2002, and Tibetans in 2003.
      Gutmann, *The Slaughter*, 239-244.

36    Author's estimates. See Gutmann, *The Slaughter*, Appendix: "A Survey-Based Estimate of Falun
      Gong Harvested From 2000 to 2008."

37    Gutmann, *The Slaughter*, 319-320.

By 2012, China was transplanting over 60,000 to 100,000 organs per year, many to foreign "organ tourists."[38] The largest transplant hospitals (Tianjin Central) and the most luxurious transplant hospitals (China-Japan Friendship Hospital) specialized in catering to foreign patients.[39]

- **Witnesses, mass medical testing:** The torture of Falun Gong, the Uyghurs, Tibetans and House Christians, including rape, humiliation, and intentional physical damage or starvation, indicate that the CCP accorded hardened criminals a far higher status than political, religious or ethnic victim groups. Guards had a free hand. Normal executions might be rewarded with an unusual or fancy dinner. Selection for organ harvesting would be rewarded with cash. These aspects of prison life emerged through extensive interviews with over fifty witnesses, including former prison guards and special police agency personnel.[40] The majority of these interviews were focused on Falun Gong who experienced everything-but-harvesting. Mass hospital testing including EKGs and urine testing. Repetitive blood-testing in camps and prisons. Buses lining up and disappearances of their fellow prisoners in the middle of the night. Prison guard threats to take organs. Visiting doctors in lab coats waiting to begin surgery.

---

38   By contrast, official CCP transplant volume was routinely reported as 10,000 transplants per year. This reporting continued for well over a decade, while a handful of Chinese transplant hospitals could easily surpass this transplant volume. Kilgour, *et al.*, "Update," Chapter 10: "Exploring Total Volume of Kidney and Liver Transplants."

39   Main nationalities: German, Japanese, South Korean, and wealthy citizens from the Gulf States.

40   If one considers other sources as valid (for example, *Minghui*, Kilgour/Matas, World Organization to Investigate the Persecution of Falun Gong, and the China Tribunal), the number of recorded witness and refugee accounts is substantial.

- **A caution here.** While they are significantly closer to the coal face than any other humans in the world, all witnesses coming out of China have motives (in many cases the desire for revenge and hatred against those who persecuted them), which can lead to lies or exaggerations. I use several interview methods to guard against this kind of distortion, including no time constraints, and being willing to leave the interview on the cutting room floor. I performed my own field research as I cannot guarantee the veracity of other people's work.

- **Medical witnesses:**
  - » Dr. Enver Tohti confirmed a 1995 live organ harvesting of a prisoner, with the words, "I did it with my own hands." Although the operation took place on a Xinjiang execution ground, and the prisoner was the only one without a shaved head, Tohti could not be certain that the victim was a religious or political prisoner.

  - » In 2006, Falun Gong investigators posed as potential organ customers on the phone. A surprising number of Chinese medical staff admitted that they had Falun Gong organs for sale: "All we have are of this type." The potential flaw was that these were not surgeon confessionals, but sale situations, with a distinctly Mainland Chinese imperative to meet consumer demand. Yet the calls were made after the Falun Gong organ harvesting issue had already become newsworthy, so the fact that the investigators were able to get any results at all while Beijing's force shields were up, still stands as a triumph of investigative journalism.

» Western doctors such as Dr. Jacob Lavee from Israel had grave suspicions about the sourcing of hearts and livers because the Chinese hospitals would arrange a transplant weeks ahead of time, and pin it to a certain day, confirming the presence of a human stable.

» Theoretically, the ultimate proof of harvesting of prisoners of conscience would be a doctor who knew the inside of China's transplant industry and had helped to construct it.

Perhaps Dr. Ko Wen-je read the hunger for the ultimate proof on my face. Anyway, here's how it went down.

In July 2008, I was in Taipei at the tail end of my Asian field research for *The Slaughter*. My fixer and translator, a brilliant young man named Leeshai Lemish, was an Israeli Falun Gong practitioner, a very even-tempered combination. We were getting less material out of Taiwan compared with Thailand and Hong Kong, so the decision to interview Dr. Ko Wen-je felt like a final bet in the casino before calling it a night. The account of what happened inside that office appeared in *The Slaughter*. I'm reproducing the important bits here because the text played a pivotal role in several Taipei court cases, a Chinese translation of the interview was widely read throughout Taiwan, and Dr. Ko is on the record confirming that the account is accurate.[41]

---

41    My impressions of the beginning of the interview—the discomfort, the harsh language—are simply my best recall. That initial section was not "authorized" by Dr. Ko, and any errors in tone or recollection of phrases used are my own. I seldom run my writing by an interview subject before publication, but I considered Dr. Ko's testimony to be extremely important. Because we did not record our interview, in the interests of accuracy I gave Dr. Ko an advance draft of the section beginning with "I blandly opened," and he signed off on it. I made a few minor edits for style. The Taiwanese court system examined the original email for comparison and found no significant discrepancies.

However, I also have two, seemingly minor, corrections, and I'll get to those.

*There's a set moment in an interview when both sides feel out each other's intentions, and initially, I thought I was the problem. I wasn't quite ready to explain to Dr. Ko Wen-Je—a senior surgeon at National Taiwan University Hospital—that Leeshai had obtained his name through the Taiwanese medical grapevine by asking for someone who might know something about mainland transplants . . . in short, that our sitting down together was an absurd long shot. Nothing about Dr. Ko's demeanor, his urbane manner, even the sophistication of his gentle handshake suggested mainland rigidity or some sort of prejudice, but the air felt distinctly ominous, as if a thunderstorm was imminent. It didn't help that both of us—I'm a big guy and Ko's unusually tall— were perched on two flimsy plastic chairs inside a cramped little office, close enough to smell each other's sweat. I blandly opened by telling Dr. Ko that I was interested in any information he might be able to provide about organ harvesting in the mainland.*

*Dr. Ko dismissed my quest as futile. With impatient authority, Ko laid down all the confining features: There is no centralized database of organ donors in China. Instead, doctors use an informal eBay-style system because it's an entrepreneurial business that operates in a gray market. Hospital staffers use their personal connections to acquire donors and recipients alike. Advertising for organ transplants appears not only on the web (bait for foreigners, and I'd seen some of those sites) but also at the street level for potential Chinese patrons—stickers in phone booths, ads in little trade newspapers, flyers on bulletin boards.*

*The similarity to escort services ran through my mind. Perhaps a minute flicker of disgust crossed my face. Perhaps not. Either way, Dr. Ko appeared to take the silence as a challenge, and his voice rose slightly.*

*"You really don't understand, do you? You can do whatever you want in China. Cut someone up. Cut their dick off if you like."*

*He showed his teeth as he presented me with a smile that wasn't pleasant. This was unsettling. Yet my real fear was not that he would call me a stupid foreigner again but that he would shut down the interview. I had no choice but to be perfectly candid: "Look, I am not from a government agency. I can't make you talk about this. I'm just a writer. I have no power to prosecute you or cause trouble for your practice. And I know that you care about your patients. By going to the mainland for transplants, you are saving lives."*

Here's my first correction. Leeshai, as an active observer (the majority of the interview was conducted in English), concurs with it. When I was trying to calm Dr. Ko down, I didn't just say "Look, I am not from a government agency," but I also added "I'm not from the CIA."

I'll come back to the significance of this.

*". . . So is it true? Aren't prisoners of conscience—Falun Gong, perhaps others, being harvested?"*

*What happened next was something I thought only occurred in the movies. Ko's body seemed to simply retract, his jaw, his shoulders collapsing. His eyes gazing at the emptiness of the wall, he fell into a barely audible hiss. "Yes," Dr. Ko said, "Yes, they are doing that. Yes, it's true."*

In Taiwan, the wait for an organ is at least two years. But Dr. Ko's aging patients needed organs as soon as possible. Ko went to the Chinese Mainland to negotiate the price of full-service transplants on behalf of his clinic.

*A glance at the web established the foreigner price of $62,000 (US) for a kidney. Because the Chinese regarded the Taiwanese as slick foreigners wearing a Chinese mask, that would be his price, too. Yet native Chinese were paying half that or even less. This injustice gnawed at him. Somehow, where so many Taiwanese businessmen before him had failed, Dr. Ko would have to convince the mainland doctors he was not a foreign devil but a brother.*

*Dr. Ko went to China and meticulously worked through the check-list of intimacy with his medical colleagues: The go-to-hell banquet. The karaoke bar. The cognac followed by the Mao-Tai. The subtle flattery and the jokes about his accent. And when the ritual was truly finished, and everyone had sobered up, the Chinese surgeons summoned him.*

*"You are one of us. You are a brother. So we will give you the family price. But we are going to do more for you than that. We noted your worries and concerns about organ quality. And we trust your discretion. So you will have no worries for your patients. They will receive nothing but the best: all the organs will come from Falun Gong. These people may be a little fanatical, but you know? They don't drink. They don't smoke. Many of them are young, and they all practice healthy Chinese qigong. Soon your patients—they will be young and healthy, too."*

*And Dr. Ko smiled and thanked them politely, and the process began. But at the point of victory, Ko had felt no relief, only something that gnawed at him far worse than before. Something he could not speak of.*

Dr. Ko claimed he wanted to change the system from within. So Dr. Ko created a "mandatory" electronic form using simplified Mandarin characters (the form exists; Ko allowed me to cursor around the English version).[42] Ko said Mainland surgeons would be forced to submit detailed information on each organ donor to justify every transplanted organ, no exceptions.

*Maybe he could even have sold the system to the Chinese medical establishment, even received some sort of compensation, and yet—that gnaw again—even if the mainland doctors adopted the system, "you would only remove 95 percent of the problem," Ko said, shaking his head. . .*

*Anyway, they rejected it. It was obvious in retrospect that it was okay for the mainland doctors to run a sort of informal auction for organ trading, done through e-mails and discrete online user groups, but Ko's forms would either cut out too many donors from the system, create too much of a level playing field, or perhaps simply leave too much of an electronic trail. It was too late in the day, and it was sickening; the rejection was passed on to Dr. Ko with the respect you give to a distant cousin who doesn't quite get it.*

*Dr. Ko was whispering now: "But something should be done. Something should be done."*

---

42    Confidential sources argue that Ko had already been paid by the Taiwanese government to create such a form for Taiwanese surgeons, and it was a trivial effort to change the characters from traditional to simplified.

Reading this now, I recognize that I was swept away by Ko the Confessor, the sackcloth doctor who tried to slip a leash on the Chinese dragon. Yet for years to come, like many Taiwanese, I quietly wondered about Ko's underlying motive in giving the interview, and his sudden shift from hostility to grim candor. Was it based on guilt? If so, I didn't know the half of it yet. Post-traumatic stress disorder? A genuine desire to make things right?

I had to wait ten years for the answer, but I won't make you wait.

In October 2018, my Chinese publisher and I had lunch with Ko's former campaign manager. She opened by stating flatly: "Ko was obsessed with you. He used to yell at the TV screen when you appeared on the news." Listening to her intensity, it dawned on me that Ko and I had made a series of miscues, slips which gave birth to one of Taiwan's longest running black comedies.

Recall that I told Dr. Ko, "I'm not from the CIA." That's an ordinary phrase for an American to use if 1) he is not from the CIA and 2) wants to point out that he is someone with relatively little power—for example, a human rights investigator. Yet in Chinese culture, a spontaneous denial often means the exact opposite—i.e., "I'm CIA."[43]

The campaign manager confirmed: *Dr. Ko was absolutely convinced that I was from the CIA.* The dramatic shift in Dr. Ko's interview style followed his internal assumption that the CIA knew nearly everything about him already.[44]

Ko had faced the dragon. Now, disguised as a portly bald man, Ko thought he was facing the eagle. Ko read the sharp eye, the hungry

---

43    The Taipei mayor's office is a formidable player in Taiwanese society, for example in its ability to withhold access from major media outlets. Unsurprisingly, Dr. Ko's former campaign manager preferred to keep her name confidential.

44    To be on the safe side, I reinterviewed Ko's former campaign manager several years later. Her answers were essentially identical.

beak, and came up with an instant plan. He would feed the eagle. Ko would confess. Not to his own transgressions, but China's.

It worked. At the time I believed that Dr. Ko was essentially innocent, and I had no desire to look further, to examine the teeth of the gift horse. As I summarized Dr. Ko's contribution in *The Slaughter*:

> *His account is the smoking gun. It represents the culmination of a long quest to find medical confirmation of China's harvesting of prisoners of conscience from an unimpeachable source.*

There is one more correction.

Although we did not discuss it until years later, Leeshai Lemish with his unblinking gaze, noticed a sentence fragment from Dr. Ko right at the end of the interview, with a single word that Lemish did not understand at the time: "ECMO."

I've mentioned extracorporeal membrane oxygenation (ECMO) machines at the beginning of the chapter. I'll come back to ECMO because that technology is central to Ko's story and the development of the Chinese transplant industry. Yet just as I had gone into the interview knowing nothing about Dr. Ko, I left without following the single breadcrumb, ECMO, that Dr. Ko, perhaps out of subconscious guilt, perhaps out of perverse satisfaction that I had accepted his gambit, had dropped in our path.

The interview had been, by mutual agreement, "informational," that is, off the record. Indeed, I had not even taken notes. Ultimately, I wanted Dr. Ko to put the interview on the record and to become a spokesman for the cause of ending Chinese forced organ harvesting. On instinct, I held back for several years while Leeshai communicated with him from time to time. When a rumor flourished in the Falun Gong community that Beijing had created a centralized database of organ donors, I called Dr. Ko just to have him explain to me again that no such database exists. By 2013, I felt that our relationship was normalized. I was closing in on *The Slaughter*, so I wrote up an account of our interview for publication and—something I never do ordinarily with a witness—I asked Dr. Ko to read it. I would not publish without his approval.

Leeshai emailed the account and added a note to Ko in both English and Chinese:

"1. Under the circumstances that we don't mention your name, specific situations, or any details, is it okay to write this content? 2. Is his draft of the story (below) according to reality? Is it factual? Because at the time we didn't record and didn't ask you too much about this direction, so there are some situations we are not too clear about, we just remember the general drift. Could you take a look and tell us where the story has inaccuracies? If it's incorrect, how should it be correctly stated?"

Dr Ko's answer: "the story seems Ok"

In January 2014, I told Leeshai to write a new note:

"We wanted to ask you if we be willing to give us permission to use your name when mentioning the things you told us. In the past, we just referred to you as an "anonymous Taiwan doctor," but it is much more credible with a name. This will help the evidence. You would be doing a great service, maybe even help save some people's lives."

Dr Ko's answer: "OK for what I say, I can be Responsible."

We asked Ko for a headshot for the book.

Dr. Ko Wen-je's response to my request for a headshot, Courtesy of Dr. Ko Wen-je

With the third, "yes" from Dr. Ko, I remember, in a moment of euphoria, dancing around my office and delivering a cryptic status update on Facebook:

*One sweet dream came true today*

I never really doubted Ko's overall story. It had plenty of detail about the Chinese surgeons, the absurd negotiation tactics, and Ko told the story, even the revelation that the organs were coming from Falun Gong, in his trademark deadpan absurdist style. And Ko was honest enough to reveal his underlying wish that a Mainland Chinese entity would financially compensate him for his medical donor form. There were even moments where I found the two of us smiling (Leeshai just kept his trademark no-blink stare). However, I can only speculate on what Ko was thinking when he signed off on his inclusion in my book. Was it a sincere attempt to join the cause to end forced organ harvesting? Personal grandiosity? An attempt to curry favor with the CIA? It may be germane that, when I called Ko in 2013, he mentioned something about Mainland China blocking him from entry (possibly a temporary restriction), so he may have been looking for warmer relations with the US.[45]

I have little to say about Ko, the politician. He was an ambitious man. The mayor of Taipei arguably stands on the best possible springboard to make a run for the presidency of Taiwan. Yet Ko also had a disarmingly low-key quality, and that same arch irony that I had witnessed in the interview. Young Taiwanese loved his idiosyncratic humor and his nerdy, approachable style. His background was neither fully "Green" (Democratic Progressive Party or DPP) nor "Blue" (Kuomintang or KMT). The Greens ended up supporting Ko, but many Taiwanese, and even many in the US State Department, simply saw Ko as a charismatic figure who could break the increasingly sterile deadlock between the two parties.

What followed in the mayoral campaign, in truncated form, is this: a few days before the Ko interview, back in 2008, I had coffee with a prominent human rights lawyer and Falun Gong activist, Tung Wen-Hsun, not far from Taipei 101. Ultimately, she read *The Slaughter* in English and translated the Dr. Ko section into Chinese. The press seized on the account and threw it onto the front pages. The emphasis was on Ko's negotiation with the Chinese transplant surgeons, not on Ko as a middleman between two medical clinics, one in Taiwan, one in the Mainland, but as an *organ broker*. I didn't say that. Ko had presented his attempt to bargain for lower transplant prices in altruistic terms, so I gave him the benefit of the doubt. I'd mentioned a karaoke bar in the negotiation process (standard rite of passage for any deal in Mainland China), but the press interpreted that as Ko cavorting with prostitutes, rather than simply having drinks with Chinese transplant doctors. In

---

45     An ostentatious but seemingly pointless visit to America was incorporated into Ko's mayoral campaign in 2014.

short, the coverage centered on frivolous issues, with little attention paid to the Chinese state forced organ harvesting of Falun Gong.

Dr. Ko, now a full-time political candidate, seemed to go into an outright panic. Over several weeks, he went through a series of contradictory denials: 1) There was no interview. Gutmann was clearly mixing Ko up with some other doctor. 2) Ko had given the interview, but Gutmann has a feverish, wild imagination. 3) Gutmann had secretly taped the interview but was withholding it, because it would exonerate Ko. 4) Ko had taped the interview. The tape is in his possession. Releasing it would exonerate Ko. 5) Gutmann had simply made up the entire thing; why else would Gutmann be hiding from the press and making no comment?[46] Ko was right about the "no comment" point. I was on book tour in Canada, and I chose to say nothing to the Taiwanese press inquiries which showed up in my inbox day after day. The reason? The Taipei practitioners had a problem. Taipei 101, the world's tallest building from 2004 to 2010, is laid out in a large and beautiful square. Falun Gong practitioners are attracted to such locations because Mainland tourists tend to be fascinated with uncensored news from China. So the practitioners ran a modest "truth clarification" booth or table in the square, as well as occasional Falun Gong exercise displays. The Concentric Patriotism Association, in essence Taiwan-based Chinese Communist provocateurs, would attack the Falun Gong installation regularly, tearing up the materials, shouting and physically threatening the non-violent practitioners.

Theresa Chu, a legal expert, and an influential leader of the Falun Gong practitioners of Taiwan (rumored to be 40,000 strong) had a friendly relationship with Ko Wen-je. According to Theresa Chu, Mayor Ko would put a stop to the CCP bullying of practitioners.

---

46    For one example among many, see English-language press coverage, Autumn 2014: Chu-min Tu, *et al.*, "2014 ELECTIONS: Ko Denies Organ Buying Allegations," *Taiwan News*, October 29, 2014.

Local politics 101. Theresa Chu, Falun Gong defender. Courtesy of Wikimedia.

From my perspective, the truth clarification booth was a second order issue, but I had a larger concern: If Mainland China had become a slave ship for Falun Gong practitioners, Taiwan was the life-raft. If the PLA invaded, Falun Gong's position in Taiwan would echo the vulnerability of the Hungarian Jews when the Nazis appeared at the border. Even if the police managing the post-invasion were Taiwanese-born, Falun Gong would be identified, rounded up, and those practitioners who did not publicly renounce Falun Gong would be shipped across the strait to Mainland re-education camps and mental hospitals with armed guards. Healthy practitioners in their mid-twenties to mid-thirties would be used as local stable of tissue types for organ harvesting on demand. I apologize for the Holocaust comparison here, but that historical event has permeated my entire working life, so I could vividly picture this potential scenario for Falun Gong.

I would stay loyal to the Taiwan practitioners even as their loyalty to me and to the issue of Falun Gong harvesting, was cast aside for political expediency. I did not contest Theresa Chu as she cast subtle aspersions on my work and attempted to mollify Ko Wen-je; I read it as fear for her people. And no matter how much it disturbed me to see my picture next to Ko's on the front page of a Taiwan newspaper with a question mark above my head, and as much as I had the distinct feeling that I had a hammer in my stomach, created by equal parts fear and impotent rage, I believed that the CCP would only fully win this scenario if it could get Dr. Ko and I into a direct fight. Ko's attacks on me were amateurish, but I knew he was getting torn up in the Taipei press, so he was passing on the pressure. We were both politically inexperienced, so in our better moments, I felt a certain amused bonding, as if we were both equally clumsy dancers asked to perform on stage.

I sat on my evidence, and the three permission emails from Dr. Ko that would have revealed the lies of mayoral candidate Ko and, very likely, cut deep into his polling lead. Ko's team interpreted my silence as weakness. Through the Falun Gong pipeline, the threats of vaguely defined legal action, of denunciation, started to come down. Underneath it all lay a hostage: Falun Gong in Taiwan. But it would all be resolved if I would only agree to re-write the Ko section of the chapter to Ko Wen-je's exact specifications.[47]

I allowed that I would "think about that." Like a game of Chinese whispers, or perhaps simply by wishful thinking, when my words reached Dr. Huang Shiwei, the Falun Gong practitioner who had suggested talking to Ko in the first place and now was handling the negotiation, he interpreted them as a "yes" and openly broadcast to the Taiwan press that the author was going to change his book. Simultaneously, the first legal letters from Ko's camp had started to arrive, demanding that my book be changed to Ko's liking and setting out their arbitrary deadlines. I huddled with Clive Ansley, an even-tempered Canadian

---

47  "On behalf of Dr. Ko... I will request you to correct these parts [in *The Slaughter*] which are not done by Dr. Ko, especially the contact with mainland China officials about purchase of organs, not to mention that these organs are from Falun Gong." Hsiu Hui Yuan, "RE: The Slaughter," Letter from Chang-Hui Law Office to Ethan Gutmann, October 28, 2014.

human rights attorney, and a veteran from practicing law in China for many years. We came up with a plan. He would send a few letters stalling for time, while also pointedly missing their deadlines. Then, when the time was right, we would throw Ko a rubber bone.

I won't quote the Ansley letter here, although it is a kind of masterwork. It praises Dr. Ko as a man who behaved honorably, shifts the blame for any misunderstanding to poor or biased translation, asserts there are cultural misunderstandings and misinterpretation of a caption to Ko's photo (that point was unambiguously true), and talks glowingly about Ko having made a significant contribution to exposing medical crimes still being committed in China.

Ko seized on the letter like a drowning man clinging to driftwood. In a televised debate, Ko's KMT opponent brought up the "organ broker" issue. Ko theatrically opened the envelope and read our letter aloud. It was the end of the issue. But not quite for me. Following a hearing at Westminster, on the eve of Taipei's election, there were a couple of Taiwan stringers in the hall. I made an impulsive statement to the Taiwanese press: "Taipei has been in a brutal political campaign. And people say a lot of things during campaigns. . . yet, as one Taiwanese reporter finally noticed, in my endnotes, I described quite clearly how I received Dr. Ko's permission to publish the interview. The Taiwan press wanted soundbites. Well, *I'm a human rights investigator, not a political kingmaker.* And the murder of tens of thousands of innocent people should not be exploited as political theatre."

For the first time in my life, I was using the Chinese principle of opposites. I'm "not a political kingmaker" meant "I'm a political kingmaker, and I spared Ko's head."

Predictably "Gutmann says he is not a political kingmaker" was front page news in Taipei (to Ko's irritation).[48] In fact, the Taiwanese

---

48    Name withheld, interview, Dr. Ko's Former Campaign Manager, 2018.

press was extremely pro-Ko by this point, so perhaps that's why my final sentence "And I stand by every word in my book" was edited out. Only one lawyer, Bob Kao from California, picked up on the charade; there was *nothing* in the Ansley letter about changing the text of *The Slaughter*.[49]

Ko went on to win the election by a comfortable margin, and he quickly fulfilled his campaign promise of getting the ersatz-CCP hoodlums to stop attacking the Falun Gong booth under the shadow of Taipei 101. The thugs were even forced to issue a written apology.[50]

I made an eight-minute video setting the record straight, telling my side of the story and the story of the publishing permission process, showing on camera the actual text of Ko's email responses and leaving nothing out. I praised Ko's courage for coming forward with the story in the first place, thereby leaving the door open for Ko to return to "something should be done." Normally this would have been front page material, but the ever-impatient Taiwan press had pulled up their tents and moved on.

For months, I had been aching to pull that hammer out of my gut and start swinging it. All that time, I had assumed that Theresa Chu knew the local situation in Taiwan, and I didn't. All that time, I wanted to be kind to the Falun Gong practitioners who had been kind to me. I had kept faith with Falun Gong, although it went against my political instincts.

What was the result? My key witness to Mainland organ harvesting now had a permanent asterisk by his name. In their rush to discredit me and *The Slaughter* to appease Dr. Ko's ever-changing explanations, some Taiwanese Falun Gong practitioners had undermined the credibility of

---

49    M. Bob Kao, "How Involved Was Ko in the Chinese Organ Trade?," *New Bloom Magazine*, December 18, 2014

50    Yu-Yan Cheng, "Taiwan: Pro-Communist Group Openly Apologizes to Falun Gong," *Minghui. Org*, April 30, 2015

the global forced organ harvesting investigation. And the great city of Taipei, *the Constantinople of our time*, was left in the hands of a deeply, perhaps fatally, compromised man—I apologize for not having seen it earlier—who was poised to become President, a potential Manchurian candidate seemingly ready to make the deal of deals with the CCP.[51]

Did that apology from the Concentric Patriotism Association make its way into a frame on Theresa Chu's office wall? I don't know, but that's the sum total that we got from the Falun Gong election strategy: a trophy. Beijing won the cup.

Three years later, Brian Wu (Wu Hsiang-hui), a prolific and talented Taiwanese writer, phoned me in London, suggesting that we meet up. If a Taiwanese political pundit with legions of enemies and dedicated followers wanted to see me, I reasoned, it was about Ko. I wanted three things:

1. To publish my book in Mandarin for Taiwan. And for the Mainland, I wanted a PDF with a simplified character version, easy to bootleg, and free of charge.[52]
2. To remove the asterisk on Ko's testimony for the world. For the Taiwanese public, to clear up any misconceptions about the interview.
3. To raise awareness within Taiwan on forced organ harvesting. To make Taiwan the central engine of research on the issue.

---

51    Brian Hioe, "Ko Wen-Je's Shanghai Trip Causes Controversy After Live Stream of Meeting Cut Off by Chinese Officials," *New Bloom Magazine*, July 9, 2019. It's germane that Chinese state-controlled television sponsored unusually positive post-election coverage on Mayor Ko for the mainland audience.

52    The previous attempts to publish a Chinese edition had been upended by a well-meaning Chinese Falun Gong practitioner who found herself pining to rewrite the book, and the fact that Hong Kong was no longer a publishing center for China-critical material.

Brian and I got together at a hotel near Paddington. He is an interesting guy, intelligent, funny, and passionate. I got down to business, and I took him on a tour through the permission emails and all the correspondence with Ko. His eyes lit up. He paused. And then without me even asking he granted the three wishes: his publishing house, Butterfly Orchid Cultural Creativity, would translate, promote, and print the Chinese edition of *The Slaughter* with full reproduction of the Ko-Lemish-Gutmann email chain. If I were amenable, he would pay for my trip to Taiwan where I would be free to promote my book and hammer on the harvesting issue.

Brian Wu, the architect of the rematch. Courtesy of Brian Wu.

Brian also made it perfectly obvious that he was an enemy of Mayor Ko. In my opinion: the Chinese character at its peak expression—that is, at war—is shattering both in its brilliance and raw aggression. Brian personified both qualities. Plotting strategy with a Chinese ally can be, in my experience, one of life's greatest pleasures. Yet Brian needed to understand my motives.

*Ethan, what is your attitude and understanding of your relationship with Dr. Ko through these two periods? 1st period—Ko as witness and revealer. 2nd period—Ko denied his testimony.*[53]

*When I spoke to Ko in 2008—the 1ˢᵗ period—he was a doctor, but also a man who appeared to have been traumatized by something in China. He seemed to feel some relief in the telling, and I respected him for the telling. I respected him much more when he agreed that we could use his name. The 2nd period was Candidate Ko: Well, politicians lie or play with the truth. It's part of the job. But I had hoped—maybe I was stupid to think this—that Dr. Ko would confirm the interview when he became Mayor. My account was accurate. I had Ko's signature that it was accurate. Even if he did not want to talk about the interview, he could join the movement to stop Chinese organ harvesting. He could join ETAC.*

*What's that?*

*The International Coalition to End Transplant Abuse in China. Or he could have joined DAFOH–that stands for Doctors Against Forced Organ Harvesting. But this silence, this denial, has lasted almost four years. So, the 3rd period, the Mayor Ko period, this is where I began to suspect that something else was wrong.*

*What do you mean?*

*I don't know. It's a feeling. But Brian, if you are asking me if I hate Dr. Ko? No, I don't. I suspect this is a man cornered by his own history. The door is still open for Dr. Ko to join ETAC or DAFOH.*

*Would you plan to criticize Dr. Ko for the ways he has changed?*

*He can redeem himself by actions. Dr. Enver Tohti stood up at a Westminster hearing three miles from here, and publicly confessed to me that, as a surgeon in Xinjiang, he had removed two kidneys and a liver from a living human being. Now Enver has spoken about that all over the world.*

---

53    This conversation is abridged from a private conversation that Brian and I had on Signal when he returned to Taiwan. He wanted the answers translated precisely. The actual conversation that we had in London was extremely similar. The initial translation was problematic because it was in the context of a negotiating a book deal.

*Dr. Ko gave, or maybe began, a confession. Now he denies it. Did politics intervene? Did fear intervene? Or maybe Chinese blackmail? But if Mayor Ko had confirmed Dr. Ko's account, would the Vatican have just made a deal with China? Would so many people in China have been harvested? A terrible question, yes?*

I knew the mayoral election was coming up in a couple of months, but I thought I could pull off a measure of neutrality. If anyone asked me who they should vote for in the upcoming the mayoral election, I would simply respond, "How are the potholes in Taipei?"

Plans like this don't last long in Taiwanese politics. When Brian returned to Taiwan, he took out a full-page ad in the *Liberty Times* on September 3, promoting my book's revelations about Ko in the Chinese language.[54] Headlines promising a Ko-Gutmann rematch quickly followed. Well, that's what a publisher does, but my instinct was that I needed to soften Brian's approach a little to maintain credibility. My long-standing literary agent, Maryann Karinch, stepped in and—with her brilliant disarming tactics—made a deal with Brian to act as co-publisher. It worked: Brian held back a little, and the book gained the stature of a joint Taiwan-US venture. Meanwhile hundreds of young Taiwanese, Ko's army, flocked to my Facebook page and began suspiciously sounding me out. If you have ever been on the receiving end of a rapidly moving social media miasma, you may understand the feeling. But it was totally new to me.

I can't say that I handled it well. Because it wasn't clear whether I was really a threat to Mayor Ko, I initially spent way too much time trying just to be liked, clowning around, trying to make people feel comfortable as if they were in a cocktail party, even as they searched for my weak points, like a mugger staring fixedly at my fake Rolex. I

---

54    Brian also held a mini-press conference in which he showed the signed book-deal contract. Although it may be routine in Taiwan, I found this slightly alarming at the time.

did, as I honestly told the Ko people, learn something about Taiwan, or at least something about Taiwanese youth culture. Enough that I could sense they were audacious on the Internet but courtly in person, much like Brian Wu.

Of course, that was then.

The eight-minute tape that I had made shortly after the election resurfaced, was translated, and went viral, racking up millions of views.[55] Most people initially concentrated on the fact that I spoke positively about Dr. Ko. The cleverer ones recognized that Dr. Ko's emails meant that he was misleading the media and his supporters throughout the previous campaign.

The Ko army, ultimately and predictably, turned, making me, or the symbolic me, the most hated man in Taiwan: Liar! Murderer! Shame! appeared repeatedly on my feed, partially accelerated by Mainland bots.[56]

I understood their anger. A foreign hired gun who couldn't even speak Chinese versus a Taiwanese folk hero. It demanded reserves of Zen-like maturity to sustain the hits. Somehow, like a burst of anti-adrenaline, a sort of shaky balance came in. I distanced myself, rationalizing that being hated was "character-building." I even mangled a James Bond haiku: "You only live twice," I told myself. "Once when you are born. And once when you look the mob in the face."[57]

The mob were clearly taking cues. Mayor Ko said that his friends (the Ko army) might come out to greet me at the airport. My male pattern baldness came into play. According to his campaign manager, as Ko watched me on television, he groused that I looked *like a hitman*, then Ko publicly proclaimed that he had inside knowledge for his

---

55  I posted it again too, just to be transparent.

56  I gleaned from a Facebook debate on my page that there was a never-fully-realized plan to take a Falun Gong woman who had recently been tortured in China and have her publicly denounce me.

57  Ian Fleming, *You Only Live Twice* (New American Library, 1964).

welcoming committee: I would fly into Taipei on September 18.[58] I responded on Facebook that I would be "washing my hair that day" to the amusement of Taiwan's newsrooms.

Nightly news program capture, early September, 2018. Courtesy of Butterfly Orchid Cultural Creativity

I was receiving long formal emails daily—mostly from university professors and other members of the intelligentsia—praising Ko's good character and beseeching me not to confront him or cause any embarrassment. These letters, with the understanding that they were written in English, a second language, had a template feel and they never addressed the central issue, that Ko was a witness who had run away from his own testimony. Yet I did receive one email which had a certain furtive urgency that seemed to burn a little brighter on my screen. It was from a medical associate of Ko's. He used a moniker (I would meet him in person later). The text was brief, urging me to look at a mainland website.

I booted up a spare computer to contain any potential virus and typed in the URL. It was a website created for a 2008 conference held in Wuxi People's Hospital, resembling an ad for a now deserted hotel that someone had forgotten to delete. Here were headshots

---

58    In an email, I had discussed that date previously but not committed to it. I took Ko's statement as an indication to confine my Taiwan communications exclusively to Signal going forward.

of the participants, a few formally posed photos taken during the conference itself, and, most critically, the conference schedule. I flipped the Chinese to English: "The 4th National Cardiopulmonary Transplantation High-Level Seminar and the First Medtronic ECMO Training Course," an ECMO conference bearing the brand name that Ko was hawking, and the keynote speaker of the luncheon on the first day? *"Clinical application and progress of ECMO" Ke Wenzhe, School of Medicine, National Taiwan University.*

*The only foreigner at the conference.* Yet it was the names surrounding Dr. Ko—hospitals and doctors—that made me catch my breath.

The schedule guide that follows is a melting pot of research, with three major sources:

1. I don't claim to have an encyclopedic knowledge of anything Chinese. The language is a massive impediment, and I have never had that gift, but as a co-author of the 2016 Matas-Kilgour-Gutmann report on Chinese transplant volume, I am unusually familiar with Chinese transplant hospitals, and the major surgeons associated with them, suspected of sourcing their organs from Falun Gong.

2. I was acquainted with a key female researcher at the World Organization to Investigate the Persecution of Falun Gong (WOIPFG), a peerless expert on Chinese transplant surgeons.

3. Finally, a small group of Taiwanese Falun Gong researchers found this conference schedule irresistible, so they ignored the never-criticize-Ko policy and, while I was in Taiwan,

they passed me some of their genius research through an intermediary. I'm very grateful for their contribution.

The original looks like this:

While we do not have information on everyone who participated, the schedule decoded, with hospitals and transplant surgeons highlighted (and annotated in the footnotes), looks like this:

## The 4th National Cardiopulmonary Transplantation High-Level Seminar and the First Medtronic ECMO Training Course

**Meeting schedule**

**2008.4.25 (Friday) (Blue Sky Newport)**

**Full-day registration**

**2008.4.26 (Saturday)**

## I. Opening Ceremony
## Wuxi People's Hospital[59] Multifunctional Hall, Zone F, Third Floor
## 8:30~9:00
## Chair: Zheng Konglin, Executive Vice President
Provincial and municipal leaders welcome speeches
Welcome speech by Ji Jianwei, Wuxi People's Hospital

## II. Special report of the conference Cardiopulmonary Transplantation
## 9:00~12:00
## Conference Chairs: Professor Chen Zhonghua, Professor Chen Yijiang, Professor Liu Deruo[60]
## 9:00~10:30
9:00~9:20 Redefining brain death with ventilator as the center—-Necessity and feasibility of starting China's "Critical Death Judgment Criteria"
Chen Zhonghua,[61] Wuhan Tongji Hospital

---

59    Wuxi Peoples' Hospital lung transplant center claims to be among the top three in the world and to have completed more than half of all lung transplant surgeries in China. Source: Kilgour, *et al.*, "Update."

60    Liu Deruo is/was a physician at the Department of Surgery in the China-Japan Friendship Hospital, a common destination for wealthy Japanese "organ tourists." Liu participated in performing organ extraction and perfusion in seven cases of single lung allotransplantation from brain-dead "donors" up to 2008. Sources: Taiwanese Falun Gong working group, WOIPFG expert, Kilgour, *et al.*, "Update."

61    Chen Zhonghua participated in multi-organ extractions from 65 "donors" from January 2000 to August 2006. When Chen ran the Wuhan Tongji Hospital Institute of Organ Transplantation in 2006, a recorded phone call captured the hospital being asked whether it could perform live organ transplantation from Falun Gong prisoners. A staff member in the Kidney Transplant Department said: "Sure, it's no problem. When you are ready, you can come over directly and we will discuss it in detail." Chen became the first Executive Chairman of the Organ Donation Management Commission of China, established in 2006. Sources: Kilgour and Matas "Report." Taiwanese Falun Gong working group, WOIPFG expert, Kilgour, *et al.*, "Update."

9:20~9:50 Progress of the International Cardiopulmonary Transplant Symposium 2007 (VAIL Conference) Chen Jingyu,[62] Wuxi People's Hospital

9:50~10:10 Improve the long-term efficacy of heart transplantation—The experience of heart transplantation in Fuwai Hospital Beijing Song Yunhu,[63] Fuwai Hospital 10:10~10:30 Discussion, tea break

---

62 The "No.1 Lung Transplant Surgeon in China," Chen Jingyu participated in performing extraction of lungs from 129 "donors" between September 2002 and December 2011. By 2014, Chen was doing up to five lung transplants per day. His team taught advanced techniques to 30 hospitals. At Wuxi People's Hospital, Chen developed pulmonary perfusion preservation solutions, doubling lung retention time to nearly eight hours. In 2015, Chen remarked, "Originally, I thought the number of available donor lungs would decrease, since the practice of using death row prisoners as donors has been abolished. However, who would have thought that we are even busier than last year. Now we perform one lung transplant every three days." Sources: Taiwanese Falun Gong working group, WOIPFG expert, Kilgour, *et al.*, "Update."

63 Song Yunhu is the chief surgeon of one of the largest heart transplant centers in the world. Fuwai Hospital began performing heart transplants as a routine procedure in 2004 and claims to have performed the most heart transplants in China (though Zhongshan Hospital claims a much higher annual rate). Source: Kilgour, *et al.*, "Update."

## Conference Chairs: Professor Gao Chengxin,[64] Professor Chen Liangwan,[65] Professor Meng Xu[66] 10:30~11:50

10:30~10:50 Problems and Thoughts on Chinese Heart/Lung Transplantation

---

64  Gao Chengxin of the Shanghai Chest Hospital was the first Chinese doctor to study lung transplantation. The hospital began clinical lung transplants in 2002, performed the first lobar lung transplant in China, and had the most bilateral lung transplants in China. It may be germane that Dr. Han Baohui, Director of Pulmonary Medicine, Shanghai Chest Hospital, reported classmate Zhao Bin to the police for practicing Falun Gong. Zhao was arrested on April 27, 2012, and was subsequently tortured to death at Tilanqiao Prison, Shanghai, on October 19, 2013. Sources: Taiwanese Falun Gong working group, WOIPFG expert.

65  Chen Liangwen from the Department of Cardiovascular Surgery of Fujian Medical University Union Hospital participated in the extraction of hearts from 111 brain-dead "donors" (average age 25 ±7 years, with no cardiovascular diseases), warm ischemia time 0-15 minutes, from August 1995 to October 2007. The hospital has successfully performed heart transplants for patients with advanced heart disease from more than 30 cities and regions of China, holding 16 "first in the country" titles. Sources: Taiwanese Falun Gong working group, WOIPFG expert, Kilgour, *et al.*, "Update."

66  Meng Xu is the founder of the Beijing Heart Transplant Center and claims to be the most prolific transplant surgeon in China, specializing in heart transplants for end-stage heart failure. He took part in heart extraction for orthotopic heart transplantation from 51 male "donors," age range 21-43 yrs, with no history of cardiovascular diseases or diseases in major organs, warm ischemia time 3-8 minutes, from April 1992 to April 2006. He claims to have independently completed nearly 10,000 surgeries, with over 800 operations every year. See also caption to ECMO conference photo. Sources: Taiwanese Falun Gong working group, WOIPFG expert, Kilgour, *et al.*, "Update."

Wang Chunsheng,[67] Shanghai Zhongshan Hospital
10:50~11:10 The Beijing Anzhen Hospital[68] Heart Transplant Experience
Meng Xu, Beijing Anzhen Hospital
11:10~11:30 Status and thinking of lung transplantation in China
Chen Jingyu, Wuxi People's Hospital
11:30~11:50 Discussion

---

67 Wang Chunsheng is Director of Cardiac Surgery at Zhongshan Hospital in Shanghai. Wang conducted heart extraction for orthotopic heart transplantation from May 2000 to April 2011 on 298 "donors" (male 283, female 15, *average age 26.8 years*, no history of obvious cardiovascular diseases or other major organ diseases). Since 2007, 60 hearts were extracted at the status of ventricular fibrillation or non-beating heart; 238 hearts were extracted with hearts still beating. Zhongshan itself is Shanghai's premier organ transplant center. In March 2006, in a recorded call to the Zhongshan Hospital Organ Transplant Clinic, it was established that the hospital used Falun Gong organs: **Investigator:** *So how long do I have to wait [for organ transplant surgery]?* **Doctor:** *About a week after you come.* **Investigator:** *Is there the kind of organs that come from Falun Gong? I heard that they are very good.* **Doctor:** *All of ours are those types.* A 2015 quote from Tan Yunshan, director of Zhongshan Hospital's liver disease department indicates the sensitivity of the hospital's extraction policy: *"All the donor livers are directly extracted at the source. Because we do the extraction ourselves and have access to the original information of the donor organ, we would know for sure whether a donor liver can be used or not. . . . We don't care whether it's from a Falun Gong practitioner or not. We don't get involved in politics. As doctors, we only care about the donor liver, about whether it meets the requirements of transplantation. If it meets the requirements, we don't care who it's from."* Sources: Taiwanese Falun Gong working group, WOIPFG expert, Kilgour, *et al.*, "Update."

68 With over 4000 employees, 1500 beds, and 31 operating rooms, Beijing Anzhen Hospital is one of China's largest and most innovative cardiac surgery centers and is noted for performing the world's first four combined heart, bone marrow, and stem cell transplants. Recipients experienced low rejection rates and required low quantities of immunological drugs. Sources: Taiwanese Falun Gong working group, WOIPFG expert, Kilgour, *et al.*, "Update."

## III. ECMO Luncheon

12:00~13:00

## Conference hosts: Professor Chen Xin,[69] Professor Zhang Lin,[70] Professor Wang Huishan[71]

Clinical application and progress of ECMO

Ke Wenzhe,[72] School of Medicine, National Taiwan University

## IV. Conference report on ECMO

13:00~15:40

## Conference Chair: Professor Li Yingze, Professor Liu Su,[73] Professor Song Yunhu 13:00~14:20

13:00~13:20 ECMO in the perioperative period of heart transplantation

---

69  Chen Xin of Nanjing First Hospital participated in performing extraction of hearts for transplantation from six brain-dead "donors" (age range, 27 to 39 years) from August 2001 to April 2003. Sources: Taiwanese Falun Gong working group, WOIPFG expert, Kilgour, *et al.*, "Update."

70  Physician Zhang Lin is Deputy Chief Physician, Department of Thoracic Surgery, at Shandong Provincial Hospital, the only certified lung transplant department in Shandong Province. Lin performed the first case in Shandong Province of single lung transplantation on January 21, 2005, plus lung extraction from a traumatic brain-dead "donor" with warm ischemia time less than 8 minutes. Sources: Taiwanese Falun Gong working group, WOIPFG expert, Kilgour, *et al.*, "Update."

71  Wang Huishan is believed to be a heart transplant surgeon and Chief Physician at General Hospital of Shenyang Military Command, PLA. Located in the "Liaoning Triangle," close to Shenyang Prison City, this hospital was identified in Gutmann, *The Slaughter*, as a key center for Falun Gong harvesting. On April 9, 2002, an armed guard in an operating room on the 15th floor directly witnessed two military doctors extract organs from a female Falun Gong practitioner. Sources: Taiwanese Falun Gong working group, WOIPFG expert, Gutmann, *The Slaughter*.

72  "Ke Wenzhe" is alternate pinyin for "Ko Wen-je."

73  Vice President Liu Su is from the Second Hospital of Hebei Medical University, a regional-level kidney and heart transplant center that performed the first living-donor kidney transplant in the province. On April 7, 2011, Liu's expert group performed a heart transplant for a 13-year-old; the hospital found a matching child donor for the patient in under a week. Sources: Taiwanese Falun Gong working group, WOIPFG expert, Kilgour, *et al.*, "Update." It is interesting that following Liu's panel at 14:20, Lin Ru of the Zhejiang Children's Hospital was presenting on "ECMO application in pediatric diseases." While pediatric transplantation is not the norm, or the focus of my research, it is undeniable that the waiting times for child or infant organs are strangely truncated and the number of children, particularly Uyghur children, that have gone missing in China, at least on an anecdotal basis, has dramatically increased over the past decade.

Song Yunhu, Beijing Fuwai Hospital

13:20~13:40 ECMO in the perioperative period of patients with severe heart disease

Meng Xu, Beijing Anzhen Hospital

13:40~14:00 ECMO support for internal medicine emergency

Li Xin, Shanghai Chest Hospital

14:00~14:20 Discussion, tea break

**Conference Chairs: Professor Yin Bangliang,[74] Professor Zhang Shijiang,[75] Professor Wang Ping[76]**

**14:20~15:40**

14:20~14:40 ECMO application in pediatric diseases

Lin Ru, Zhejiang Children's Hospital

14:40~15:00 Clinical application of ECMO

---

74   Yin Bangliang is hospital director, and Chief Physician, Cardiothoracic Surgery, in heart and heart-lung transplantation for the Second Xiangya Hospital of Central South University. He participated in two cases of combined heart-lung extractions from "donors" in September 2003 and in April 2006. His hospital ranked 19th among the 100 most competitive hospitals in China in 2015. The surgeons are kept busy: "Transplant surgeons often have to work for over 20 consecutive hours performing surgeries. They will start another round of operations after they rest for three or four hours. . . . They often conduct a dozen operations over a period of two to three days. They once performed nine kidney transplants in one day." Sources: Taiwanese Falun Gong working group, WOIPFG expert, Kilgour, *et al.*, "Update."

75   Zhang Shijiang is Chief Physician, Department of Cardiothoracic Surgery at Jiangsu Province People's Hospital. Zhang participated in extracting lungs from four brain-dead young male "donors" during June 2006 to January 2007. Sources: Taiwanese Falun Gong working group, WOIPFG expert.

76   Wang Ping, based on the composition of the panel, is believed to be Deputy Chief Physician, Department of General Surgery, Jiangsu Province People's Hospital. From October 2004 to April 2006, Wang participated in the extraction of livers from 117 "donors" (no history of liver diseases, malignant tumors, or obvious hepatic steatosis, also negative serologic test results for Hepatitis B). Sources: Taiwanese Falun Gong working group, WOIPFG expert.

Li Binfei, People's Hospital of Zhongshan City,[77]
Guangdong Province
15:00~15:20 ECMO in the perioperative period of lung
transplantation
Zheng Mingfeng, Wuxi People's Hospital
15:20~15:40 Discussion, tea break

**V. Cardiopulmonary transplantation**
**15:40pm~17:30pm**
**Chairs: Professor Chen Jingyu, Professor Jiang Gening,**
**Professor Meng Long**[78]
**Professor Qu Jiaqi, Professor He Jianxing,**[79] **Professor Lin**
**Ruobai**15:40~15:50 Double lung transplantation treatment of
simultaneous cardiac repair for Eisenmenger syndrome
Qu Songlei, Beijing Anzhen Hospital District
15:50~16:00 A case report of long-term survival of
cardiopulmonary transplantation
Wang Chunsheng, Shanghai Zhongshan Hospital
16:00~16:10 A case report of long-term survival of heart

77    Zhongshan People's Hospital has been associated with numerous extractions: livers from 32 "donors" from May 2001 to October 2005; "fast extraction" of livers from nine "donors" (male, age range 41-60 years) between January 2001 and 2004; hearts in 2002 from two brain-dead "donors" (age 23 and 19 years), no history of cardiovascular disease or drug abuse, warm ischemia time 3 to 4 minutes; hearts from six brain-dead "donors," age range 19 to 30 yrs, no history of cardiovascular disease or drug abuse, June 2004 to April 2005; hearts from two "donors" in April 2004, warm ischemia time 0 minutes, and October 2005, 4 minutes; heart extractions from 16 brain-dead male "donors," age range 23 to 40 years (June 2004 to January 2008). Sources: Taiwanese Falun Gong working group, WOIPFG expert, Kilgour, *et al.*, "Update."

78    Meng Long, Chief Physician in Shandong Provincial Hospital, performed the first single-lung transplantation in Shandong Province on January 21, 2005, from a brain-dead "donor," warm ischemia time, 8 minutes. Sources: Taiwanese Falun Gong working group, WOIPFG expert, Kilgour, *et al.*, "Update."

79    He Jianxing, Director, Department of Thoracic Surgery, First Affiliated Hospital of Guangzhou Medical University participated in the extraction of lungs from nine "donors" (January 2003 to August 2006). Sources: Taiwanese Falun Gong working group, WOIPFG expert.

transplantation Han Zhen,[80] Harbin Medical University
Second Hospital

16:10~16:20 Experience and Experience of Cardiopulmonary
Transplantation

Yin Bangliang, Xiangya Second Hospital of Central South
University

16:20~16:30 Diagnosis and treatment of lung transplant
recipient Aspergillus infection

Zhu Yanhong, Wuxi People's Hospital

16:30~16:40 Experiences and Lessons from 3 Perioperative
Nursing of Lung Transplantation

Lin Ruobai, Fujian Union Hospital

16:40~16:50 Diagnosis and treatment of chronic rejection after
lung transplantation

Meng Long, Shandong Provincial Hospital

16:50~17:00 Thinking from 4 cases of lung transplant patients
experienced

Zhang Weidong, Tianjin First Central Hospital[81]

17:00~17:10 A case of double lung transplantation experience

Zheng Mingfeng, Wuxi People's Hospital

17:10~17:30 discussion, tea break

---

80  Harbin Medical University Second Hospital's organ transplant center was the first in Heilongjiang
Province to carry out standard and combined transplants. There have been suspicious cases of
young "donors" harvested at the hospital. For example, in January 2004, Han Zhen participated in
a heart extraction for transplant from a brain-dead "donor" (age 37 yrs, apparently healthy), warm
ischemia time less than 5 minutes. Sources: Taiwanese Falun Gong working group, WOIPFG
expert, Kilgour, *et al.*, "Update."

81  Tianjin First Central Hospital's Oriental Organ Transplant Center is the largest in Asia and has
ranked first in China in cumulative volume of transplants performed since its establishment in
1998. Liver and kidney transplants became routine surgeries in 1999. The hospital began to accept
and treat South Korean patients in 2002. It converted the 24th and 25th floors of a nearby hotel
into wards for patients awaiting transplants, with an estimated 500 beds in full use at any given
time. 85% of the patients came from over 20 countries and regions. Tianjin Central's transplant
volume is estimated at 5000 transplants annually. Sources: Taiwanese Falun Gong working group,
WOIPFG expert, Gutmann, *The Slaughter*, Kilgour, *et al.*, "Update." See also Matthew Robertson,
"A Hospital Built for Murder," *Epoch Times*, February 2016.

**VI. Dinner Banquet, Blue Sky Newport Ballroom (1st Floor)**
**18:00~20:00**
**Xinfu Pharmaceutical Reception**
**2008.4.27 (Sunday)**
Wuxi People's Hospital Multifunctional Hall, Zone F,
Third Floor
9:00~11:00
1. Heart/lung transplantation, cardiopulmonary
transplantation video
2. Toronto in vitro double lung transplantation video
3. ECMO double lung transplant surgery demonstration video
11:30~12:30 Lunch (Blue Sky Newport)
12:30 Organized sightseeing, Lingshan Buddha
18:00 Dinner and dispersal (Blue Sky Newport)

*Dr. Ko Wen-je's central role as an instructor incorporating ECMO into the Mainland's practice of live organ harvesting prisoners of conscience with the use of advanced American technology is illustrated in this photo, retrieved from an abandoned website created for the Medtronic ECMO conference 2008 at Wuxi People's Hospital, China. Medtronic is a blue-*

*chip medical device company originally based in Minnesota. Dr. Ko Wen-je, the former mayor of Taipei, is third from the left. As the only foreigner at the conference, he claimed to be an authorized salesman for Medtronic equipment. In China, Ko's proposed application of Medtronic equipment could theoretically triple the profit margin of organ sales. To the right of Dr. Ko are two surgeons, self-identified as Dr. Ko's "students." Second from the right: Dr. Chen Jingyu, a close associate of Dr. Ko who extracted lungs from 129 live "donors" before 2011 and was the creator, along with China Eastern Airlines, of "Green Lanes," airport expedited lanes for human organs (in Xinjiang the Green Lanes appear to be export-only). By 2014, Chen claimed that he was performing five lung operations per day. The informally dressed man on the extreme right, Dr. Meng Xu, extracted hearts from 51 live males, age range from 21 to 43, with no history of cardiovascular diseases. He claims to have independently completed 10,000 surgeries, with over 800 operations every year.*

* * *

I contacted Brian's assistant and told her: *Things have changed. Brian needs to schedule a press conference during my book promotion in Taiwan.* She called me back and said: *Brian isn't sure he can control what people might do* (the *to you* was gently implied) *at a press conference. But he will look into it.*

On October 2, Maryann Karinch and I stood at the entrance to our central Taipei hotel (the old Ritz) while Brian introduced my two bodyguards. *The best in Taiwan,* Brian said. Like a true rookie, I explained to them that *I'm glad you are here, but it would be best if you could be discreet because I prefer a low profile.* They smiled; every idiot who has never had a bodyguard thinks they are *a man of the people,* and they all say the same thing. Anyway, it was the last time that Maryann, my wife, or I would see the hotel from the entrance again. From that point on we would make our way through the kitchen to the garbage collection point, thus avoiding heated political demonstrations and the tabloid press, which staked out the hotel on a 24-hour basis.

In the van on the way to the press conference, I was laughing about something with Maryann, when I noticed that a great storm was coming in. I became aware of a kind of raspy, white-knuckle, jungle rhythm playing in the background. Maryann claims that she didn't hear this, and the storm was merely a single cloud.

We got out at some enormous venue, walked in, two doors swung open, and fifty cameras went off simultaneously.

"The 2nd biggest presser in Taiwan history." Gutmann flanked by bodyguards. Courtesy of Brian Wu

Brian spoke first, then Maryann, and I delivered a lengthy PowerPoint on the evolution of Chinese forced organ harvesting. I'll spare you the presser details because only two moments really mattered:

The first moment was defined by the first question following the presentation. A mysterious guy with dark glasses smiled broadly and asked me in broken English: *Do you think Doctor Ko is a liar?*

*Yes.* I paused. *Next question please.*

It was an honest answer. Of course, Dr. Ko is many things besides that. Perhaps I might have said that. And yet, based on the viewing numbers, most of Taiwan's population had seen my eight-minute tape. With Brian in his pundit role hammering that point home every night on television, most papers had tacitly accepted the fact that Ko had signed off on an interview that he now denied, like a child insisting that he "didn't do it." Yet I was the childish one. If the reporters were impressed by the sincerity of my PowerPoint delivery, giving a one-word answer was viewed as impolite. Suddenly, I was back to square one, the arrogant foreigner.

I imagine that Ko's legal team popped a champagne cork. But wait half an hour and your chance may come. In this case, it was the raised hand of a lovely young woman with swollen, tear-streaked eyes. She sorrowfully noted the difference between what I said about Dr. Ko on my eight-minute tape four years ago and my attitude about Mayor Ko today. What had changed?

She was a Ko partisan, and yet the young woman's question was sincere, the first presser question without an underlying political agenda. I called up a slide, while the lights dimmed and addressed her directly:

Falun Gong practitioner interview, Bangkok. By Leeshai Lemish.

*Thank you. Fair question. If you ignore the guy in the middle, this is a pretty good mathematical representation of what happened to Falun Gong.*

"All these Falun Gong women were in labor camp. All were tortured. One was sexually abused. And the woman on the left, Jing Tian was examined for her organs." I moved to the left of the screen. "Before ECMO, if Jing Tian had been harvested alive and tissue matched to foreign organ tourists in various Chinese hospitals, she was worth $200,000, maybe $250,000 if we throw in the corneas. Let's call it $225,000."

I know Jing Tian well. We presented evidence together in Vancouver. She's an intelligent and brave woman. As I spoke, I impulsively touched her image on the screen.

"After ECMO? Jing Tian was worth $680,000. About 200 percent more. It's simple math. And a roomful of women 'donors' that was worth just over a million dollars, about 30 million NT, was now worth three-and-a-half million dollars, about 100 million NT dollars."

I paused to let the translators catch up.

"I think all the men at that ECMO conference in 2008 understood this calculation very well. No matter what the original intentions were, bringing ECMO to China created a perverse incentive to kill Falun Gong, Uyghurs, and Tibetans. We don't know how many. And we don't know exactly how much Dr. Ko contributed to ECMO in China. But I have no doubt that ECMO accelerated the killing. And made it easier to use organs extracted in Xinjiang in East Coast transplant centers. And I have no doubt that it is a contributing factor to the spectacular growth of the transplant industry in China and the human rights crisis that we see in Xinjiang today."

About ten minutes later, the reporters started packing up. Brian and the bodyguards ushered me and Maryann to a side door. The bulk of the presser, marred with errors of tone, translation, and technical difficulties, did not matter anymore. The first round went to Ko. This was the second round, and the networks, God bless, went with it.

The rest of my time in Taiwan was a series of vignettes.

After the presser, Brian had organized a celebration banquet for perhaps twenty people on top of some spectacular building, and my wife ended up sitting next to a doctor named Su Ih-jen (we know him in this book by his English-language name, Dr. Vincent Sue). She told me later that apparently Doctor Sue had an important story about Dr. Ko. I shook Dr. Sue's hand that night, but all I really wanted to do was smoke cigarettes and share a bottle with Brian and his broken English. The friendship with Dr. Sue would come years later.

Dr. Sue revealed that Dr. Ko carried out the first live organ harvesting of comatose patients on Taiwanese soil. Perhaps other doctors knew about the scandal as well, but the difference is that Dr. Sue openly spoke about these facts in the Taiwanese media and brought it to the attention of the Control Yuan, a sort of internal FBI that investigates government corruption. Sue later explained to me: *When you stood up, that's when I decided to go public.*[82] The difference was that I would fly home from Taiwan in a week or so. Sue would have to live with the consequences. Dr. Sue's courage in standing up alone against Ko's army was far greater than mine, and the evidence he submitted was irrefutable. Ultimately, in a private session with the Control Yuan, Dr. Ko confessed that Dr. Sue was right.[83]

The day after my press conference, Taiwan's Ministry of Health held a small press conference of their own. They showed a surprising new transparency regarding the number of Taiwanese organ tourists who went to the Mainland for organs, illegal under Taiwanese law, and resolved to enforce penalties on those who continue to flaunt Taiwan's

---

82    Interview with Dr. Sue, September 2023.

83    Interpretations of the Control Yuan questioning of Mayor Ko and his response may differ, but this
      is my best understanding.

regulations.[84]Two days after my press conference, Ko brought criminal charges for defamation against me, based on my agreement with the statement that Mayor Ko is a liar.[85] I was in court for eight hours that night, stirring hope in the Ko legal team. In fact, the judge was visibly appalled by Dr. Ko's efforts to re-write my book. The entire case against me boomeranged, stimulating the Control Yuan to begin looking into Ko's medical and financial activities.[86] Ko said he would pursue me all the way to the UK to get justice.[87] Ultimately Ko initiated three legal proceedings against me, and by 2023, he lost all of them.[88]

I had several extended interviews at major Taiwanese television networks. They never aired. Taiwan media retreats to self-censorship, particularly if there is top-down legal action in the air.

84    Lee I-chia, "Ministry to demand transplant information," *Taipei Times*, October 4, 2018. See also Lin Huiqin, \"Minister of Health and Welfare: Incomplete overseas organ transplant registration indicates plans to withhold medication reimbursement 境外移植器官登錄不全 衛福部長： 擬不給付藥物," *Ziyou shibao* (Liberty Times), October 3, 2018.

85    Lee I-chia, "Ko accuses US author of slander," *Taipei Times*, October 5, 2018.

86    Briefly reported in a now-defunct online journal. From memory: two days after my appearance in court, the Taiwanese prosecutor declared that Mayor Ko "has no case" (the phrase has much the same meaning in both Mandarin and English). Cryptically, she added that my material had opened a new line of investigation or words to that effect. I suspect she was referring to the Control Yuan.

87    Ko's paranoid style extended into his relations with the Democratic People's Party (DPP): "Ko has further accused the DPP of hiring American author Ethan Gutmann to defame him with regards to organ trafficking allegations made by Gutmann in a book—never mind that such allegations actually date back to 2014, when the DPP endorsed him, and not 2018, when the DPP did not endorse Ko." From Brian Hioe, "Ko Wen-je Announces Formation of New Political Party, Likely Will Run for President," *New Bloom Magazine*, August 1, 2019.

88    Chang Wen-chuan and Jason Pan, "Court rejects Ko's defamation case," *Taipei Times*, September 8, 2023.

One that slipped through. Taipei Times, October 8, 2018. Permission of the artist, Lin Lung Jiuh.

When I was preparing to return to London, someone in the Ritz hotel staff leaked my flight information to the press the night before. Concerned about getting pummeled with squashy tomatoes at the airport, I was instead met by the Taiwan press corps firing all their shutters again, like an old friend waving goodbye. "I believe in the Taiwanese legal system," I said and left it there.

In his first run for mayor, Dr. Ko was swept into power by a margin of 244,000 votes. On November 24, 2018, Mayor Ko won re-election by 3000 votes.

He was greeted by an extraordinary letter—it resembled a blackmail note, as if penned by a long-term mistress–on social media from his Mainland colleague, Chen Jingyu, the "No.1 Lung Transplant Surgeon in China."

*"Now that Ko Wen-je has won the Taipei mayor election again, I want to congratulate him. . . . As a medical specialist you've come to*

*the mainland 33 times, teaching the mainland how to use ECMO.*
*You are the teacher of ECMO to mainland China, and you have a*
*deep academic connection with the mainland. We, the doctors of the*
*mainland, wish that your reelection can help increase cross-strait*
*cooperation, and deepen relations of the two sides of the Taiwan Strait*
*as a single family! Push forward for unification with the motherland!*[89]

Not long after he won the mayoral race for a second time, Dr. Ko's
office contacted me through my secure e-mail. The writer presented
himself as a Ko campaign operative. Over the course of our exchanges,
it became obvious that it was Dr. Ko himself on the other end.

Ko said that he would not be a politician forever. Therefore, at
some time in the future, he would like to go back to being a doctor. Dr.
Ko praised my work and said that we shared the same goals. I read this
as a statement that he wanted me to help restore his medical reputation.
Maybe he still thought I was CIA, and I had the power to call off the
dogs of the Control Yuan. I responded that if he acknowledged our
interview, and joined the movement to stop forced organ harvesting,
I would have no choice but to publicly embrace him. Ko's response
was to negotiate: Which exact part of the interview would he need
to confirm?

My response was that the Chinese harvesting had reached a new
level of urgency: 13 million Uyghurs blood-and-DNA-tested. Nine
crematoriums constructed in Xinjiang. Urumqi's crematorium hired
50 security guards. The time for negotiation and equivocation was
finished.

In a world of negotiated peace and incremental change, perhaps
my reply can be seen as pig-headed. Ko was untrustworthy, but his
potential return to "something must be done" might have strengthened

89    Translation by Paul Huang.

the global fight against Chinese forced organ harvesting. Yet I could not grit my teeth one more time and bring myself to return Ko's praise, to say that I respected what Dr. Ko had done. The communication flickered, flared, and went out.

In the heady days following the Taipei presser, a friend of mine remarked that if Ko were not re-elected as mayor of Taipei, he could always get a job as a doctor in China. We both laughed. Now Ko was telling me that wasn't true. It had never been true. Ko would have found himself falling out of a Shanghai window or dying of mysterious organ failure in Wuxi People's Hospital, because Beijing does not reward failure.

Ko doubled down on his political potential, creating the Taiwan Peoples's Party (TPP or the "Whites"), a vehicle for a presidential bid when his mayoral term was up. Ultimately, the TPP would win eight seats, a kingmaker position between Blue and Green, but former mayor Ko was thrown for a loss, coming in third place with 26% of the presidential vote.

In 2024, Ko was indicted for corruption relating to a real estate deal. Ko was alleged to have received the equivalent of half a million US dollars when he was mayor. He was also accused of embezzling the equivalent of two million US dollars from TPP campaign contributions.[90] The prosecution asked the court to sentence Ko to 28 years.[91] As we near the end of 2025, Ko was recently released on bail amounting to the equivalent of over two million US dollars, contingent on restricted communications and an ankle monitor. His medical license has lapsed, and a political comeback, let alone pushing forward for unification with the motherland, seems implausible at this time.

---

90    I had no knowledge of any of this; I suspect the CIA didn't either.

91    Koh Ewe, "Taiwan's ex-presidential candidate charged with corruption," *BBC*, December 25, 2024.

We may never know the full extent of Ko's activities on the Chinese Mainland, or how many Taiwanese power players received transplant assistance for their relatives from Dr. Ko's Mainland connections. Yet ECMO took on a life of its own in China, particularly as organ harvesting shifted to Xinjiang. Chinese hospitals and transplant centers also abandoned Medtronic's relatively large and clunky machines for Hemovent, a German-engineered mobile ECMO, a practical response to the logistical challenges of transporting oxygenated organs to China's East Coast.[92] Auction records on portable ECMO machine sales to Chinese hospitals indicate a steady upward sales trend from 2017 on, and fully 50 percent of the sales are to hospitals and medical centers that we identified in the 2016 Kilgour-Gutmann-Matas Report as likely organ harvesting and transplant centers that exploit prisoners of conscience.[93]

One wrinkle: Hemovent ECMO machine sales abruptly end in June 2020, replaced by orders for ventilators, suggesting that there may have been a secret Covid outbreak earlier than is commonly understood.[94]

After that, the auction records shed less light because the Jiangsu Saiteng Medical Technology Company produced the first Chinese domestic ECMO machines and began the registration process in

---

92    Keystone Perfusion, "Hemovent Is Developing the World's Smallest and First Self-Contained and Fully Portable ECMO System," *Perfusion Blog Posts*, March 10, 2016.

93    The auction records were collected by an intelligence entity that prefers anonymity. I'm grateful to two individuals in that entity, and to David Campanale for arranging the connection. See also Kilgour, *et al.*, "Update."

94    The shift to medical ventilators is so abrupt that it seems unlikely to be explained solely by gray-market Chinese domestic production of less expensive mobile ECMO devices.

August 2020.[95] Hemovent was acquired by Shanghai-based medical device company MicroPort in October 2021.[96]

Dr. Ko was the only doctor outside Mainland China who knew with confidence the exact off-label procedure that explained why Chinese transplant hospitals were purchasing mobile ECMO machines in such volume—and who they were being used on. Dr. Ko's melancholy emails were correct; this is his true home, and now, his legacy.

95    "China's first portable ECMO system begins registration process, brings hope for domestically-produced machines," *Global Times*, August 9, 2020.

96    "ECLS Company Hemovent has been Acquired by MicroPort and Receives Investments in Expansion of German Operations," *Businesswire*, October 4, 2021.

# 3

# INCH BY BLOODY INCH

I wasn't exactly the right guy to do this, but I'll get to that.[97]

In late 2013, I received an indirect hint that something might be happening in Xinjiang. Leeshai Lemish, my Israeli fixer, translator, and Falun Gong whisperer for more than half a decade, mentioned something about unusual physical examinations in inner China and began regularly sending me articles from *Minghui*, sometimes translated as "Clear Wisdom" in English.

*Minghui* could be described as an online spiritual bulletin board for Falun Gong practitioners and an underground information conduit from China. It's also a tightrope walk for the authors. Too many personal details or too specific a location could lead to detention, torture, and death. For many Mainland practitioners it was the first time, perhaps the only time, they would publish anything in their life. So they made it count. From the Falun Gong perspective this meant

---

97    The title of this chapter is a phrase I picked up from my former associate Jaya Gibson. It was my understanding that "inch by inch" referred to trench warfare, a metaphor for the glacial pace of Western political action on harvesting issues.

infusing stories with spiritual insights and moral lessons.[98] But the entries that Leeshai was sending me were different—stark, minimalist, as if written in Morse code. The articles, all from different authors, formed a consistent pattern: *In at least five Chinese provinces, police were entering the homes of Falun Gong practitioners, those not in detention or under house arrest, and taking blood samples and cheek swabs.*[99]

Even by CCP standards, breaking into a home and plunging a needle into an elderly woman's arm was a little transgressive. Taking a cheek swab, a method to gather an individual's DNA, had taken on a new significance for Falun Gong investigators working in Europe and North America. They had found, or hacked into, Mainland medical references and online conversations discussing a recent medical advance in "tissue typing" or "cross-matching," the process of determining whether an extracted organ would be compatible within the new host. The stakes were high: if the tissue match was not close enough, the new immune system would "assess" the transplanted organ as an enemy and attack it, and without immediate countermeasures the immune system would kill the patient. The standard procedure had been to extract the "donor's" blood, analyze it, and compare it to the new host's blood sample. Yet there were always errors: David Kilgour often spoke of a third-time's-the-charm case involving a foreign billionaire; his body rejected two kidneys from two different "donors" before the Chinese hospital finally got it right on the third kidney. But that was then. Now, Mainland surgeons agreed that a DNA sample could produce accurate

---

98   While the Party's 6-10 office perpetually scan *Minghui* looking for clues and potential arrests, Western China analysts and journalists ignore it. Yet, as this case demonstrates, practitioner accounts can act as an early warning system.

99   *Minghui* correspondent from Liaoning Province, "Falun Gong Practitioners Forced to Submit to Blood Tests," minghui.org, July 19, 2014; Tian Jian, "Why Does the Chinese Regime Collect Blood and Tissue Samples from Falun Gong Practitioners?" minghui.org, December 18, 2013. I'm grateful to Simone Gao for explaining the scale of the home testing in Guizhou, Liaoning, Hunan, Beijing, and Hebei provinces.

tissue typing as well, or better, than a blood sample. Any argument was resolved in favor of *exploiting both the blood sample and the DNA* as a guarantee against errors. (The DNA process was subsequently simplified. A few drops of blood from the larger blood sample could be used for a DNA test-kit work-up, and the cheek swab would be largely abandoned.) For now, even if the local police did not fully comprehend the purpose, blood-sample-plus-cheek-swab was the key to a successful and profitable Chinese transplant industry.[100] The handful of practitioners who were keenly aware of the implications of home testing involving blood and DNA read it as a portent of accelerated organ harvesting for Falun Gong, even *a final solution.*

*Too dramatic*, I countered. By 2013, Mainland practitioners, even in rural isolation, must have made the theoretical connection between blood tests and organ harvesting. Therefore, the theatricality of six policemen forcing their way into a house could just as easily be seen as a CCP scare tactic, a pantomime to scare local Falun Gong into behaving. Practitioners in the West were—quite justifiably, in my view—proud of their global resistance and perseverance. When I addressed Falun Gong audiences, I was calm, even optimistic: *Nearly 15 years from the beginning of the Falun Gong persecution, and the Party is still looking for the elusive knock-out blow*—a line that always elicited smiles, if not spontaneous applause.

Long wars can make a guy kind of callous. So I quietly reasoned that even if—just for the sake of argument, you understand—the Party was making a genuine attempt to hook up non-incarcerated Falun Gong organs with paying customers, that attempt undermined

---

100   Dr. Charles Lee of the World Organization to Investigate the Persecution of Falun Gong (WOIPFG) pointed out to me that while DNA collection could be exploited to ID practitioner family members, in the search for a Falun Gong gene (yes, some Party members actually believed in this), or in quest of a gene-specific biological weapon, the DNA and blood test *combination* was a strong indicator of cross-matching for transplant purposes.

Beijing's recent claims that their transplant system was switching to a voluntary system of organ donations, just one more piece of evidence that Beijing was lying about medical reforms. Tactical thinking, a little ugly, yet in 2013, I was close to many Falun Gong practitioners, so my final, secret thought felt truly illicit.

Here's what I knew. The Chinese voluntary donation system was simply a Party public relations campaign, a chimera. Death row prisoners with high rates of hepatitis and drug addiction were poor substitutes for healthy Falun Gong members.[101] So perhaps the forced home testing was exactly as it appeared. Perhaps the "final solution" had always been a partial solution—organ harvesting as a method of culling the Falun Gong ranks—and it had already occurred. But there was a financial side. The unprecedented expansion of the Chinese transplant industry since 2001 was constructed on the glut of Falun Gong organs. There were no signs of an industry retraction over the last decade. Chinese transplant volume was a hungry beast.

One possible interpretation is that Beijing had gone soft on keeping Falun Gong in detention, but that does not jibe with Public Security Bureau (PSB) memos over the years, which consistently called for more arrests of Falun Gong. And there's a more plausible explanation. Perhaps the years of persecution—tens of thousands of relatively young practitioners killed for their organs, the torture and the hunger-striking that degraded otherwise healthy organs, the practitioners who had been driven mad and met premature deaths, and the aging of those practitioners not selected for harvesting in the first round—had radically diminished the remaining Falun Gong population of Mainland China. In a scenario that many practitioners

---

101    "Over 60% of prisoners in China have hepatitis. That means the organs of most prisoners are unusable." From David Matas, "Speech at Rally at Hong Kong Government Headquarters," August 21, 2016.

still find too depressing to acknowledge to this day, perhaps *the Chinese Communist Party was running out of Falun Gong to harvest.*

In short, a substantial number of Falun Gong were locked into the Laogai system, but in dramatically reduced numbers and, increasingly, at highly undesirable ages.[102] The other possibility is that *Falun Gong had won*, that overseas practitioners had successfully outed the Chinese transplant industry in the Western media, and the Party increasingly perceived that harvesting Falun Gong practitioners *en masse* was too risky for China's reputation.

Either way, the Party needed a new, discreet, and definitely more youthful, organ source.

I went through the potential victim groups, starting from the assumption that sourcing from several victim groups simultaneously would exponentially increase the risk of external detection. The Party would have to choose.

**House Church Christians**, commonly estimated in the tens of millions, were growing, but were decentralized and thus highly vulnerable. Perfect targets of convenience. There was even a precedent: a couple of Falun Gong refugees had told me that in the early years of Falun Gong blood testing, around 2003, the guards had also systematically drawn the blood of Eastern Lightning, a House Church Christian group who believed that the lord Jesus had returned and was hiding out in China.[103] I had published that finding, but it hadn't gained much traction in Christian circles, probably because Eastern

---

102    Witnesses in the Xinjiang camps mention Falun Gong in detention, with one practitioner whose disappearance can be clearly traced to harvesting (see Chapter 5). Having said that, information on Falun Gong incarceration is increasingly scarce, correlating to the reduced number of Falun Gong refugees escaping from China in recent years. While it seems unlikely that it will ever surface in Party communications, it can't be ruled out that the tireless campaign against the organ harvesting of Falun Gong was ultimately successful in changing Chinese Communist Party (CCP) policy—not in ending Chinese forced organ harvesting *per se*, but in persuading the CCP to concentrate on sourcing from a different victim group.

103    Gutmann, *The Slaughter*, 239-40, 280, 302.

Lightning was seen as heretical. And yet if the Party were planning on expanding the testing to more mainstream congregants, there was a potential tripwire in the form of communication channels with Bob Fu, an activist Chinese Christian leader in Midland, Texas. Fu not only had the physical courage to rescue Christians from the Chinese mainland but was so self-effacing about his record that he had won the trust and respect of many established Western Christian organizations. The PSB in turn had learned not to underestimate Fu. If the Party began to harvest House Church Christians at scale, even the self-neutered, China-curious Vatican might be forced to respond.

**Tibetans** also had been targets of organ harvesting, just a year after the Eastern Lightning blood tests.[104] The logistics and potential security risk of bussing Tibetan monks hundreds of miles north to be examined in modern medical facilities kept the initial numbers in the hundreds or low thousands, but local Tibetan hospital facilities were modernizing.[105] As a key "enemy" of the Chinese State, the Tibetan cause had burned like a comet during the late 1990s–think back to the Tibetan Freedom concerts on the DC mall–gradually smoldering into embers. But even if Tibetan activism had cooled, every foreign correspondent in China felt obliged to go to Lhasa at least once, and the US Congress had a vestigial but unusually robust and bipartisan response mechanism to Tibetan abuse. In 2008, the Chinese Communist Party genuinely feared that the Tibetan uprising in Lhasa had the potential to destroy the Summer Olympics in Beijing. I suspected that the Tibetan stalemate would persist.

**Uyghurs** had far less clout in Washington, London, or Brussels in 2014. For example, half of the policymakers I met in Westminster

---

104    Gutmann, *The Slaughter*, 240-44.

105    The Dalai Lama is aware of organ harvesting allegations but, inexplicably, his research staff has chosen to maintain a low-profile stance. See Gutmann, *The Slaughter*, 245-46.

weren't sure how to pronounce *Uyghur* or even *Xinjiang*.[106] The Uyghur cause had almost no foreign lobbyists. As Muslims, they weren't considered orthodox enough to interest the Gulf States, and Turkey, the center of the Uyghur diaspora, such as it was, regarded Uyghurs as only a step above the Kurds. The former leader of the Uyghur human rights movement, Rabiya Kadeer, was so charismatic that I would have personally followed her command to physically go over the top of a trench, but she didn't speak English. The Uyghurs were an acquired taste, with even fewer defenders in China. The Party had relentlessly taught the Chinese public to see the Uyghurs through three different lenses, depending on what level of emotional heat the Party desired at any given time: 1) primitives whom China was morally trying to advance, 2) shiftless charity cases, or, 3) Muslim separatist terrorists.

The internal Party view was a little more straightforward. You weren't supposed to say it, but it was okay to regard the Uyghurs as an inferior race. Yet from the Party perspective, what set the Uyghurs apart from, say, Africans, was their potential to act as conduits of infection from radical Islamists, or vectors of Central Asian or Russian intrigues. Collective Uyghur Muslim practices such as the celebration of Ramadan were viewed with grave suspicion, leading the Party to slaughter of hundreds of protesters in Ghulja in 1997. The Party's response to the 2009 Uyghur uprising in Urumqi, which in turn was sparked by Chinese bullying of Uyghur men in a factory far from Xinjiang, elegantly combined the Party's fears and its bigotry. The Public Security Bureau didn't simply mobilize Chinese paramilitary units and carry out mass arrests of Uyghurs; they openly played to Han Chinese

---

106     For the record, there are at least two competing spellings, including Uighur or Uyghur. For what it's worth, I tend to use Uyghur. It's okay to pronounce either spelling simply as *wee-gur* in English. The word Xinjiang is a Mandarin name meaning "new" (xin) and "territory" (jiang). It's okay to pronounce it as *shin-jahng* – the jah portion as if one was using the German word for yes, or the Rastafarian term for God. Most Uyghurs find the Chinese term "Xinjiang" to be insulting—or at best, willfully ignorant. The traditional established name for the region is "East Turkestan."

machismo, escorting packs of crudely armed Chinese vigilantes to beat the crap out of Uyghurs on the streets.[107] Inside the detention centers, several Uyghurs reported that the PSB was administering blood tests again.[108] Yet from Beijing's perspective, the management of the Uyghur problem was not ultimately punitive, but realpolitik.

The valuation of Xinjiang has shifted dramatically over the last twenty-five years. In 2013, Xi Jinping designated Xinjiang as the launch pad for the major overground portion of the Belt and Road Initiative. The Silk Road was a familiar cultural concept to Uyghurs— one could even argue that *they invented it*—so they were the ideal advance men to deal with the Kazakhs, Kyrgyz and Uzbeks. Yet the Party's planned exploitation made that sort of cooperation impossible for anyone but the odd Uyghur traitor or soldier of fortune. Beneath the Xinjiang landscape lay enough resources to meet China's energy needs for decades to come, with approximately 20 percent of China's rare earths simply waiting to be mined. The years of the *bingtuan*, the PLA-run cotton-plantations that dotted Xinjiang, had whetted Chinese appetite not only for the luxury of Uyghur forced labor, but for ownership of traditionally Uyghur land. In any legal dispute with a multi-generational Uyghur farm family, the courts would favor the Han Chinese settler. Theoretically, it could go further. Chinese engineers have apparently speculated—and according to rumor, have begun rudimentary construction, on a diversion of the vast Tibetan plateau water table to make the Tarim Desert bloom. *En passant*, this has the potential to alternately produce water scarcity and flooding throughout the beating heart of India. The first gambit is planned mega-dam construction on the Brahmaputra River, right at the Tibetan border,

---

107 The Party liked this technique so much they subsequently used it on Hong Kong University students a few years later.

108 It's an ambiguous finding. There were no explicit reports of DNA testing, so any blood testing may have been routine medical checks in detention.

thus threatening both Northeast India and Bangladesh.[109] What a move on the chessboard, but for Beijing to have a fig-leaf of deniability, it would be wise for any redirection to have a Chinese entrepreneurial angle. Either way, the Uyghur and Tibetan pawns must be cleared from the center of the board.

After 2009, the Xinjiang Internet was shut down then re-opened as a controlled and patrolled Intranet. The isolation of the Uyghurs was nearly absolute. The term "Autonomous Region" had a special meaning in the Chinese principle of opposites. It meant that the Party could do whatever they wanted to, with no meddling interference from the Dalai Lama, Bob Fu, or *Minghui*. Xinjiang was China's once and future secret laboratory, from the first nuclear tests in the 1960s, to the first live organ harvesting in the 1990s. Now, in the year of our lord 2014, the Party would return to the dedicated harvesting of Uyghur organs ". . . as a dog returneth to his vomit."[110]

Following the Gutmann principle of opposites, I pushed these thoughts down to my soul.

In Spring 2014, the first large advance purchase of *The Slaughter*, approximately 35 copies, came from a street address that matched the Public Security Bureau (PSB) in Beijing. By the time the book was published on August 12, 2014, I suspected that the Party had drawn some practical conclusions. The first was not to let your victims or your "trusted" transplant doctors leave China.[111] The second conclusion was to commit to an alternate narrative. Two weeks after the book came out, there was a Chinese rumor of a splashy announcement regarding

---

109    Fred Pearce, "China's Mega Dam Project Poses Big Risks for Asia's Grand Canyon," *Yale Environment 360*, May 14, 2025.

110    Proverbs 26:11 (KJV).

111    The ultimate moment of potential CCP exposure occurred in 2012 when Wang Lijun, a protégé of Bo Xilai and director of the Jinzhou City PSB Psychological Research Center—more accurately described as an organ chop-shop—attempted unsuccessfully to defect at a US consulate. Gutmann, *The Slaughter*, 262–69.

organ harvesting in the works, and on December 4th, the rumor was confirmed: former Chinese deputy health minister, and the apparent spokesman for overhauling the Chinese transplant industry, Dr. Huang Jiefu, announced to the Western press that beginning on January 1, 2015, China would no longer harvest prisoners for their organs.[112]

The significance of that announcement is that the Chinese police began to routinely allow harvesting of executed prisoners as early as the Late Eighties. By the mid-1990s, they were experimenting with live organ harvesting. Any remaining inhibitions about exploiting Uyghur political prisoners for their organs collapsed in the wake of the Ghulja Incident, in 1997.

The West didn't become fully aware of the harvesting issue until notable dissident Harry Wu engineered a Congressional hearing, complete with a credible Chinese physician testifying on the routine practice of harvesting prisoners in 2001.[113] In 2005, alerted to ongoing Western research into the organ harvesting of Falun Gong, Huang Jiefu made the decision to preempt the issue publicly. Huang chose the lesser plea of China harvesting the organs of death-row prisoners, murderers, rapists and the like.

In 2006, *Bloody Harvest* was published by David Matas and David Kilgour, the first comprehensive study of Falun Gong practitioners being targeted and exploited for their organs. In the Western transplant world, there was little comment. Dr. Tom Treasure, an London-based cardiothoracic surgeon and a peer reviewer for *Bloody Harvest*, stepped up to the plate, and wrote a sober piece in a respected British medical journal asking why the larger medical community was not responding to the Kilgour and Matas' credible allegations.[114] I contacted Treasure,

---

112   "China to stop harvesting executed prisoners' organs," BBC, December 4, 2014.
113   "Kill and cull: China rejects doctor's testimony," CNN, June 28, 2001.
114   "Tom Treasure, "The Falun Gong, organ transplantation, the holocaust and ourselves," *Journal of the Royal Society of Medicine*, March 2007

we became friendly, and we submitted a modest joint proposal for research funding to the Wellcome Trust, a behemoth in the UK health research world. Given Treasure's reputation and his contacts, Wellcome's approval seemed little more than a formality. Yet Wellcome suggested to Treasure that we meet with a young visiting German scholar, an acclaimed medical history investigator, who was a great favorite in London at the time.[115]

The young scholar opened the meeting by stating that he had no knowledge of our actual investigation. The message was that he was too important to look at the reading list we had sent in advance, so I began an elevator pitch on the evidence, but in less than sixty seconds, he cut me off: *I personally consider the probability of the Chinese state harvesting Falun Gong to be nonexistent.*[116] The pattern was set. After a few more rounds, I found myself covering my face with my hands, and a silent Dr. Tom Treasure, wearing a grimly neutral expression, saw our visitor to the elevator.

I despaired because I needed Wellcome's research funding, not because I was personally offended. I knew the hitman had not come for me. As the Chinese idiom goes, "Kill the chicken to scare the monkey," and, like a chicken with my head cut off, I wasn't sure as to whether the Wellcome Trust had financial investments in China—okay, I do remember that some Wellcome grantees were working in China, under some form of Party oversight. Yet I knew one thing with certainty: Treasure's professional legitimacy was under threat.

A few months went by, and Treasure was asked to contribute an essay for *State Organs*, an edited international volume comprising doctors and researchers expressing solidarity against Beijing's forced

---

115  I have forgotten his name, and I wouldn't put it in print anyway.

116  When I attempted to bring our discussion, such as it was, to Rifkin's research on the Nazi doctors and motivation, he responded as an aging jazz aficionado might to an adolescent mentioning "Take Five."

organ harvesting. In response, Treasure submitted a piece identifying the American right wing as the true global enemy of ethical medicine. The editor assigned to his chapter was David Matas. Treasure refused any editing: *take it or leave it.* Treasure must have calculated that Matas would turn the chapter down. Matas did, and Treasure gave me a defensive, but apologetic, call. I was polite. I appreciated the gesture, and, at the end of the day, I didn't blame him. Treasure had made a real effort to swim against the tide. The London medical establishment interpreted such behavior as eccentric, and they staged an intervention. Treasure would stay on the shore.

I've spent undue time on this minor parable because the Western transplant world seemed to find itself perpetually wearing a grimly neutral expression–repulsed by their Chinese counterparts yet anxious not to be somehow left out of *the Chinese future.* When challenged on China's organ harvesting, Western medical professionals would invoke Chinese official denials as evidence that the allegations were already refuted or even repeat the Party whispers that Falun Gong's adherence to traditional religious values resembled that of conservative American evangelical Christians. In DC, the China skeptics were largely Republican. The full bipartisan congressional alliance against China–in some respects, the only area of agreement between the two parties—had not yet emerged. A few surgeons, and some journalists as well, would skip the China hogwash and simply refer darkly to American right wing political interference, the same station where Dr. Treasure left the train.

Perhaps it needs to be said. David Matas is a traditional Canadian human rights advocate and immigration lawyer, while David Kilgour was a beloved Canadian politician who routinely expressed Socialist leanings. Having worked at both Brookings Institution and Free Congress Foundation, I could be plausibly associated with either political side in DC. Yet all of us swung both ways, left and right, when it came to finding alliances and supporters on the harvesting issue. None of us had family who were Falun Gong. None of us were romantically involved with a practitioner. Matas is a practicing Jew. Kilgour took me to Sunday service at his local Presbyterian church in Ottawa. I'm as religious as a cabbage.

We happy few. David Kilgour, David Matas, and the author, at the Senedd Cymru

(Welsh Parliament), 2014. By Simon Gross.

Many practitioners encouraged us to try the Falun Gong exercises because they felt we lacked passion. Perhaps we did, at times. We also looked slightly absurd together, yet anyone who waded into our material quickly realized that our combined harvesting allegations were solid. One early adopter, a Hill staffer at the Congressional-Executive Commission on China (CECC), Toy Reid, read everything, and from the very early days stood up for us. Yet, as his seminal work on the lab origins of Covid-19 would ultimately demonstrate to the world, Reid's an evidence freak. He had moved on from the CECC years before, yet Toy's legacy at the CECC—the one guy who sat down and read our stuff—would create a hinge moment in the years to come.

I'll get to that. But at the time, Kilgour and Matas, with my published articles arriving later, created a slow-motion crisis for Western transplant practitioners.[117] One of them was Francis Delmonico, an advisor to the World Health Organization on organ donation and transplantation since 2006, the President of The Transplantation Society (TTS) from 2012 to 2014, and a Pope Francis appointee to the Pontifical Academy of Sciences in 2016. By 2012, Delmonico recognized that transplant ethicists could not continue to nibble round the edges—the "dead doner" rule, the definition of brain death—but had to convince the Chinese to swear off the practice of harvesting prisoners, *all prisoners*, full stop. And observing Chinese motivations, he thought he saw a potential end-run around the Chinese Communist Party: *personal engagement with his Chinese counterparts*. In exchange for the Chinese reforming their transplant practices and moving to a voluntary system of organ donation, the TTS would grant the Chinese transplant industry clemency and legitimacy going forward.

There are many mysteries in China. How to handle foreigners is not one of them. When Huang received Delmonico, I suspect Huang followed the basic template: *You came to the right man. China has progressive forces. I'm a leading member. But it also has dark forces, traditionalist forces, which you and I will have to fight, like blood brothers. China is complex, China is political, but if the Party can avoid losing face, transplant reform is possible. We can make history. Everything is contingent on your discretion.* To prove his sincerity, Huang did not send Delmonico back empty-handed. Huang publicly vowed that this great transplant reform would take place within the next five years. There would be bumps in the road, just as Huang had predicted. Even Huang had gone dramatically back and forth on a total ban. At one point, Delmonico had even written an open letter expressing his disappointment with the

---

117    Ethan Gutmann, "China's Gruesome Organ Harvest," *Weekly Standard*, November 24, 2008.

Chinese inability to commit firmly to forswearing the use of prisoner organs. Now, at the end of 2014, Huang had come in two years ahead of schedule. The TTS and the World Health Organization were invited to declare that Chinese transplant reform was a reality. "We shouldn't always dwell in the past, always concerned about the page of death row inmates," Huang Jiefu said, "Flip over the page and look at the future. . . ." [118] This was the signal that TTS, which had always avoided the issue of Falun Gong (and Tibetan, Christian, and Uyghur) organ harvesting, should publicly declare victory.

Within the TTS, a minority advocated a "trust, but verify" regime, including Dr. Jacob Lavee, arguably the most influential transplant surgeon in Israel, who advocated spot checks of Chinese hospitals. Yet Francis Delmonico put his faith in continuing to build cooperative relationships with the Chinese surgeons themselves rather than some tricky verification regime that would lead to further arguments and tension.

I personally asked Delmonico about this point. It was in the summer of 2016, when the tide was suddenly turning in our direction. By pure chance, I saw Delmonico sitting in one of the Congressional canteens, less than an hour before we would be sitting together to testify to the Foreign Affairs Committee. Delmonico has an informal yet courtly manner. He also cut a lonely and sympathetic figure in the afternoon light. I approached and smiled faintly, suggesting that I might sit down? He recognized me, and was gracious, his eyes invoking the irony of the situation. What followed was anticlimactic. There would be no argument—time enough for that later—so I fell back on my safe space, my Beijing business consultant role, and just asked questions, mainly about what it was like to negotiate with the Chinese surgeons.

118    Shar Adams, Larry Ong, and Matthew Robertson, "China's Horrific Live Organ Harvesting Revealed in Documentary," *Epoch Times*, April 19, 2015.

Delmonico was proud of how he had handled the Chinese, particularly that he had gambled the whole agreement on the open letter. And it had *worked*, he told me vehemently. So rather than asking him if China would need voluntary donations by a factor of ten to meet their obligations—I knew he wasn't able to discuss our evidence seriously—I invited Delmonico to tell me about what evidence convinced him that the Chinese transplant system was truly changing. His answer: *The young Chinese surgeons desperately want a reformed and ethical transplant system. I could see it in their eyes.*

It was the look in Delmonico's eyes when he said this that troubled me: the elation of a *cultural breakthrough*, the father forgiving *the prodigal son, the man who would be king.* So many foreigners come to China (just as I did at one time), ostensibly to help. In a purely transactional environment, they believed they made an emotional connection, or a clever deal, until the day when rational outside observers pointed to the wreckage left behind. Usually, it was financial loss due to counterfeiting. In Delmonico's case, it was the squandering of the TTS reputation, and his own.

There were so many things to be said, but not at the weighing-in ceremony. I shook Delmonico's hand and made my excuses.

An hour later, I presented my view of how the TTS mission gone astray. How a Chinese doctor testified to Congress on the harvesting of death row prisoners in 2001. How it caused a ripple, not a wave. How the TTS, underneath it all, were deeply concerned by the optics of medical professionals harvesting prisoners of conscience, yet had initially, *temporarily, just for tactical purposes*, denied their own motives, as I stated at the hearing:

> "*. . . the Chinese medical establishment promised to move to voluntary sourcing within 3-5 years but wrapped it in a semantic trick: The*

*phrase 'end organ harvesting of prisoners' was acceptable. The phrase 'end organ harvesting of prisoners of conscience' was unacceptable. Thus the Chinese could avoid speaking about a vast captive population that doesn't officially exist, while the acceptable phrase allowed Westerners to hope that 'prisoners of conscience' was just a subset of 'prisoners.' By avoiding the taboo phrase, both sides could maintain their illusions."*

The polite evasion of the central issue back in 2012 led directly to the "verification tours" of select Chinese transplant hospitals in 2015. But verification devolved into the first Potemkin hospital tour where the Chinese surgeons were sincere, the patients recovered on schedule, and no Western surgeon requested that a locked door be unlocked.

One junket would have been enough. But success, or even failure disguised as success, has many fathers, so a new entourage emerged.

The second tour held even less pretense of medical fact-finding. One of the main protagonists wasn't a surgeon, but a man of the cloth: Bishop Sanchez Sorondo, an Argentine who rose to Chancellor of the Pontifical Academy of Sciences in 1998. A book could well be devoted to Sorondo: his charisma, his influence on Pope Francis, his contempt for the West, the United States in particular, and his stated belief that China was—not only for Catholicism, but for the world—"assuming a moral leadership that others have abandoned."[119] In short, while Sorondo was not the central architect of the Vatican's surrender to Beijing in the critical area of CCP control over the appointment of bishops, he was the key enabler in making sure that the rumors about Chinese organ harvesting did not kill the deal.

---

119    Reggie Littlejohn, "Praise of China's Adherence to Catholic Social Doctrine Flies in the Face of Facts," *National Catholic Register,* February 9, 2018.

Bishop Sorondo wades in. By Gabriella Clare Marino/Wikimedia

There were still respected members of the TTS such as Jeremy Chapman, whose motivations centered less upon Chinese victims of organ harvesting, and more around saving the world from Chinese medical experimentation. I had a tense phone conversation with a member of the TTS leadership cabal (name withheld by request)[120] who quietly revealed his suspicion that the Chinese medical experiments in growing human organs within pigs could cause an epidemic down the road (eerily prescient). However, his solution to this problem was marred by his own retentive tendency towards preserving even the Chinese medical right to secrecy at all costs; the tragedy of assuming that everyone outside the medical field was an idiot would play out in Covid as well.[121] Unlikely that the TTS could have changed any of these outcomes, but either way, the TTS facilitated a lot of once-in-a-lifetime Australian junkets for Chinese surgeons who operated out of some of the most lethal transplant hospitals in China.

Finally, there was tag-along Campbell Fraser, an Australian

---

120   Although the conversation did not contain any major surprises, I'm withholding his name here because I appreciated his taking my call. He did not have to, as the standard operating procedure of the TTS was to avoid informal overtures, and the privacy level of our conversation was not determined.

121   I had barely scratched the TTS surface. Matthew Robertson systematically established communications with several members of the TTS leadership over time. It may be ancient history to some, but I have a nerdy interest in Robertson's account, forthcoming.

third-tier academic with such a severe case of writer's block—I'm actually being sympathetic here—that it was never quite clear how he made it onto the guest list. Fraser had personally received a kidney for a congenital condition and then staged a Tintin-style investigation into Egypt's shadowy organ broker network. Back in Oz, he turned his breathless style on Falun Gong—I'm *not* being sympathetic here—blatantly lying about his motivations to gain access to practitioner refugees, only to label them as "wretched people." In mainland China, surrounded by TTS doctors, Fraser told Xinhua that "an evil religious organization" (Falun Gong) had "falsified data" and then had personally threatened him and his colleagues "who are continuously getting the harassment. They are crying. They are upset."[122]

With no alternative comment from the Western press, China observed a series of apparently high-profile Western thought leaders sanctifying perverse Party beliefs. Falun Gong was a malevolent cult (Fraser). The West allowed Falun Gong free range to destabilize China (Chapman). It was a desperate attempt by America to derail the shining Chinese century which lay ahead (Sorondo).

We, an informal coalition to stop Chinese forced organ harvesting, had held fire to give the TTS room to negotiate. Yet whatever Delmonico's original goals, the follow-up TTS strategy was not about prisoner rights in China, but about genuflecting to Chinese power and gratuitously jeering at the victims whom the CCP had murdered—yet refused to acknowledge. Even Huang's agreement with the TTS to end organ harvesting of prisoners was purely for foreign consumption. Early in 2015, in the Chinese internal press, Jiefu and his associates clarified matters: *Chinese death row prisoners were citizens. And Chinese citizens could volunteer to have their organs harvested, if the appropriate*

---

122  "Academic's painful experience with Falun Gong," Xinhuanet, February 22, 2017. See also "Australian Academic Investigated for His Support of China's Anti-Falun-Gong Campaign," Bitter Winter, August 4, 2018.

*documents were filled out.*[123] Aside from the laughable premise of citizen-prisoners on Chinese death row thoughtfully considering the pros and cons of donating their organs in a meditative, stress-free, environment, this wasn't even the first time around for this reform. Within a year of Kilgour and Matas publishing *Bloody Harvest* back in 2006, the Party announced that prisoners were now obliged to sign donation forms before their organs could be extracted.

In short, Chinese transplants in 2015 would operate in the same regulatory environment as 2007. Only the messaging of "transplant reform" had changed, and only in the English language.[124]

For well over a decade, I had always assumed that I was writing about history. Surely, Beijing will fix this transplant issue in a year or two? Surely, they cannot continue on like this? It was too illogical, too self-defeating. There is an obvious paradox in the Chinese Communist Party's actions regarding forced organ harvesting of religious, racial, and political prisoners in China. And while I've never been able to fully solve it, I want to lay out the puzzle.

My China background was not really forged in academia, but in business. As a Senior Counselor at a leading American public affairs firm, APCO Beijing, my job was to find and assist clients who wanted to make money in China, and I was given a wide berth to explore sensitive issues. One insight that I picked up from my Chinese business associates, just over two decades ago, ran like this: China's medical future—financially, reputationally—will not be found in medical services, of which the Chinese transplant industry is a subset. These are interim financial sources, one of many. *China's future is in pharmaceuticals.* For Beijing, it's a *pillar industry.*

Global success in pharmaceuticals requires brains, education,

---

123    Didi Kirsten Tatlow, "China Bends Vow on Using Prisoners' Organs for Transplants," *New York Times*, November 16, 2015.

124    None of the TTS leadership have ever directly acknowledged this point.

well-financed research, access to materials, production of scale, and speed, both in testing and bringing the product to market. China has comparative advantages in virtually all these areas, particularly in an environment where humans can be tested as if they were lab rats without complications from the media or legal recourse. But no matter how good the product is, the development of pharmaceuticals and the international financial success that follows requires widespread confidence in the Chinese medical industry.

The Chinese transplant industry provides an organ match, easy payment, live extraction, transplant, and managed recovery, all at an unprecedented scale and tempo. The entire procedure, from contact, to arrival in a Chinese hospital, to surgery and full recovery can theoretically occur in *less than a single month*. That's a great product, a product that should build confidence in the entire Chinese medical system. It explains why so few stories have emerged from resentful organ tourists. Yet the secrecy and obfuscation regarding the source of the organs, the bribes that foreign organ tourists are obligated to pay, and the whiff, the rumor, even the denial, of live organ harvesting and innocents-killed-to-order is an open wound that prevents China from dominating the world's pharmaceutical industry.

The last two paragraphs were written before Covid-19 emerged, which caused a further erosion in confidence in China's medical expertise.[125] Yet China's pharmaceutical confidence game was essentially lost in 2015, four years before the pandemic. While I was not striding around China with a clipboard and interviewing its

---

125    Anyone reading this knows how much further China's medical image has deteriorated since then. It doesn't matter what China's Western defenders—the World Health Organization, TTS, honorable mention to the Vatican—say publicly. We are all looking at the same evidence of secrecy regarding Covid-19: gain of function research, disregard for international medical cooperation, false pandemic reportage, inexplicably casual control of Chinese international borders, protective equipment profiteering, incompetent and opaque vaccine development, and vile nationalistic propaganda.

transplant surgeons—and obviously, there are no documents on this most forbidden topic—it's possible to form a theoretical picture of Chinese motivations behind what we call *transplant reform*.

Let's start with what we know: Huang Jiefu was technically lying when he made the English announcement that prisoners were not to be harvested after January 1, 2015. But it's far easier to tell a lie if there is sincere intentionality, however technical, behind the mask. Chinese surgeons could keep a straight face with Americans, Australians and Vatican officials when they spoke about their intent to end the practice of harvesting prisoner organs, because, from their perspective, *death row prisoner organs are unhealthy. Voluntary donations are good for optics, but prisoners of conscience or despised ethnic minorities have healthier organs and can be selected, killed-to-order from a large pool of tissue types.*

Huang Jiefu needed reform, but it had little in common with our conception of the word. From Huang's perspective, there *was* a crisis within the Chinese transplant industry: *the vulnerability to information seeping out of China (witnesses slipping through the cracks) but also the state of near-anarchy, the eBay gold rush, within the Chinese transplant industry.* Huang needed to start fresh. The foreigners required a story, and the Party required a rational, predictable, approach to harvesting internal enemies of the state. The "reform" then, was to create a dual system.

The foreigners were the easy part. The first move would be to create a plausible world of voluntary organ donations—an app, volunteers who would show a delicate rise over time, and a few orderly, seemingly transparent transplant hospitals for show—with just enough bedside manner to attract high-paying foreign customers. These qualities can be seen in this promotional English-language video of a Chinese "traditional medicine hospital" that also specializes in organ transplants with an attractive Muslim canteen and prayer room for the paying customers. The clients from the Gulf States are presumably looking for organs from people who don't eat pork (such as Uyghurs and Kazakhs), sometimes referred to as "halal organs."[126]

The internal shift was more challenging. It required Chinese medical staff to be conversant in false numbers (the voluntary donations), while keeping track of the living organs' flight status. It required doublethink, willful blindness, and compartmentalization. Chinese transplant surgeons already had a reputation for suicide far above the norm.[127] Most of the reported deaths involved jumping out of high windows (the question remains how many of the surgeons were actually pushed), but if Beijing could limit the harvesting of organs to a finite group of tough and loyal surgeons in a finite geographical area among people whose Mandarin comprehension was weak, perhaps this could be the nucleus of Huang's transplant reform. The Party could focus its resources on controlling a population, creating a combination of medical facilities and the carceral infrastructure that would transform a single province (or "autonomous zone") into the center of China's organ sourcing.

* * *

Until now, I've been describing the TTS and the CCP as a nearly unbreakable unit, full of action, and my associates and I as sullen spectators. Of course, it wasn't like that at all, and the public push-back started an hour after my lunch with Francis Delmonico.

"Bloody Harvest/The Slaughter: an Update" (Informally we called it the "2016 report" or the "Transplant Volume Report"; here it's the "Update") was an unusual document by DC standards—over 700 pages,

126    An edited version of the video can be found on Erkin Sidiq's YouTube page titled "An Example of Muslim Organ Transplant Hospitals in China," posted on June 14, 2020.

127    Frank Yue, "Chinese Medical Expert's Suicide Draws Attention to Questionable Organ Transplant 'Model,'" *Epoch Times*, March 16, 2021; Wang Youqun, "Chinese Doctor's Suicide Casts Light on Forced Organ Harvesting in China," *Epoch Times*, February 16, 2023.

the title wildly understated. We purposely did not include an executive summary because we wanted journalists to wade into the hospital data. I won't create an executive summary here either. The report is easily found on the web. It is germane that Matt Robertson's seminal piece in the *Epoch Times*, "A Hospital built for Murder" was highly influential in informing my own approach to the numbers and contributed strongly to the breadth and decisiveness of the report's conclusions.[128] But the only advance copies of our report for outsiders went to three mainland Chinese employees of the Congressional Executive Commission on China (SECC), the premier human rights watchdog for Congress. The Mainlanders' sole mission was to keep garbage out of the committee. Over a period of months, they explored the report's 2400 footnotes, 90% of these referencing mainland Chinese sources, and declared it kosher for a Congressional hearing.

David Matas, the author, Dr. Francis Delmonico, and Dr. Charles Lee at Foreign Affairs hearing, 2016.

By permission of *Epoch Times*, photographer Li Sha.

---

128    Matthew Robertson, "Investigative Report: A Hospital Built for Murder," *Epoch Times*, February 4, 2016. See also Kilgour, *et al.*, "Update," 59–63, and *Organ Harvesting: An Examination of a Brutal Practice: Hearing before the House Foreign Affairs*, 114 Congress, 2nd session, June 23, 2016.

Congressional testimony allows fewer than seven minutes to make one's case. It's a no-pain, no-gain exercise that forced me to condense a doorstop of over 700 pages to a single paragraph:

*"The Chinese medical establishment commonly claims that China performs 10,000 transplants per year. Yet imagine a typical state-licensed transplant center in China: three or four transplant teams. 30 or 40 beds for transplant patients. A 20 to 30-day recovery period. Patient demand: 300,000 Chinese wait-listed for organs, not counting foreign organ tourists. Would it be plausible to suggest that such a facility might do one transplant a day? 146 transplant facilities, ministry-approved, meet that general description. And that yields a back-of-the-envelope answer. You can do it right here. Not 10,000, but 50,000 to 60,000 transplants per year. Suppose we actually hold those same hospitals and transplant centers to the actual state minimum requirement of transplant activity, beds, surgical staff, and so on? 80-90,000 transplants per year. Yet how shall we account for the emergence of Tianjin First Central Hospital, easily capable of 5000 transplants per year? PLA 309 military hospital in Beijing? Zhongshan Hospital? The list is extraordinary. A detailed examination yields an average of up to two transplants a day, over 100,000 transplants a year. Now the figures that I have just given you are based on Chinese numbers. Not from official statements, but sources like Nurses Weekly."*

At this Foreign Affairs hearing, Congressmen Chris Smith and Dana Rohrbacher had never heard of *Nurses Weekly*, but they knew something about the Chinese Communist Party. So, they put Dr. Francis Delmonico into what Rohrbacher called "the hot seat," and Delmonico, with a speed that took my breath away, threw his

Chinese transplant associates and, for good measure, most of the TTS, under the bus.

> *"Mr. Smith: How do you independently verify that even though he [Huang Jiefu] may be very sincere that anything he says, zero foreign customers for organ trafficking in 2016, how do you independently verify that when there has been such a backdrop of terrible duplicity, lies, and deception on the part of the government? Trust and verify. How do you do it?*
>
> *Dr. Delmonico. I am not an apologist. I am not here to tell you not to worry. I am not here to verify. That is not my job."*

Delmonico didn't know how Chinese organs were sourced. He admitted that the TTS had no access to the Chinese military hospitals, although "That doesn't mean that I condone it." Delmonico couldn't confirm that China had reformed their transplant system. He allowed that there were cases of foreign organ tourism, but "it is not my job to say to you that it is eradicated or completely stopped." When Smith confronted him on our report, "Dr. Jeremy Chapman, as we know the former president of the Transplantation Society, called the estimates in your [motioning to me and Matas] report 'pure imagination piled upon political interest,'" Delmonico stayed silent.

Finally, under cross-examination, Delmonico revealed that his TTS travel and hotel bills in China were paid for by a Chinese foundation, financially supported by a "benefactor hotel magnate." This turned out to be Li Ka-shing, the Hong Kong shipping billionaire famous for buying up Panama Canal assets on China's behalf.[129] When

---

129  For more on Li Ka-shing's role as a CCP runner, see testimony of Randolph Quon, Hearing on S.1315, "The U.S. Markets Security Act of 1997," Senate Banking, Housing and Urban Affairs Committee, November 5, 1997.

asked if there was any TTS conflict of interest, Delmonico replied that "Well, it is not for me to answer for everybody else. . . . China is not paying for me to be here today."

The longer I listened to Delmonico—I could practically feel the sweat emanating through his jacket into mine—the more I admired his chutzpah for showing up at all. By the end of the hearing, every Congressman in the room knew that the Western transplant community's attempt at a soft reform of the Chinese transplant industry had either 1) stalled or 2) was actively being exploited as a smokescreen for continuing forced organ harvesting of prisoners of conscience at a wider scale than previously understood.

I don't generally reach out to individual reporters. So it was a sort of end-the-war-by-Christmas fantasy that prompted my call to Didi Kirsten Tatlow. She had been the *New York Times* Beijing correspondent since 2010 and had distinguished herself as a "color writer." I didn't consistently read the NYT; from my perspective, the beloved paper of my college days had slid into an American version of *Pravda*, the Party-line of the elite, rather than the paper of record, for at least two decades. Yet that's probably why the Central Committee in Beijing respected and even feared the paper; one or two paragraphs describing my work on live organ harvesting in a David Brooks column had probably saved more lives than my book.[130] I have a healthy respect for reality. The NYT had the power to break the Chinese stranglehold on the TTS. And I also liked Tatlow's writing, especially compared to the NYT China correspondents I'd known in Beijing. Tatlow, because of her fluency, covered the eclectic, even seemingly trivial items like the Chinese high heel industry, yet somehow cast light on the vast contradictions of China. Reading her work made me feel like I had

---

130    The book was Gutmann, *The Slaughter*. The column that probably saved some lives was David Brooks, "The Sidney Awards, Part II," *New York Times*, December 22, 2011.

returned to a place that I had once called home. Anyway, I used a secure line and caught her at her Beijing flat.

I went through the evidence for the organ harvesting story for at least twenty minutes, while she said almost nothing. Investigator to investigator pitches are potentially competitive, so I was careful to use a combination of evidence and sources, downsizing my contribution, avoiding drama. When I finished—we both knew the full stakes of her investigating the story with the *New York Times* imprint—she remained uncannily silent, as if the line had gone dead.

Tatlow finally replied that she had already been thinking about the problem. And had written "...about organ wastage, due to transport difficulties—traffic jams, uncooperative airlines—and followed the threads. They're still untied of course."[131]

There was that quirkiness again. Her mother was said to be German so that might have explained her propensity for engineering. I'm not sure if she mentioned train schedules in the original conversation, so any resemblance to the early ground-breaking research into the Holocaust was probably only in my head. I also sensed that Tatlow had been expecting a call like this one, *like a visit from the Grim Reaper.* But hey, I know the victims, and Tatlow knows the train schedules.

*Ethan, I have two kids in pre-school.*

*Are they Chinese? Anyway, you know they'll be okay, Didi. They don't go after...*

*But you know the kinds of stories I write...*

131  My Tatlow quotes are taken from a conversation on Tatlow's Facebook page where I thanked her for writing "Angry Claims and Furious Denials Over Organ Transplants in China," on August 24, 2016. My understanding was clarified by Tatlow's prepared testimony for the China Tribunal. See Sir Geoffrey Nice, *et al., China Tribunal Judgement* (September 29, 2020), 494-497.

*Yeah, I do.*

*And you think I'll still have access?*

It was my turn to be silent.
*No, Didi. You won't.* [132]

Didi Kirsten Tatlow, Beijing correspondent for *The New York Times*. By permission.

Before I thanked her for her time, I gave her a couple of names. One was Dr. Jacob Lavee, the Israeli heart surgeon who had been the driving force behind the Knesset's decision to ban Israeli citizens from going to China for organ transplants in 2008. Technically, the ban was limited to Israeli HMOs financing organ tourism, but Israel's medical establishment claims that Israeli citizens have universally respected the directive.

Lavee is a confident man, relaxed and even humorous at times, but it all rests on a highly developed sense of tragedy. So, it was predictable that Tatlow and Lavee would develop a bond. Tatlow confessed to him that, at an informal discussion in a hospital canteen, Dr Chen Jingyu (Dr. Ko Wen-je's effusive associate from Wuxi People's Hospital)

132    Best recollection of conversation.

and Chen's friend, Dr. Tong, assumed that Tatlow wasn't fluent. Chen reminded Tong that the Party line was that all the organs were voluntary donations now, and not to mention either prisoners or Falun Gong as an organ source to a foreigner.

In short, Tatlow was silent when I first called because she knew the allegations of forced organ harvesting were true. As Tatlow put it, "My own path into the issue was not ideological, but rather observational."

An unacknowledged comparison to the Holocaust, however distant and garbled, was on the line with us on that first call, too. But when Tatlow learned that Dr. Lavee's father was a survivor of the camps, it streamlined things. Lavee was a Jew. Tatlow was German. And from the Tatlow perspective, she confessed to Lavee that she found herself in a situation of non-negotiable debt.

Tatlow pitched the story to the NYT editorial staff. As she explained to me, "I had tons of pushback along the lines of 'What's new here?' And yet it was never properly reported in the first place, nor any of the bigger issues explored." The editorial staff's next line of defense was that Chinese forced organ harvesting was no longer a story. And yet based on a series of events—the publication of the Kilgour-Matas-Gutmann report, the Foreign Affairs Committee hearing, and the controversial TTS decision to hold the annual conference in Hong Kong—interest in Chinese forced organ harvesting would crescendo in 2016.

Tatlow knew these objections were insincere. *The editors sensed that Tatlow would not be pushing the story unless she knew that the allegations were true.* The editors were right. As Tatlow said, "there are very few non-Chinese who understand what's going on, but when you personally hear Chinese transplant surgeons discuss the use of prisoner of conscience organs for transplant, and the government says 'it's OK to report on the illegal organ trade just be sure you're clear that Xi Jinping is going to crush it,' you have to believe your ears."

*But the NYT did not want to present evidence on forced organ harvesting of prisoners of conscience in China.*

"Overall, the media is deeply contradictory. Far too often their work method is not deductive, but inductive. Start with your assumptions and particular culture and write from that. . . ."

Tatlow approached the story by keeping evidence at arm's length, transforming the forced organ harvesting conflict into a drama, specifically, a black comedy. I remember the story this way, in my mind's eye: *It's the first day of the TTS annual convention in Hong Kong. The streets are plastered with posters, and Falun Gong practitioners near the entrance to the convention center say that the Chinese authorities are harvesting Falun Gong prisoners for their organs. Pro-China counterdemonstrators say the Falun Gong are liars and cultists. Mainland Chinese transplant surgeons are flooding into the convention center. Tension is rising.* However she actually wrote it, Tatlow slipped in the reference to harvesting Falun Gong, the first time that the issue had been referenced in the *New York Times*–through the side door. By creating a series of precedents, Tatlow constructed a set for a series of vignettes to play out. From the TTS perspective, the NYT was friendly media, so Tatlow was given the freedom of movement enjoyed by a court jester, with the solemn respect given to "the paper of record." She used this freedom to publicly question the TTS representatives about Beijing sourcing organs from prisoners of conscience, the very question that the Western surgeons were too timid to ask of their Mainland colleagues. TTS representatives, relative novices at handling this sort of controversy, erred on the side of not saying anything at all. The beauty of the NYT editorial direction was that Tatlow was released from the responsibility of resolving competing views for the reader. On this stage, evidence *per se* didn't matter, only credibility.

Somehow, that message got through to the TTS, and the safe approach was apparently unbearable for certain doctors. At least one member of the TTS clique, acting president Phillip O' Connell, said the quiet part out loud to the Mainland surgeons in a breakout session:

> It is important that you understand that the global community is appalled by the practices that the Chinese have adhered to in the past," Dr. O'Connell said he told them. "As a result of these practices, the Chinese transplant centers have allowed a trenchant political opposition to their government to prosper.[133]

From the perspective of the "trenchant political opposition," opinions varied on whether O'Connell's remarks represented a tragedy for the entire field, or just more black comedy gold. David Matas pointed out that O'Connell delivered his critique as if the TTS were a private consultant to the Chinese Communist Party. The TTS might aspire to that status, but the Mainland surgeons' antennas were tuned to a different frequency: O'Connell's consultant act came across as condescending. O'Connell had carefully phrased his accusations in the past tense, signaling his acceptance of the current Chinese claim of transplant reform. Yet the Chinese perceived that his motivation was, first, to defend the TTS image, and second, to strike a pose of virtue and tough love for the approval of a female NYT reporter. Just this once, Chinese paranoia may have been correct on all counts.

Following China's supposed transplant reform in January 2015, the obvious imperative was for the TTS to build a legitimate transplant

---

133 Didi Kirsten Tatlow, "Chinese Claim That World Accepts Its Organ Transplant System Is Rebutted," *New York Times*, Aug. 19, 2016.

hospital verification regime so potentially intrusive that the costs of creating a deceptive Chinese transplant system would be greater than the transplant profits of forced organ harvesting. O'Connell's moment came close to what could have been a constructive clearing of the air. Yet O'Connell couldn't bring himself to say that he had—*currently, right now*—doubts about the credibility of his Chinese counterparts. The TTS had seemingly committed themselves in their "victory tour" with Bishop Sanchez Sorondo, when the desirable imprint of TTS legitimacy was not used to open locked doors at the transplant hospitals, but to denounce Falun Gong for the cameras of China Central Television.

Like an exorcist, Tatlow had brought the TTS floating above the bed back down to the mattress, revealing the callow, performative aspect of the entire TTS-China enterprise. The TTS clique had previously attended several transplant conferences on the Mainland, but the TTS annual conference in Hong Kong was the high-water mark of public fraternization with the Chinese medical establishment. It ended in embarrassment. Instead, the NYT got a story, and Tatlow's credibility stress test produced a Western scalp. To complete her collection, she needed a Chinese one.

One year later, Bishop Sanchez Sorondo had approved a Vatican conference designed to finalize the great achievement of Chinese transplant reform. China had many human rights problems, but, in a testament to our collective efforts perhaps, organ harvesting had somehow become the final impediment to normalization with China; the Pope would allow the Chinese Communist Party to have some form of secretive power on the selection of Mainland Catholic bishops in exchange for—well, it was never quite clear, but I suppose the Pope wanted what Christians have wanted even before the Jesuits arrived in the 16th century: an officially sanctioned Christian movement in the most populous country on earth, 1.4 billion souls.

To bring down the house of cards, all Tatlow had to do was to write a hard-breathing piece asking whether there might be some credence to the charges of organ harvesting of prisoners of conscience. And why was the Pope sanctioning a man like Huang Jiefu anyway?[134] Several English papers that had published breezy, optimistic stories about the same exact conference 24 hours earlier, immediately fell into line and cast shade on the Chinese presence in the Vatican.[135] But the *Tatlow Effect* did not end there. An audience with Pope Francis following the Plenary session was scheduled. He never arrived, having proffered an excuse about other commitments. And just like that, the moment of China's benediction, the photo-op of gentle Pope Francis posing with a grinning Huang Jiefu, was lost forever. What I wouldn't have given to have been a fly on the wall in business class on the Rome-Beijing flight that night.

The *New York Times* headquarters, against the advice of the regional editors, pushed Didi out the door in 2017 for having taken the *irrational* stance that prisoners of conscience (not just death row prisoners) were being exploited for their organs and for having questioned the CCP's official portrait of their transplant industry. Didi, a true professional, won't vindictively name anyone at the *Times*, yet she did give me a parting epitaph: "I followed my conscience without fear or favor and did what I could under the political and institutional circumstances, and sadly it wasn't much, though I tried and pushed for much more."

Now she was back in Germany. Honestly, I don't remember who

---

134    Didi Kirsten Tatlow, "Debate Flares Over China's Inclusion at Vatican Organ Trafficking Meeting," *New York Times*, February 7, 2017.

135    Example of the *Tatlow Effect*: Stephanie Kirchgaessner, "China may still be using executed prisoners' organs, official admits," *The Guardian*, February 7, 2017.

initiated the call, but I do remember that Didi asked me somewhat pointedly:

*Ethan, how does one make money doing human rights?*

*Didi, when I have the answer to that question, I'll let you know.*

Considering how much capital Didi had invested to pay her German debt to the Jews, she may not have appreciated my borscht-belt reply. Anyway, I was rewarded with another long silence.

In 2017, Human Rights Watch (HRW) came out with a report confirming that Chinese authorities were forcing all Uyghurs above the age of 12, approximately ten million people at a minimum, to undergo mass physical examinations.[136] The Party called them "health checks." Ultimately the tests would incorporate Kazakh, Kyrgyz and possibly, Hui, nearly half the population of Xinjiang/East Turkestan.[137] The Han Chinese were exempt from the tests, thus ruling out the possibility that Beijing was concerned about infectious disease.[138] None of the Uyghurs/Kazakhs reported receiving medical results or follow-ups from the health checks. In short, the tests were not aimed at improving individual health.[139] Radio Free Asia exposed internal PSB chatter confirming the scale, and Enver Tohti, using his contacts on the ground in Urumqi, established that the standard blood sample was compatible with tissue typing. In a private phone call with the Dutch researcher behind the technical aspects of the HRW report, I

---

136  Human Rights Watch, "China: Minority Region Collects DNA from Millions," news release, 2017.

137  "Xinjiang spends 4 bln yuan on universal health checkups," Xinhuanet, March 18, 2019; see also "Uyghurs Forced to Undergo Medical Exams, DNA Sampling," *Radio Free Asia*, May 19, 2017.

138  Author's interviews with "health check" participants, Turkey, October 2019, and Kazakhstan, January 2020.

139  Author's interviews with "health check" participants, Turkey, October 2019, and Kazakhstan, January 2020.

confirmed the Party's mass use of DNA testing kits, which required only a few drops of the detainee's blood sample.[140]

The evidence seemed clear to me that Uyghurs were now the main target for organ harvesting, but HRW interpreted the utility of the tests in a single word: *surveillance.*

Surveillance, in this context, the ability to identify family lines based on DNA samples, was logically a useful by-product of the tests, but was it the Party's sole purpose? I had seen ugly partisan politics, or perhaps just distaste for Falun Gong, corrupt interpretations of human rights evidence for many years, particularly with the Amnesty International secretariat.[141] To avoid a repetition of this grim pattern, and with the apparent stumbling block of Falun Gong's "controversial" beliefs out of the picture, I asked Sophie Richardson, the China director of Human Rights Watch, if she would meet with me privately in her DC office.

In what appeared on the surface to be a friendly meeting, it became obvious that Richardson was determined to avoid grappling with any of the established history of the Chinese transplant industry, and even more determined to ignore the cross-matching implications of blood and DNA tests on Uyghur subjects. Richardson avoided even acknowledging the blood testing that yielded DNA results as if not saying the words gave HRW license to bind itself further to the inexplicable position of accusing the CCP of invading Uyghur *privacy* and *confidentiality.* In fact, my early career in human rights was all about Chinese surveillance techniques. I acknowledged that the Uyghurs had

---

140    This, and the company that had provided the DNA tests, Thermo Fisher Scientific, was confirmed by my friend and colleague, Maya Mitipolova, Director of Human Stem Cell Laboratory at the Whitehead Institute for Biomedical Research, Massachusetts Institute of Technology.

141    In the Amnesty International Secretariat in London, a research director furtively whispered to me that, based on her own witness interviews, she personally knew that *the allegations of Falun Gong harvesting were true.* Apparently, it would have been considered heretical to make such a statement openly.

been fingerprinted, biometrically photographed, and their voice prints recorded. Yet I could not go along with HRW that Uyghur civil rights and dignity were on the line, but Uyghur lives were not.[142]

Richardson clearly didn't, or perhaps wasn't allowed to, have an open mind on forced organ harvesting of political or racial prisoners, though she encouraged my belief in witness confirmation. It was a nod to my fieldwork expertise and seemed to leave the door open, just a crack. The truth is that I liked Sophie. I suspect she liked me too, but our conversation gave me the sinking feeling that everything was being recorded, perhaps just for her records. I suspected that Richardson was trying to mollify me just enough so that I wouldn't publish a denunciation of HRW.

Time has passed. I expect I can talk about it now, particularly as I still have no idea what Richardson really believed.[143]

Sophie got me wrong. HRW had produced a research breakthrough. While I was disgusted by HRW's criminal misinterpretation of the DNA tests, a public denunciation coming from me could have easily been perceived as sour grapes. In truth, I was feeling my immobility acutely now because all my Uyghur harvesting theories seemed to be coming true. I would ultimately verify the following two points: first, that all Han Chinese in Xinjiang were exempt from the health check requirement., and second, that none of the Uyghurs were given follow-up medical treatment. I would eventually see the grainy, poorly focused

142  According to the Uyghurs/Kazakhs whom I interviewed in Turkey and Kazakhstan, the one universal feature of the mass testing was *not* a DNA test, but a large blood test compatible with cross-matching for organ transplantation, thus ruling out theories by human rights organizations that the health checks were solely given for surveillance/anti-terrorism purposes. A blood test can also be exploited as a DNA sample, so, in essence, approximately 10 million Uyghurs received the same combined cross-matching test used on select Falun Gong members three years previously.

143  Several years later, Sophie Richardson met with Susie Hughes, Executive Director and co-founder of the International Coalition to End Transplant Abuse in China (ETAC), and Matthew Robertson, China Studies Research Fellow at the Victims of Communism Memorial Foundation on Chinese forced organ harvesting. According to Matthew, the meeting yielded similar results to my own.

footage of the health check lines at the local hospitals, captured on cheap phones, and smuggled out through illicit electronic means.

Perhaps these were people offended by the assault on their privacy. They were certainly people who hate standing in line. But I thought I saw the unmistakable image of one woman who felt she already had one foot in the grave.

The eternal face of fear. Frame from Uyghur forced "health check" footage, probably 2016, Xinjiang, China. Image courtesy of Enver Tohti.

*　*　*

Let's wrap up some early returns before the intermission.

- Sophie Richardson continued her nothing-to-see-here policy on forced organ harvesting. She later left HRW to co-direct Chinese Human Rights Defenders (CHRD), a coalition of Chinese and international human rights non-governmental organizations that works in tandem with the equally dismissive United Nations.[144] The CHRD's current medical policy consists of a "Watch List" focusing on "Depriving medical treatment to individuals in custody."[145]

- Capitol Hill lacked the full killer instinct while the Western medical consensus appeared to engage directly with China. For example, Resolution 343, "regarding persistent and credible reports of systematic state-sanctioned organ harvesting," passed the House but never made it onto the Senate floor. However, Congressman Chris Smith never relinquished the fight. In 2021, he introduced the Stop Organ Harvesting Act, which, like the Magnitsky Act, would ban those directly involved—in this case, Chinese transplant surgeons—from entering the United States. Bipartisan Congressional support is building for passage of the bill, but the final legislative outcome remains currently unresolved.

- The Falun Gong practitioners, supported by ETAC, the International Coalition to End Transplant Abuse in China (founded by Kilgour, Matas, and myself), and DAFOH, Doctors Against Forced Organ Harvesting, provided logistical support on what would ultimately become a "people's tribunal," held in London. Led by Sir Geoffrey Nice, the prosecutor of Milosevic, the Tribunal served as a powerful counterweight to HRW, Amnesty International,

---

144 The CHRD website briefly mentioned forced organ harvesting ten years ago. "China's Response to UN Torture Investigation: Nothing to See Here," Chinese Human Rights Defenders, December 24, 2015.

145 "Watch List of Detainees and Prisoners of Conscience in Need of Medical Attention," Chinese Human Rights Defenders, June 24, 2014.

and the human rights establishment in Geneva. However, while the Tribunal invited both the TTS and representatives of the PRC to testify, only the TTS replied with statements of limited evidentiary value. Like the Chinese, the TTS refused to appear before the Tribunal. The Tribunal examined the evidence, in detail, for a full year. In June, 2019, the Tribunal announced that the allegations had been "proved beyond reasonable doubt" and would ultimately produce the China Tribunal Judgement, the most thorough and broadly objective study of Chinese forced organ harvesting produced at this time.

• With Didi Kirsten Tatlow gone, the *New York Times* withdrew from the Chinese transplant game. As if Tatlow's extensive reporting had never existed, ambitious Metro desk reporters staged a breezy, facile attempt to neutralize the harvesting issue in 2024, in the context of a highly focused attempt to tar Falun Gong's Shen Yun dance troupe as a cult. Tatlow would testify to the China Tribunal on condition of a closed-door session. I didn't take notes, but I hope that I've accurately captured some of her main points in this chapter.

• An in-depth study by Jacob Lavee, Matthew Robertson, and statistician Raymond Hinde showed conclusively that Beijing's claim of exponential growth in voluntary organ donations from Chinese citizens was constructed, not on accurately reported data, but on a relatively simple equation.[146] While the actual number of voluntary organ

---

146    Robertson, *et al.*, "Analysis of official deceased organ donation data casts doubt on the credibility of China's organ transplant reform."

donations remains unknown, falsified numbers seemed to indicate that China had not successfully moved to a voluntary organ donation system. Lavee and Robertson would follow this with a second study which outlined the widespread use in China of organ removal as an execution method.[147]

- Bishop Sorondo's overt anti-Americanism and increasingly extravagant praise of the Chinese Communist Party rule became a serious problem for the Vatican, particularly in the age of Covid. He was replaced as Chancellor of the Pontifical Academy of Sciences in 2022. Within hours of Pope Francis passing, Beijing took advantage of the vacant Holy See to unilaterally appoint several bishops.

As the story broke about the mass "health checks" in Xinjiang, The Transplantation Society, or TTS, chose not to deny the medical significance of the tests for cross-matching or, alternately, publicly recant on the claim that the Chinese transplant industry had reformed, or send a second open letter to Xi Jinping. Instead, TTS went silent and exited the public stage, while occasionally rising up behind the scenes to denounce those perceived as threats to Chinese medical interests. This imperative would carry into the crucial period when Covid-19 was emerging and was still exclusively spreading throughout China. TTS would double-down with a stubborn defense of the hapless Tedros Adhanom Ghebreyesus, director-general of the World Health Organization. The long-term damage to Western medical credibility was incalculable.

---

147    Matthew Robertson, Jacob Lavee, Execution by organ procurement: Breaching the dead donor rule in China. *American Journal of Transplantation*, April 4, 2022

*　*　*

It's interesting that Delmonico did not go on the second Potemkin hospital victory junket. Perhaps, as the man who had performed the most delicate surgery—the relationship with Huang Jiefu—he sensed that Chinese Communist Party harvesting would quickly relapse. Delmonico did not prevent Harvard University from making relationships with Chinese transplant hospitals—engagement was his idea after all, but he dropped the overt activism. Perhaps all Delmonico really wanted was to declare that he had tried, and to ride off into the sunset.

At the end of the hearing, I had the same impulse. I can't fully explain why.

I knew that Congress couldn't really move to serious legislation against forced harvesting without the support of the medical world. A man like Delmonico was unlikely to declare the engagement with China dead any more than Henry Kissinger would say that the opening to China was a failure.

For seven years my wife supported the family. Now, it was my turn. At some point soon, I would have to face reality: We would lose. Yes, of course, history, in the form of Wikipedia or whatever deeply flawed system that humans use to measure these things, would ultimately vindicate our side: TTS leadership would pass from the scene, while the China Tribunal Judgement and our books and reports would still reside on the Internet, along with Didi Kirsten Tatlow's brief, glorious run. These ensured a certain facticity. Ironically, the overwhelming human resolve to hold our collective fists in the air would only occur under certain specific conditions: after human organs could be 3D-printed or perhaps grown in pigs, rendering the issue technically moot. After Kilgour and Matas (and most likely Delmonico, Treasure, Gutmann, and Sir Nice) had passed away. After it was too late to save even a single life in a land far across the sea called China

I rationalized the subtle change in my attitude, not as an abandonment of my supposed status as a human rights defender, but as simple maturity: "When I was a child, I spake as a child, I understood as a child, but when I became a man, I put away childish things." Yet they kept pulling me back in, so I put my back into it: the BBC appearance, the documentaries, the conferences, and the testimony. I would be heard at hearings in DC, Brussels, London, Dublin, Paris, Jerusalem, Canberra, Prague, and Tokyo, but increasingly, it all felt like a case of mistaken identity. I would swim in jet lag. I would drown in it. I would wake up in a hotel room marooned in a time zone, start the kettle for my instant coffee, brush my clenched teeth, and play a song by Electronica, an obscure Eighties band: Getting Away with It. Indeed, the bathroom mirror told me that I'd been getting away with it all my life.

If it sounds as if I'm complaining here, I'm not. It didn't matter if they were buttoned-down members of the Japanese Diet in Tokyo or a mob of rowdy anarchists in a Brighton movie hall, I genuinely loved, and I still love, presenting witness evidence to a room full of people. But I never craved an audience waving my book in the air. I wasn't doing this to promote a documentary, a website, a march, a dance performance, or even a petition. Johnny Appleseed wandered around America planting trees; I wandered into the venues to get one or two people in the audience—I could usually identify them by their eyes—to read *something*. It didn't have to be *The Slaughter*, it could be *Bloody Harvest*, or our collective *update*, or one of Jacob Lavee and Matt Robertson's long-form reports. Unless a person went into the bat cave alone and grappled with the evidence, critically, allowing their skepticism to run free, they would never fully believe in that which they supposedly were so eager to spread. Their activism would be inauthentic. They would be worthless to the cause.

Many people whom I otherwise liked and admired pushed me to simplify what I was saying for maximum impact. Tell the audience that *together we can save lives*. Aside from one family where I may have helped to save at least one life—I'll get to that—I will *never* be certain that I, or the movement against Chinese forced organ harvesting *saved any lives at all*. In fact, Chinese cover-ups—shutting down a camp or prison for example—were often very lethal affairs. So many on my side believed that *messaging* was more important than evidence. I spent a weekend politely listening to a highly intelligent young entrepreneur repetitively promoting the need for a slogan like "Save the whales," or "free Tibet." I had operated as a public affairs specialist for several years in Beijing, but this obsession with advertising techniques and public relations—ultimately with propaganda—the younger activists were positively saturated in it. I was constantly encouraged to use the word *genocide*, as if it weren't already the most misused word in the human rights world. Even then, I sensed that in a couple of years, the word *genocide* would be bloody worthless currency.

Perhaps my young friends were right in some respects. Messaging has its place, and the elevator pitch is a necessary evil, but this is not only a long war—*inch by bloody inch*—but, very rarely, it can become a war of maneuver. *The Party's primary organ source had just shifted to the Uyghurs. It had happened in the blink of my unseeing eye.* No slogan or phrase can capture the Party's elusive harvesting strategy because it isn't even based on a single impetus. It's not about transplant profits, not exclusively. Nor is it about destroying young Falun Gong or Uyghurs exclusively. It's about both, and—yes, although it's genuinely ironic in a horrible sort of way—vaporizing past atrocities plays no small part in keeping the Party's perpetual motion machine going as well.

Every minute spent on a slogan is a minute not used for evidence. And the single element that held Huang Jiefu, Francis Delmonico, and Bishop Sanchez Sorondo from publicly ridiculing and then shutting down our harvesting investigation at that time was the "Update," our comprehensive study on China's transplant volume. Their side had contradictory Chinese state numbers, medical conformity, an incurious media, a reckless Vatican, and well-established human rights groups who stared at their shoes, played word games and favorites among victim groups, and ultimately twisted the implications of their own research findings. They had messaging. We had mass: a stockpile of replicable and peer-reviewed work. Thousands of footnotes. Months of taped interviews. That evidence was the rock, our *on ne passe pas* at the critical moment.[148] It seemed clear to me going forward that without the drip, drip, drip of new evidence, however intermittent and unpredictable the timing, Bishop Sanchez Sorondo or Dr. Chapman or some AI version of Don Draper would simply craft new Chinese Communist Party slogans, and whatever phrases my young friends came up with, no matter how pithy or rhymey, would sound hollow and fade. Maybe on a personal level all that shouldn't have mattered to me, because I wasn't really an activist. I was just getting away with it.

Ad interim, the Party had learned from the Falun Gong case. Uyghur camp refugees who had made it to the West were a trickle, and only a fraction of the evidence going forward could be gleaned

---

148    Translated, "They shall not pass". French Army General Robert Nivelle, Verdun, 1916.

by sitting at a computer.[149] And that haunted me. Because I was also confronted with a recurring image, or maybe just a foreboding, as subtle as the shift from daylight to twilight on one's skin. It was of a place where the signal drops, where the winds were laughing, where something was hidden over the horizon. I was headed for all that, but I just didn't know it yet.

---

149   Parting thoughts on the evidence/journalism problem: As you may have noticed, state-sponsored forced organ harvesting was never justified in what we might call "normal" Party terms. Only internal medical discussions, little slip-ups in messaging, such as the one that Didi Kirsten Tatlow experienced, individual hospitals bragging about their transplant volume, or witnesses (medical personnel or refugees) create an evidentiary trail. Obviously, that trail is slow and circuitous. Western legacy media reporters will always prefer insta-legitimacy from the PRC National Health. Commission to the Gaza Health Ministry, and the World Health Organization, uncritically printing their statements and numbers, no matter how suspect or contradictory. Investigative reporting, as we saw during the medically illiterate reporting on Covid-19, is becoming a lost art.

# 4

# OVER THE HILLS

"We are two wolves in the same valley," Enver Tohti liked to say.[150] It meant that we two form a multitude, with all the loyalty, trust, and howling at the moon that a pack provides.

I've only mentioned Enver Tohti briefly, identifying him as a Uyghur doctor who had removed the kidneys and the liver from a living human being, a prisoner of the Chinese state, on a Xinjiang execution ground back in 1995. On a professional level, Enver was "my discovery." From the moment he raised his hand in a Westminster presentation on organ harvesting and said, in a heavy accent, that he did not have a question for me, but "I want to tell you a story. I did this with my own hands," Enver became my living proof that China's live organ harvesting of prisoners was not a myth. From that day on, we would ride together.

Enver Tohti and the author. Verdun.

There are some unique individuals, Holocaust survivors like Elie Weisel, civil rights warriors like Rosa Parks, who could tell the same story again and again, with only slight variations depending on the audience. Enver told a different story each time: the EU Parliament got the sheepish, hangdog Enver, whispering apologies over a crime he never actually identified, while the Irish Parliament got a cold medical technocrat, "I did not feel anything, but a fully programmed robot doing its task."[151]

The inconsistency troubled me. Exploring Enver's credibility on a train from London to Edinburgh, I began to sense that a perpetrator's state of mind might be far more anarchic than, say, a victim like Elie Wiesel, and there was an emotional progression during the actual surgery. Terrified by the gaze of the armed police, Enver hissed at the anesthesiologist to *do your job*, yet he knew that other than one sickening lurch when Enver's scalpel broke skin, the victim was "too weak to avoid my action."[152] As the man on his table went completely

---

151     Enver Tohti, "Surgeon Testifies Houses of Orieachtas Ireland," International Coalition to End Transplant Abuse in China, July 28, 2017.

152     Tohti, "Surgeon."

slack from shock, Enver's inner voice broke into a scream: *I'm a killer. Like a killer I am too afraid to even look at his face.*[153] Then, as Enver's hands regained their familiar power, he became *a fully programmed robot.*

The first two responses, anger and guilt, are universal, even *expected of a decent human being.* Yet Enver the robot gnawed at Enver the man. Something unspeakable had been briefly released in Enver's psyche, and, as if he bore an open wound that refused to close and heal, a callous formed. Underneath, the infection spread into his life. Forced to do a repetitive task pertaining to professional norms, such as rechecking academic footnotes or retaking a Medical Licensing test, Enver sometimes found himself just slipping away. Delivering the same speech was torture. Enver would freeze mid-stream, like a film projector jammed on a single image, and while the film crisped and melted, Enver would describe something new, contradictory, and strangely authentic: *You know, this man's bullet wound was not fatal. I could have operated and saved him. But instead, I removed the kidneys and liver and I killed him.*[154] It was the opposite of deception. For Enver, testifying meant picking off a hunk of the scab every time.

Enver personally confirmed to me that live organ harvesting was real, so much so that I found myself being cruelly sarcastic when my British colleagues expressed even a hint of incredulity. We were wolves in London, a city that, for all its international airs, has become, with the end of empire, comfortable, diverse yet oddly provincial, and circumspect. Enver was invited for coffee by a self-identified British intelligence agent. After inquiring about Enver's confidential health problems, in effect demonstrating that he had accessed Enver's private phone calls, the agent casually mentioned conspiracy theorists, *some who are no longer with us.* Following a long pause while the threat sunk

---

153    Gutmann, *The Slaughter*, 19.
154    From memory, Westminster hearing, 2017.

in, the agent politely told Enver not to speak to big audiences about harvesting anymore, only small ones.

I couldn't confirm if this agent was real, a fantasist, or just a hired thug for some sort of Beijing mind game. But Enver and I drank vodka and plotted.

A week later, just a few steps from the Foreign Office entrance, I held an ostentatious denunciation of this shadowy "agent" with a couple of London human rights kingpins, standing in the middle of King Charles Street, as if we owned the joint. I fancied that spot had good fengshui; it certainly had second-to-none surveillance. To my surprise, the exorcism seemed to work. The "intelligence agent" left a few messages on Enver's phone saying Enver was doing "a good job," and after six months, fell silent.

As my friend Conor Healey observed, "once you get into these things, you become responsible for people."

Now the wolf was at the door, and Enver was asking me to go on a road trip from London to the plains of Hungary for a festival honoring Attila the Hun. This sounds like the beginning of a joke, involving a Uyghur, an American, and a Rabbi, but it was apparently all in service to Enver's most recent vision: a plan to resettle persecuted Uyghur Christians in Hungary.

"Enver, what will the Uyghurs do in Hungary, build an arc?"

Enver smiled apologetically.

"Ethan, I don't want to drive alone."

I don't fully believe that was the whole story. Enver had become responsible for me, too. He sensed that I was flailing. By mid-2017, we both understood what was emerging.

- Beginning in 2015, CCP authorities ordered construction of camps across the Xinjiang/East Turkestan region. The

claim that by the end of 2016 at least one million had
been arrested, tricked into entering, or otherwise detained
in the camps[155] was initially met with Western media
skepticism.[156] The archipelago of camps that the CCP was
constructing in Xinjiang was initially validated by local PSB
chapters bragging about the percentage of males they had
incarcerated,[157] then by witness accounts,[158] and finally by
camp construction activity captured by satellite imagery over
time[159]—all on a scale unprecedented in recent history.

- From 2016 on, Uyghur and Kazakh witnesses describe
  several mass executions of male camp detainees—we don't
  know the reason for the killings—that overloaded local
  disposal systems, such as crematoria.[160] Local crematoria
  also acknowledged occasionally burning bodies from
  the camps,[161] while Uyghur cemeteries were routinely
  bulldozed.[162] As early as 2017, local authorities put out a

155   Author's interviews with camp refugees, Kazakhstan, January 2020.

156   Two diametrically opposing accounts from the same time period: Ajit Singh and Max Blumenthal,
      "China detaining millions of Uyghurs? Serious problems with claims by US-backed NGO and
      far-right researcher 'led by God' against Beijing," *The Grayzone*, December 21, 2019; versus "Expert
      Estimates China Has More Than 1,000 Internment Camps For Xinjiang Uyghurs," *Radio Free
      Asia*, November 12, 2019.

157   Shohret Hoshur, "Nearly Half of Uyghurs in Xinjiang's Hotan Targeted For Re-Education
      Camps," *Radio Free Asia*, October 9, 2017.

158   "China: Massive Numbers of Uyghurs & Other Ethnic Minorities Forced into Re-education
      Programs," Chinese Human Rights Defenders, August 3, 2018.

159   Mark Doman, Stephen Hutcheon, Dylan Welch and Kyle Taylor, "China's frontier of fear," *ABC
      News Australia*, October 31, 2018.

160   Author's interviews with Kazakh/Uyghur refugees and Enver Tohti, Sweden, Turkey, and
      Kazakhstan, 2019—2020.

161   "Xinjiang Rapidly Building Crematoria to Extinguish Uyghur Funeral Traditions," *Radio Free Asia*,
      June 6, 2018.

162   Matt Rivers, "More than 100 Uyghur graveyards demolished by Chinese authorities, satellite
      images show," *CNN*, January 2, 2020.

directive to construct nine new crematoria across Xinjiang.[163] The first completed crematorium, located in Urumqi, placed an ad in the Chinese press to fill 50 security guard positions with a salary of 1200 USD per month, extremely high by local standards.[164]

- Surveillance in Xinjiang was now universally listening and watching, even in the toilets, while an infrastructure of human checkpoints and electronic readers to determine race (yes, video cams could differentiate between Han Chinese and Uyghurs) and stress levels (which cameras read off the skin) ensured an orderly arrest and incarceration process.[165] All travel and all fraternization, defined as any group of three individuals or more, was monitored and controlled.

- Western reporters allowed into Xinjiang came back with choreographed footage of Uyghurs singing and dancing. Outside of China, they had tapes of relatives emoting and weeping. But actual human stories from inside the camps were rare. The Uyghur and Kazakh camp refugees who theoretically could talk about the camps were in Central Asia where the risks were theoretically manageable, yet Kazakhstan didn't come with the bragging rights of visiting Chinese territory. Only a handful of Western reporters asked camp refugees about medical exams or disappearances.

- It was that last point that chewed on my guts. *The Uyghur camps are news. Why can't the legacy media handle the Uyghur*

163  "Xinjiang," *Radio Free Asia.*
164  "Xinjiang," *Radio Free Asia.*
165  Author's interview with Uyghur software engineer, Turkey, October 2019.

*harvesting story? It's established. And because the legacy media are established, they aren't likely to be arrested in Central Asia. And they aren't walking around with a tin cup. They have the means. The BBC are no longer network virgins on harvesting: they have interviewed Enver, me, and one of their own stringers on World News Report, the biggest international program in the world. I didn't hold back with the BBC. I sprinkled all the breadcrumbs. Just follow them.*[166]

Enver caught me howling at the moon. The next day, we drove through the Chunnel and into the European summer and the German *autohofs*. The further east we drifted, the more superstitious we became. It began in the morning. As Enver warmed up the engine, he would lead me in a prayer:

*God, please help us as we drive. Protect us from evil spirits on the road. Give us speed. Let our dust choke the enemy and blind their eyes. Permit us to reach our destination safely. Let us accomplish our sacred mission.*

Like a truck driver framing his cab windows with lace curtains, Enver had bought a case of diet Coke because you can drink it or "just use it to wash your hands." He had purchased a large mock-brass cross with a matching chain for my chest, presumably to protect me and my Jewish-sounding name from Hungarian bigots. Near the Swiss border, we were stopped and searched by a mobile unit of German plainclothes police. Inexplicably, I had brought along my own talisman, the German-language edition of *The Slaughter*. As I explained to the

---

166  At their invitation, I've provided internal briefings for the BBC, Channel 4, the main BBC competitor, and Al Jazeera. The BBC is the only network who came through with an initial story. Now, the BBC are sitting on some interesting raw material for a follow-up report. The BBC's inexplicable self-sabotage suggests that the Chinese Communist Party has threatened to limit the BBC's internal access in China if they report on the story a second time.

police that we weren't transporting drugs, that book suddenly became very useful.

Eventually we reached the Great Kurultaj, the Festival of Turkic Nomadic Culture in the Southern Great Plain region of Hungary. Spread across a green field, large yurts, wrapped in white material to ward off the July sun, had been erected, each one draped with the flag of a different country: Bulgaria, Turkey, Azerbaijan, Uzbekistan, Kyrgyzstan, Kazakhstan, Mongolia, even Japan. Enver and I headed into the yurt marked with the blue and white flag of East Turkestan. Inside, mustachioed Hungarians and Uyghurs with beards resembling fly whisks were ten minutes deep into a traditional folk tune, familiar enough to everyone that the individual musicians could improvise. A few of their home-made instruments I had only seen in Uyghur restaurant wall murals in Beijing. Most of the players seemed to recognize Enver by sight, so we relaxed on the hand-knotted rugs and stretched out like cats in the intense afternoon heat.

From my first exposure to Arabic music as a child to my first contact with Uyghur culture in late 1990s Beijing, my heart lifted to these horseback rhythms.[167] Yet this was a deeper sensation. Maybe it was heatstroke, but just for a minute, I felt swept away by the dream of a nomadic brotherhood stretching from the Tarim Desert in Xinjiang to the Great Hungarian Plain, vast, yet as close as a mother and child cruelly separated by discarded imperial armor and Soviet checkpoints half-buried in sand. I had never discussed the concept of the Hun's shared legacy with my China expert friends, but I knew that when it came to the Silk Road, they would roll their eyes, and tell me it was a political construct, or a romantic myth. Perhaps it was. But

---

167   Uyghur music and dance is often recognized as the greatest entertainment in Central Asia. When I lived in Beijing, the Uyghurs effortlessly outclassed most Chinese performers as well.

like a sandfly, the Silk Road had somehow burrowed its way into the Hungarian and Uyghur consciousness, and now, into my own.

I won't say much about the days that followed: the achingly beautiful women riders, the men incessantly cracking whips on the plain, and, while the concession stands seemed to draw the line at serving horsemeat washed down by *kumis*, or mare's milk, the seemingly endless supply of horses.

Enver and I would drive back to Hungary the following summer, although this time, the Hungarian government would pick up the petrol expenses. We had been invited to give a briefing on Chinese organ harvesting at a side event of *Tusvanyos,* a Hungarian cultural celebration. Doubling as a political vehicle for Hungary's President Orban, the big draw was still a massive music festival that went on for days.[168] At this intensely social, liquor-soaked affair, we met Hungarian ministers in the "VIP lounge"; I knew that Enver was under pressure to explain the denomination of Uyghur Christians that might come to Hungary and his proposal for their resettlement, yet Enver seemed to resist this mechanical task of simple lobbying. Perhaps it didn't matter. On our last night in Hungary, we had a lively meal of borscht and sour cream with local farmers. As we made our drunken goodbyes, they produced a gift, a case of their homemade palinka, a highly potent Hungarian fruit brandy. Early the next morning, we set off for London. The palinka exploded in the Chunnel.

The boozy SUV symbolized the closing of Enver's Hungarian dream. Yet one wolf had steadied the other. And the tarmac itself was the intervention. Time and the shifting landscape conspired to let us

---

168    Held in a forest valley, surrounded by cliffs and pines, Tusvanyos took place at the eastern end of Transylvania, Hungarian land until Woodrow Wilson decided to award the whole lot to Romania in the 1920 Treaty of Trianon. The Romanians countered this modern invasion by shutting off mobile Internet, and they possibly had something to do with the sewage back-up in the tent where Enver and I gave our talk.

think aloud and rediscover long-forgotten identities. Enver told me of his adventures with Kazakh hospitals, African women, and the English health system. I told Enver about my rather tame fieldwork adventures in Thailand.

But fieldwork was changing. A new tension had crept in within a single decade. The entire time I spent in Bangkok interviewing Falun Gong refugees, I barely thought about Chinese Communist Party surveillance. It wasn't being called "wolf-warrior" just yet, but China's confidence now extended far beyond the sarcasm of its diplomats. Central Asia was being electronically transformed by the long arms of both China and Russia into a Cold War landscape where human rights researchers were classified as Western spies, or just easy prey.

Even if fieldwork was in my blood, I had observed an internal failing during my low-stakes road trips with Enver. It wasn't just that I was tightly wound, although I've always been on the intense side. It was my inability to control it. I kept nattering at Enver, complaining, assuming the worst, assigning blame for not fulfilling our sacred mission.

Enver was cool, existential, a bit like my wife. In Taipei, when I haltingly told her that Mayor Ko Wen-je was bringing *criminal charges* against me and I would have to leave the hotel room tonight to go to a Taipei court, she just smiled:

"Ethan, you have all the facts. You have the documents. So relax. Have fun. It's just another ride on the roller-coaster."

If it was *smiert spionam*–death to spies–in Central Asia, I would have to learn to think of it as *The New Great Game* and find a way to enjoy the ride.

My interview skills felt rusty, so I told Enver I would pick up the tab if we stopped in Germany along the way so I could interview resettled Uyghurs about their families. There was something jarring about the experience. Several parents said that their son or daughter had been sent to the camps but given the PSB's lockdown on communication—at one point a father assumed a character in Animal Jam, a children's online game, to speak with his daughter confidentially—little verification was possible. It confirmed my suspicion that secondary accounts have potential emotional impact, but listening to a refugee's searing disconnected pain under the umbrella of an outdoor German biergarten had become an inflated currency, a lazy way out for journalism. The reader's goal is not to share in pain, but to assess what is occurring in the camps. I conducted a couple of successful camp refugee interviews in Europe and one in Turkey, very productive interviews that strongly confirmed the presence of organ harvesting selection in the camps, but these findings on their own could not supply a sense of scale. China scholars in the West may be able to construct a fairly accurate flow-chart of the Party committees that make up the architecture of Uyghur repression, but when it comes to mass murder, human beings need some sense of the proportion involved. And given the ongoing atrocities on a global scale that compete for their daily attention, they have an absolute right to that information.

The Party would not repeat past mistakes. Beijing would hold Uyghur camp refugees in Xinjiang—no passports, no cars with Xinjiang plates miraculously appearing at Tiananmen Square,[169] no trips to a foreigner compound to knock on the door of a *Washington Post* reporter.[170] The Party also insured that any Western reporter's foray into Xinjiang was, at best, a performative but ultimately empty exercise. At worst, if real information was transmitted to the reporter through

---

169    "Tiananmen crash 'incited by Islamists,'" BBC, November 1, 2013. Enver Tohti has pointed out that it would be impossible to drive a car with Xinjiang plates from anywhere in Xinjiang to the center of Beijing without being stopped and interrogated.

170    Ethan Gutmann, "A Darkly Sinister Accusation," endtransplantabuse.org (International Coalition to End Transplant Abuse in China), September 14, 2017; author's conversation with Simon Denyer of the *Washington Post*, in 2017: "Why haven't I heard about this? Why hasn't anyone come to me personally?"

a whisper or a crumpled note, it would condemn real people, probably family members, to death.[171] If I wanted untouched virgin testimony of actual refugees from the camps, the only people who could shed light, however cloistered, on the organ harvesting puzzle, were the ethnic Kazakhs, the secondary inmates of the camp system. A small fraction, perhaps a thousand or two, were able to use their family connections to arrange a bribe. A few Kazakh officials had greased the wheels enough with Chinese counterparts to arrange release. Now most of these refugees had disappeared somewhere in Kazakhstan.

I knew that some Western reporters and academics had made the rounds in Almaty. They would do a few interviews in a hotel lobby, film a native dance or perhaps a secretive protest. If they were an academic, they might hand out questionnaires at a meeting, make sure they were handed back in, and take a cab to the airport.

There was another breed, typified by a young Russian-American activist named Gene Bunin, who wanted to interview *everyone*—camp refugees, family members of someone in the camps—and build a database of victims.[172] This is the bread and butter of human rights. If everyone speaks out, the theory is that witnesses would be protected by the principle of safety in numbers, and like a great wave, it will shatter the prisoner's dilemma that is the core of Party control. Yet it's a leap of faith to think that an internet-accessible database on the internet constitutes a total solution. In fact, a successful database usually creates further questions. Constructing a working database also means operating out in the open. That's a legitimate and gutsy approach, but in my experience, it's also true that some of the most critical witnesses are afraid to lose family members if they speak out openly. They suspect

---

171    A close colleague of mine lost a valuable "deep throat," a source deep in the PSB. The Party "announcement" that his asset had been exposed was a photo of the mutilated corpse.

172    Gene Bunin's Xinjiang Victims Database is a remarkable achievement and a practical tool that I used to cross-check many of my field interviews. See Shahit.biz/eng/.

that the Chinese Public Security Bureau will ultimately persevere. I follow their pessimistic lead. Perhaps it comes down to the political sensitivity of the investigation (organ harvesting and say, biowarfare testing, would rate as most sensitive), but it also simply comes down to personal style and how much potential guilt the investigator is willing to take on. By this point in the book, you know my fieldwork style— less interested in cattle calls and collective action, more interested in the distinct human being underneath the victim designation.[173] And when it came to that distinct human being, the shared code of our wolfpack—Dr. Tohti is a good example here, as he was very careful about revealing sources' names and locations—was casually related to our shared belief in *first, do no harm*.[174] In other words, take your witnesses' safety—and secrecy—seriously. If the witness believes that the investigator is sincere in protecting them, that secrecy has the potential to create unfiltered candor.

However, we would have to enter quietly and leave no trace.[175] The snag was that both Enver and I had become moderately famous on the Internet over the years. Kazakh national security forces would stick to us like glue from the minute we disembarked at Almaty Airport (ALA). Everyone I interviewed could look forward to a follow-up visit from an agent or a policeman. I ruled out ALA from my future. Yet the

173   There is a tension here between two different approaches. When a man comes to you with a picture of his wife who is being tormented inside a Xinjiang prison cell, you will ask questions, you will take his paperwork, and you have the option of telling him that you will give it the US State Department. But, in my experience, State has limited resources and will do little. Another option is to write up the case of the man's wife and put it in a corner of the Internet because memory and the recording of injustice is a primal human need, one that Bunin has dedicated his life to fulfilling.

174   Enver took the most serious risks on by himself. See Cliff Glaviano review of "Death on the Silk Road," produced by Richard Hering and Stuart Tanner, Channel Four Dispatches, July 1998.

175   It might fairly be charged that by taking the quiet approach we are tacitly confirming the inevitability of Chinese power into the foreseeable future. That's partially true. Our perspective, perhaps it's the perspective of aging men, is that there is no 'arc of history' and nothing 'bends towards justice.' In a world of uncertainty, the "leave no trace, do no harm" credo is simply meant to lower the chances of an individual dying at the hands of the Kazakh National Security (KNB) or the Chinese Public Security Bureau (PSB) because of an interview.

Hungarian road trips had opened up the possibility that any destination in Central Asia was theoretically accessible by car. Reporters just didn't enter Kazakhstan that way. Kazakhstan, by length, is almost identical to America, Atlantic to Pacific. Journalists certainly didn't enter at the "wrong" Kazakh border, via the Caspian Sea, the entrance that truckers used. With enough border crossing stamps behind me, if I could keep cool, the Kazakh authorities wouldn't be looking for someone like me, and I had at least a fighting chance to enter the country without recognition. To be candid, while jail time would undeniably generate public attention, I feared cracking under pressure and implicating companions and witnesses. But mission failure, just being turned back at the border, was a hundred times more likely and didn't even include bragging rights. And yet, going around the tree one more time, back to the branch where I started, I honestly couldn't come up with an alternative plan that would minimize the risk to my future witnesses.

As my plans for the ultimate road trip started to firm up, Enver announced with an unfamiliar tightness in his voice that he had pre-existing warnings never to return to a country—I won't name the country here—that we would have to pass through on the road to Kazakhstan.[176] One wolf could not leave the valley, and Enver's words hit me like a punch in the stomach. For many reasons beyond our friendship—I'd simultaneously lost a vehicle, a second driver, and a fixer/translator—I did not accept his answer as final. I pressed Enver. I showed him alternate routes to Kazakhstan. I snarled. But I didn't taunt him. This was a man who had single-handedly gone back into Xinjiang to copy confidential hospital files on Uyghur cancer rates.[177]

A week later, I asked Enver: *Have you thought about going?*

*Ethan, I think about it every night. And every day. I can't do it.*

---

176  I'm withholding the name of the country to avoid repercussions for Enver's associates.
177  Glaviano, "Death on the Silk Road."

Of course, my proposed alternative routes were theoretically viable, but I still feel foolish about challenging Enver's decision. Enver had led me down the European garden path to the outer limits of the Schengen Zone. He could go no further. It's obvious to me now that he was right.

Consider how the German plainclothes police had zeroed in on us near the Swiss border: Suspect One: a tall, aging white man with shaven head and close-set eyes. Suspect Two: a tall, middle-aged brown man with shaven head, eyes with epicanthic folds. I suppose the police, given the Western European context, could had written us off as an aging, multiracial, and ultimately harmless gay couple. But they didn't. It had taken us fifteen minutes to talk our way out, even with the German translation of *The Slaughter* in hand, *and we were telling the truth*. In the Asian/Muslim context the police would see a more streamlined version: two supposed tough guys in a nice SUV, on a job, a mission with a *secret purpose*. Every route to Kazakhstan would have failed.

The more I thought about it, the more I realized that Enver pulling out provided an interesting blank slate. Perhaps I could get a relatively untraceable car. Perhaps I could arrange local fixers in Kazakhstan ahead of time. But I couldn't go it alone. Every border cop in the world would Google my name, just out of human curiosity. I briefly toyed with changing my name by changing my gender. I'm a dual UK/US citizen, and the switch could be accomplished legally in a month or two on the UK side. I wouldn't make a very convincing female, and it would wildly distort any interviews in a Muslim country. But all this free association was leading me to the right track: The whole thing had to look like *a proper joyride*, like the Motocross races that ran through Turkmenistan and Uzbekistan just for fun. What I needed was someone sitting in the front seat next to me to counter-balance my close-set eyes—young, Caucasian, female, and preferably blond

\* \* \*

Ten to fifteen years ago, my wife and I used to leave London habitually to summer for a couple of weeks down in an Italian villa in Tuscany. The place belonged to an old and dear friend of mine from the US, Ben de Haan and his wife, Sophie. Over time, our families had become close, and I was particularly fond of Ben's middle child, Josephine. Like so many middle children, Josephine was prone to feeling neglected and the odd girl out. Several years running, we invited Josephine to come stay with us in London and act as an au pair for our son.

Josephine had the occasional flare of genius and some of the madness of it, too. One of those summers—I think she was just about 16 at the time—Josephine achieved a sort of adolescent trifecta: making self-destructive noises, writing horrible things in her diary, and developing a penchant for wielding sharp objects. Ben and Sophie were both devoted parents but had simply lost control. After a particularly rough evening in the villa, I invited Ben to let us take over for a while. We would legally become Josephine's guardians, temporarily, and see if we could successfully induce her to finish her final year of high school in London. Ben agreed. Josephine finished. And, although the road ahead was twisted, Josephine ultimately made it into a top art school in London, settled in with another genius but slightly mad boyfriend, and peace was restored for Ben and Sophie.

So for a year or two, I had a daughter, and I took the responsibility seriously. When she developed an infection, I accompanied her to the hospital every day for a full week, until the NHS finally agreed to operate on her. When she left a bag of pot lying around, I flushed it down the toilet. I took her to the London Olympics. I took her bowling. I always enjoyed watching her mind work. I regretted nothing.

I mention all this because Ben felt he owed me a sort of friendly debt. And while Ben had never understood precisely what I did for a living, he respected it. One August night I was informed that a Uyghur witness had a conflict with the Swiss immigration authorities, so I began packing to leave Ben's merry palazzo to catch an early flight to Bern. Ben suggested that he might come along.

*Why do you want to do that Ben? I mean, what would you do?*

*Um, hold your coat?*

Now Ben was in London staying with me and my wife for a night. Over drinks, I explained my Kazakhstan dilemma. I had a young woman in mind, but I suspected that MI6 had other plans for her. Ben believed the solution was obvious: Josephine. She was a quick study, with high emotional intelligence, and, while she had never learned to drive, she could read a road map like a naval officer. She had become a beautiful young woman with radar-scanner light blue eyes, the perfect visual foil to my sunken-neck hit-man demeanor. I worried aloud about the risks—less to the investigation, more about the potential danger to Josephine's safety. Yet the more I thought about it, the more I had to admit that she was the critical piece in the puzzle.

It was better to travel sooner rather than later. I had already assumed a winter framing for the investigation, so I laid out the miseries that Josephine would face. The first of the ten plagues— the travel vaccines—would come six weeks before departure. This would be followed by the tedium of the endless road: isolation, cold, exhaustion, weird food, squat toilets, seasickness, desert, snow, and police harassment. I knew that Ben would brief her on every one of these points, and I sensed that my next conversation with Josephine would be a formality.

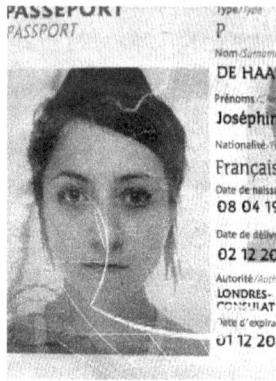

Josephine's French passport photo.

I spoke on Signal with an old friend who works in US intelligence. He didn't think the overall idea of driving to Kazakhstan was insane, and he confirmed that a pre-2005 vehicle could theoretically avoid tracking. But he cautioned me that if I maintained connectivity while using a virtual private network or VPN, we wouldn't electronically disappear.

*Ethan, every app that you use has a little electronic signature. It rubs off. It leaves traces of you everywhere. So no Google maps, no email, nothing. The surveillance in Kazakhstan is run by the Russians. They don't miss anything. Don't use credit cards or debit cards either. They're poison. Just bring cash. Use burner phones. That's pretty much it.*

Through a random London connection, I'd made a casual friend who worked for British Naval Intelligence. I visited his flat in London and laid out what I was trying to do. He confirmed the no-chip, radio silence policy and told me that, given my age, I had an advantage because I could drive with a map and a compass. I nodded. He smiled at me and said: "You are growing a beard, aren't you?"

* * *

When you wake up with an unfamiliar beard, the first thing you should do is scratch it really hard. My next task, at 4 am on the 3rd of December, 2019, was to gently wake up Josephine downstairs because Enver Tohti would already be parked outside waiting to drive us to the airport. The night before, Josephine and I had done some final gift shopping for Kazakh children at a pound store, and on impulse we darted into a noisy Woolwich Arsenal pub, famous for catering to munition workers and sailors during the Second World War, to raise a pint, or two or three, as we took leave of beloved London.

Now I was buzzing Enver into our flat and heating a pot of espresso as Josephine stirred on the couch. Enver and I lugged two massive duffel bags to his SUV. Along with our warm clothes, the bags contained inexpensive English products that might appeal to Kazakh families, extensive road maps, a mini-library of used travel guides from Romania to Mongolia, home-made binders of photos and maps devoted to snow leopard behavior and locations, watercolor sets and cotton paper, fur hats from the Turkish souk, and two gender-specific sets of skis and poles.

Half the money we would need, 10,000 in US currency, was sewn into the flannel lining of my jeans.[178] The other half of the cash that we could legally travel with, a mix of British pounds and Euros, was wedged into a weighted Diet Coke can with a hidden screw-off bottom and a hollow detangling brush with clumps of Josephine's hair as a potential repellent. These items would live in Josephine's bag along with a vintage SLR camera, 35 rolls of Ilford black and white film, a first aid kit including a collection of heavy-duty prescription antibiotics, malaria pills, and codeine. My carry-on included a small Dictaphone, soft and

---

178 I won't go into the money at this point in the story. Thanks to six different sources, and one major patron– (see the Acknowledgements for the details), we had enough to do what we needed and maybe enough to handle a contingency.

normal-looking electromagnetic field shielding cases ("Stalinbags"), specialized anti-facial recognition glasses ("Reflectacles"), and two compasses.[179]

I went back upstairs, kissed my wife, and joined Josephine in Enver's SUV. It must have been 4:30 am. I told Enver we were flying Ryanair, and I drifted back to sleep.

My first fixer/translator in Kazakhstan came through Uyghur Christian circles I had encountered in Northern Germany. This was parlayed into communications with a Uyghur Christian of some standing in Turkey, which led to my direct contact with "Ranger," a talented Uyghur Christian guy in Almaty, Kazakhstan. His English was so fluent that he had to be a prodigy or a spy (I definitely ruled the latter out when I met Ranger's children who clearly shared the same natural talent for languages). Ranger was also a skilled Central Asian negotiator. He wore me down until I finally blurted out that I could pay him fairly for his services—at human rights rates—but I couldn't pay him enough to reflect the very real risks that I was asking him to take. He accepted and promptly made a brief foray into Kyrgyzstan, a decision which would have a multi-year impact on the investigation down the road. He also led me to a dedicated human rights lawyer in Almaty, Aiman Umarova, who could act as a backup if any problems arose with the police.

The second fixer—I knew that I had to hedge my bets because I assumed that I could only make it into Kazakhstan once—came to me through my relationship with Gulchehra Hoja, the Uyghur reporter from Radio Free Asia, and Rahima Mahmut, my translator and fixer, particularly in the Rukiye case. The three of us toured London one

---

179    I endorse Stalinbags for data security and Reflectacles to prevent facial recognition. I'm not endorsing Ryanair, unless you are working within a tight human rights budget: Given the oversize/ extra bag charges that we ringing up, any other airline transport from London to Frankfurt would have been approximately three times more expensive.

afternoon, meaning that they used me as a human selfie stick. Over fish and chips, I received my reward. I asked Gulchehra for a name of someone who could help me in Kazakhstan. She immediately replied that there was a Uyghur guy in Almaty who was already instafamous for creating a series of webpages called Uyghurland. She called him "Bavi," and she believed that he would work.

I contacted Bavi using Threema, a messaging system reputedly more secure than Signal that Ranger recommended. Bavi's English ability was rudimentary over the phone, but his sincerity came through. He did not even bring up payment. Over the shaky connection, I sensed that he had the potential to be a fisher of men.

Ranger had a sophisticated understanding of the investigation at that point, so I encouraged him to meet up with Bavi in Almaty. I wanted them to cooperate, and I also suspected Ranger's negotiating skills might come into play over the flat issue. Bavi supplemented his income as an apartment locator. Ranger knew that the flat had to be 1) cash only and completely off the books, 2) have a balcony, two bedrooms, and, most critically, 3) a nice domestic setting for interviews. The location of the flat didn't have to be abnormally discreet, but a tight, friendly neighborhood wouldn't work. A vast and anonymous apartment complex, ideally with parking, was preferable.[180] I estimated that we would reach Almaty by Christmas Day, and I would contact Ranger by burner phone when we were close.

That left one more crucial element: the vehicle.

Peter Recknagel is a German Falun Gong practitioner who had built a successful consulting business over the same years that I was building a reputation as a scholar of the conflict between the Chinese State and Falun Gong. He became a natural patron; every couple of

---

180    Ranger and Bavi knew that if they revealed the apartment would be occupied by Europeans or Americans, the price would double.

years we would renew contact, and he would re-affirm that he could help with some business expenses. He kept me going with iPads and provided a new iPhone for Enver Tohti when we met Peter for lunch in Frankfurt during our road trips. In the late summer of 2019, we picked up the conversation again:

*Ethan, what do you need?*

*What I really need, Peter, is a car. A car that I can drive to Almaty. And make it back to Europe.*

*What sort of car?*

*Probably an SUV? Anyway, it must have four-wheel drive. We'll be going during the winter, probably around Christmas when Kazakh security gets a little more relaxed. But I've been told by someone who used to live out there that the snow can get pretty crazy.*

*Anything else?*

*Yeah. Sorry. This is, actually, you know, the hard part. The SUV has got to be older than 2005. That's when they started putting chips in everything, around 2005. So it's pretty easy, you know, with the chip. If the Kazakh guys want to track us, they can do it, pretty much at will. But we need to get through the Kazakh border and then just, you know, vanish into thin air.*

*So. A used SUV. 2004 or older. Okay. Good. Anything else?*

*Yeah. A universal ski rack on top. Enough to hold two sets of skis. Plus poles. Maybe a dashcam if we have to drive in Russia. Walkie talkies could prove handy too.*

*You are going skiing, Ethan?*

*Yeah, well, I need people to think that we're going skiing. Almaty has a ski resort. I have the skis. I have this theory that if you want to disappear,. . . you need visibility. It's like wearing a beanie, that American hat with a propellor on top. I want something silly on top of the car. Something that tells a story.*

*Ethan, let me see what I can do.*

Peter and his crew purchased a 2003 Toyota RAV4 (Recreational Active Vehicle with 4-wheel drive) in early November 2019. In true German fashion, Peter's staff spent several weeks with mechanics ensuring that there would be zero breakdowns, that the CD player worked, installing the ski-rack, and stripping out back seats to give us extra room (a single jump seat, foldable, remained in the back).

The RAV4 is the poor man's SUV. It's basic, just a little black box really. Perfect. Just as the quality of a wedding invitation signals how much money the wedding guests are expected to spend on a gift, the car would be a signal to the Kazakh police as to how much they could reasonably expect to receive in a bribe.

*Plus,* as I explained to Josephine as the plane taxied to our gate in Frankfurt, *if we run out of fuel in the Kazakh desert, the black paint will absorb the Winter sun, while the small, enclosed space and our body heat will slow down the onset of severe frostbite. If that fails, there are wild horses everywhere. We could cut one of them open and use the heat of the dying animal as a sort of...*

*Shut up,* Josephine said, channeling her inner vegetarian. *I've actually been having a recurring dream about us wandering in the freezing desert.*

*Josephine, what makes you think your dreams are so special? It's the same for me. Every night. But, you see, my dream involves a horse...*

*You think your dream is funny, that's your fucking problem.*

Peter's staff met us at the gate—they didn't recognize me because of the beard, a promising sign—and led us directly to the RAV4. We shoved the bags in and strapped the skis and poles to the top. I started the engine. It was a good moment with gratitude and trust on both sides. Fleeting hugs. I threw the clutch into reverse, then 1st, and we waved. Short of a physical tracking device, we now had an electronically untraceable car, so the strategy was to *turn everything off.* Five minutes later we were in double Mixmaster Hell.

Over the years, attorneys representing Yahoo! and other Internet companies were legally obliged to call me because there "was a breach in my account"—in other words, I had been hacked—and, employing charm and the *don't say anything for two seconds if it's China* routine, I established that Beijing hackers were behind the breach, every time. I was certainly not the only one: Beijing bored into certain accounts in New York State (Falun Gong), in Dharamsala (Tibetans), and in Munich (Uyghurs). Ultimately, China would hack the Pentagon. During the Doctor Ko uproar, Mainland bot accounts commented directly on my Facebook page. I theorized that the poor Chinese sap in charge of my case file probably used Facebook as a lazy way to monitor my location. So before I left, I put together a series of Facebook posts—"Happy New Year!"—that sort of thing, with a photo of myself, in full winter gear, hoisting a beer in a location that screamed *London! I'm still in London!* I gave my son access to my FB account with strict instructions to post these innocuous messages on specific dates, just one or two a month. Enough that the poor sap in China would think it was *all quiet on the Gutmann front.*

Then, last night, I shut down my devices, completely cleansed of any controversial content, and stowed them in the Stalinbags.

Josephine and I had talked it over. There was always the slim possibility that the PSB was monitoring Josephine, along with my wife and son, even several years after she had moved out of our house. We had a flurry of recent communication. So, when the plane landed, we would err on the side of caution. Josephine would shut down and stow her phone, perhaps just as a way of getting in practice for what lay ahead. It all seemed clean and logical, even virtuous.

Yet here we were, Josephine focusing on our European road

atlas, shouting out exit numbers, my missing them, exiting anyway, struggling with an unfamiliar clutch to get back on the Mixmaster again, until I cried: *Just use the phone!* Josephine rummaged through her bag like a congestive heart failure patient trying to find nitroglycerin and emerged smiling like a cat as her thumbs moved like lightning on the screen. Sixty seconds later we were out of quadruple bypass spaghetti junction and en route to our destination for the night, Prague.

Now we were into the first of the many road CDs I'd put together, perfect for licking wounds. We briefly tried a teach-yourself-Russian CD, got annoyed with the authoritarian style, and, after I taught Josephine a couple of useful Russian phrases, we segued back to Lee Hazlewood and Nancy Sinatra and "Some Velvet Morning." We didn't dwell on our first failure, because. . . joyride. Instead, we gratefully followed our progress on Google Maps, entered the state of European road Zen for 320 miles, and as the streetlights lit up on the outskirts of Prague, we pulled into a Soviet-lite motel with a shiny Vietnamese restaurant tacked onto the side. It was the first of many nondescript budget accommodations. We avoided using Airbnb. Even though most motels would make a copy of our passports, they wouldn't use them unless the police were already in pursuit, and motels take cash. My experience with Airbnb hosts is that they demand cards or electronic payment, and if one doesn't follow every minor rule, no matter how eccentric or intrusive, some hosts are quick to invoke higher authorities. As for the sleeping arrangements, we're both private people and bad sleepers, so, apart from sharing a cabin on ferries, I'd budgeted for two rooms all the way to Almaty and back.

Before we left London, I had gone through the potential routes to reach Almaty. I ruled out the "Southern Route," essentially driving east through Istanbul and northern Turkey. Erdogan was being rough on the Uyghurs at that time, and some journalists were rotting in prison or under detainment (domestic Turkish journalists, not foreign, but still). I ruled out the "Northern Route" through Latvia, then into Russia and exiting into Kazakhstan just north of Aktobe, because I feared the Russian border crossing. That left the middle road of Czechia to Slovakia to Romania to Moldova to Ukraine. We could shorten that by following Google's first choice: straight east to Poland, then Ukraine all the way, but it looked like a soul-sucking drive to save three hours. The problem was, after Ukraine, then what? I was vaguely aware of the situation in the Donbas, but I was certain that the Russian border was to be avoided unless there was a good reason.

Perhaps it sounds like I knew what I was doing? Well, I didn't. I was going on a feeling about the crossings: follow the lines of commerce. Safety in numbers. Lots of eyes. *Batch processing.*

When I was in my late teens I had served for a year in the Merchant Marines on a ship named the S.S. American Argosy. Some merchant seamen became truckers. Maybe the life of isolation, of men, of constant movement, was the same.

The solution was to reserve tickets on a budget Black Sea Ferry line that seemed to cater to Ukrainian truckers. The ferry left from the Ukraine (Chornomorsk near Odessa) on December 8th and docked in Batumi, Georgia, approximately two days later, weather permitting. Either way, it would give us two days to recharge from the driving.

Waking up in Prague on December 4th, we had four days to make Odessa, just under 1200 miles away, about five-and-a-half hours of driving a day. I think, going from memory here, we made it as far as Liptovský Mikuláš, in the middle of Slovakian ski country, a six-hour drive. The next morning, we walked to the central Christmas market. As if they were expecting us, a white-bearded Saint Nicolas (or Father Christmas, or Grandfather Frost) came out of the Church, accompanied by an "angel," a smiling young blond woman, dressed in a sort of elf costume. The gravitational pull of Western Europe was fading. Without forethought, Josephine and I had inadvertently mimicked the Slavic Father Christmas figure with his cute sidekick.

Over the course of the second day, off-road madness set in. For three days, my captain's log, a short diary that I would attend to at the end of the day, becomes unintelligible. I'm sure that one of the musicians from the East Turkestan yurt at the Attila the Hun festival made lunch for us in Romania because Josephine has photos of us laughing it up. At a service station, I gently backed into a Slovak truck in the darkness, scuffing his fresh wash and wax. The driver kept yammering about *polícia* and started calling his trucker buddies over. In my madness, I raised my hand with a wad of cash like a panda brandishing a gun, Banksy style, and theatrically peeled a hundred dollar bill off for him. In an American ghetto, such an act would have been followed by theft and possible death. Yet everyone just got back in their vehicles, with no *polícia*, and drove off.

We found ourselves deep in Transylvania, through Romani villages that Josephine giddily compared to a Tintin adventure and, when it became hopelessly dark, we followed signs to a hilltop hotel. There was no breakfast—not even tea—just fixed stares from a group of Eastern Orthodox clergymen in the morning, so we drove east into the morning mist and split a Red Bull, only stopping for a Jewish cemetery with concrete headstones on the side of hill. A traditional marching song sung by Mark Pidgeon came on the CD player:

> *So fall in lads behind the drum*
> *With Colours blazing like the sun*
> *Along the road to come-what-may*
> *Over the hills and far away.*

And it was as if we had broken the chains of Western Europe and England.

*If I should fall to rise no more*
*As many comrades did before*
*Ask the pipes and drums to play*
*Over the hills and far away.*

I felt what can only be described as profound ecstasy, which had reduced us to idiots who so loved the freedom of the road such that we would dedicate our bones to that anonymous hilltop, if we could just keep driving on this enchanted highway, this ancient mountain range, for an hour more.

Road in Eastern Europe. By Josephine de Haan-Montes.

We dropped into a canyon deep, so steep and cavernous that Josephine said she could smell the brakes reaching their limit. Then, the spell was broken, and we found ourselves in a modern Romanian strip mall. With Internet connectivity returning, the Black Sea Ferry website announced that the Batumi ferry was delayed. We had an extra day to make Odessa, so we took rooms in a highway hotel. We had two border crossings in our way, Moldova and Ukraine. But we had already completed a practice session at the Romania border, a textbook border crossing, which involved four standard elements:

1. **Triage:** It begins with a barbican or subtly fortified gateway to a castle. An official in a booth asks the driver for the passports of everyone in the vehicle and briefly examines them. Assuming there are no obvious problems, the official hands the passports back and directs the driver to the (usually open air) carport ahead.

2. **Customs:** The distance between triage and customs is generally one hundred feet or more, theoretically allowing border security a chance to react to a suspected terrorist. At the carport, the driver turns the ignition off while customs agents examine the undercarriage for contraband with under-vehicle search mirrors. Typically, a border agent will tell the driver to open the rear hatch to allow access to luggage. This can be a gentle search, a conversation, with a bit of poking around. Some countries allow trained dogs to search the vehicle for drugs or explosives. An aggressive search includes removing the luggage and running it through a scanning machine and pulling components of the car apart.

3. **Immigration:** After filling out a form and waiting in line, or just crowding around a border control window, the driver and passengers will usually be subjected to questions over the purpose of the trip: duration, location, potential financial issues, and vehicle status. The first issue is translation, which, as one leaves Europe, is unreliable. The second issue—and the hinge-point for me—was that the border agent can look

you up on the Internet at any time. So, the trick is to be interesting and pleasant enough in person, and close enough to a known quantity—the enthusiastic, eccentric foreigner—to engage the border agent, yet not be *too* interesting. The objective is that all the vehicle occupants' passports receive an entry stamp.

4. **Surveillance:** Certain countries will also require a biometric face scan, fingerprints, and other identifying materials as the final step before entering the country. As the driver and passengers return to their vehicle, there is usually a final once-over, in person and remote, looking and listening for emotional behavior or compulsive repacking before the border gate opens.

Romania joined the European Union in 2007 but hadn't joined the Schengen Area fully until 2025. So the border formalities felt like an anachronism. Never mind the skis, Josephine had a French passport, mine was British,[181] and the car was registered in Germany. Romania was Neptune, part of our solar system, and they had to let us pass.

The Moldovan border was Pluto, not even a planet, and the first test of our cover story. We were in stage 2) Customs, when a young border policeman asked me to step out of the car. He gestured at the skis, told me to open the back hatch, and peered in. Then, perhaps because Moldova is a long way from any ski slopes, or perhaps because he just wanted to seem engaged, he said: *Where is your tent?*

Of course, these were downhill skis, not cross-country. Yet explaining that downhill doesn't generally involve camping out would come across as condescending, so I just smiled as if I didn't fully

---

181    This was still during the Brexit transition period.

understand the question. After unzipping a bag or two, he waved us off. Yet the policeman had made a critical point: the skis had worked their diversion magic, but our luggage was neat. It needed to reinforce or expand on the ski story. The travel guides should be spilling out, the files on finding the elusive snow leopard needed to be front and center, maybe even the watercolor sets. Skiers should be attractive. When I left the SUV, Josephine should have joined me.

In stage 3, the questions all had to do with the ownership of the car. I explained it was a company car, which they ultimately accepted, but I realized we would have to get written communication on company stationary from Recknagel and print it out. The border guards always seemed to feel better if they had something that could be photocopied.

Josephine watched as our passports were stamped. We'd been lucky, and we chewed over all the details of what we did and didn't do as we—the only vehicle on the road—headed into the poorest country in Europe. As if on cue, the weather shifted from a sunny and chilly December day to a threatening storm with high winds lashing grey sand, almost like asphalt, against the RAV4. Josephine had barely had time to process the brutalist Soviet-era high rises of Slovakia, Hungary and Romania. Now nothing but dreary brown single-family homes lined the horizon, and she briefly panicked. I understood the feeling but remained calm. We would both experience odd moments of panic in the weeks to come, but they were personal, tripped by different stimuli. Fortunately, we never freaked out at the same time.

In the early evening, we made it into Chișinău, the capital of Moldova, on the Stefan cel Mare si Sfant, a showcase main street of statues, government buildings, shopping, and even a packed Christmas market. Just off the boulevard, it turned into a ghetto, where we spent an hour in the alleys trying to locate a bed and breakfast that only existed in the imagination of the Internet. Finally, we spotted

The Cosmos, a massive late-Soviet-era hotel. The rooms came with a bed-radio console and push-button phone, (something I had only seen in Moscow during the 1980s, and this one still had a dial tone), separate shower and toilet, lenticular Bambi images on the wall, and each balcony had a complimentary wasp nest. We found some grub and tried to go out clubbing. I figured that's what a 24-year-old female might enjoy after a tough day, but Josephine's sweatpants, standard going-out gear in London, was judged too informal for Chișinău's disco dress codes.

It was a disappointing evening. But the next day, I woke up early, went down to the lobby and had a Soviet-style buffet meal, late Eighties communist comfort food. Josephine showed up at the table, sniffed at all the processed food on display, choosing only to drink black coffee while Google-mapping our route to the Ukraine and Odessa.

We followed the highway for an hour until the road signs abruptly switched to Cyrillic, and the highway became an avenue lined with red and green flags bearing a hammer and sickle,[182] alternating with the Russian tricolor flag bearing a double-headed eagle clutching a scepter and orb, a throwback to the Tsarist late imperial period.[183]

We had stumbled into the city of Tiraspol and somehow, as established in a back-and-forth using my primitive Russian, we had to undergo a Russian Federation checkpoint in an essentially unrecognized, country/border zone called "Transnistria." Because Google primly didn't recognize these silly Russian claims, Google Maps had sent us smack-dab into a not-real-country occupied by hulking Russian soldiers in plain green uniforms manning a sophisticated border checkpoint where we were the only customers.

A soldier told us politely to leave the keys in the vehicle, and we

---

182    Apparently, this is the same flag that the Soviet Union used for the Moldovan SSR, before the establishment of the Republic of Moldova in 1991.

183    Presidential Standard of the Russian Federation.

were directed into a medium-sized hall with sliding glass windows. As two humorless Russian soldiers examined our passports, I tried to explain, in my infantile way, that we were simply on our way to Odessa and the Black Sea ferry. The younger soldier of the two—cropped brown hair, intelligent face—responded coldly with something that, to my ear anyway, sounded a lot like that old Communist classic: *Your papers are not in order.*

Alarmed, I retreated to a document table to see if I could find the number of the Moldovan British or US consulate in my bag. These were the two consulates I had not written down on my country list as it had seemed insignificant.

Josephine broke the deadlock. My strategy on border crossings is to *find someone who is on your side. There is always one.* While I debated calling London, an escalation that would likely backfire, Josephine softened up the younger Russian soldier. He was smiling now and even chatty as he translated Russian into French on his phone and she responded on the same phone with French to Russian. Finally, Josephine skipped over to me calling out:

*Daddy, Daddy, I think they want to help us!*

I hustled back to the glass windows, where the soldier, looking bored now, retranslated the Russian to English and held the glowing words up to the glass:

*maybe we can help you*

Then the soldier typed a short phrase and held it up to the glass:

*65 euro*

It's all legal, Josephine explained. Something about a highway, or an exit fee, *or a Transnistria military bake sale! Like we fucking care! I thought.*

*Blagadorio vas* (my thanks to you both), I said solemnly, bowing my head slightly, while pulling a 100 Euro note out of my wallet.

The soldiers, both very relaxed now, passed me some crinkled bills in non-convertible Moldovan currency. Since we were all friends, I didn't count the money, and they didn't seem to feel any pressing need to stamp our passports. Everyone waved goodbye as if we had been on a cruise ship.

After a ten-minute drive through the sliver of Transnistrian territory, crammed with barracks and equipment, the Ukrainian border felt like checking into an artist's colony. The border guard noted the skis approvingly, opened the back of the RAV4, and Lonely Planet guides and Snow Leopard location files cinematically tumbled out onto the asphalt. The letter establishing the use of the Recknagel consulting car was produced, passports were stamped, and we made Odessa by nightfall.

I'll spare you the nightmare of the next day: the short trip to the port of Chornomorsk on the Black Sea, the fruitless attempts to locate the ticket counter in the suburbs while I asked over and over: *Gudyeh lodka?* (I kept saying "lodka" which I thought meant "ferry," although the full phrase actually means "Where's the rowboat?"). As time before departure grew short, we found the ticket office and then headed down a mile-long road with trucks ominously parked on both sides to what looked like a trucker leisure center. Standing in front, looking confused and anxious, an older trucker—short, bearded, and serious—approached us. Critically, he was Azerbaijani, which explains why he was not irritated by my childish Russian. With great decency, he took us under his wing. We had cars. Everybody else had massive rigs, so he lobbied the ferry staff to ensure that our vehicles would be the first to drive onto the ferry, and we would share a table with him and his friends in the ship's mess. That evening when Josephine and I stepped into the ferry canteen, full of animated truckers from Ukraine, Georgia, Armenia and Kazakhstan, the conversations suddenly ground to a halt as if they had never seen a woman before. Josephine was poker-faced. I could read her inner stress, but our Azerbaijani buddy was sitting at the far table, and he even spoke a little French.

Josephine and I went out on deck after dinner. It was a beautiful night with an unseasonably warm wind gusting the Black Sea waves like a school of flying fishes. I poured bison grass vodka into our Coke cans; open drinking was against ship's discipline. While we waited for the gargantuan ferry to sail out of the dock, we were joined by two truckers, both Ukrainian. The older one had a whiskered feral cat appearance and an aging hipster vibe. The younger one, clean-shaven, friendly and sincere, spoke English well. The conversation was fluid. The old hipster shared the secrets of living well: he had the best slim cigarettes, whiskey that beat that Polish shit that I was drinking, and he even offered to share his *salo*, little slices of pork fat, with us. The ship refused to move, it was past midnight, and we were all laughing, and it became gradually apparent that he was infatuated with Josephine. Josephine's an all's-well-with-the-world sort of drunk, so she was oblivious to the aging hipster's signals. When she wandered off to use the facilities, the younger man assumed a conspiratorial posture, keeping his voice low.

*Please tell me, if you don't mind, what is your relationship to this woman?*

*You mean Josephine?*

*Yes. What is your relationship to her?*

*She's my daughter.*

I smiled gently and the young man translated this back to the old hipster. As if a knife had been plunged into his stomach, every muscle seemed to spasm inward. He glanced at me for a fraction of a second, his eyes conveying deep shame, and then he stared blankly at the emptiness of the deck, his face a Greek mask of pain.

The vast ferry began to silently push back from the dock. Josephine made it back to the table, while the two Ukrainians quickly retired to their shared cabin. We would not see them again during the trip.

I felt sorry for the romantic old trucker—I can still see his stricken face—but he'd confirmed a central tenet of the Hun code of honor: *Father-daughter relationships are sacred. And that was good, because from the moment the ferry pushed back, we were dependent on the Hun brotherhood, as surely as if we were sharing a* lodka, *not a ferry.* When we walked into the mess hall the next morning, conversation paused, and then, like an engine skipping a single cylinder, it started up again, just as strong. The word had spread about Josephine and her dad, and the ferry was on an even keel.

A big Ukrainian trucker who resembled Robert Duvall befriended me, partly as an excuse to practice his rudimentary English, but also because when he had asked about where we were going (Almaty), and the route we would take, he expressed alarm. On the day we were scheduled to arrive in Batumi, he told me to bring my maps, and, sitting at the table overlooking the Black Sea, we went over our route: From Batumi in Georgia across the Caucasus Mountains to Baku, Azerbaijan—yes, he approved. From Baku we would take the Caspian Sea ferry. Yes. Then, on the Kazakh side of the Caspian, we would head south to drive through Uzbekistan to Kyrgyzstan to Kazakhstan. . . .

*No. You drive through Kazakhstan. On this road.*

*But look at that road. It's not direct. It goes north, then East, then south again. It's shaped like a house. Unless we cut across the desert. . . [He was laughing now and shaking his head]. . . Okay, okay but, the road really is longer. It's more time. Look at the distances. And this southern part. It goes through the desert. For a day, two days, there's nothing there. Not even petrol.*

*No. You bring petrol. Road is good. Uzbek road is bad.*

*We have four-wheel drive...*

*No. You drive with trucks. You drive with us. On Kazakh road.*

Our eyes locked. He held. It was an intervention and the map lost.

A few hours later, Josephine and I heard some commotion from the top deck, and we headed up. Lit up like fire, in the late afternoon sun, was an incredible scene. It was land—Georgia and the port city of Batumi. On the right side, in the black waves, perhaps a dozen dolphins raced alongside the ferry, guiding us in, while the truckers pointed and laughed. Behind it all, looming above the port, was my first view of the Caucasus Mountains, perhaps the most distinctive range I have ever seen, resembling ginormous pointed teeth. In general, the more I age, the less fear, but something about the peaks and cliffs, the dark blues and greens, the theatrical verticality of it all, made my heart sink and set my teeth on edge. It resembled a detail from a mysterious poster in my sister's room, when I was a little boy.

The premonition. Detail from The Land of Make Believe

As mentioned, Josephine and I had different triggers, and we rarely synced up. But travelers develop a sixth sense about each. I expect it's a survival mechanism. Anyway, she asked me what was going on. I pointed mutely at the mountains. I wanted to say that we were headed to the Wicked Witch of the West's house—okay, the East—either way, we were doomed. I didn't want to creep Josephine out, so I pushed the feeling down into my guts. My wife always says that I have no psychic ability (She does, but that's for another book), but the premonition had come in on little cat feet. Perhaps it was linked to the "Red Bridge" checkpoint between Georgia (Christian) and Azerbaijan (Muslim), reputed by my Ukrainian trucker friend to be the best of bad border options.

Josephine and I went down to the hold and sat in the RAV4—Josephine was always happy when we were in the vehicle. We waved and smiled at the truckers we recognized and watched the rigs pull out with barely inches to spare on both sides.

The border agent who interviewed me at Georgia immigration spoke English so well that I effusively told him: *We are going to ski in Almaty. And then in Mongolia. I told my daughter that if she graduated from college with honors, I would give her the trip of a lifetime. And here we are. On the trip of a lifetime.* This cornball line raised a smile from the border agent and brought down two passport stamps in quick succession.

Like a computer game, every mile from Western Europe meant a checkpoint of increasing difficulty, yet somehow, the credibility of our cover story seemed to increase as well. The strategy became *if you want to appear to be a crazy Westerner, then your passport stamps need to begin in a crazy Western country like Germany. No shortcuts. And you need to develop a nomadic crust. Like the rigs, your vehicle needs to feel as personal as a home.*

We made it to a Batumi guest house late that night. After I made sure that Josephine was satisfied with her room, I drank a glass of vodka neat. East of the sun and west of the moon, I said aloud, as if that would close the door on the incident, and pulled the covers tight over my shoulder.

We headed out again, climbing the Georgian plateau, where the landscape became the Land of Make Believe made flesh, capped only by the dreamlike effect of snow gently falling in night-time Tbilisi. The next morning, we walked over to a bustling outdoor market and found a guy who sold remainder cell phones in bulk. One box featured a ring programmed with an idiotic dance phrase in English, *Are you serious!?* At 10 dollars each, they were perfect burners; if customs searched the RAV4, we could plausibly say they were novelty gifts. I purchased fifteen, and we drove off to the Azerbaijan border and the fabled "Red Bridge" crossing.

The Triage of our passports went smoothly. But on the extended approach to Customs, there was a steep hill to the right. Josephine pointed to the silhouette of a soldier, armed with an AK-47, in low ready position. Josephine, who had been on kind of a high since the Transnistrian crossing, began moaning in shock and fear. I talked fast: *Armed guards are standard in this part of the world; you just don't see them. They protect us from terrorists.* And so on. I felt guilty because automatic weapons had not been on my Josephine warning label list. But Josephine rapidly cooled down as Customs went smoothly: guidebooks and watercolor sets fell out of the rear hatch right on cue. We moved on to Immigration, which consisted of two mini-office booths, surrounded on all sides by shouting, cursing men of all ages. I parked the car. Josephine and I joined the mass struggle. The men stared and gave us a little room, but it was hard to gauge between "aggressive" and "normal" pushing.

If I could say we were carried away by the mob and held hostage in a cave, it might be good for book sales, but a common-sense strategy had emerged from the checkpoints: *Don't be afraid to look human or stupid.* Using a child's matter-of-fact tone and volume, Josephine announced she had to use the toilet. This gave me an excuse to approach one of the armed guards who was standing around watching, and I was able to explain in crude Russian that my daughter had a *"problema."* The men parted for the armed guard, as he escorted us to the visa office window. In less than 60 seconds, an aging female in military garb stormed in—an Azerbaijani version of Rosa Klebbs[184]—and efficiently led Josephine to the facilities. Whether Josephine really needed to go or not, everyone had gone relatively quiet, so there was no pressure to relinquish my spot at the window while we rapidly went through the questions: Immediate destination? Baku and the Caspian Sea Ferry. Ultimate destination? Mongolia. Purpose? Eco-tourism. Skiing. Find the snow leopard. Vehicle: RAV4, company car, no drugs. The Azerbaijanis generated a series of forms including a receipt of entry from the Commonwealth of Independent States (CIS), a post-Soviet hangover that presumably mimicked the European Schengen zone (but without the benefit of open borders or a common currency).

Smiling very faintly, Josephine reappeared by my side. With no further surveillance, we got back in the car, and, just like that, we were in Azerbaijan. All that stood in our way was approximately fifteen Azerbaijani men, shouting and blocking the RAV4. Josephine involuntarily flinched and cried out. *Don't show fear, Jo,* I barked at her, exposing a little anxiety myself. I explained that these guys probably just wanted us to change money and, if they were lucky, serve as our guides. In truth, I needed a fixer at the entry, so I put the car in park, got out, and stood in front of them. A strategy floated into my mind:

---

184    Ian Fleming, *On Her Majesty's Secret Service* (New American Library, 1963).

*Find the evil face. This is the man who can help you.* And like some sort of orientalist vision, there he was in the back, quietly smirking. Tall, with almost comically sinister features, he wielded a beard resembling a jambiya, an obscenely curved dagger. I pointed to "Jafar,"[185] and just like that, the men dispersed.

Somehow Jafar and I were able to work out that I needed Internet connectivity with a name, *any bloody name,* in Azerbaijan for a week. I also needed an anonymous phone chip that would operate in Kazakhstan. The strategy here was to *go black but have a back-up—* should we get overrun by the Kazakh police, maybe we could send out a text. The British Naval Intelligence officer had specified that if we had a single shot, it should go to the US side, not the UK. *Think of* Jurassic Park, *he said. Who actually shows up on the beach?*

Jafar's commission was reasonable, because we both knew that I had tipped him in advance by singling him out as the serious guy at the Red Bridge crossing. Ninety minutes later, we were on the road to Ganja, the Azeri halfway point.

The next morning, we headed out for the Caspian Sea and Baku, Azerbaijan's capital city—a light day, only 225 miles. We were really feeling invincible at this point (the Red Bridge toilet break, Jafar, all our little victories), and we changed the music to heavy metal/rock to celebrate—well, ourselves, but also Route E60. On this two-lane Mad Max extravaganza, we passed Jeepney-style contraptions, repainted Soviet transport trucks, three-wheeled farmer mini-pickups, and cars carrying crushed appliances, bound together, literally 20 feet high and swaying from side to side. On the shoulder of the road, there was even a bicyclist, furiously pumping away. . .

*Uh, Josephine, you see that guy? On the bike? See him?*

*Yeah, I see him. What's he doing?*

---

185    Jafar is a cartoon villain, the Sultan's Royal Vizier, in Disney's *Aladdin.*

*Can you get a picture?*

*No, too late. I'm sorry. Ethan, can you slow down?*

*No chance Jo. Look at that rig behind me. Jo, I mean, was that guy white?!*

*He was hairy. Full beard. It's hard to tell, but yeah, I think he was European maybe? He had, like, trainers.*

*Was he nuts?*

*Yes, Ethan. He was definitely crazy.*

As if I had just turned over a tarot card, the image of the lone traveler whispered to me: *Don't take yourself so seriously. You think you are brave, but there is always someone braver.*

His name was James Stram, but I'll get to that.

The Baku entrance was easy. Perched on the side of the Caspian, a hotel with relatively cheap rooms, a ballroom restaurant, and live music every night took our fancy. The next day we drove 50 miles south to the Port of Alat to buy tickets on the elusive ferry to Kuryk, Kazakhstan. I say elusive because the Caspian Sea ferry has no set schedule.

The otherwise modest port had a vast concrete parking area with hundreds of rigs forming a series of meticulous alleyways where the truckers could grill meat, pray on mats, hang washing, gamble, and, as a trip to the latrine tent confirmed, overwhelm the septic system. All booze had to go under lock and key at the entrance to the port, so at least the women toilet attendants—always women once you enter the old Eastern bloc—while fighting a futile war on human waste, didn't have to put up with drunkenness.

There was no sign of life at the ticket office and no departure schedule on the chalkboard, only satellite information on Josephine's phone confirming that the ferry was still anchored in Kazakhstan. Even if the ferry left for Alat immediately, we had approximately 24 hours before the ship arrived on our side of the Caspian, and, we were told, a full 12 to 24 hours after that to allow for loading and unloading. That's just under a two-day notice, and Baku was one hour away. In a moment of weakness, using my new-found belief in picking the fixer with the most sinister face, I gave seventy-five dollars as a holding fee to a grizzled camp fixer who promised to set up tickets and provide the latest rumors as to the ferry's departure. Other than endlessly sending texts to Josephine such as "save yourself from sorrow. come to Alat now," regardless of the ferry's actual position, he was useless.

On the way out of the port, we stopped at the Port of Alat café, a basic little coffee shop with a few hot meat trays. I ordered some lunch while Josephine protested with black coffee. Through the window, I could see a bearded young man with what looked like *trainers* biking up to the café. He walked in and ordered. I casually mumbled something in his direction about traffic conditions on the road from Ganja. James Stram, half-Jewish, half-Armenian, lives in New Orleans. He had begun this particular journey, documented on his travel blog, "James on a Bike," in Spain. Yeah, he'd brought a tent. With a burst of high-pitched laughter, James casually told a story about wild dogs attacking him on the way over to the port this morning. If this was courage, there was something effortless about it, and the friendship that followed. A few minutes later another cyclist arrived at the cafe. Younger than James, he had ridden all the way from Israel.[186]

The afternoon was fun in a familiar expat way, but I had no appetite for roughing it in the concrete jungle. We returned to Baku, the gem of the Caspian, where the hotel manager kindly took over the circuitous problem of purchasing the ferry tickets, so Josephine and I took our first vacation. We had a long outdoor lunch at the biggest McDonalds in Baku, and we purchased blankets, as the ferry reputedly

---

186    Perhaps the only misstep of the afternoon was that Josephine suggested the two cyclists should ride together.

had infested bedding. I even purchased a second Kazakh-network-capable SIM card as a back-up,[187] but the uncertainty surrounding the ferry's movements dampened our days in Baku. Josephine was restless, her mind on the road, so we took to repeatedly playing a melancholy pop song about rumors and waiting for news that never came.[188] The ferry was apparently still in Kazakhstan, so to save ourselves from sorrow, the soundtrack on the drive home remained the same.[189] But Josephine had subtly changed. When we first entered Eastern Europe, I could see the shock of endless Soviet housing blocks reflected in her eyes. Now she was comfortable playing the game of the authoritarian world; passing a billboard with Azerbaijan's President-for-life Ilham Aliyev waving to the nation, Josephine smiled and waved back.

On our third day, with ferry tickets in hand, we made a fascinating day trip to a Zoroastrian fire temple. On the road back, Josephine announced that the ferry had left Kazakhstan and was apparently making good time across the Caspian. We could sleep in the hotel tonight, but that was it.

By noon the next day, we were back in the Port of Alat as the ferry came in. By 6 pm, we began drinking illicit vodka shots with James, Omer the Israeli, a Georgian named George, and his Kazakh buddy "Buzz." At midnight Josephine and I drifted off in the RAV4. At 3am, all the truck engines started up, followed by a port official screaming at us in Russian to put our bags through a scanner. Josephine really had to go to the toilet this time, and the only positive was that

---

187    The man who sold me the chip registered under a false name, was clearly one of the rare Jews of Azerbaijan. I could tell he was trying to read my face to see if I was a member of the Tribe. In fact, I'm Jewish on my father's side and Josephine is a quarter-Jewish, also on her biological father's side. I did not pursue the connection because I had no idea of his allegiances or what pressures he faced in the Azeri diaspora – this sort of prohibition against casual conversation was a tragic constraint throughout our travels.

188    Pet Shop Boys, "King's Cross," on *Actually*, Parlophone 0190295826222, 1987, compact disc.

189    Pet Shop Boys, "King's Cross."

the hard-bitten women who ran the ferry's sleeping arrangements took pity on Josephine and quickly assigned us one of the cabins. We slept in late, until I heard George bellowing (apparently, he defaults to English when he is on a bender) from his porthole: *I did it! I'm guilty! Take me away!*

"Let me off this filthy ship!" George on the Caspian Sea Ferry. By Josephine de Haan-Montes.

Coffee was non-existent, but liquor seemed to be everywhere, and seen from the perspective of the lounge, the whole ship was blotto. When I stood up to go find Josephine, a young blond Ukrainian truck driver decided to confront me with the information that the finest meal in Kazakhstan was horsemeat, while he searched my eyes to see if I would flinch or break into tears like a little girl. When he registered my deadpan reaction—hmm, he had given me an idea for a very profitable food stand at the next Attila-the-Hun festival—he moved on to James and began to berate him about. . . well, nothing really, although it was somehow connected with James being Jewish and all. James laughed it off, and his subtle body language—a distance biker is, pound for pound, physically much stronger than a truck driver who sits on his ass for a living—conveyed that he could lick the Ukrainian if he had to.

On December 19th, we docked in Kuryk, Josephine shut off her phone and stashed it in the Stalinbag. George the Georgian, drove just ahead of us as we exited the ferry and joined the Kazakhstan immigration line. We had huddled with George over our precious cans of coffee a few minutes before, and with just the faintest of hints, George grasped that our trip had little to do with skiing. He assured us he would try to smooth the way with the border guards.

The Triage began as an elderly Kazakh military man, flanked by police, approached our RAV4 and demanded our passports. After a moment of scrutiny, he ordered Josephine out of the car and into a waiting van. Other than her bathroom break at the Red Bridge, we had crossed every border together, and we hadn't really discussed how we would handle it if we were questioned separately. Like a wildcat, Josephine let out a low growl and using three different languages, she eloquently implored the old soldier to let her stay with her dad. I understood a little of the elderly military man's Russian—it seemed to come down to a regulation: one vehicle, one driver. *Don't worry, it will be fine,* I said to Josephine, and attempted to smile.

A lone soldier manned the Customs station ahead. Mongolian features, cold and grim, he had two well-trained German shepherds and a selection of tools that could quickly and efficiently remove any part of our car he wished to examine. He went after George:

*What are these packages?*

*They are wine. House gifts for my friends in Kazakhstan.*

*Really? How nice. Well, what is there for me?*

*What!? Oh, for God's sake, nobody ever tells me anything! That's crazy.*

*Of course I would have brought something for you, Officer! And next time, I promise I will. Just let me know what you like.*

*You really messed up. I know who you are. Next time then.*

*Officer, can I ask you a question? What are you going to do with the black car behind me? You know, with the guy with the white beard?*

*That guy? I'm going to rip his car apart.*

*Wait, wait. You don't have the full story. That guy is a foreigner. He is here with his daughter. First time ever in Kazakhstan. They are coming here for* New Year's. *You know what that means? They are going to spend* New Year's *in Kazakhstan. And that guy is from America. That's very important. Because first impressions are* everything.[190]

The soldier waved George on.

I drove in slowly, stood outside the car, and opened both doors so that the soldier could let his German shepherds jump through the car and have a sniff. The soldier, still glaring, politely asked me in Russian if I had any drugs or alcohol. *Nothing,* I said. *My friends drank my vodka on the ferry* (on the final night, James and Omer had requisitioned my last bottle). The soldier, seemingly annoyed by his own restraint, waved me through.

The final hours were filled with forms, fingerprints, financial and length of stay questions, and a full facial scan. Now, unless I was wearing Reflectacles, the biometrics of my features could theoretically be recognized by any surveillance camera in Kazakhstan, and linked up with my passport and my dossier, but did that thumbnail really go much beyond my passport data? Unless my dossier was already filled in with my human rights background.[191] Yet no official asked a single question about my professional life. Instead, when I mentioned

---

190    George's charisma was the critical factor that allowed us to enter Kazakhstan without extra surveillance. We're very grateful.

191    We would be stopped by Kazakh police a handful of times and they often accessed my passport. I suspect my dossier was nearly blank.

our search for the elusive snow leopard, I had a strong feeling that the Kazakh authorities were hearing it for a second time. Josephine, wherever she was in the compound, had played her part perfectly.

We were all reunited in a parking lot in the shadow of the Immigration structure, where George filled me in on his prep work with the soldier. We had made a slight leap of faith with George, and the lesson here was to *never underestimate what a friend can do for you at the critical moment.*

Now we would all disappear into the paper map, and the first hours would go smoothly. We woke up in an Aktau hotel, just an hour up the coast of the Crimean Sea, on December 20th. We spent the morning finding our way to the automotive part of town, secured a 20-liter metal jerry can for extra petrol, and found our way through trial and error to the highway that would lead us east, to Beyneu, a Kazakh desert city. Suddenly, the Kazakh horizon opened up before us. We saw small herds of camels walking around free, and Josephine was laughing and crying at the sight, and the wind was howling, and on the side of the highway, in the distance, there was a now-familiar figure. We passed James and pulled over. He dropped his bike and sprinted to the RAV4, cranking the heat volume to the max.

James defrosting his hands. By Josephine de Haan-Montes.

He politely refused our offer of a lift, explaining that despite the wild wind and intense cold, the only problem was his hands, and to a lesser extent, his feet. Anyway, there was a village coming up in a couple of miles where he could warm up again. Ultimately, he was headed for the southern route across Uzbekistan, while, after a night in Beyneu, we would turn north according to the Ukrainian trucker's directions. Josephine dug out some gloves for James and gave him a sandwich with Soviet-style mystery meat for the road. "See you in Almaty," James said, smiling.

It was late, and snow was coming down when we arrived at the Beyneu guesthouse I had selected back in London months ago. Josephine had managed the local directions perfectly from a faded print-out.

The next morning, December 21st, we woke up in an exuberant mood, and decided to send Christmas cards to our families to let them know that we were okay. We would leave my name out of it by sending both cards to Josephine's family address in Italy. Ben would presumably pass my card to my family in London. Bearing the theme of Grandfather Frost and his young blonde sidekick, the Snow Maiden, we wrote innocuous messages—*Merry Christmas! I love you!*—on them and left the envelopes open so the Kazakh police state could examine them. When we reached the counter at the Beyneu post office, instead of simply letting us pay for overseas postage, we were told to follow a tall, middle-aged woman with a blue uniform. She led us into a large room so brightly lit that it gave the impression that there were no doors or windows. The lady then sat down at her desk and carefully ignored us, not even offering us a place to sit. We stood for thirty minutes and watched her type. Since we assumed we were being monitored at this point, we did not speak to each other, and we attempted to project a sort of quiet optimism.

Finally, she looked up, informed us the cards were okay, and I went back to the end of the line to pay the bill in Kazakhstani tenges. The strategy going forward was clear enough: *Don't do stupid unnecessary shit.*

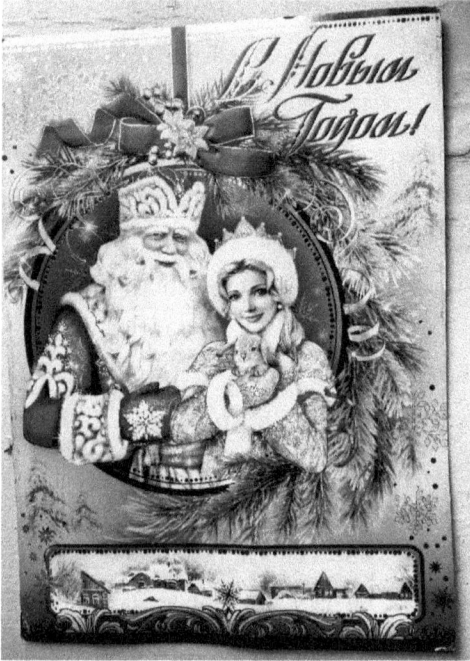

My stupid unnecessary Christmas card to London. From the author.

We couldn't wait to get in the RAV4 and start driving north. The goal was to reach the small city of Makat by nightfall. There, the road north would become a Western highway for another long day of driving, perhaps eight hours, ending in a larger town called Kandyagash. This would be followed by the longest day of the excursion, the intense drive south through the desert to the edge of where the once great Aral Sea had been, a former port city called Aralsk, the coast now long gone due to failed Soviet agricultural projects.

Kazakhstan is very thinly populated, particularly in the West, but my London Internet searches showed that all these destinations had accommodation, food, and at least one gas station. Again, I'm not psychic, but I kept referring to Makat as "a town called Malice," to Josephine's amusement. At one point, purely on impulse, I tried to bypass the grid pattern and the town called Malice by taking a shortcut which would lead us directly onto the eastern highway.

The shortcut had once been asphalt, but neglect and the Kazakh winds had turned the road into great chunks of rock and stone. We drove for perhaps 200 yards then realized the RAV4 could not handle this for even ten feet more, so I turned the vehicle around painstakingly, and we barely made it back.

Outskirts of Makat. By Josephine de Haan-Montes.

Makat was distinguished by its sprawl of muddy roads, pipelines, and bleak houses. We quickly became lost—we couldn't even find our way to the East/West highway—so we stopped and asked for directions from a team of appliance movers. Even with my bad Russian, I sensed something odd in our broken conversation. I didn't want to believe it at first, but they were sizing us up. The unblinking smiles, the confident posturing, the peering at the windows of the RAV4, and the trace of a leer as they assessed Josephine were all strangely universal. Perhaps too politely, I broke off contact and we found our way to Makat's main street. At an intersection, I pulled to a stop in front of two beat cops, and, as I began asking for directions, they noted my German plates, averted their eyes, and race-walked away. This same behavior was repeated several times over a single hour in different sections of the city. At one point, Josephine was certain that a policeman had bolted around the corner before I had even noticed his presence.

But there was a lodging house in Makat center, so we decided to stay there, and that night the movers stole the 10k in cash sewn into my jeans and, while I was out cold, they tied Josephine's hands with... okay, none of that happened. But it could have. On paper, we were in a police state, but the fact is that we had money, a beautiful girl, and all the evidence suggested that Makat was mob controlled. So what really happened? We were thrown for a loss: without Internet, our only apparent choice was to drive 80 miles back to the coast to a quasi-resort town on the Caspian Sea, Atyrau, where we would spend the night in an old Soviet hotel and looked out our windows to see three policeman forming a defensive triangle of fire just across the street. I looked out again around 4 am. They were still there.

In the morning, we headed back to Makat to find the eastern highway. The day was still beginning, people were leaving their houses, and, even if they did not really understand me, pointing at the map and making driving noises got us close enough. We found ourselves turning to the right off a mud road that encircled Makat onto something much bigger and dirtier. It was, apparently, the lost highway. Somehow, the realization that we would drive on a huge dirt road for God knows how long excited us: Adventure! Kazakhstan revealed! Free from useless chunks of asphalt, the Cheshire Cat police, the false pretenses of legitimacy and modernity. Even our German map was in on the big fat lie, depicting this overgrown mudslick as Kazakhstan's major east-west thruway. Every ten minutes a colossal rig would rumble by on the opposite side, proving without a doubt that there could be no other road. Yet the dashboard navigation compass I had bought for the car was in on the deception too, consistently indicating that we were going straight south. Josephine speculated that there was some sort of magnetic force inside the car that was overruling the magnetic pole, so I pulled the RAV4 over, dug out my hand compass from our luggage, walked about 10 feet from the vehicle and took a measurement: Dead east. Exactly what we wanted.

Compass check. By Josephine de Haan-Montes.

It's hard to explain, but from that morning to 1 pm, when the snow began, these were the happiest hours of our journey.

First snow, enroute to Kandyagash. By Josephine de Haan-Montes.

By 4:30 the light was fading from the sky, the snow was accumulating, and the first hills began. I had neglected to tell Peter that we needed snow tires, not all-season. The slips and the sense of drift began. Next to us now was an actual asphalt highway, a relic of China's belt and road initiative funding, somehow gone cold, unfinished and unused. The dirt road traversed the top of the dead highway, switching back and forth, leading us on long, sweeping arcs, in fresh snow, like a skier making first tracks. Then, as if a giant child had lost interest in his blocks, the asphalt highway simply disappeared again. The hills grew steep, the clouds, thick, and I had to nurse the vehicle through the pitch dark for two hours, until at the top of the final hill, we spotted the glow of Kandyagash on the horizon. The light turned out to be a sprawling appliance store. I went in to ask for directions. The sales staff were all young people, very attractive, and none of them spoke English. But they were awfully excited to see a foreigner, and they danced around me clamoring for selfies. I made up some excuse to hurry back to the car because I was worried that they would post a picture on social media. The next stop was a wedding reception. There was a middle-aged woman eager to help us find a place for the night, but she seemingly could only speak convoluted Russian. When I asked her to *please slow down*, she would simply say the exact same sentence in the same rhythm but louder, as if I were deaf. We finally found a club. Behind the bar stood a young woman who, it seemed, was the only English speaker in town. I was beginning to freak out a little bit at this point, so I had to steady myself with a drink. Josephine and I tucked into the bar snacks, and the young woman took pity and took charge. Eventually, after an hour or so of calling around she was able to acquire two rooms for us in a college dorm. After saying goodbye to the young woman who had become our patron saint for the night, Josephine and I found ourselves walking out of the blizzard and into an enormous red hall resembling the Court of the Crimson King. There we found a student suite with two bedrooms, both of which had the heat on maximum. We slept dreamlessly.

The next day, we found ourselves mushing through several feet of snow to a small breakfast joint. The appliance store excitement flared up again, so we raced back to the RAV4. We were now entering the moment that we had alternately anticipated and dreaded: The southern turn to the empty corner. But the asphalt was back. We had the feel of the road now. We had the jerrycan full of petrol. We had the cooler full of bread, cheese, meat, and pickles. We had blankets and burner phones that could be quickly enabled. On the other side, we had our fading nightmare of abandoning the car and staggering through the snow.

After a couple of hours of driving, the final roadside attractions—hand-drawn signs and a kind of tumbleweed—disappeared, and it was pure desert, the camels and horses long gone. There was something intoxicating about the sheer flatness, as if we had set sail. Driving straight south, the problem was that the climate had shifted, too; in place of snow, there was sheer ice.

Neither plow nor salt nor gravel—the road to Aralsk. By Josephine de Haan-Montes.

Back in my safe London home, I had estimated the drive as 8 or 9 hours. Now, with our reduced speed—I wasn't willing to slide off the road going above 45 miles per hour—I would get us into Aralsk after 12 hours of driving, with no stops.

Without landmarks, distances between vehicles became hard to judge and the vanishing point, deceptive. There was no life at all. As the twilight, and then the night came, my perception changed too.

*Josephine, are we going down?*

*No. What do you mean?*

*We are driving down. Like, for the last ten minutes. Losing altitude. We're coming off some sort of plateau, right?*

*No, Ethan. Really, we're not. Everything is just the same. Ethan, are you okay? Do you want to pull over?*

*Not here. Maybe a little later. Did I drink all the Cokes? It still feels like we are going down.*

We stopped for a compass check several times. It always read South. The words of the British Naval Intelligence officer came back to me: *You know how to read a compass.* I suppose that's why I kept stopping, to hear his voice, but also to assess the ice on the road, which would grow thinner and then thicker again, like a vast pendulum.

Just before midnight, we saw the lights of Aralsk. Never had a gas station looked so inviting. I could see a trucker hotel two hundred yards away. They were wrapping things up in the kitchen when we came in, but they gave us some sandwiches and beers, and we took our rooms. The only *problema* seemed to be one old woman who had it in for foreigners. I'd not met a battle-axe quite like this, not even in the old Soviet Union. I fell asleep on my bed immediately and within 30 minutes the old woman was banging on my door and demanding extra money. I wordlessly handed her a $20 bill. That mollified her for the night—she even gave me an unpleasant smile—but the US currency was a tactical mistake. The next morning, December 23rd, while we had breakfast, she was screaming in the kitchen about "Amerikanski." When I checked out, she blatantly doubled the price. Because I suspected she was a paid informer, or at least aspired to be one, I paid what she asked in tenge and tipped her with another $20 bill, which raised another ghastly smile. I don't regret this action, especially when we were so close to our goal. The strategy: *No confrontation with bit players.*

Something was wrong with Josephine. She seemingly could not communicate. To divert her, I led her to the Aralsk bazaar, and, out of habit, I ended up looking for some burner phones. Something about the repetition, that I was befriending the most evil-face-in-the-market (like the Red Bridge), or that we stood there while he fiddled with the phone (like the Beyneu post office) upset Josephine further. I bailed on the market and pulled her into a fast-food restaurant. She didn't want to eat anything and was beginning to cry. I tried driving her to a spot that I had promised we would see, small Aral Sea ships now rusting in the sand, but when we reached the edge of town, it became clear that the boats were much further across the ice-glazed plain, and we would not be able to make the journey. I took her to a small museum of Aralsk history. I took her back to the car. Then she started bawling, as people walked by. I wanted to give her a hug, yet if I so much as held her hand, a bystander would see an older man touching a young woman who was crying uncontrollably, easily reported as an abduction gone wrong. I've questioned what I could have done in this situation many times, but all I know is what I did. I decided to give Josephine some privacy, so I let her know that I was going to change money, and I let her cry it out.

After 20 minutes, I returned. Josephine was more relaxed now, yet still uncommunicative. The obvious point hit me while I was standing in line to change money: Josephine was in a state of post-traumatic stress disorder, PTSD, a delayed reaction to driving through the empty quarter. I figured the best cure was simply to hit the road. And that's what we did, and her mood lifted, and after a couple of hours, by the side of the highway—no ice this time—we spotted a tree, the first in two days.

That evening we found ourselves at the entrance to a city of light, Kyzylorda. Population of over 200,000. A big international oil-deal center, glistening with Christmas decorations. A vast Avenue lined with massive hotels. A breathtaking song came on the CD player: "Nomad" by Luc Arbogast, French Medieval revivalist, sampling from Borodin's transcendent *Prince Igor: Polovtsian Dances*. Josephine had previously called it *our theme song*. Now she told me it was a sign that I should pull into the spacious courtyard of the "Hotel Nomad."

Kazakhstan has an absolute zero policy towards driving under the influence. Tonight, on Christmas Eve, we would take a taxi into the city and have a meal and a drink just like normal folks. The hotel, beautiful and lavish, was essentially uninhabited, so I bargained for a 12-hour stay and received a huge discount. We went to our respective suites, changed, and met in the floor lounge next to the elevator. There was something cinematic about having it all to ourselves. I concocted two vodka martinis and underneath the glistening modern chandeliers that bespoke an oil-rich Kazakhstan, we toasted each other, yes, *and our courage,* and we wished each other the merriest Christmas of them all. And just for a second, it was. Of course, the restaurant overcooked Josephine's salmon and overboiled my lamb, but I'll always remember that first martini, because beyond all the shock of her morning breakdown, we had made it around the horn, and I was so proud of her.

It was Christmas Day when the final aftershock hit. We had lunch in a basic road joint in the town of Turkistan. But when we got out the air was filled with dense, choking fumes. I don't know where it came from, a factory on fire perhaps, and I didn't really care. Yet it was a premonition. We got back in the RAV4 and headed east, but then, in the valley below, we saw the outskirts of Shymkent, a Kazakh industrial city bordering Tashkent, the Uzbek metropolis. Like a cat's tail standing on end was a great plume of ginger-orange smoke and haze. I could see Josephine beginning to shake.

*Ethan, what is that?*

*It's industrial pollution, Jo.*

*Oh my God.*

*Jo, half the world lives with pollution like that. And most of them will live longer than we will.*

I don't remember the rest. It was our first and only fight on the trip. I pulled the car over to the shoulder and Josephine got out of the car and walked into the woods. She walked back after two minutes, sat down in her seat and said: *Why are you so mean?*

I don't remember how I replied. Maybe I apologized. Maybe it doesn't matter. Because I knew in my heart what I was doing. Josephine, just for a brief time, had gone PTSD. And that was a security risk. And

I didn't want her to do it again because the investigation was my main priority—and that was mean—and I didn't say any of that. I didn't need to. Josephine knew it anyway.

I have no strategy to offer here. But somehow the argument, as brief and truncated and unsaid as everything was, cleared the air.

We had been in Kyzylorda. We were going to Taraz. And it was only a few minutes after the argument that just under a hill, the kind of hill where you don't brake quite quick enough, the police had set up a dragnet. Four cars had been stopped. I was just one more, but the policeman, seeing my foreign plates, ordered me to walk to the police vehicle at the front of the line. Inside there was a police captain of some sort, and he pleasantly ordered me to take the passenger's seat beside him. Despite my limited Russian vocabulary, my adrenaline spiked, so I remember the gist of the conversation quite clearly:

*You were going too fast. Give me your passport.*

*I'm new to your country. I'm sorry.*

*Sorry just won't do it, Mr. Gutmann. I'm going to have to take you to the station.*

*I can't leave my daughter. I'll pay my fine to you right away. I need my passport.*

*Good. Put your hands down here. Like mine, you see? Yes, there, below the camera. Now give me 500 dollars.*

*No, I can't.*

*What do you think is right?*

*100 dollars.*

*No, no, no, Mr. Gutmann. We'll drive to the station now.*

Eventually we settled on $250, put our hands on our hearts to symbolize our understanding for the other's position, shook hands, and said goodbye. Utterly humiliated by the transaction of course, and yet I knew that if the captain had scanned and reported my passport the investigation might have been compromised. And if he had taken me to the station? Josephine was at risk. *If you meet the devil on the road, give him his due, but protect the mission.* The police in Kazakhstan have an unusual system. It's considered a plum job. And because it's a plum job, the police actually have to go into debt to buy the badge. They are expected to extort drivers, particularly foreign drivers, to settle the debt.

Taraz is cop city, the main training ground for the Kazakh police. We didn't know that when we picked a place on the map to spend the night. So, when we drove from our modest hotel to the mall that was the main cultural center, the police recruits were constantly trying out their newfound power, pulling people over, screaming through their megaphones, blasting their sirens. Given that I was $250 down for the day, this was hard on my nerves. Josephine, by contrast, had made a complete recovery and went ice skating in the mall and even made a young Muslim friend, a 14-year-old girl who wanted to show us the city. We drove back to the hotel with the itchy feeling of constant hot pursuit.

The next morning it was obvious that some VIP had arrived in Taraz because there was a policeman stationed every ten yards for miles on the same route we had to take to return to the highway. I kept to the speed limit carefully. It was now December 26th, and the madness of the last few days felt a little raw. The highway was broken, half dirt, half paved, and the road switched back and forth as we made our first burner call to the Ranger. He was excited to hear my voice, and he told me that a couple of people were very nervous when we did not call on Christmas Day.

We finally reached the outskirts of Almaty, where we slowed for a mammoth ice floe with hundreds of cars trying to navigate around it through a slurry of ice and mud. That led us into the actual metropolis. With no map of Almaty, we drove around blind for four hours, in a kind of hysteria borne of exhaustion from the road. I don't know why I didn't call Ranger. I suppose it was pride. I finally stopped and asked someone on the street, *where's a hotel?* He pointed mutely to a karaoke bar and a hotel next to it. We checked in. I called Ranger and arranged to meet him the next day. Josephine was amused to find a complimentary condom carefully laid out on her bedside table like a mint on a pillow.

Journey's end, Almaty. By Josephine de Haan-Montes.

I spent the next morning cleaning off the desert dust and mud caked into every crevice of the RAV4. We met with Ranger for shashlik, Bavi joined us, and, with their help, we moved into the anonymous flat. Then, for a very long time, we sat together at the kitchen table in the fading afternoon light, four wolves in the same valley.

# 5
# THE PERFECT 28

*This is the numbers chapter, a detailed account of 20 refugee interviews on camp disappearances. The majority of the interviews were conducted in Kazakhstan, and no witness testimony has been excluded. All witnesses came from different camps. Their collective testimony yields a plausible range–a minimum and a maximum annual death count—of Uyghurs, Kazakhs, and other Turkic groups selected for organ harvesting. The order of the witnesses in the chapter is loosely thematic and has no special significance.*

*This is human data, distorted by perception, memory, bias, and trauma, but free from intentional lies or propaganda. To verify that statement, I'll take you behind the curtain as far as I can without compromising the safety of the witnesses, their families, or their associates.*

*I strongly prefer that you draw your own conclusions based on actual testimony. Realistically, however, journalists and staffers are often under crazy time pressure to report hard numbers and central findings, so you'll find the equivalent of a short executive summary, beginning with a chart, at the end of the chapter.*

## KAZAKHSTAN. WITNESS 1: "FATIMAH"

Bavi found us a cash-only, no-name, no-lease apartment with a balcony, somewhere I could smoke, I'd requested. Our high-rise terrace looked out over the southern Almaty skyline, and, to Josephine's relief, our floor floated just above the smog line, which always seemed to settle, like a sleeping gray cat, four flights below.

It was still the period between Western Christmas and New Year's Day, down time even for camp refugees. And we had gone to the mattresses, our final attempt to shake off any attention we might have attracted in those first chaotic hours entering Almaty with nothing more than a schematic map. Perhaps, come January, we would break the isolation, go directly to the witnesses, and travel freely, but for now we kept our movements outside the apartment complex to a minimum. I parked our RAV4 in an extended snowdrift, a line of cars visible from my bedroom window where the police would be forced to approach on foot and crane their necks to see the German license plates.

Despite our self-imposed inactivity, this was turning into a good day. Bavi had crossed the avenue to collect a witness at a pre-arranged cafe. Sharing a cigarette, Josephine and I watched the tiny silhouettes of Bavi and a woman, backlit in the late December sun, as they made their way along a winding concrete path to our complex in the newly fallen snow. We waited at the elevator door.

The refugee, a slim woman in her thirties, dropped her phone in my Stalinbag without comment. Bavi had briefed her on the way over.[192] Josephine, with her angelic smile from the other side of Eurasia, gently clasped the woman's hand and began brewing tea for everyone. The second translator gave me a quick briefing: *This woman has kept a*

---

192   Bavi would tell the witness to turn off their phone and explain the purpose of the Faraday bag. Theoretically the woman's phone could give away the location of our safe house, but I theorized that someone publicly handing over their phone carried its own security risks, or that the witness might fear that they were getting scammed.

*very low profile since her release from the Xinjiang camps. After crossing the Kazakh border, she had made her way here but avoided contact with refugee support groups.*

The refugee explained that she had family back in Xinjiang who were currently incarcerated. So, she had conditions.

First: "no name" ("Fatimah" is an alias).[193]

Second: "No recording." Not on a computer, not on my Dictaphone.[194] Handwritten notes were okay—I kept these to a minimum, in any case—but *nothing* about her background, not even to indicate Uyghur or Kazakh identity.

Third: "No locations." For the purposes of the book, Fatimah agreed that it was safe to say that the interview took place in Almaty.

My father used to say that interviews sometimes resemble a seduction process. I reminded myself that underneath her demands (in fact, Fatimah would turn out be one of the only witnesses who didn't allow any recording) lay a traumatized woman trying to impose order on a confessional situation. On my side, when it came to camp survivor interviews in Kazakhstan, I suddenly felt like a sweaty-palmed virgin, so I simply agreed to everything.

Josephine and Bavi had worked on the setting, a plate of fresh

---

193   Real names are provided here when it would not put witnesses or others at risk, but if there is any ambiguity on that issue (Kazakh authorities began to forcibly deport Chinese passport holders of Uyghur or even Kazakh origin less than a year after our departure), the default throughout this entire chapter is to use aliases suggested by the witnesses, or, in a few cases, I made up the names entirely. "Fatimah," for example, was chosen simply because it's a Chinese Communist Party taboo to name a newborn after the prophet Muhammed's daughter. Uyghurs and Kazakhs can be sent to the camps if they ignore it.

194   My notes, written in a doctor's scrawl that even I can't always decipher, reflected only a few points, but I have an unusually good memory for dialogue. Nearly all the camp refugees allowed recordings, allowing me to use the voice memo function on my iPad, provided it remained disconnected from the Internet until I returned to the Schengen Zone. A few opted for my antique Dictaphone. The analog tape recording would be the only copy in existence, protecting a witness's identity from CCP hackers who could theoretically match the distinctive voice print found on a digital recording. Microcassette tapes have wildly uneven sound quality, and are hell to transcribe, but I stood by my promises.

Kazakh fried sweet bread in the center of an oversized kitchen table, the afternoon light from the balcony bouncing off the Formica. And Fatimah's conditions actually meant that instead of spending hours on specific camp conditions (other witnesses would fill in those gaps), I could simply plunge into her personal story.

Fatimah had been in the camps from 2017 to early 2019. In other words, she had been in Kazakhstan for less than a year. Her main "concentration camp" (her phrase) was home to approximately 2000 prisoners, with the males outnumbering females two to one, so the woman's portion stood at approximately 650. Without mentioning anything pertaining to organ harvesting, or even using the term "disappearances," I slipped in a neutral question about people leaving the camp "early."

Other than a few very old people who were hospitalized or died in camp, only "two kinds of women left the camp early," Fatimah said.

The first group of women were "very young," about 18 years old on average. The camp authorities said that these young women were "graduating," the euphemism for going off to work, usually in a factory out east. This was announced respectfully, sometimes with careful pronunciation of the factory's name and the usual bromides about this "great opportunity," as if the girls had completed finishing school.

"Usually, they announced it at lunch, in the canteen," Fatimah said. Sometimes, she said, the camp authorities even encouraged light applause.

The other women who left the camp early disappeared "in the middle of the night." That is, you would go to sleep with them. If the cell was crowded enough and cold enough, you might even spoon for warmth, and then in the morning, they were gone, and only their toothbrush remained. By midday, that would have disappeared, too, and if you mentioned their name, even to a relatively friendly guard, they would look through you, meaning that you were not to speak of this person again.

Fatimah's cellblock held about 60 women. Within the first month, following a camp-wide physical exam, "about ten days before," one woman went missing.

"The woman who went missing. How old was she?"

"28."

Josephine dropped the tea tray.

* * *

It was somewhere past Aralsk, when the first trees had started to appear by the side of the road, indicating that we were safely out of the Kazakh desert, when Josephine asked me *how are you going to handle these interviews in Almaty?*

The question was late in coming. My apprehension over what would happen, or what would not happen, in Almaty—I was gambling my reputation and funding from several patrons—was deflected every waking day by Jo's fixation on the unfolding road. As if on a magic carpet, she sat cross-legged, cat-like satisfaction in her eyes. Her immediate concerns—Would it be a squat toilet at the next truck stop? Would they have anything to eat that was sort of vegan? Would the police stop us today?—and my alternate reassurances and teasing tamped down my pointless anxiety over potentially finding an empty pot at the end of the Kazakh rainbow.

Josephine did not know my state of mind. From her perspective, I'd done everything right. We had cash, vaccinations, four-wheel drive, burner phones, alibis, and not one, but two fixers waiting in Almaty. We even had an aggressive Kazakh human rights attorney if we had to pull the ripcord.

*Jo, I know there's something here. No state would give blood and DNA tests to 10 million people unless there was a plan.*

*You say that you can get the numbers by talking to people who have been in the camps. But what's the method? What exactly do you think they have seen?*

*You're asking me for "the one weird trick" that would prove that the Chinese are selecting Uyghurs from the camps to extract their organs. Well, okay, there are two patterns. The first is that there must have been a blood test or a health check—usually it's within a week or ten days—that guarantees that the product is, you know, fresh. That there are no blood disorders. That the tissue type is still the right tissue type. That there hasn't been a mix-up.*

*And the second pattern—yeah, maybe it's kind of a weird trick—I mean, it was discovered by accident. A couple of years ago, a bunch of Falun Gong medical researchers, the World Organization to Investigate the Persecution of Falun Gong, had somehow downloaded, or maybe hacked into, a cache of organ extraction and transplant records, Chinese surgeon's records.[195] The records were straightforward as it goes. This "donor" was harvested, and these organs were transplanted. And the "donor" had died of "heart failure." And the "donor" was a male, or sometimes it was a female, but again and again and again, the "donor" was 28 years old.*

---

195    A decade ago, I was involved in the English-language editing of several major reports by the World Organization to Investigate the Persecution of Falun Gong (WOIPFG). It is germane that in the period while we were examining the surgical records, Dr. Charles Lee (he currently heads up WOIPFG) and I disagreed on the average age of Chinese transplant targets. Specifically, I believed the average age was about 28, while Charles believed it was closer to 29. While I still favor 28, I mention both ages in this book, and it doesn't change the concluding numbers. Two of the reports that I edited are: *The Final Harvest: A Comprehensive Investigation into the Chinese Communist Party's Live Organ Harvesting of Falun Gong Practitioners* (WOIPFG, 2016) and *A WOIPFG Investigation Report on the Chinese Communist Party's Ongoing Crime of Live Organ Harvesting against Falun Dafa Practitioners* (WOIPFG, 2017). In my experience, WOIPFG reports tend to be evolving documents: some information drops away over the years, while new evidence fills in. With that proviso in mind, many WOIPFG reports and documents can be accessed at www.upholdjustice.org.

*What? Seriously?*

*Right? Who fucking dies of heart failure at age 28? Maybe one in 100,000? Anyway, I used to fix up the language on the English version of their reports, but American or Chinese, we all noticed the pattern. My buddy Charles Lee used to say that the average age of the "donor" is actually more like 29. Okay, maybe anywhere between 25 to 35 is okay for successful organ transplants. But it's right in there: 28 years old, or 29, if you like. Anyway, my theory is your organs have stopped growing at 28, but you haven't started to die yet. You're in perfect health. Like the best that you'll ever be.*

*Shit. Ethan, that's so fucked up.*

*Yeah. And we all agreed—it's not like there's another explanation out there—that the surgeons were selecting these people in their late twenties "to order," that is from a large pool of tissue types, a large pool of prisoners. And given the health problems in the hard-core criminal population—the majority had hepatitis—that large pool was Falun Gong. A million of them in Chinese detention. And most of these "donors" were alive when they were put on the operating table. That never changed.*

*Why would they do it when they're alive?*

*Live organ harvesting improves the odds of the organ being accepted by the new body. Like cutting a flower under running water before it goes into the vase. And harvesting a body all at once keeps it simple and helps cover up the crime.*

*Okay. But how would a prisoner in the camps know about any of that?*

*They won't. But maybe a prisoner noticed when their friends started going missing. Not why they went missing, and I'm not going to ask them about organ harvesting unless they bring it up first. Look, it's just my personal theory, Jo. I could be way off. But if someone disappeared, I'll ask 'How old?' And maybe they'll say the magic number.*

\* \* \*

Josephine dropped the tea tray as if that one weird trick was black magic, as if I had hypnotized Fatimah. But it also meant that what we were doing had meaning. For Josephine, Fatimah's response was a potential portal out of the drudgery of human rights work—the long waits, the initial formality, the witnesses carrying on about their passports being held by the Chinese authorities—into something fascinating and simultaneously, unspeakable.

For me, hearing "28" translated from a new language wasn't surprising—more like slipping into a comfortable old pair of slippers. But I readily admit that Josephine's reaction brought it all back: *I remember that moment. That moment when you know it's true. And how that moment made all the difference.*

\* \* \*

"There were two other women who went missing in the middle of the night, about two months later." Fatimah said.

"Did you all have a health check around this time?" I asked.

"Yes, a week before."

"How old were these women? Did they have any special characteristics?"

Fatimah groped around: One of them was maybe 27. She thought the other one was 28 or 29. Or maybe even 30.

A blood test a week before. One 28-year-old, one 27, the other 30. Within her cell block of 60 women, "three women went missing like this over six months."

At a minimum, one out of 20 women, in their late twenties or early thirties, after being blood- and DNA-tested a week before, were being removed in the middle of the night. But I needed to rule out systematic sexual exploitation.[196]

"I'm genuinely sorry to ask this question, but I have to. Were these three women beautiful? Were they sexually attractive?"

"It's not nice to say this about anyone, but no, none of them were good-looking."

"What did they have in common then? Anything?"

"They were healthy."

*Fatimah's camp had a harvesting selection rate of 5 percent.*

## SWEDEN. WITNESS 2: SAYRAGUL SAUYTBAY

Sayragul Sauytbay and her husband, Uali Islam in Swedish refugee housing. By the author.

This was only my second pre-Kazakhstan interview, so, lacking context, it initially raised more questions than answers.[197] In September 2019,

---

196   I asked the sexual exploitation question to approximately 7 camp refugees before abandoning it. They all had similar responses, with the majority confirming that the likely targets of sexual slavery would inevitably be found in the younger, "forced labor" group.

197   Kaiser ÖzHun and Dr. Enver Tohti translated the interview reproduced here. But I still had questions about Sayragul's access to medical files, the average age of the prisoners who disappeared, and their ethnicity. in November 2023, with Salih Hudayar translating, I was able to re-interview Sayragul, just after her election as Vice President of the East Turkistan Government in Exile. I have built her clarifications into the text.

I interviewed Sayragul in purpose-built immigrant housing. She's an ethnic Kazakh, an accomplished teacher with medical training, and has written a well-received book about her experience in a Xinjiang camp.[198]

I'll summarize. In November 2017, on pain of losing her family to detention, the Chinese authorities recruited Sayragul to teach Chinese at a camp. The "offer" initially came as a relief, but she quickly grasped her cell was nearly identical to any prisoner's: cement floor, a plastic cover for her to sleep on, a bucket, and a surveillance camera. The only difference was that regular detainees had a minimum of 17 people sharing the same size cell, while she slept alone.

"So, you were one step above them."

"Yeah, I wouldn't be considered the same as the detainees. I was assigned to teach, but my treatment is the same."

"Did you have any power? Say, if someone disobeyed you? If someone did not study Chinese vocabulary, could you have them punished?"

"It's not my job to punish them and they don't dare to break the rules. There were two armed police in my classroom."

"What was the name of this camp?"

"No special name... I guess... it was the "Transformation through Reeducation" camp?"

The same name as so many others, just a different address. The CCP had learned from the publicity given to certain centers of the Falun Gong persecution (Dragon Mountain, Masanjia, Shenyang Prison City), *don't give an evocative name to your torture chambers.*

I encouraged Sayragul, as a doctor, to give me a health assessment:

"There is a nurse inside the camp. But never a doctor's presence.

---

198    Sauytbay Sayragul, *The Chief Witness: Escape from China's Modern-Day Concentration Camps* (Scribe, 2021).

Even if somebody was ill or sick. Sometimes doctors come. But only to take a specific blood sample drawn by the nurse."

"How often would the blood samples be taken?"

"Sometimes twice a week."

"Why so often?"

"It's overcrowded. To prevent a pandemic."

"Was there ever sickness in the camp? Did you get sick? Typhus?"

"The hygiene is so poor, and there's no toilet. If the bucket is full, then you have nowhere to go. You just have to wait until the next morning when the bucket is emptied. So, for that reason, many people sometimes. . ." Sayragul gave a fatalistic shrug. "So, the hygiene is. . . it's just very, very dirty. It's a kind of pandemic, technically. It's common to see people vomiting. Along with diarrhea and temperature. Sometimes it looks like everybody's sick. And no doctor will come even if you complain that you are sick."

Sayragul paused, as if to check that her voice wasn't carrying to her immigrant neighbors.

"And sometimes some people will disappear. They will take them away."

"How often did that happen?"

"One per week. Or two per week? Sometimes one disappeared, sometimes two or three. They are taken away, sometimes nobody is taken away. But yeah, there are always people sick."

"Did people disappear for other reasons?"

"Sometimes the police came to my class with a list of names. For example, one time they took five. And then a few hours later, two came back, beaten up, and the other three never came back."

"Did you see any of the physical examinations that were given to the other people in the camp?"

Sayragul had not witnessed the examinations, but she saw the medical results. From the beginning, Sayragul embraced the key survival method of camp life, from the Gulag to Auschwitz: *Make yourself indispensable.* Trained as a doctor, Sayragul saw printouts of the camp blood tests piling up in the little office that served as a faculty lounge for low-ranking workers like herself. She offered to file them. She spent a week cleaning up and sorting the confidential medical files of the entire camp.

Sayragul said that there were "documents on everyone. *And there's the mark, the red mark. . .* Just the people who have been marked in red are taken away. If there is no mark, you probably will not be taken away."

"Did that pattern have to do with sickness, or something else?"

"Everybody gets a [medical] checkup. When the report comes back, some people will be marked red. And those people will disappear one by one. Yeah, sometimes two, sometimes one."

"What was the average age with the red mark?"

"30."[199]

A patten was coming into focus, but I wanted to avoid contaminating Sayragul's testimony. I tried a deflection tactic–as much for myself as for her—wondering aloud if perhaps the red check people had been "troublemakers"?

"There are no troublemakers. Because if you make any trouble, *you lose your life.* All inmates are psychologically dead. Nobody dared to make any trouble there. They were healthy. *Healthy people.* And they were taken away. After being marked red. Only innocent people."

"When the red marks appear, did the people disappear within the next week?"

---

[199] The word "average" is often interpreted as "range" in Uyghur and Kazakh. Sayragul had said that the age was "30." And then added, "Up to 50," but in her second interview she clarified that the average age to receive a red check mark hovered around 30. In other words, red check marks could extend as high as a 50-year-old, but she considered that an outlier.

"Within two days."

For the camp bureaucracy, the red checkmark meant ". . . there will be paperwork. And then someone will come to copy all this person's medical records. Then this guy, like from special forces with weapons and everything and wearing a mask, will come to take all these documents away.... That means the [red-marked] person will never come back."

"Where did you think they went?"

"At the beginning we thought because since they have just been sick, they're taking them to the hospitals. For example, there was a man marked as red. I thought that he was taken to the hospital. Then, after I left the camp, I met someone from that exact hospital. I asked him if he had seen the man. And he said, 'Really? His family filed an appeal to see him. And what his family was told is that he is in the reeducation camp.' But we both knew that he was not there. So, he [the red-marked man] disappeared, and both sides thinks he's over there [in the hospital, or in the reeducation camp]. Right?"

Sayragul knew there were approximately 2500 Kazakhs in camp. Then there were the Uyghurs, about half that number, and then an even smaller portion of Kyrgyz. Yet the relevant point to Sayragul was that the proportion of red checkmarks didn't seem to favor any specific group.

"Were these medical files connected with tissue typing?"

"I don't think anyone was thinking that way. I never thought about it that way myself. The government doing experiments or testing people's blood for the purpose of organ harvesting? First, it's *forbidden* to think about things like that. Second, there's always a watchdog in the room. *Always.*"

To make herself indispensable, Sayragul had put one foot forward and stepped into quicksand. So Sayragul retreated to the path of least resistance, consciously avoiding counting red marks, let alone in relation to the camp population. She finished the filing quickly and efficiently.

Yet back on solid ground, Sayragul could not help but notice that in her class of 30 people, one person, around 30 years of age, went missing about ten days after a camp-wide blood test. There was so much more, but that was the solid rate. She didn't dare revisit the files to see if there was a red checkmark.

*Sayragul's camp had a harvesting selection rate of* 3.3 percent.

## TURKEY. WITNESS 3: GULBAHAR JELILOVA

Gulbahar with Rahima Mahmut translating (right, reflected in mirror) in Istanbul. By the author

You may recall Gulbahar—the "look at yourself!" woman in the first chapter (her interrogator exposed himself, implied that she should perform fellatio, and humiliated Gulbahar for invoking his mother). In October 2019, Rahima and I interviewed Gulbahar in a far-flung neighborhood in greater Istanbul.[200]

Gulbahar added several pieces to the organ harvesting puzzle. First, Gulbahar remembered that three out of approximately 40 women

---

200    Gulbahar had previously testified remotely to the China Tribunal. She was a compelling witness, but had left behind some loose ends on color-coding.

had vanished before she left the camp. I'm not counting it because it was not the number of disappearances that she vividly recalled, but a sort of color-coding that appeared in her camp about a week after the camp had undergone a health check. The camp guards had affixed an orange or pink plastic bracelet to several women, purpose unknown. To ask was unthinkable.[201]

There's a history of color-coding prisoners. In Dachau it became a standard for the whole Nazi camp system: red triangle for a Communist, pink triangle for a homosexual, black triangle for the "work-shy," while two triangles intersecting made a neat little star of David for the Jews. A red triangle with a pink triangle over it would indicate the trifecta: a Communist homosexual Jew. Sewed onto prison uniforms, they served as a useful pecking order for guards and prisoners alike.

In Gulbahar's camp these colored bracelets just made a fleeting appearance on the inside of a sleeve, but the women who wore them "went missing" a few nights later. After the guards—inevitably—raped Gulbahar, she was sent to the camp hospital for about ten days, in wards where the color-coding was more explicit. As Gulbahar's statement to the Uyghur Tribunal shows: "In the hospital there were people with clothes of different colors. Depending on the color different things happened to them. There were some people in orange clothes, according to a roommate they will be taken away for "sleeping." I asked her why they can't sleep in the room. Then she told me they will be killed via injection. . . . She also told me they have to sign a paper before they will be taken away, and family members are not informed. Those with blue colored clothes got a sentence of 15-20 years."[202] According to Sayragul, color-coding also appeared in people's medical files, so, it

---

201    Gulbahar was difficult to translate because she often shifted from topic to topic as she recalled the outrages of the camp. Watching the emotions playing on Gulbahar's face, I sensed that we were stepping around a complex minefield brought on by trauma. I'm grateful for Gulbahar's cooperation and to Rahima for working through it.

202    Gulbahar Jelilova, *Witness Statement: Hearing before the Uyghur Tribunal* (June 6, 2021).

can't be ruled out as a sort of medical execution signal. Perhaps like a shoulder brand on cattle, in a code known only to the guards and the camp administrators, it might have indicated that, however little time was allotted to their lives, these women were organ carriers potentially representing significant profit for the camp—protected assets until they were butchered.

Gulbahar made a concerted attempt to recall how many women in the camp had "left," but ultimately, she admitted that she was not confident speaking about the whole camp. Could she just tell me about her cellblock? Gulbahar confirmed that during a three-month period, one woman—she knew that one woman was in her late twenties, and there was a blood test around that time—had "gone missing" in the middle of the night. Gulbahar's cellblock numbered approximately 40 women. If she included the orange bracelet women, the percentage would rise, but we both felt more secure sticking to one woman out of 40.

*Gulbahar's camp had a harvesting selection rate of 2.5 percent.*

## KAZAKHSTAN. WITNESS 4: TURSUNAY ZIYAWUDUN

Qalmyrza and Tursunay Ziyawudun in our Almaty safehouse, December 2019.

By Josephine de Haan-Montes

"I always felt myself to be Chinese. I was very proud that I was Chinese. Everything was normal. Then, in 2008 I went to the passport office to renew. A Chinese officer looked through my documents, and he was like, 'Oh, you're a Uyghur. It's not allowed.' From that time on, I started to think about everything. . . . For years, I didn't say anything bad about China. They pushed me to do this, right? I'm doing this now because I'm the person that they created. They brought me here."

Technically, Tursunay was here because the first person that we met in Almaty was Aiman Umarova, a human rights lawyer who operated on the knife's edge of Kazakh's authoritarian society. She briefed us on her clients.[203] Tursunay, like most camp refugees, was still a Chinese citizen. Having abused her in the camps, China wanted her back. Her husband, Qalmyrza, was a respected physician and a Kazakh citizen, and Tursunay was willing to go public with her struggle.[204] I admired their courage. We would interview Tursunay for two days, first on the detailed conditions of her camp, and then moving on to disappearances.

"Why were you arrested? Because of the Kazakh connection?"

"If you communicate with foreigners, if you have relatives there, and they call you. . . and if you answer them once—only once!. . . Or if they [the PSB] see you have a phone number from Kazakhstan or some other country? Yeah, you will be put in concentration camp."

For the first couple of months, Tursunay was kept in a "vocational school. To learn to be like, a cooker, like a hair stylist...." But then she

---

203   I suspected that Tursunay had been raped in the camps. Qalmyrza stayed by Tursunay's side for two days of interviews. If Qalmyrza had not been present, perhaps I would have asked. When the BBC interviewed Tursunay in Istanbul around a year later, Qalmyrza was not present, and Tursunay spoke frankly, and at times cathartically, of rape in the camp. Serikzhan, the head of Atajurt, who was accompanying Tursunay in lieu of her husband, wept when he heard it and said, 'Why didn't you tell me?' Anyway, the BBC got the information out to the public.

204   Sensing that even Turkey would not provide a safe haven for such a public case, I broke my own security rules and visited the US Consulate in Almaty to lobby for Tursunay. With Bob Fu's help, she ultimately made it to America.

was moved to a re-education camp for nine months. The camp was still under construction, but they were herded in anyway. "At first it was like men and women about 1000 [total]. After one week it was 3000." Then the medical exams began: "Put us in line. Big, big bus. Like a clinic, but it's on wheels. So, you go into this makeshift hospital or whatever it is. The first thing is the ultrasound."

"What about an EKG?"

"They did that. Then they took some people away. They said that some people had 'contagions.' There's an older lady. And there's two younger ladies like in their 30s or something like that. And they said one had a problem with the liver. But they took those, those kind of people from different places, from different cells. . . . So these two women did not return. These two women, who were about 30."

"Was there a hospital nearby?"

"County People's Hospital. And it's about maybe 10 to 15 kilometers from the airport."

"Does this hospital do liver transplants?"

"Organ transplants. They don't let Uyghurs and Kazakh [doctors] perform those operations. No extractions, they don't let them."

Tursunay's husband Qalmyrza broke in, "Those kinds of hospitals, they're not in the cities now. They take them, they build them somewhere far away from populated places, in the mountains, in remote places. Where nobody knows. And minorities don't work there. Only Chinese."

Shortly after the exams, Tursunay noticed women vanishing from her cellblock.

"Some people just disappear. And we would say, 'What happened to them?' [And the guards said,] 'We moved them to another Grade.' [Guards imposed a system of Grade A, B, and C based on inmate behavior]. But you know, we don't see these ladies. We don't know where they are, they just disappear.... But we can see other people, even from the 'C Grade.' You know, when we go outside, we are only separated by mesh.... Other ladies were transferred to other grades. And I saw them."

"Let's stick with this for a second, Tursunay. What's the average age? If somebody put a gun to your head and said: estimate the average age of the women who were disappearing...?"

"There was a 28-year-old girl. She was with us for months. She was in her cell.... Somebody took her. Everything. Her clothes, everything. Yeah, they just took it all away."

"Was the 28-year-old woman transferred to C grade?"

"No, she was not there. I was looking for her.... But that 28-year-old lady, I still remember her."

"Where was she from?"

"Kumas. She was pretty good-looking. She had curly hair, you know? She's healthy. She looked healthy, too. Her name was Aliyah.... Then there were two Kazakh girls [both in their late twenties].... Raised in China, but they were screaming and saying that 'We have Kazakhstani citizenship.' Screaming and kicking and... three days later... well, the guards took them away.... They would never let them go to Kazakhstan, because they will tell people everything that's happened, right? The last time we saw them was at midnight. We didn't see them again."

Tursunay noticed that I was hanging on her words. Perhaps she thought I was skeptical.

"Those that are [officially] released, they're not released during the night. They're released during the day... So, you know, I started thinking, what is going on? But it all happened before we could ask for their names, what are they up to? ...We didn't even look at them. I didn't care for anybody at that time. So, I didn't look. They could be dead."

Tursunay was not thinking about death but about her friend, a 25-year-old woman who was being raped repeatedly. At the time, Tursunay interpreted the medical checks as related to birth control. "Yeah, we're going to put the [IUD] spirals in, and then we're going to check your blood, blood-testing, and then, you know, vaccination."

*Tursunay suddenly looked very tired.* By Josephine de Haan-Montes

Seconds after the photograph, Tursunay was sprawled on the couch while Qalmyrza explained to us that, ever since the camps, his wife's heartbeat occasionally became irregular. Given that Qalmyrza was qualified to make medical decisions, I fished his phone out of the Stalin Bag, and we gave them privacy. Several hours later, Tursunay felt well enough to rejoin us in the kitchen. To avoid further stress, I cut to the chase, asking Tursunay to make an estimate of the women in their late twenties to their early thirties who had disappeared during her nine months in the camp.

"In nine months... I don't know. Probably not the ones that they're taking to work, but just disappeared...? About 16."

Unlike most witnesses who are only describing disappearances in their cellblock, Tursunay was considering the entire female area of the camp, about 1000 women. And the way she described it, while there was a constant influx of detainees, there was also a steady rate of five disappearances every three months. I rounded out Tursunay's observation of 16 disappearances over 9 months to an even 20 disappearances over 12 months.

*Tursunay's camp had a harvesting selection rate of* 2 percent.

## KAZAKHSTAN. WITNESS 5: BAQYTALI NUR

"Three blood tests in one week. . . I found this very troubling. . . [and then] they are taken during the night. 12 midnight, 1 am. . . we don't know where they will go. . . It's always the young guys. Between 20 to 30 years old. Old people don't disappear, only young people."

Baqytali's interview, conducted within the cold bare walls of the Atajurt office just off the Green Market, was interrupted several times by curious Kazakh activists. Yet Baqytali is a serious man and a Kazakh master of the plain statement, so we were able to move quickly through the material.

He initially wanted to speak about the surveillance structure of the camp where he was incarcerated from October 2017 to November 2018, but in the first fifteen minutes, he also mentioned "disappearances," telling the story of a young boy who cried every day because his father was in the same camp, but on the 5th floor. They could catch glimpses of each other, but communication was strictly forbidden. The Chinese had sentenced his father to 13 years; instead, though previously thought to be in good health, he was "pronounced dead" at 46 years old. The family was denied access to the body.

Baqytali's initial arrest came as he was transporting fruits and vegetables across the Kazakh border, and the local Chinese authorities told him to come in for a chat. The pincers closed. The Chinese police seemed to take a certain professional pride in reinterpreting Baqytali's cross-border trade as a conspiracy with a foreign government. Baqytali was incarcerated in a camp with no name, formerly "Chapchal No. 3 Middle School," but now home to 5000 detainees, mainly Uyghurs, with some Kazakhs as well. "No. 3" was one out of a cluster of "five camps," Baqytali estimated, "comprising 30,000 people."

When I heard the number, my eyes widened.

Baqytali shrugged. "I knew a man who was in a Ghulja prison camp with 100,000 people in it. He knew a lot of things," he said with a faint smile. Yet from the beginning, Baqytali felt there was something off about his camp. It wasn't just the endless "health checks" and obsessive blood drawing that never seemed to identify his or anyone's health problems, but the large multi-story hospital, "750 meters from camp." Within that compound there was "a secure hospital within the hospital," that specialized "in liver and lungs. . . The operating rooms were on the first floor. And when it became a camp hospital, they moved in Chinese surgeons from inner China."

After he had been in the camp for eight months, Baqytali caught a pretty serious infection. Hospitalized, he observed two distinct patterns of care.

The first was "prisoners being brought in who had their legs broken and were screaming for treatment." They were seen as a distraction.

The second group was healthy and passive. Baqytali saw "doctors putting on surgical masks to operate on people who were silent." These doctors weren't general physicians but "lung, heart, and liver specialists." One Han Chinese doctor quietly confided to Baqytali that "I am actually from Shandong. We were pushed by the government to come here." They were all, it seemed, from inner China. Rumors swept the ward that other hospitals with exclusively Han Chinese surgeons were close by.

Baqytali also knew that the local airport was just 10 kilometers away, but, confined to his ward, Baqytali was never able to establish how often the medical vans went to the airport. Nevertheless, Baqytali willingly made a rough estimate about disappearances, and, unlike most witnesses who only feel confident talking about disappearances from their cellblock or Chinese language class, Baqytali preferred to make estimates–it's a "feeling," he said—for the full 30,000. About 5000 people left the camp every year. One in four, about 1250 people, met the criteria that we discussed: good health, between 25 and 35 years of age, had received a medical exam or blood testing within the last two weeks, and were "taken in the night."[205]

*Baqytali's camp had a harvesting selection rate of 4 percent.*

\* \* \*

By this point, five witnesses in, the reader may sense a systematic pattern. I noticed it very clearly in the Almaty interviews. But outlier witnesses, both high and low, matter as well. While their observations may be distorted by personal circumstances, bias, or disinterest in individual cases, every camp refugee has a story to tell, and just as a deal is a deal, a study is a study. So, I'm going to delve into the five outlier cases out of 20 interviews.

## KAZAKHSTAN. WITNESS 6: "MUJAHIT" (OUTLIER INTERVIEW)

Mujahit is an alias. This individual did not want to be identified, photographed, recorded, or any identification including the Central

---

205    Postscript: I ran into Baqytali at the Uyghur Tribunal in 2021, where, with the guidance of Enver Tohti, Baqytali made a public request for asylum. He didn't recognize me for a few minutes without my beard. It's my understanding that Baqytali is now a resident of the United Kingdom.

Asian country where he was interviewed. Given my movements that could be Kazakhstan, Kyrgyzstan, Uzbekistan or Tajikistan.

Chinese authorities incarcerated Mujahit in a camp that had "between 2000 to 3000 prisoners." Mujahit told a now-routine story of incarceration and reeducation: scarce food, long periods sitting in a fixed position, wildly overcrowded cellblocks with a single toilet, ubiquitous surveillance, arbitrary interrogation and torture, and humiliating rituals of thanking the Chinese Communist Party in song and dance. When I asked about sexual abuse, I thought I saw a strange motion in his eye, while he denied knowing anything about that.

Mujahit is relatively young, mid-30s perhaps. He's a clean-cut, good-looking guy. I suspect he was gang-raped, and that he has post-traumatic stress disorder (PTSD). Quite emotionally, almost shouting at me, Mujahit estimated a 20% annual disappearance rate for organ harvesting.

I think if you lower that by 50% to reflect the 25 to 35-year age-range—he admitted that he found it hard to think about people's ages and he didn't follow people going into the hospital—a 10% rate is far more plausible, although still far higher than any other interview.

Very much an outlier, Mujahit was in the camp for at least one year, and no matter how damaged he may be from the experience, this was his testimony. Given what happened in his country of exile since the interview, it's highly likely that he was forcibly deported back to the Xinjiang camps.

Out of this mess then, an estimate:

*Mujahit's camp had a harvesting selection rate of* 10 percent.

## KAZAKHSTAN. WITNESS 7: "ARMAN" (OUTLIER INTERVIEW)

An alias, Arman means "a dream." While Arman wanted to avoid any identification, he did agree to a digital recording.

Arman was incarcerated in four camps. The first was a brief spell in a detention center. The second camp had approximately 5000 detainees with 3500 men and 1500 women. I asked Arman about individual disappearances, and he replied that the Chinese guards moved approximately 750 men out and then moved another 750 in ". . . and that was the flow. But there were no [individual] disappearances." The third camp had similar numbers and again, "no disappearances." The entire camp was in the process of becoming a women-only structure, so after 60 days, a new camp was established for 6000 men. Arman said that "[t]here was a building outside with about 200 men confined in it. No disappearances, but you don't really know what's happening."

While most witnesses didn't report suspicious disappearances in the gentler holding pens (for example, short-term detention centers and career training centers), Arman stands alone in reporting zero disappearances in three separate concentration camps. Arman also mentioned that "the majority [of the detainees] were Kazakhs." Arman's region comprised approximately 250,000 people, with 125,000 Han Chinese, 95,000 ethnic Kazakhs, and 30,000 Uyghurs. In my experience, Kazakhs (and Kyrgyz) are generally not selected for organ harvesting at the Uyghur rate.[206] Selection may have been less perceptible in camps where Kazakhs outnumbered Uyghurs 3 to 1.[207] Arman also mentioned that there was a hospital built into the third camp, streamlining the "farm to table" aspect of selection: unless one is really looking for disappearances, the declaration that someone is "sick," then hospitalized, is easy enough to accept.

---

206    Sayragul disputes this, and she told me that the rate was about equal in her camp, although she may be the exception that proves the rule.

207    The reason why the Kazakhs are not generally harvested at the rate of Uyghurs is common-sense in my view. The Kazakhs are not as strongly associated with separatism, and the majority of Kazakhs have some relatives, however distant, in the bordering nation-state of Kazakhstan, which, theoretically can create problems for Beijing. The same logic can be applied to those of Kyrgyz ethnicity in China.

Arman is a no-nonsense survivor, with a relaxed style. That's valuable. Theoretically, a guy like Arman might have had at least a whisper of a chance of making it through Auschwitz, and, again theoretically, I would have tried hard to be his wingman. Yet part of his seemingly effortless survival involved wearing blinders. Arman was uncommonly good with crowd estimates, yet he never mentioned a single individual in the interview, a distinctly male pattern of perception that I've run into from time to time. For example, he wasn't sure if detainees actually returned from the hospital or not. Near the end of the interview, I asked Arman, "Would you have known if anyone went missing?"

"I don't know," he replied with the trace of a smile.

With reservations:

*Arman's camps had a harvesting selection rate of* 0 percent.

## NETHERLANDS. WITNESS 8: OMER BEKRI (OUTLIER INTERVIEW)

Omer Bekri (left) speaking with Dr. Enver Tohti (right) in the Netherlands. Photo by author.

Omer's interview, the first in the investigation, led to the idea of interviews in Central Asia. Born to Uyghur and Kazakh parents, Omer is a Kazakh national, and his arrest was "an error." Han Chinese guards were confused by Omer's potential legal status and equally afraid that his declared public refusal to cooperate could make them look weak. The solution was to use solitary confinement, 223 days of torture and starvation, to "break" him. Omer refused to cooperate. However, after the guards released him from solitary, Omer, praying for imminent release from the camp system, avoided contact with other detainees and simply kept his head down for 20 days.

Omer's camp comprised approximately 1000 young men—75 percent Uyghur and 25 percent Kazakh. The guards told Omer that everyone's re-education would take a year, and no one would leave before that year was up, so Omer was not looking for disappearances. Yet Omer provided one clue that I had caught a whiff of the Xinjiang Procedure. In Omer's initial detention, prison officials administered a series of medical tests: urine, blood, "full body check," kidneys, ultrasound, EKG, and lungs. As sweat poured down his face during these trials, Omer was convinced that the medical staff were preparing to "extract my organs."

Omer's description of his medical tests is nearly identical with Falun Gong prisoner descriptions of harvesting selection ten years prior, with a few modern tweaks: extensive use of ultrasound and attention to the lungs (when Falun Gong was the main organ source, lung transplants were far less common). Since Omer was approximately 40 years old at this time, his organs would normally be considered at the outer age limits for transplant purposes in China's increasingly selective transplant industry. Yet from the Chinese perspective, Omer was a healthy giant, a troublemaker, and initially viewed as a man without a country. Omer was forced to wear a black hood throughout these examinations. Hypothetically the staff was aware that Omer might live and identify his Chinese doctors to a third party in the future. Or perhaps the medical examinations were simply a scare tactic to break Omer's resistance. As a Kazakh citizen, Omer's detention became sensitive, particularly with the Kazakh public. As Omer had hoped, the Kazakh authorities visited Omer after twenty days and granted him a temporary visa to Kazakhstan, ultimately creating the conditions for Omer to flee from China to Kazakhstan and then to the Netherlands.

Omer's flight to Europe was extremely unusual at that time. I interpreted this as a warning: by confining interviews to the European or North American diaspora, my safe places, I would receive limited or distorted results.

With reservations shared and acknowledged by the witness:
*Omer's camp had a harvesting selection rate of* 0 percent.

## KAZAKHSTAN. WITNESS 9: "MILQA" (OUTLIER INTERVIEW)

As her family's residency in Kazakhstan was under threat, "Milqa" and I agreed to make up an alias for her and leave out dates and locations from her story, including which method of recording I used. I'll only add that she was interviewed in Almaty in January or February 2020, and she was warm and friendly to Josephine and me.

Milqa was born into a sheep-herding family in 1992 and was raised by her grandmother. Because her family were nomads half the year and farmed the rest of the time, Milqa did not attend school until 1999. In 2017, she was in Kazakhstan on her way back to China when Chinese border personnel stopped her. "They scanned my phone. Opened up the back, took down the codes and said, 'Okay, you can go now.'" The authorities told her to "check in" near her home and gave her a date a few months later.

At 9 am on the appointed date, Milqa went to the police station in her village. "They said, 'We can tell from your phone calls that we are going need to have a longer conversation.' They put me in a vehicle. When I asked where we were going, the policewoman was silent."

By the afternoon, Milqa found herself in a room with 30 Kazakh women as the police prepared cells for about 10 persons each, with a 60/40 split favoring the Uyghurs.

"Were you scared?"

"Well, we started talking. The Kazakh women showed me the cameras in the cell. . . . Yeah, so we were talking about their cameras, then one of the women just said something, and someone [a disembodied voice of authority] responded. I was shocked."

"Okay. So, you were all in good health?"

"Everybody appeared to be in good health. Except there was one [young] Uyghur woman who had high blood pressure. She was taken to the hospital that day. . . One other girl was also taken from interrogation. She had heart problems. During the interrogation, and the torture, something happened to her heart. Found out that she had had a weak heart after that. Do you understand?"

"Yeah, I do. But what happened to her?"

"She had heart problems before. She was born with it."

"Had you been given the 'health check' previously?"

"Yes, in China? Yes, well before that day."

My first thought was that the local CCP authorities must have forced the young Uyghur woman with the "weak heart" to have the same mandatory health check as Milqa. This included an EKG. Assessing the heart, an organ with a potential value of over 150k, was critical to the Xinjiang health checks, particularly for harvesting. But perhaps Han Chinese doctors who administered the tests just didn't catch the weak heart. They probably wouldn't have told her if they did. To repeat, not a single camp refugee reported any post-health-check medical follow-up. Or perhaps they understood the condition. Perhaps they even informed her that she had a congenital heart defect, but the brutality of the interrogation had brought her heart to crisis. Or perhaps the "weak heart" explanation was simply planted by the guards to keep prisoners like Milqa from thinking about her removal from the camp.

Milqa did not know what had happened to the young Uyghur woman: "In my cell, the youngest woman was 40, the eldest was 72," so they were out of the loop—and didn't have particularly valuable organs. Anyway, Milqa did not consider it "a disappearance."

"Okay. During this time [2017 to 2018], you said there were women constantly arriving. So, they did not make anybody leave...?"

"Once you get in there, you don't go out. Nobody just leaves."

"Were there medical tests?"

"Sure. There was a major medical check in December—blood, eyes, ultrasound, EKG, everything, even nail samples–and then one vaccination."

As the interview continued, several more cases of medical problems emerged, always mentioned in passing.

"One woman did [disappear] after the medical test, as they found out that she had AIDS. So, they took her out of there."

"Okay, how old was she?"

"I thought she was a druggie. Anyway, she was about 27 years old."

With another woman it was "high blood pressure." While most camps in this investigation adopted a blinders approach to disappearances, removing people in the middle of the night or forcing the detainees to look down at their shoes, in Milqa's camp, women in their late twenties -following camp-wide health-checks—were taken away on the pretext of medical conditions.

Milqa saw it differently. Those who disappeared had special connections or were being unfairly rewarded. "For the rest of us," she said plaintively, "you could die, and they wouldn't care. It doesn't matter how you feel. Even if you're sick, you don't say it. You have to go through the motions. You have to go to the classroom. . . ."

When Milqa was moved to a new camp, I asked her about the transfer process.

"They took us, the healthy ones. After we moved to a new camp, they did a medical check-up and discovered 14 pregnant women from our camp. They were taken somewhere else."

I brought up the possibility of rape. Milqa who had previously acknowledged that very young women were, in fact, being raped in the camp, ignored my question, very likely because her husband came back into the interview room at that exact moment. In tacit sympathy with Milqa and her husband, I avoided questions about how these women magically became pregnant without contact with any males other than Chinese camp guards. It must have taken place not long after they entered the camp; most women in the camps stopped menstruating altogether after a couple of months, possibly from malnutrition, stress, or, more likely, the mysterious flu vaccinations.

Or were these women pregnant at all? As a thought experiment, if you ignore the medical rationales that the guards supplied, the disappearances in Milqa's camps would calculate along these lines: 500 women in Milqa's camp. Six "medical" disappearances works out to over 1 percent annual disappearances. If there were no actual pregnancies, then it would be 6 plus 14, that is, 20 disappearances, translating to 4 percent annual disappearances.

Yet consider Milqa's vantage point. As she acknowledged, everyone in her cell was above the age of 40. No one ever woke up to find someone missing. Given the highly sensitive listening devices that extended to showers and toilets, even prisoner gossip was self-censoring, and speculating on disappearances was forbidden. Any information

Milqa received was usually a repetition of whatever medical rationale the guards had planted. Yet Milqa was a smart woman, and she kept referring to "vaccinations." I dove into that.

"So, okay Milqa, I need you to give me a real sense of what happened with that vaccination."

"One gets a bit forgetful. You don't care about what's happening outside. You are kind of in a euphoric state after those 'flu vaccinations.' You don't know if you've slept or you're not sleeping."

"A lot of people have described it to me and sometimes it sounds almost like a narcotic...."

"You don't even want to go home. Yeah, before that, you really want to touch base.... Normally, when everyone goes to call their families, then you go call, too... After that, there's not really a strong will to do this anymore. You don't even want to talk to somebody or call somebody. You just want to read a book, and that's all... We're supposed to read whatever Chinese propaganda is around... but I just wanted to read other books about... motivational stuff or ecology or something."

"So why do you think they gave you the vaccination?"

"So, they say 'this is a vaccination against the flu.' But the flu vaccination doesn't do all that stuff. There's only one flu vaccination. It's all over the world. But hey, if they want to make us forget? Or make us docile?"

"Did you get a physical side effect of this vaccination?"

"Right. You don't feel any pain, but you kind of feel cold at times? But you know it's not real. It's like they have you on drugs."

I wasn't at Milqa's camp, so Milqa's "0" rate of disappearances is the final word here. Her interview is an outlier in terms of the annual rate of disappearances, but her interview sheds light on two methods of Chinese gaslighting. First, Chinese authorities framed disappearances as medical problems. Second, purported "flu vaccinations" rendered an intelligent woman like Milqa docile enough to accept the authorities' framing.

With reservations:

*Milqa's camps had a harvesting selection rate of* 0 percent.

## KAZAKHSTAN. WITNESS 10: "THE TEACHER" (OUTLIER INTERVIEW)

A corpulent man with an intelligent face, The Teacher requested an alias (he is, in fact, a teacher) and asked me to keep the details confidential. I interviewed him and his close friend "Ear Man" twice, first at the Atajurt offices and the second time in our Almaty flat. They both took a while to warm up, but the Teacher's candor and his rural deadpan style made him one of my favorite witnesses. His experience in his local camp—I won't give the dates—was brief, about half a year. His narrative was defined by his deep Kazakh nationalism and the size of his camp, fewer than 100 Uyghurs and Kazakhs.

As if the camp were a local CCP afterthought, the teacher claimed that the Chinese had recruited several local "non-entities" into the camp security detail. In their smart new uniforms, they barked orders at the former bulwarks of the small community, now reduced to prisoner status because of the "idiotic" CCP. The Teacher could talk circles around these "losers," and with his imposing physical mass, he challenged their authority at every step. Like a principal stepping into a classroom where an assistant teacher has lost control, the Chinese overlords threw the Teacher into solitary confinement for a month, yet he never changed his attitude. The Teacher was immensely proud of his actions, claiming that his insistence on pre-camp standards of behavior, and his willingness to bear the burden of solitary, contributed to a camp that had little serious torture or sexual abuse.

None of that ruled out discreet selection for organ harvesting, yet the Teacher and Ear Man were far more interested in talking about the dangers of the vaccines that the camp was forcing upon innocent men and women. I still needed answers to my central question:

"Did anyone disappear?"

"Not among the Kazakhs!"

"Well, what about the Uyghurs? Did any of them go missing?"

"I only care about the Kazakhs!" the Teacher replied, laughing.

I laughed along with him. Theoretically, naked tribalism shouldn't be rewarded, but comic relief is scarce in my business. Anyway, it's conceivable that Beijing's selection for harvesting imperatives slipped for the Uyghurs in his relatively small camp as well. I hope so. At any rate, of the four interviews that reported "0" disappearances, I found the Teacher's the most credible.

Without major reservations,

*The Teacher's camp had a harvesting selection rate of* 0 percent.

## KAZAKHSTAN. WITNESS 11: "EAR MAN"

It's not ideal to interview two witnesses at the same time, particularly if one—the Teacher—has a larger-than-life personality. In other words, other than acting as the Teacher's wingman, I have far less information on "Ear Man," my alias for him, other than what I picked up when the recorded interview was over, and the two witnesses were just hanging out. If memory serves, Ear Man was also a detainee in a camp. Approximately 200 prisoners were in Ear Man's camp, which was, if I understood correctly, geographically quite close to the Teacher's camp. Ear Man did not seem to differentiate seriously between Uyghur and Kazakh prisoners, and his best memory was that three individuals in their late twenties had inexplicably disappeared following a standard health check. He was speaking about a six-month period. Rounding out that rate of disappearance to a full year, yields 6 people selected out of 200.

*Ear Man's camp had a harvesting selection rate of 3* percent.

## KAZAKHSTAN. WITNESS 12: TURSYNBEK QABI

Tursynbek, like many Kazakhs born in China, used to regularly cross the Kazakh border. Returning to Xinjiang for a family funeral in September 2017, the Chinese border authorities detained Tursynbek. He would not return to Kazakhstan until February 2019. The snag, from my perspective, was that he was under house arrest that entire time, except for a single week confined in a concentration camp.[208] I doubted he could add anything, but Serikzhan encouraged Tursynbek to follow Bavi up to our safe house.

Tursynbek was born in Emin County, China, bordering Kazakhstan, the youngest male of 12 children. Now a filled-out construction worker with a prize-fighter face in his late forties, his eyes still bore a trace of the canny, observant boy. Tursynbek began with an articulate explanation of how Uyghurs and Kazakhs had always felt like second-class citizens, but in 2017, when his brother was killed, he recognized that the CCP crackdown had entered a sickening new phase. He recited a common anonymous text message: "20,000 renminbi for Uyghur women to marry Han Chinese males." Even under house arrest, he explored the exponential expansion of Chinese surveillance through carefully designed sorties in Xinjiang urban settings, calculating that "Every 700 meters, there is a police station with five cars. *Xinjiang had become a perfect police state.*"

When the Chinese police finally transported Tursynbek to the local camp, he was confined to a cage, like an animal. But he used the time to observe. After several days of interrogation and torture,

---

208    According to the Xinjiang Victims Database, the confinement took place in late September 2018.

Tursynbek saw a young male Uyghur being escorted into the neighboring cell, who whispered to Tursynbek that police and medical personnel had given him "a series of blood tests" the day before. The next morning, the young man vanished. Tursynbek asked the guards about him, and they replied, "'He hanged himself.'"

Tursynbek knew it was physically impossible to pull off such a stunt in the cellblock. Anyway, he had briefly observed a pink line on the young man's neck—the mark of a choke wire, a common police tactic to ensure that a prisoner could not speak in his own defense in a courtroom or any other official setting. "They had control of him," Tursynbek said. "Throughout his life in the camp, they had control of his body."

"Tursynbek, how old was this young man?"

"Age 28."

I kept my questions neutral, but Tursynbek had his own conclusions: the young man's disappearance in a single day was "predictable." The guards' obsessive medical tests meant that the young man was "used for his organs."

Tursynbek subsequently learned that whatever remained of the young man's body was delivered to the camp, "wrapped and taped." The police told the young man's family, "You are not to touch his body. No Muslim washing. Just bury him like this." The family suspected that "They took his organs. They couldn't see the body, but they believed it had been bleeding." His widowed bride initiated a legal case for restitution. The Chinese legal system responded by sentencing the widow's lawyer to 20 years in prison.

Tursynbek's interpretation was that Chinese authorities preparing a body for "Muslim burial" was simply a euphemism for organ extraction. Those code words will come up again in this chapter, so this seems like a good place for a supporting witness.

Start here: The CCP practice of extracting Uyghur organs before burial began in the aftermath of the 1997 Ghulja Massacre (or Ghulja Incident, according to the CCP) and scattered clues from the Uyghurs, and, more recently, the Kazakhs, suggest that it never fully ended.

According to Serikzhan Bilash of the Atajurt Kazakh Human Rights group, a single grave proves that practice still exists today. A few months before I arrived in Almaty, Serikzhan could sense a tremble behind the text message sent by a young man identifying himself only as "the son" of a man who had died in Chinese police custody. The watchfulness of the Chinese security forces at his father's funeral—no one was allowed anywhere near the corpse—sparked the son's suspicions. The son waited patiently for an overcast night, and then, in the wee small hours, slipped into the cemetery, silently dug out the grave's entrance, and slipped down the chimney-like passageway down to where his father's corpse lay. Beneath the Muslim funeral wrap or *kafan*, easily removed, his father's entire cadaver was encased in industrial-strength plastic. Hacking away at it for what seemed like hours, the plastic shell finally yielded and could be folded back to reveal his dead father's torso. Too cramped and dark to visually examine the body, the son made a painstaking assessment with his hands: his father's chest and abdomen had been surgically opened and barely stitched together. The son cut the stitches. There was no heart. The lungs were gone. Possibly the liver too. Gasping for breath like a diver who had plunged too deep, he clawed his way back up the chimney, pushing the loose earth aside to gulp in the cold night air.

The son said that he would only tell his story if Serikzhan met him in an isolated rural setting. I asked Serikzhan to reconnect. I would have offered the same conditions, but the son had disappeared.

Serikzhan constructing a model of a *Kafan*—a Muslim burial wrap—as he explains how a son

discovered that his father's organs had been pillaged before the burial. By Josephine de Haan-Montes.

Seven days in the camp, yet Tursynbek remained alert. He estimated, with no hesitation, that the camp had 6000 detainees. Based on the familiarity of the prison guards with the rituals of organ harvesting—the final tests, the injections to keep the victim docile, even the guards' sick jokes—Tursynbek estimated that, "at a minimum," there had to be *at least* one case of organ harvesting every week, 52 cases out of 6000 people.

Tursynbek caught me giving a skeptical look to the translator when he laid out that number, and he followed up in rapid Uyghur. The translator sensed a potential conflict, so it was only after we had made our goodbyes that he translated Tursynbek's remarks.

"This guy [Gutmann] was not in the cellblock. I was. And what I saw looked like a machine with extra oil; the guards treated the prep-work for the young Uyghur's death as completely routine."

"Like the town dump will be open tomorrow morning at 8 am?"

"Like that. Exactly," the translator replied.

*Tursynbek's camp had a harvesting selection rate of* 0.8 percent.

## KAZAKHSTAN. WITNESS 13: "AISHA"

At her request, I'm going to limit her personal details. In 2015, at age 25, Aisha was told to go to the hospital by the local cadres, and, together with her friends, received her first health check. "Blood was taken. [They examined my] liver, kidney, heart, lungs. Everything."

Aisha was detained in 2017, ostensibly triggered because she visited Kazakhstan. But when the police questioning went nowhere, they gave Aisha a list of around fifty "'crimes'" that justified detainment and, like a student asked by a busy professor to write their own letter of recommendation for the professor's signature, Aisha was ordered to pick two infractions from the list as a justification for her "re-education."

After a brief stay in a detention center, Aisha was transported to a concentration camp until the end of 2018. Initially they bunked in a traditional medicine hospital, as new camp buildings were constructed around it. Every week, there were 30 incoming detainees, ultimately reaching 8000 detainees camp-wide.

Aisha's cell contained 50 women, mostly Uyghurs with some Kazakhs. But the camp was a carousel of other suspected enemies of the Chinese State. It was rare for any of my witnesses to mention Muslim Hui people, but Aisha recollects seeing a handful of them. There were also Falun Gong: Aisha mentioned meeting a 50-year-old female practitioner, Han Chinese. The woman did not strike Aisha as a rebel or an activist, more a target of opportunity, as the CCP had seized her home as a windfall. Aisha also met a 40-year-old middle-aged lady, also Han Chinese Falun Gong. She had been sent to the camp after years in prison. Born in inner China, until her arrest, her home, too, was in Xinjiang. Yet constant surveillance meant it was not possible to talk to her and verify with which crimes, if any, she had been charged, and whether she was also a property owner. Neither woman disappeared. Both Falun Gong practitioners seemed resigned to eternal incarceration.

"Four people per day would leave." Aisha said. She theorized that one of four, the pretty ones, were taken away for some form of sexual slavery. Another young one, always a teenager, was taken away to do forced labor, and that wasn't even a secret. Aisha said the third would be older, perhaps a more difficult and hard-headed woman. She would be transferred to another camp for reasons unknown. Or perhaps known: "If you don't agree with the rules of this camp, if you don't tell the truth, you will be moved," the camp teachers would say every day.

The fourth would be "30 years old and sometimes as young as 25 years old." There was even one perfect 28, just like herself. Aisha recalled:

"These ones who are leaving, leave in the middle of the night. Or at other times... like during a safety drill... and there are ones who are leaving, you are forced to assume the 'stare at your feet' position while they're being loaded... black hoods over their heads, handcuffed, shackled... Into the black vans with the smoked glass.... These people who leave are healthy. They are not the most attractive. And they're not the sick people, the ones who didn't get the black hoods."

Aisha had heard the rumors. Only Uyghurs were taken away. Or it was Uyghurs and Kazakhs too. Or that the nine cameras per cell, including the toilet cam, were switched off when the people were transferred into black vans. Everyone agreed that "it was mostly young people who disappeared."

Aisha didn't need my explanations.

"The sons' and daughters' bodies are hidden from their parents because their organs have been stripped.... The young guys who pray? They have clean bodies. They have clean organs. They are 'accidentally dying' because of Chinese policy of stripping their organs."

Aisha explained, "You have to bury them without washing and

cleaning. They are wrapped in white cloth. Those whose bodies have been stripped of their organs are stuffed with rubbish. And you have to bury them *today*."

If, on average, one out of four people left daily in the black vans, that comes to 365 per year. Given Aisha's camp estimate of 8000 people, it follows that:

*Aisha's camp had a harvesting selection rate of* 4.5 percent.

## KAZAKHSTAN. WITNESS 14: RAHIMA SENBAI

Rahima came from a family of shepherds and traditional Kazakh nomads who summered in yurts and wintered in cement-block houses with an outhouse in the yard, like the one that we visited. Growing up, she lost several siblings to illness, and in 2013, her family settled into a more permanent base just across the Chinese border, in Tekes County.

Rahima knew the quiet crossings and the security lapses at the Kazakhstan-China border. Following the Urumqi demonstrations of 2009, she suspected a Uyghur crackdown was coming.

Rahima had four children in a marriage that ended in a difficult divorce in 2016. She chose her preferred side of the border and applied for Kazakh citizenship.[209] In Autumn 2017, Rahima was called back to China. "I was somewhat naïve," Rahima acknowledged. Two days in, she was taken into detention for seven days. By mid-December 2017, Rahima was incarcerated in a concentration camp.[210] In October 2018, she and her children fled to Kazakhstan.

---

209 One month before our interview in early 2020, the Kazakh authorities finally awarded Rahima citizenship.

210 Ostensibly, Rahima was in the camp because she had downloaded WhatsApp on her phone. Yet even the camp investigators seemed bored by this fig-leaf, so they pestered her with questions: Why Kazakhstan? Who are you in contact with? What do you know about terrorism? You could have met those terrorist people in Kazakhstan. With little help from Rahima's innocent, smiling manner, the questions changed: Who had radicalized her? Was she aware of the religious corruption in Kazakhstan? She was indeed a blank slate, and I gathered that her interrogators ultimately lost interest in her.

Rahima received no blood tests before December 2017. Alone among all my witnesses, a true nomad, she never got caught in the health check dragnet. Upon entering the camp, the guards made her run the full gauntlet of medical tests.

Rahima was aware that rankings, A, B and C were assigned based on behavior, but it didn't seem to matter because her cell of 30 women was initially in flux. Only one thing remained constant.

"It's a daily thing. We kind of got used to it. Twenty-year-olds were taken out at night. Some returned. Some did not."

"Were they raped?"

"I haven't seen that happen, but it could be. When they return, they're different. . . . You know, it's not like their hair is messed up, but they're crying or they're very quiet. . . . We don't know why some of them don't return. . . . There were not so many young unmarried Kazakh women. Many of the Uyghur girls were not married. And Uyghur girls, you know, are good-looking. On the virgin side. But when you ask them what happened. . . they just stay silent. We heard, you know, that they were raped. But in the camp? You don't understand, you don't know what's happening. Because it's all hush hush. And everyone is kept under so much fear. I don't know about the men, but it's very different, it's just difficult, for women."

Rahima felt the firebreak between the camps and the outside world eroding. Previously, no Uyghurs married Chinese or had any contact with Han Chinese men at all. Now she described the forced marriages between Han and Uyghur as a form of *legalized rape*:

"Now the CCP are saying, you know, 'We are one family.' And there's all this propaganda about unity. But the truth? It's just forced marriages. And the Han Chinese men know *nothing* about Xinjiang. And they don't know who they are marrying. . . So, for the women it's heart-wrenching—no choice, no freedom."

Rahima retreated into her friendship with one Kazakh girl, Araya: "We shared a bunk."

Araya's husband was a cleric with a 25-year sentence. Araya's kids had been put into an orphanage.

"Araya used to say, 'I'll never get out of here.' She was like my sister. I worried about her children."

Rahima does not know how to calculate the disappearances. But she is relatively sure that 2000 of the people in the camp were women. "They usually take girls two at a time. . . . There were 45 girls in my class and five of them went missing." That's an 11 percent disappearance rate. Rahima acknowledged that some of those women were younger–too young–and they could be lost to sex slavery. But Rahima was certain about her own cell of 30 women. Her friend Araya—27 years old, healthy, and—Rahima only noticed because the bed had gone cold—quietly taken from their shared covers on a winter's night.

*Rahima's camp had a harvesting selection rate of 3.3 percent.*

## KAZAKHSTAN. WITNESS 15: NURLAN KOKTEUBAI

"In May 2017, my wife was invited to China for two weeks," Nurlan said. "And she did not return."

Nurlan was born in 1963. At that time, his parents received government salaries for running a village. Like other minor bureaucrats in Xinjiang, his parents were non-practicing Muslims. Nurlan grew up identifying with his family's People's Liberation Army family background, and only secondarily as a Kazakh. Over time, Nurlan became a math teacher in the Chapchal region, and had two sons and a daughter.[211] Perhaps it was that innate confidence in the Chinese

---

211   An expanded bio for Nurlan can be found in his entry within the Xinjiang Victim's Database. See Shahit.biz/eng/.

system that led Nurlan to leave Kazakhstan for China that August "to clear things up."

By September, Nurlan was detained and arrested for "international terrorism." The Public Security Bureau was after Nurlan's contacts in "Kazakhstan and Syria," although Nurlan could prove that he had never visited any other country outside Kazakhstan. The PSB sent him to have a forced medical exam, "EKG, everything, totally comprehensive," and forced Nurlan to pay 500 RMB for the blood test on a technicality. The doctors injected him with a "flu vaccine" that led to unstable blood pressure and heart arrhythmia, which would confine him to hospital three times.

Nurlan's new home was a cell of 16 very crowded square meters in Number 3 Middle School, Chapchal County. With a ratio of two men to one woman, Nurlan estimated 15,500 people in the camp. Nurlan further noted 155 toilets, one for every 100 detainees.

The combination of the crowding and the lingering effects of the flu vaccine on his heart led to an outright heart attack in January, so Nurlan was transported to the Chopchal County People's Hospital.

"It was huge. . . three kilometers from the camp and 20 kilometers away from Ghulja airport. . . . The hospital had special force guards, paramilitary guards. . . and Uyghur patients always had a double guard assigned to them. They would follow me. Make sure I stayed silent. . . And there were cameras in the hall, maybe in the room."

Nurlan observed a mocking, jeering attitude among some of the hospital staffers. He hadn't seen a female Uyghur up close for months, until he happened to glimpse a doctor treating a female Uyghur patient. She was naked, and "the doctor was inserting a long stick into her vagina." There were no guards around. The door had inexplicably been left open. The Han Chinese doctor stared at Nurlan impassively, almost, he thought, with sadistic pleasure. "Perhaps the doctor was treating her? But he was also exposing this naked woman in a way that resembled torture."

About halfway through his 18-day stay, Nurlan received a blood transfusion, then an intravenous injection. A nurse came in and looked at him wide-eyed. She whispered to Nurlan frantically, "Drink five liters of water as quickly as possible, or your organs will become liquid.'" The nurse said something about 'kidneys,' but Nurlan was busy forcing water down his throat. When Nurlan recovered, he heard a rumor that the nurse who had saved his life had fled the hospital.

Nurlan had no explanation for the organ failure episode. Yet he consistently indicated that "there were mainly young people in the hospital," and that many of them "went missing." In March, a special bus drove into the camp perimeter. Cellblock after cellblock lined up and, one by one, medical examinations took place in the bus.

"There were police surrounding us. I can't estimate the number of people taken.... I asked a doctor: 'What kind of bus is this?' 'Shut up!' the doctor replied."

In April, after a final body check to make sure he wasn't carrying documents, Nurlan was released from the camp.

Basically, eight out of 100 went missing on a regular basis, taken from men "20 to 40 years of age." In other words, the seasonal rate was 8%, and the annual rate was potentially stratospheric, particularly with the addition of the "Shut up!" bus. Nurlan said that only about half of those disappearances fit into the 25 to 35-year age range. The actual disappearance rate associated with organ harvesting would be half of 8%.

*Nurlan's camp had a harvesting selection rate of 4 percent.*

## KAZAKHSTAN WITNESS 16: GULZIRA AUELHAN

"Celebrity witness" Gulzira, with Bavi and Ethan. By Josephine de Haan-Montes.

From a nomad family, born in 1980, Gulzira was clearly of the people, salt of the earth, her face simultaneously hard and unblinking, yet with a smile as guileless as a little girl's. All these qualities made her popular—if not in the official Kazakh media, then on Kazakh YouTube—and finally, with Josephine and me.

Gulzira told TikTok stories, little riffs that made the concentration camps come alive. The women entering the camps had to stick their head into a hole where their hair was shaved. In the morning you only had two minutes to use the toilet. A guard would accompany you. If you took too long, the guards, one for every two women, would shock you "on the head." After 7 months in the concentration camp, Gulzira "graduated" to a trade school camp and finally to forced labor with a sewing machine. In lieu of a coffee break, they had a daily break that everyone called "the two minute cry." Gulzira said, "You miss your children," and then, sarcastically, "But the Party is nice, so it gives you two minutes to vent." Within the factory, Gulzira was forced to dance for foreign visitors, presumably journalists.

The problem with a popular witness is that in the act of retelling, their story loses spontaneity. Even tears can be part of a performance. Rather than make her dance, I moved the questions the into less familiar journalistic territory of medical exams and disappearances.

Gulzira's camp was in a place called "Nine Directions" near Ghulja, the nucleus formed by a maternal/infant care hospital. Ten days in, Gulzira got her finger pricked for blood testing. Thirty days in, the doctors gave her "a big blood test" with 6-inch containers, followed by ultrasound, EKG, urine test and an abdomen test. Three months later, the doctors vaccinated Gulzira and she was told "you will feel tired for a week." The doctors showed a great interest in IUDS, pregnancy (presumably for immediate abortion and sterilization), or any signs of sexual activity. The doctors were "all Han Chinese."

With the tests completed, "There was tension in the room. . . Some of the Uyghur nurses had tears in their eyes. They felt that bad for us. . . . The doctors would ask these questions: 'Who is divorced? Who is widowed? Who is [not] on contraceptives?' They would black tag these women. . . those that did not have coils installed, the widowed, the divorced. . . and they would be taken away. . . . And they wouldn't come back. . . . There were many people that disappeared. Even children disappeared." I asked Gulzira for the women's ages and she estimated 21 to 37, average age of disappearance, 29 years old.

When someone was taken, the guards played a perverse game. They would ask the women: "'Do you know where she went?' And we would answer, 'Yes, oh sure,' as if we knew. Even though we had no idea. If we expressed any uncertainty, the guards would say, 'You haven't changed,' and you would be subject to interrogation or torture."

Gulzira recalls a guard teasing the women, "You should be happy that you have all your intact organs inside of you."[212]

---

212    One Falun Gong practitioner, Yu Xinhui, mentions the guards using similar taunts during his time in Guangdong prison. See Gutmann, *The Slaughter*, 248.

Gulzira became increasingly observant about the disappearances over time: "If there's 24 people, there are 2 people gone. If there are 30-something people, there are 3 people gone. If 17 people, there is 1 gone." Put another way, Gulzira said that "[e]very three or four days, someone would disappear," although she allowed that "[s]ome [who disappeared] were good-looking" and "[o]ne woman, a 37-year-old, was taken away in the middle of a class." So Gulzira agreed that approximately half of the disappearances could be for sex slavery or, with the older women, forced labor, or even skilled work of some kind. *Medical disappearances* meant: "They are taken away at night. But the bed would already be reoccupied when you woke up."

Medical disappearances, one woman taken every 8 days, works out to about 45 women a year out of a camp of 800 women.

*Gulzira's camp had a harvesting selection rate of 5.6 percent.*

## KAZAKHSTAN. WITNESS 17: "BRIGHT MORNING"

Male witness, mid-thirties, alias, refused to give any personal details, including his ethnicity, and preferred to be recorded on the Dictaphone. Like so many camp refugees, he was concerned about familial repercussions.

Or maybe it was something else. As Bright Morning pointed out, "Ordinary people, often Uyghur or Kazakh, were [sometimes] used to staff the camps. For the simple jobs." Yet any job in the camp, even cleaning, was seen as part of the larger CCP surveillance structure and could theoretically build resentment among the detainees, amplified in a camp of only 168 people. At least for part of the eight months that Bright Morning spent in the camp, he was earning a salary of 5000 yuan per month, a considerable sum, indicating that the Han Chinese guards considered him a trusted asset. He hinted that the police had previously used him as a sort of neighborhood snitch. Perhaps Bright Morning had to do some things in the camp that he was ashamed of.

We'll never know. Bright Morning had only limited special privileges: Chinese doctors gave him a typical comprehensive medical exam. The police gave him an iris scan and made a voiceprint. Shower once a week, ten minutes to use the toilet, then "vaccination," followed by Bright Morning collapsing: "Dreaming of freedom, my nails became thin because there was no light. I had no energy. Eight months in this dark and dismal place."

Bright Morning grasped the significance of the disappearance question without any prodding on my part. The ones who left were transferred to an "infection hospital. . . a few kilometers away" The 7th floor was reserved for prisoners and had cells instead of hospital rooms.

"There was an imam who disappeared. The camp had a truck that was used to transport dead bodies. Within the compound, the camp had a hole in the earth. . . . One time I was passing by, and I saw some bodies before they filled it in. The cloth had slipped. I recognized the face of the imam. Eventually the gossip made its way to the imam's family. But they didn't want to believe it. Eventually, after two months, they wanted to make an issue of it. The camp guards went to their house and said 'He was killed in an accident, and the body was destroyed.'"

Six disappearances are of interest.[213] Five were Uyghur or Kazakh, "about 30 years old." One was "about 40 years old," and he was Falun Gong, kept under strict surveillance. Bright Morning knew him as a "a local guy, a metal worker-locksmith guy," but the rest of the camp was told that he was crazy because he spoke about how Falun Gong was good. Given the history of Falun Gong harvesting and the fact

---

213  Eight people went missing over eight months. Two of those may have been murdered or euthanized: One was Chinese male, 60 years old, who was in the camp for complaining to Beijing about seizure of agricultural lands, and the other was Uyghur but was 78 years old. Neither individual is counted in the organ harvesting tally.

that the Chinese transplant industry commonly prized the teetotalling and non-smoking Falun Gong practitioners for their healthy organs, I assume that he would have been a candidate for harvesting despite his relatively advanced age.

If we extend the rate of 6 disappearances over 8 months into 9 disappearances over 12 months, keeping the 168 individuals camp size as a constant:

*Bright Morning's camp had a harvesting selection rate of 5.3 percent.*

## KYRGYZSTAN. WITNESS 18: OVALBEK TURDAKUN

The first interview with Ovalbek took place on a snowy afternoon in Bishkek, in what was meant to be little more than a visa refresher run. I'll go into the rescue of Ovalbek and his family a few chapters on—I also refer to him as Joseph—and will only summarize his key observations here.

Regarding the disappearances:

"They press down your head as they take them out, so you are essentially looking at your feet. Sometimes you are in that position for a long time. That's when they're removing somebody. They're pressing your head down, so you don't see them going. Old people who would die in the night? They would be carried out [openly] on a stretcher."

Ovalbek described trying to track who disappeared as a sort of shell game or three-card monte: "When we start wondering about the disappearances, they 'shuffle up' [move detainees from cell to cell]. So that we don't know where they've gone, or who's who. They do it in the dark."

Regarding numbers:

"Three out of 20 per month disappearance [from the cellblock]. Seven out of 50 per month, that's [in the] classroom. About 32 years of age for the young ones. About 50 [years of age] from the older ones.

Doesn't give me a real average, but I'm assuming there's more young ones than older ones that disappear."

Ovalbek's estimate of classroom disappearances (14%) is very close to his cellblock estimate (15%). To represent accurately Ovalbek's observation that there were two groups at risk—one group about 50 years old on average and the other 32 years of age on average, we can cut these ratios in half to get a crude estimate:[214]

*Ovalbek's camp had a harvesting selection rate of 7.5 percent.*

\* \* \*

The final two witnesses were not camp refugees, but both maintained a relationship with their local camps' associated hospital and either observed or participated in the preparation for organ harvesting. This is highly sensitive material, even in Kazakhstan. I've left out locations, used aliases, and avoided personal details.

\* \* \*

## KAZAKHSTAN. WITNESS 19: "MINA"

Mina was a fashion entrepreneur, the director of a factory with 68 employees. I opened with: "When did your troubles begin?"

In 2014, the Chinese authorities ordered Mina to enforce full company compliance with the Chinese State's new medical testing regime for Uyghurs: "Cheek swab DNA tests, blood tests, and a hospital check that included checking our organs." The associated hospital, Mina noted, was a 40-minute drive to a major airport. For good measure, Mina said, "they also confiscated our passports."

In 2016, the police ordered voice checks, iris scans, and a second

---

214    The 15% estimate as opposed to the 14% estimate is reduced by 50% here to reflect Ovalbek's impression that the younger group disappeared at a higher rate than the older group.

round of blood tests and DNA cheek swabs. In an unguarded moment, a Chinese government representative told Mina that the Party's purpose "was to try to find the same DNA as Uyghur rebels and warriors of the past." Mira suspected Beijing wanted to strangle future Uyghur leaders in their cribs, or at least to prevent them from mating.[215]

This time around, the experience was no longer curated to conform with the company's production schedule. Mina found herself and her workers crushed into a hospital reception with hundreds of Uyghurs and Kazakhs. When it was her turn to register for her "health check," Mina looked into the eyes of a somehow familiar hospital staff member sitting at the long table. He craned his neck towards her. She lowered her head as if she was trying to concentrate. Ignoring the chaos, he whispered softly but clearly:

"Don't get the DNA test. Just the blood test."

"Why? I want to complete all the medical tests."

"I will put down that you have already been checked for DNA. Just don't do the DNA test. And then, just leave."

Mina reasoned that the staffer "knew that the voice recognition was being put together with the DNA as an identifier. Somehow, he knew that I was planning on going abroad." But later, Mina realized that there was something else. "He really wanted to help me. So why would the medical staffer warn me not to take the DNA test? Well, there was a Kazakh guy [at the hospital], an official. He was responsible for my DNA tests. But I had paid for his mother's care in hospital. He was returning the favor."

Mina paused, then said very quietly: "Everyone was afraid to talk

---

215 While this may seem superstitious or irrational, the CCP is clearly fascinated by DNA. For example, there is a belief at the highest levels of the Party that 10% of the Taiwanese have Japanese blood – and that specific DNA is the main impediment to Taiwan's reunification. My source is an American at the US Embassy in Beijing.

about organ harvesting. It was a rumor. *Yet I knew that DNA was being used to check our organs.*"

By the end of 2016, it was widely understood throughout the Uyghur and Kazakh community that there was a quota for arrests, and then, by the end of 2017, for camp disappearances. When night fell, Chinese police would transport 20 people to "3rd Uyghur Middle School," since transformed into "a concentration camp" with a "capacity of 3000." There was a five-level hospital close-by, split in half, one side "normal," the other, "the dark side," assigned to camp detainees.

In 2018 ("It was spring. It was a little warm.") Mina checked into the hospital's "normal" ward for a ten-day treatment. But she found herself slipping away to the coffee shop and a kebab stand just outside the dark side. "I'd have a rest or a smoke at the table for lunch. The food was better outside the hospital. I was there for 10 days. And I would go down there eight times a day from morning to 10 pm." At night, all the lights were turned off in the main entrance and hallway of the dark side, "but the drugstore just across the way gave a view and provided a light."

At twilight, the show began. Like watching a meteor shower, you had to keep your eyes on the entry area, or you would miss it: Two male guards marching another man (handcuffed, shackled, bag on head) through the doors and down the hall. She was positive that all the men were from the camp. "Sometimes they were going out, but most of them were coming in."

Mina knew that the age range of the camp was 18 to 80. "But the average age of the hospital prisoners was 25 to 45." Very late one night she saw a male prisoner, "a youngish guy," going into the hospital.

"His head was covered. How could you tell he was young?"

"He had tapered jeans. Fashion jeans."

"What time?"

"That was at 10 pm." After that, the food stands were closed, Mina explained. To be out there looked suspicious. "I tried to look ignorant. I tried not to look at the prisoners going in. I tried to look down. I tried to ignore them, but I could still see things."

"Why were the detainees dressed in their civilian clothes?"

Mina thought for a moment. She was aware of photos that had been taken of young Uyghur men in prison uniforms with their eyes taped shut in a train station, the ones that had made it out to the West. She speculated that the Han Chinese authorities wanted to avoid that sort of exposure. But really Mina felt that the guards used the clothes to make the camp prisoners feel calm, maybe even happy: *I'm getting my own clothes back. I'm getting out of the camp.*

"Why do you think these prisoners were brought in? What's your theory? What was going on?"

"A couple of times they wanted to make people think that these people had just passed away inside the concentration camps. They even gave the bodies [to the family] for burial. But they said, 'Just bury them. You can't open the wrapping.' And the police watch all the time, so the family cannot examine the body. But what's happened to that body? The family cannot research the cause of death. No autopsy. The police say: 'We already washed [the corpse]. Just bury him.' Some of our people think about that, and they say: 'they could have been organ donors—they [the Chinese] harvested the organs.' But none of us can talk about it. . . . They always took the people who were in good health... so at that time, I started to think that too, that they could be organ donors. That's why the police force us to just bury them without seeing the body or the face. They were wrapped like mummies. . . yes, I believe it was organ harvesting."

Mina had personal experience as an organ recipient. "There's a 6-month organ wait time. I needed a kidney, and I paid RMB 75,000 [approximately 11k USD] for that kidney. . . . I wanted to personally thank the girl for the kidney [donation]. I wanted to meet her. But the authorities said that it was against the rules. Nobody knew about the operation."[216]

Through her workers, Mira was aware of the daytime disappearances inside the camp as well: "Forty-year-old people, men and women, married couples sometimes, too. They were sent to inner China to work. . . . About 60 people went to the work camps." Mira held her company together, but by 2018, Mira had to make a deal with the camp authorities. Mina gave up three workers a month. "No more. We need to finish an order. So yeah, I gave up some workers to forced labor. And they will be leaving the camps. . . . It is better that way. They will suffer in inner China. But they will not die."

I called it *the Schindler Quota.*

Because Mina was never incarcerated in the camps, she was less accustomed to controlling her emotions, and this came out at the close of the interview:

"If we hear something in the night and we are eating, the food no longer matters. Maybe they have come for us? And we cannot even swallow what is in our mouths. We know that the treasures of our life—our house, or money, the wealth of our life—these things don't matter any longer. We think only of the concentration camps. And we know that one day we will be there."

Mina was near tears as she summarized her thoughts: "Only survival matters. . . . You cannot sleep. Listening for these tiny noises. If the noises are not there you think okay. I'm okay. Today, they won't get me."

Through a combination of bribes, Mina "crossed the border to Kazakhstan with only my coat and my bag."

---

216    Theoretically, this could be a case of a Uyghur or a Kazakh receiving a Falun Gong organ.

Mina had a house, a bank account, and a business, but "I couldn't take anything. . . . I told my minder: 'I don't need to take anything because I will be back in two days.' I was so lucky and happy just to have a passport. . . . I had 2000 RMB [300 USD] in my pocket."

Mira believed that the annual ratio of prisoners being sent off to do forced labor, about 60 a year, compared with prisoners entering the hospital for organ harvesting (minus the prisoners coming out of the dark side, and the middle-aged prisoners ) worked out to about 3 to 1—in other words, about 180 detainees a year (or 182, as she also expressed it as one prisoner harvested every two days).

*Mina's camp had a harvesting selection rate of 6 percent.*

## KAZAKHSTAN. WITNESS 20: "SAMAL"

"I crossed the Kazakhstan-China border illegally on May 5th, 2018. . . . I've been here for nine months already. I was introduced to different reporters. I went to the American Consulate a few times. But I never told this story to anybody."

Samal paused for a beat. "I hope that the fascism that is being perpetrated in China will finish one day. My destiny, my fate, is not decided yet. I could be put in prison for the cause."

Samal stopped and stared at the wall, as if it was too difficult to look at me, Josephine, or the translator. "This is the truth, only I know, only known to me," she said with quiet resolve. "The reason I ran away from China was my impending incarceration in the camp. And this is what I'm going to share with you."

Then Samal began to shake and then broke into great heaving sobs. I got up and handed her a box of tissues. After three minutes, she stopped and said: "The person who did that, and saw it, and did it with their own hands—this was somebody close to me."

At the end of 2017, a veterinarian was sent to the local "political education camp" to serve as a doctor. And this person, Samal explained, had high blood pressure and a cough. "So, this person was given like half a day off work. That's when we met." It was outside the camp, Samal explained, smiling faintly. Just a flicker.

"And this person said to me, 'It's better you go to Kazakhstan because there could be danger waiting for you. I cannot see everything, but it's pretty dangerous for you now. You've been in Kazakhstan many times. You know a lot of information. You could be sent to the camp, or you could even be sentenced to seven to ten years.'"

The vet explained the situation inside the camp to Samal: "'The people that used to work as guards to police the camps were originally Xinjiang Chinese or other minorities. Now they're bringing people from inner China that don't really care because they're not local. They're really hardened and callous. And they just have no pity or mercy. There's 14-year-olds, 13-year-olds even, all the way up to 78-year-olds. That's the age range. Some of them cannot walk. And the hardest thing is that people die. *Like seven or eight people die a day*. People don't care about them. They can just walk over them. At midnight or one in the morning, they're taken very deep underground. I don't know how. I don't how deep it is. It's very cold. Dark. And there's three medical clinics there.'"

As Samal described the underground medical compound, I realized that she was no longer giving a second-hand account. *Samal had been down there. She had seen it. That's why she cried.* Like a psychiatrist listening to a patient free-associating on a couch, I remained silent, afraid of breaking the spell.

"There's no surveillance down there. Instead, there are two armed guards before you enter into the clinics, black masks over their faces. They never move, but they hold their guns at the low ready."

Inside the compound, there was an assembly line—or more

accurately *an extraction line*—a system for the processing of corpses, manned by a team of eleven doctors, one Kazakh, the rest Han Chinese. As the vet had noticed, "When they talk on the phone, their Mandarin dialect was not our local Chinese dialect, but always a dialect from outside Xinjiang."

Their station was the first on the line, and the only one that was not shielded behind the carefully locked doors of the three clinics. "Today there were three bodies," Samal said. "The doctors told us that their intestines will start rotting, decomposing. You have to. . . clean the intestines or take them out." Indeed, there had been a previous case of an imam's body that was "'so stinky'" that it had nearly led to the complete evacuation of the medical compound.

Still, the veterinarian's job was the lowest, most unskilled part of the line. Perhaps the surgeons were grooming the veterinarian to work in the advanced clinics. But one day everything came apart when the veterinarian recognized "a young mother from my village. And I said, 'I will not cut this person's body.'" When the police heard about this, "they started beating the vet very hard. After that, it's like the vet almost went crazy. Something happened. A nervous breakdown. . . . So after that the vet was told to take out *only* the intestines. And put them in a black bag. Like a plastic bag or something. But there was another corpse. *We didn't know their nationality or whether he was Han Chinese, Kazakh or Uyghur. His face was covered somehow.*" The covering was apparently a new feature, brought on by the veterinarian's reaction to the young mother. Perhaps it was another corpse that the vet could identify.

Samal never explained how the vet had engineered it so she could work as the vet's assistant, but she did formally confirm to me that the vet took her down to the operating room many times. Back to her narrative, Samal said that two or three days later, there were seven corpses.

"Again, the faces were wrapped with something. . . so that you wouldn't know who that was."

"Approximately what age?"

"Mostly about 57 or 58. But one. . . by looking at her breast, we could tell that she was not an old person. . . she was young. . . around 30 years old. We cleaned her intestines—not much food in the intestines or in the stomach. She wasn't fed anything when she died. . . [Then] the doctors were working on her. They were cleaning something inside, doing something. . . ." Samal trailed off for a moment. "But it was also like: Another day, another seven bodies. . . . Nobody is supposed to use, you know, minority languages. . . only Mandarin [was allowed]."

"The next time when we went there, it was four people. There was one male out of the four bodies, in his 20s. There were many wounds on his body. Lots of blue [bruises]."[217]

Samal was an attractive woman working as a medical assistant with a high level of clearance. She wanted to reveal everything that had taken place in the camp, and the following story came out in a confessional rush.

One night, around 1:00 am, Samal was taken into a black room with no surveillance cameras. There were two "tables" and six Han Chinese in the room.

"Take off your clothes."

When Samal started to answer back, they said, "You don't have the right to ask us why. You're supposed to do whatever we tell you to do."

They tore off her clothes. Samal scratched someone's face.

---

217   "But the vet discovered that one of the corpses had four kidneys. The vet had never seen something like that. He was pretty terrified and screamed out. This looks like four kidneys, but they're connected somehow to each other. The other doctors were pretty happy. There was lots of phone calls, you know. Maybe they called Beijing or somewhere else. All at about 3:00 in the morning."

Someone hit her on the head, perhaps with a weapon, and it all went black.

"It was maybe one or two hours later. I don't know how long. I woke up. It was very cold. . . and I felt someone penetrating my vagina. Then, I felt like I was being torn apart. There were two other men holding my arms. They were smoking. It's this older Chinese guy. He's raping me, and I was freezing, and I've just woken up to this. . . . And these other two, the other two Chinese there, took off their clothes and they were, kind of, getting ready. Waiting for their turn. It was like 15 minutes. After the old guy finished, the other two continued for another 20 minutes. There. Now you know. . . and I got pregnant. I was pregnant and they made me abort, have an abortion, and I was taken to the hospital for the abortion. And after the abortion, I was sent home to recuperate for a month."

Samal slowed down and said, "You know, that's when I talked to the vet again. We talked in the basement because all the apartment blocks in China, they also have a basement with a room to store things. There's no electronics down there. . . that night, we drank about four glasses of alcohol together."

The vet told her that three days after they had cleaned the body of the man with the dark blue bruises, something happened. The vet was relaxing at home. But suddenly it was "hard to breathe, and my eyes felt like they were going to pop out of their sockets." So the vet crawled down the corridor, was put on a stretcher and taken to the hospital. "Three days later, I woke up. They told me to go home and rest. But after midnight, I think, at 2:00 in the morning, five people came to my house. They took me and strapped me to a chair, and they said, 'Everything you saw in the camp. And everything you've heard? You're not going to share it with your parents. Or your spouse. We know you have two daughters. Not them either. If you tell anybody about this, anyone who has any connection to you will be in a very difficult situation. You know, you cut out their intestines. And we do Muslim ritual washing. So, we can give the wrapped bodies back to their relatives and they can have a Muslim-style burial."

The scope of the lie, the threats to family, started to play on the veterinarian: "'Something was developing, you know, like a drinking habit. And talking to myself. Screaming sometimes.'" The vet went back to the camp to work but was no longer allowed "to go do an autopsy" or "prepare for burial" or whatever they called it, but his temporary removal from the clinics allowed the veterinarian enough distance to internally confront the purpose of the clinic.

"The vet told me that the people that were killed in the camp. . . . The bodies would be put in the black body bags and taken outside the camp to be used."[218]

That confession, in turn, started Samal thinking about how warm the bodies were sometimes, particularly the young ones. Like they had just been slaughtered, not that they had died naturally. The vet told Samal, "There are many cells in the camp underground, at least three or four levels underground. So, we clean up their intestines. But we don't know the content of the other rooms. What's inside? What kind of instruments? We don't know. Not allowed. I've seen a special glass, like a container. . . they put organs in there."

The vet had seen a kidney in the glass container, another time, a liver. When the vet casually asked the Han Chinese doctors about the organ removals, they explained that the person had hepatitis. One

---

218    In Samal's description, every trip the vet made to the morgue included at least one corpse very close to the ideal age of 28. And while most organ harvesting in China is performed while the "patient" is still alive, Samal's camp may have been the exception that proves the rule. Put another way, if perfusion methods are used, live organ harvesting is clearly desirable, but not fully essential. Given that at least one of the three dead young people was a male covered in "blue" with wounds on his body, the camp director may have made the judgement to exploit the organs of prisoners who are tortured to death, which appears to have been a fairly routine occurrence.

of the worst forms. Very contagious! So, we need to extract it, and put it in "seclusion, like this." That way, when it's buried, it doesn't "'cross-contaminate.'"

Of course, there were no such safeguards with the intestines, which were either cleaned or removed, just as long as it didn't stink up the funeral or the clinics. But it was all lies, the veterinarian said: "The camp might give the body up, but they will not let you do a Muslim ritual washing: If they have some [dental] fillings, normally you would extract the gold. You would take off any earrings. You would tie the head up so the chin will not fall open. You would wrap the private parts. But they don't allow that. They just wrap the body in cloth. They tape it. And no one can un-tape it. And if you open that cloth, you'll go to the camps. They'll take your family, too."[219]

The veterinarian asked Samal the closing question: "So, after the camps, what happens next?"

Samal stayed silent.

"Your situation is pretty dire. Because of the things that are happening in the camps."

"What things?"

"'What I've told you. . . . This place, they're telling you it's a vocational school. They're telling you that you're learning things. They're telling you this and that. But. . . people are dying here. . . . You know what happens to the bodies. . . *You can be an organ donor. They can do that to you. This is what's happening.* And I cannot tell you all of this here.'"

"No, I'm not, I'm not going to tell."

"Life is so dear. You're a Kazakh. In your ID it says that you are a Kazakh. That's your ethnicity. You can go to Kazakhstan. And people

---

219 The veterinarian added that at the actual funeral: "'You're not supposed to read Quran at the burial. You're not supposed to put them on the special carrying stretchers, Muslim style. You are not supposed to wail.'"

like me? Uyghurs. We cannot go. . . . I'm probably going to die inside this camp.'"

Samal was exhausted. It was early May 2018, 4:00 am, and she still couldn't sleep. Over the last couple of days, a Chinese interrogator had openly stuck his hand into her pants while he was talking to her as if assessing the ripeness of a piece of fruit. She had protested, talking about her rights as a citizen and invoking the Kazakh authorities.

"Oooh, so you can share this with the government in Kazakhstan. You know *all* the laws." The interrogator mocked Samal. "So that's why we're interrogating you. Because there are 27 countries on the *terrorism list*. That's why you're here. Because Kazakhstan is on that list."

They finally let her out, "'Go and get your passport,' they said. 'Come back at 7:30 [in the morning]'. And I was thinking about it all night."

Samal slowly got out of bed and called a taxi.

"I resolved to try the trading zone between Kazakhstan and China, the buffer trading zone. If I will be caught. . . ? I couldn't. . . well, it could have ended differently. But when I ran away, I ran to Kazakhstan. . . . Of course, I knew I could never be in touch with the vet ever again."

Before she left, Samal had tried to reassure the veterinarian that she would never lose contact, that the evidence that the veterinarian had uncovered would be revealed to the world "The WeChat app has a feature that you can, like, store something, save something for the future," Samal explained. And she installed the app on the vet's phone. Samal occasionally logged into the veterinarian's WeChat account: "For two months, the vet did not log into WeChat at all. And three months later, I tried to log in again. And at that time, all the passwords were changed. . . . I think the vet was taken into interrogation."

There are complexities and mysteries scattered throughout Samal's account, particularly regarding the extraction line. I wish that

I'd asked more clarifying questions. Following the tears, it was if Samal had entered a hypnotic state. The confessions just kept coming, and then the gang rape, and I was reluctant to interrupt. When Samal finished, she was embarrassed and highly vulnerable. Although we were all polite and sympathetic to a fault, it was getting dark, and she clearly wanted to get out of our flat.

I don't like telling readers how to think about witness statements, but a lot of non-verbal communication and side-chats take place around an intense interview, and I think my interpretation might clarify things:

1. The "three clinics"—the medical compound—does not focus on autopsies, but organ harvesting. The cover story was that the medical staff prepares bodies for Muslim burial.

2. The cleaning or removal of the intestines could be seen as unusual in an organ harvesting context. When Samal brought up "the case of the stinky imam," I didn't initially understand why she mentioned it. Setting aside the red herring of his imam status, the significance is straightforward: one man's bowels could disrupt the entire clinic, exacerbated by the limitations of a ventilation system four stories down.

3. It is also germane that the veterinarian and Samal were working on the front end, "Exhibit A" of the Muslim burial cover story. Muslim burial preparation requires the removal of excrement. Traditionally, a same-sex family member will prop the corpse's chest up slightly, while pressing down on the stomach, and clean up whatever emerges. The

veterinarian handled the problem like a mortician: cutting into the intestines and flushing them out with a hose or removing the intestines altogether, but still consistent with Muslim cleansing.

4. When the clinic began to have doubts about the veterinarian's discretion, poison appears to have been administered, followed by a message delivered in the middle of the night: *Shut up about the clinic's activities. We do Muslim burial preparations. End of story.*

5. The veterinarian knows this is a lie and explains to Samal privately that many of the steps required for Muslim burial are not being followed. Instead, the veterinarian recounted glimpses of Han Chinese surgeons handling containers with extracted organs and overheard conversations (the vet could apparently understand Mandarin well enough to pick up regional differences) proving that the clinic was part of a transplant chain. Were actual transplants taking place in that specific compound, perhaps using a separate entrance? Or at a nearby medical facility? That remains a mystery.

6. One last point. The veterinarian explicitly warns Samal that the clinic, or some other medical facility, will harvest her organs sooner or later. It's their final conversation. Samal's faith in the vet's prediction, combined with the prospect of further sexual abuse, drives Samal's extremely risky decision to leave all her worldly assets behind and try her luck at the Kazakh border.

I suspect the veterinarian saved Samal's life—not only by warning her, but through sacrifice, perhaps hoping to mollify the Chinese security services by transposing one scalp for another. Yet Samal was emotionally drained, so I simply asked, "About how big is the camp?"

"Let's think. Maybe six or seven thousand."

"And how many people, do you believe, disappear?"

It was the wrong question. Samal never woke up in the middle of the night to find her bunkmate missing.[220] She was in the front lines. In her experience, and that of the veterinarian, *every night* at least one warm 30-year-old body was brought down to the medical compound. Samal estimated 365 bodies with this profile in a single year, out of 7000.

*Samal's camp had a harvesting selection rate of* 5 percent.

\* \* \*

At one point, near the end of the interview process, Josephine asked me why we didn't have more refugees from the camps who cried during their interviews. Perhaps she was thinking of something she had watched on YouTube. I replied that the translators, following my lead, were making a conscious effort not to distort or incentivize the witnesses through our reactions. When Samal broke down and wept, I handed her the tissue box. "Gutmann does not believe in tears," I said to Josephine.

In other words, in an interview like Samal's that contains truly toxic allegations, sympathy is a luxury. Any signs of exuberance over

---

220 "At night, women disappear. They're gone. Two or three people. Every night. It's the young girls. Beautiful, young girls. And divorced or unmarried woman. Not too old. They put bags on their heads. They're taken at midnight. So, in the morning, they bring back those that they want to bring back. But those that are not brought back? They say she's moved to another camp...And of course they're being raped. It's, you know, what they did to me during interrogation and...you know...they're giving them birth control pills. They're putting the coils inside."

testimony that supported my working thesis would have tainted the results as well. Nor did I badger "Milqa" (outlier witness 8, who claimed that all the disappearances in her camp were for valid medical reasons), but I did ask how the flu vaccine affected her—a subject on which Milqa spoke articulately.

So yes, Josephine was right to ask. Because it was a tight ship and a cold process, but it was the only way I knew to keep the compact with the reader that I stated in the beginning: witness testimonies *free of intentional lies or propaganda.*

This chart shows the raw data.

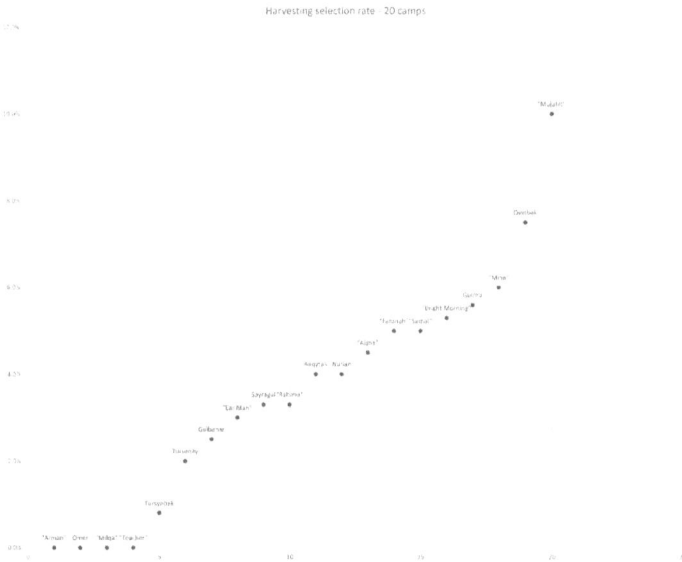

Harvesting selection rate · 20 camps

And the next chart is where I place the "zone of probability," between 2.5% and 5% selection for organ harvesting.

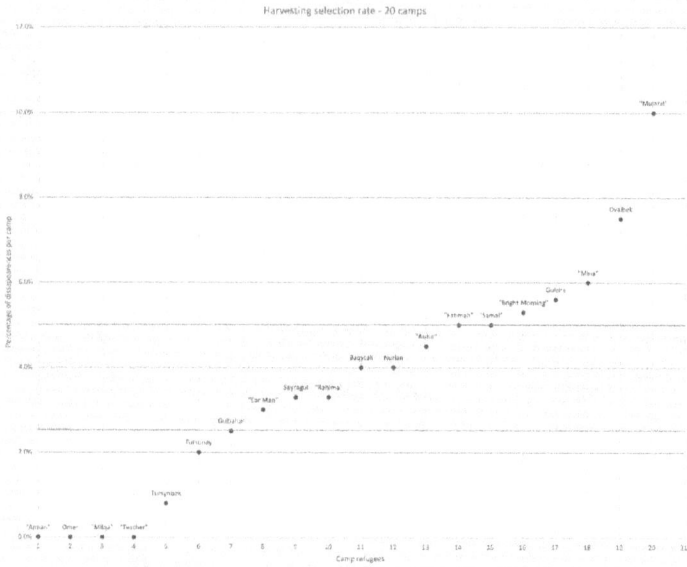

As I stated in the opening, this is human data distorted by *perception, memory, bias, and trauma.* The outlier cases reflect this: "Arman," (no *perception* of individual cases); Omer, (no *memories* to work with); "Milqa," (*bias*, stemming from psychoactive effects of the "flu vaccine"); and "Mujahit" (personal response to *trauma*). Perhaps other outliers rang true. For example, at camps below 100 detainees, such as the one "The Teacher" describes, a disappearance would be far more suspicious. As for the higher selection percentages, my China experience informs me that one could easily circumvent strict quotas, and Han Chinese prison guards are not immune to bribery. It's hard for me to discount Ovalbek's 7.5% estimate, far above the routine quota, simply because he was one of the most perceptive witnesses I have ever encountered. Yet the overall effect of my camp refugee testimony suggests that by 2017, Beijing had imposed a rational system where every camp was permitted to secretly harvest a range of its inmates in their late twenties/early thirties every year.

One caveat. Looking at the distribution of points on the chart, it would certainly be possible to express the zone of probability between 2% to 6%, except for one factor: the average.

The midpoint of 2% to 6% is **4%**. The midpoint of 2.5% to 5% is **3.75%**. The actual midpoint of the 20 witnesses in this chapter is: **3.59%**. Pretty close. For those readers who really love precision, if we subtract Omer (which I debated doing, because he frankly admitted that, following the tests on his organs, torture, and deprivation for over 200 days in solitary, he was in no shape to track other's people disappearances during his final twenty-day stint in the camp cellblock), the average selection rate according to the 19 witnesses is **3.78%**, essentially identical to the midpoint of 2.5% to 5%. And that yields the following summary:

1.  Xinjiang camp prisoners are being selected for organ harvesting at a rate of 2.5 percent to 5 percent annually.

2.  With one million people in the camps at any given time, that selection rate translates into 25,000 to 50,000 Uyghurs, Kazakhs, and others of Turkic ethnicity, harvested every year.

3.  Assuming that the rate of selection for organ harvesting from the camps has stayed constant since 2017, the death toll of Uyghurs, Kazakhs and other Turkic ethnicities, in 2026, is—*again, at a minimum*—200,000 and counting.

*Addendum: Given that a single body can be exploited for two (or theoretically, as many as six organs) the minimum number of prisoners selected (25,000) from the Xinjiang Camps can easily supply **60,000 organs per year**, the estimated minimum annual transplant volume of China.*[221]

---

221 See Kilgour, *et al.*, "Update." The calculation in this chapter assumes a minimum baseline of one million in the camps at any given time, although, as the selection rate variance between individual camps suggests, there is play in the system, and Beijing can theoretically dial up or down the selection rate for harvesting with existing detainees to meet China's transplant industry requirements. Some researchers have recently speculated that the camp population may currently be as low as 500,000. Their evidence is not fully based on satellite data (which the Party has learned to manipulate) or systematic witness accounts (the Party has ensured that these are scarce on the ground) but represents a general feeling that the current camp system is currently more oriented around forced labor rather than reeducation. There are plenty of experts, such as Sayragul Sauytbay, who dispute that there has been any significant reduction in camp population at all. I'm not in a position to know, although the general move to a forced labor focus from reeducation feels correct. Yet lowering the numbers to create a coherent picture of the forced labor focus implicitly plays along with Beijing's strategy to lower the volume of global chatter surrounding the camps, so I'll just make a few observations: *First, 500,000 detained is as low as any serious researcher can plausibly go.* The recorded legal sentencing of Uyghurs and Kazakhs is above 500,000 according to every source that I've examined. *Second, there's a missing piece here.* An accurate count of unrecorded and extralegal measures of the *Laogai System* (long-term detention centers, prisons, psychiatric hospitals, combined prison/hospital facilities, and so-called "Black Jails") is currently unknowable. Based on my previous Falun Gong interviews regarding their incarceration patterns over time, extralegal forms of detention quite plausibly doubled the total number of Falun Gong in captivity at any given time. In the Uyghur and Kazakh case, this would easily bring the total to over a million or more. *Third, given the relatively tiny population of Xinjiang, the per-capita level of medical attention that Xinjiang receives already is well above most Chinese provinces.* The current construction of new medical sites in Xinjiang suggests a countertrend—that the harvesting of Uyghurs and Kazakhs is not slowing down but accelerating. See Allegra Mendelson, "China 'to triple number of Uyghur organ-harvesting centres': Campaigners fear six new medical sites in Xinjiang could be used for forced 'donations,'" *Telegraph*, July 3, 2025.

# 6

# AND FAR AWAY

Our entry into Almaty was like a magic show that ends with the levitating table crashing to the floor. When we hit our stride, confidence became second nature, and then, my vulnerability.

Hitting our stride meant finding camp refugees who were willing to talk. There were several days in the beginning when we found no one to interview, and Bavi and the Ranger would kindly come over to the flat just to hang out. The waiting ended after I met Serikzhan Bilash, the head of Atajurt, at that time the leading activist and research group on the Xinjiang camps.[222] A block away from Almaty's central Green Market, Bavi and I were interviewing Baqytali Nur in a spare room within the Atajurt offices, and Josephine was taking photographs, when Serikzhan walked in. I paused, introduced everyone, made it clear to Serikzhan that I was familiar with his reputation, and thanked him for the use of the Atajurt facilities. Serikzhan responded in English that he knew my name well and made it equally clear that he was familiar with my work on forced organ harvesting.

---

222     The "leading activist and research group" description was indisputably true in Kazakhstan. When it came to direct contact with camp refugees, in early 2020, I would argue that they were second to none in the world.

We bonded easily. Serikzhan may be many things, but he has a big heart. He is also a charismatic showman, and, like a rockstar, he operates on impulse. I don't know where it comes from, but I have a predisposition for feeling comfortable around that type of guy. I stay loose, borrow a fraction of their ego, and slip into the role of trusted advisor. A few days later, I met Bekzat—Atajurt's vice president at the time—and we spoke sincerely about common goals for an hour. Having passed these tests, I was in, and I met many of Atajurt's dedicated staff. They were admirable, serious men and women, with a highly developed sense of tragedy. All of them shared contempt for their competitors, the human rights groups that were working with the Kazakh state. Clearly the Kazakh government had promoted the growth of human rights groups as a way of co-opting and deflecting the explosive movement that had grown up around Kazakh ethnics in Chinese concentration camps. Yet this was not my struggle. I was here because the camp refugees were here and Serikzhan and Bekzat knew that.

Serikzhan recorded at least one video every day. These messages all began with Serikzhan saying in a calm voice, *Attention, attention*, and I could boil down his central message to this: *The Kazakh state has failed you. They have allowed China to seize our sons and daughters. And the human rights groups that the Kazakh state allows to operate? They will fail you too. If you want justice, come to me.*

Atajurt operated on the knife's edge. Technically illegal enough to be fined by the Kazakh state, but too hot for the state to prosecute fully. Serikzhan had a weapon that none of the other human rights groups had: The people were with him. You could feel it in every room. *Attention, attention* went viral online. On any given day, the Atajurt office was jammed with supporters and victims alike. Other than funding, all was well. The disappearances among the core group of

Atajurt, the first death in Kazakh police custody, Serikzhan's detention, and following his release, Serikzhan's clumsy move to an anti-Uyghur public stance, his ultimate exile in the United States, the mass arrest of Atajurt's staff, including Bekzat—these were all in the works, but had not yet been put into motion.[223]

Serikzhan understood that I wanted a low profile, but the day after Bekzat interviewed me, Serikzhan opened one of his YouTube videos with a statement: *A famous author has come to Almaty. If you were in a Chinese camp, and you have a story to tell, then you should talk to this man. Just contact Atajurt. I'll do the rest.*

In better times. Left to right: Serikzhan, the author, and Bekzat at Atajurt headquarters.

By Josephine de Haan-Montes.

Serikzhan made that announcement unilaterally, but I was secretly relieved that he did so. Yes, Kazakh security might be alerted to our presence, but every day now ran like a well-oiled machine. Serikzhan would make the pitch. We would go down to the Atajurt office—everyone understood that we would only communicate in person—and Atajurt staff would send witnesses to an establishment

223  Regarding Serikzhan's move to a Uyghur-critical stance, my working theory is that the Kazakh authorities broke him during his detention by putting members of his family under direct threat.

close to our flat, where Bavi or Ranger would collect them. Serikzhan and Bekzat never knew our actual location.

We needed to refresh our Kazakh visas, so, accompanied by Ranger, we made an overnight trip down to Bishkek, Kyrgyzstan. Ranger's advance work allowed us to interview an important new Kyrgyz camp refugee, Ovalbek Turdakun (or K-man, as I called him).

It also allowed me to pull out some cash from a Bishkek ATM. I didn't really need the money, but a cash withdrawal would send a Wow! signal to my wife—she watches financial transactions carefully—that I was alive and well in Central Asia.

In hindsight, this dramatic gesture was an unnecessary risk. I previously gave my blessing to Josephine to call her parents and her boyfriend using three of our precious stock of burner phones. I could have easily told Josephine to tell Ben to call my wife and inform her of our progress. We were already ignoring our rules: burner phones weren't supposed to be used for anything but short, informational calls. And while the use of a Kyrgyz ATM seemed harmless (the chances that Kazakh and Kyrgyz security were fully linked up seemed remote) both of my North Atlantic intelligence contacts had cautioned me against this exact behavior.

One morning, I sent Josephine and Bavi off to meet with Serikzhan. It felt like a good team-building exercise, and their body language signaled how much it delighted them to be on their own. A few days later, I sent them off again. Mid-morning, I took a leisurely drive down to the Green Market area, parked, and put my Reflectacles on to avoid electronic recognition from the surveillance cameras in the area. An obvious plainclothes informant was standing outside the entrance of the building containing Atajurt headquarters. I could have waited, or I could have turned around and gone home. Instead, I'm certain the agent recorded me as I stalked into the building.

A week later, there was a blizzard, and I parked my car in the deep snow, not far from our safe flat. I wasn't sure if it was a legal space, but I assumed the snow would disrupt parking regulations even if it was not. On my drive down to Atajurt the next morning, I was pulled over by the police, and while I assumed that they were just looking for a bribe, they directed me to the front of the RAV4 and pointed wordlessly at the space where my license plate had been. After they explained that the local police were probably holding my plates somewhere, I was so visibly upset that the policemen retreated to their vehicle. Using up one more burner phone, I contacted my lawyer friend, Aiman Umarova. Aiman advised me to chill out. She identified the correct police office, went down to the station, raised the roof, and ended up passing the plates to me from the open window of a taxi as she made her way to the airport. It was magic—and such a frivolous waste of Aiman's formidable skills. It also pared down our operation to a specific neighborhood.

When a Uyghur orchestra came to Almaty, we went along to the theater with Ranger. The Uyghur musicians were superb, *the finest entertainment in Central Asia*, Ranger said. Josephine loved the dancers, and the costumes, and it was a lovely reward for all of us. But we were the only foreigners present, and the audience undoubtedly contained Kazakh security agents, so we probably shouldn't have been there at all.

While I suspected that our collective shelf-life might be coming due, a sign of my own deterioration appeared at home. The ground level convenience store for our flat, a Kazakh 7-Eleven, had figured out exactly which vodka brand I favored, and about what time during the night I might drop by. To my irritation, the owner would have a bottle waiting for me next to the cash register without my even asking. Is there a strategy to be drawn from this? Not really. Just that, like a convex mirror, *I was rotting faster than I appeared.*

It was around this time, near the end of February, that Ranger made a unilateral decision to give us a smartphone. It was clean, he said, registered to someone completely unconnected to our circle. The Ranger's motive: *I'm sick of you guys getting lost in Almaty.* By now, Josephine and I were used to life without the internet. Having brought a small library, we read books and listened to Kazakh folk music on Josephine's transistor radio. So we virtuously ignored the new smartphone, only turning it on in the car. But I did sneak in a couple of minutes to catch up on the news.

A coronavirus was apparently spreading throughout China. Most of the world appeared to be untouched, aside from France, Japan, and South Korea, but there was obviously a lag in reporting new cases, and, based on the original Chinese SARS crisis, I suspected the Chinese Communist Party had leaned hard on its health ministry to suppress the actual case count of SARS-2, probably by a factor of ten, or perhaps much more.

*Ethan, what do you think of the coronavirus?*

*I don't know, Jo. For what it's worth, I took an epidemiology course back in college. I guess the good news is that it doesn't look like it's very deadly, especially for youngbloods like you, but based on the way it's moving, I suspect it's really, really, contagious.*

*I was thinking that I might go ahead and buy a mask? I saw some at the mall drugstore.*

*Yeah, maybe go buy some masks. But please don't start wearing one Jo. We don't even know how it spreads. A mask will draw so much attention. Two whites wearing masks? Everyone will think we have it.*

*Okay, so we do nothing. . . ?*

*No. . . . Look Jo, I'll tell you what I'm really worried about. Countries are going to start checking people's temperatures. There will be quarantines.*

*And then, at some point, they'll panic and close the borders. And the ferries won't run. And it will all happen really fast.*

*Shit.*

*It's just a question of time. Or you know, Jo, maybe it will just fizzle out? But there's a real chance that we could get stuck, maybe here, maybe even in Europe.*[224] *If we get stuck here, Kazakh security will go through everything.*

*Ethan, you have the interviews. Maybe we should start thinking about driving back.*

*Yeah. And maybe using the fast route this time.*

*Russia?*

*We would need visas. I'll ask around.*

The strategy was to *adapt early to changing circumstances. Stay mobile. Don't get stuck.* There was a well-lit travel agency in the building next door. Our return home began with me and Josephine making the short walk over to that building the following afternoon. A few days later we were at the Russian embassy with a female Kazakh travel agent who whispered, *Your British passport is okay, just don't say anything about being American,* as she introduced us to the Russian Senior Consular Officer. We each received five-day visas to drive through Russia.[225]

It was at this moment that James Stram came biking into Almaty, with amazing tales of his travels (and hardships, which he laughed off). He also confirmed what the Ukrainian truck driver on the Black Sea ferry had said to me. The southern road, through Uzbekistan, was so terrible that James had taken to just riding through the desert for long stretches.

James claimed that he had always suspected that we were doing

---

224   As awareness of Covid-19 became widespread, James Stram would get stuck in India for nearly a year.

225   We did not have to specify dates, but we had to pick the Russian entry point (Orenburg Oblast) and the exit to Estonia (Pskov Oblast, said to have shorter wait times).

*something* other than skiing, so we made him an honorary member of the team for two aborted efforts to get the interview sound files, my notes, and other documentation out of Kazakhstan.

The first failure occurred at DHL, the Eurasian equivalent of FedEx, within walking distance of our flat. We put all the materials into a DHL box, filled out the forms, sealed it, and handed it to over the counter to the DHL rep. But as we hit the street, Bavi told me that the rep had almost imperceptibly whispered to him: *Kazakh security will go through these things.*

*Ethan, if they go through it, they can get the witnesses. I don't think this is okay at all.*

Bavi was a little nervous, confronting me. But I embraced him, saying *my mistake, you're right. Let's run back to the office.* With the faintest trace of a smile, the DHL employee told Bavi that he had not gotten around to sending the package out. We retrieved everything.

That night, we had a few drinks and decided to try to send the electronic files (mostly interviews) via Wetransfer.com. Suddenly our Internet slowed to a crawl. I had experienced this in China on a sensitive date like June 4th or when one was under targeted surveillance.[226] I felt suddenly sick as a wave of paranoia washed over me. The careless mistakes were coming due. We'd soon have the police at the door. I hid the materials inside the stove cooker hood.

*I did it! I'm guilty! Take me away!* As I quoted George the Georgian's bleary words on the Caspian Sea ferry only half-jokingly, I calmed down. Josephine calmly suggested that she could simply photograph the notes: *Ethan, think about it. How many border crossings will have a darkroom, and all the equipment necessary to develop black and white film and print contact sheets? Wasn't that our plan all along?*

---

226    The slowdown probably stemmed from our devices updating everything after a long absence and WeTransfer not liking the sender's location.

While James and Josephine fixed lights on the documents and took photos, Bavi and I sat down together and came up with an approach. We would put the interview sound files on data sticks— one was even disguised as a lipstick case—and Bavi would populate the data sticks with a million stupid images, sound files, and other electronic trash. I came up with the idea of keeping those data sticks in the RAV4's coffee holder, in plain sight, next to chewing gum, a half-eaten sausage or an apple core, and lipstick-smeared Kleenex. We would turn the RAV4 into a trashed hotel room from a vacation's final days—*some velvet morning*—and drive the rat's nest across the Russian border.

Was this a good strategy? Well, it seemed a decent improvisation under the circumstances. Kazakhstan is an advanced electronic surveillance state by all accounts on the level of, if not fully controlled by, Russia's Foreign Intelligence Service (SVR).

Testing Reflectacles' facial recognition interference on Chinese surveillance products in an Almaty retail center. By Josephine de Haan-Montes.

Transferring sound file interviews through the Internet, even to a safe corner of the cloud, may, or may not be, be a secure process.[227] The answer may be different for other Central Asian countries, but for Kazakhstan, I can only offer lukewarm strategic advice: *Currently, I am not aware of a failsafe procedure to export information from an advanced high-surveillance police state. Maybe in the future. Follow the evolving technology.*

\*   \*   \*

The next night, the final night, Josephine and I threw a party for the four wolves. Ranger brought his kids. Bavi DJed. Even our Kazakh friend "Buzz" from the Caspian Sea ferry showed up.

Final night in Almaty. James, "Buzz," the author, and Josephine. By James Stram.

The next morning Bavi helped us carry our bags down to the car, and then he turned to Josephine and me. We all embraced, and for

---

227   In China, my working assumption is that even a short burst of secure messaging or file transfer would give away one's location and could be followed by arrest.

those two minutes, Josephine and I felt so deeply sorry to be leaving Bavi behind.

As we hit the road out of Almaty, Mark Pidgeon, the British pub singer, who had somehow unlocked the marching cadence behind a familiar traditional song, came on the CD player again. We were back on that unfinished highway construction site, with the familiar dirt roads crossing back and forth over the Chinese-financed tarmac.

*O'er the hills and o'er the main*

*Through Flanders, Portugal and Spain*

And we swerved around the curves to the marching rhythm, swinging to the left and right, roaring:

*King George commands and we obey*

*Over the hills and far away*

We planned on making Shymkent by nightfall, but the clouds and the snow came in fast. On the top of a hill, all the traffic came to a dead halt. The Kazakh police were closing the highway but annoyingly made us wait while they did it. I finally made an illegal U-turn in the twilight, and we found ourselves painfully retracing our steps back to Taraz—*Cop City*—for one last night. In despair, we even chose the same hotel.

Over the days and nights that followed, we faced a rerun of the desert drive, but in unplowed snow, which somehow seemed preferable to ice. At least this time, I was free of the illusion that we were descending or ascending into heaven or hell. At the end of the empty quarter, where we had to turn onto a highway heading west, a police car pulled us over for no reason at all. A tall, young policeman gestured for me to come back to his vehicle.

By now this was routine, the fifth time in Kazakhstan. Negotiate the bribe, aiming for 100 dollars, or the equivalent in Kazakh currency. Pull the cash out discreetly. Keep your hands below the camera. But this time the young policeman sitting beside me had a fixed smirk, a deeply disrespectful look. Behind him, sprawled out over the back seats was a middle-aged policeman, likely a lieutenant, sleeping. The vehicle reeked of booze and sweat.

The young policeman announced in simple Russian: *We are taking you down to the station.* He started the patrol car, and, as it began to move, I cried out like a four-year-old Russian child: *Stop it! Stop the car. My daughter—in my car. She does not know how to drive. If you take me away, she. . . .*

*We are going now.*

*No. No! You will see.*

I pulled out my wallet, and the patrol car stopped, and the young cop's eyes were fixed on my hands, but instead of a wad of cash, I handed him the business card of a friend at the US consulate in Almaty. I was intending to explain that I was, you know, well-connected, but instead, the lieutenant roused himself from the back seat, and snatched the name card from the rookie cop. The lieutenant stared at the great seal of the United States—*eagle incarnate from Rome to Washington.* He looked at me, linking the generic American name to my face. Then he yelled to his subordinate:

*What the fuck are you doing!! Get him out of the car! Immediately!*

*No, Officer! We have to say our proper goodbyes!*

And I made a production of slapping my right hand on my heart and then making the young rookie candyass grip my trembling cold hand. I walked back, slowly, to the RAV4 and Josephine, my heart leaping out of my chest.

*Well, how much did you give them?*

*Nothing.*

*Ethan, I'm so proud of you,* Josephine said, laughing.

Regarding strategy: *Yes, I got away with it, but I do not recommend pretending to be a member of the US diplomatic corps, even if it's a case of mistaken identity.* And yet, that night, having settled into whatever cheap truck stop we landed at, all the crap of the Kazakh desert fell off my shoulders, and I slept like the dead.

It snowed throughout the night. The next day, we passed a handful of trucks jackknifed in the drifts, including at least one fatality. Our last night in Kazakhstan, we made it to a town near the Orenburg exit to Russia, which had an overheated hunting lodge for rent. We toasted cheese sandwiches, downed Belenkaya vodka shots, and made endless jokes about nothing that I can remember, while snow piled up on the windowsills. It was our Dr. Zhivago moment, just before the reckoning.

Approaching the Russian border the next morning, we stopped to fill up on cheap Kazakh gas. I threw my codeine pills into the trash, since the Russians have a zero-tolerance drug policy, even for legal prescriptions. I pried open the cover of my Dictaphone, tore out a couple of vital components, and reassembled the device. It had taken me a month to find that antique Dictaphone back in London. It would take the Russians a week to find an antique Dictaphone that could play those cassettes with their precious interviews, and between that and the facilities and chemicals needed to process black and white photographic film, they would have to hold us at least that long. Then Josephine and I spilled the contents of every suitcase into the RAV4, transforming the vehicle into a highly curated pigsty.

We were the only customers at the border. Customs and entry had been streamlined into a single office. We were told to leave the RAV4 and wait in an unheated single-line hall covered with slush, while two female border agents addressed us. They were sitting on opposite sides of the well-heated office, staring into their high-end desktop screens. We went through the usual questions with the woman closest to us, careful to speak only in English. We sensed that she was the junior partner, but at least we could see her eyes. The senior associate, the one we could only see from the back, began slowly delivering skeptical questions, like an artillery barrage increasing in intensity as it closes in on the target. My Russian is poor, but this was my approximate understanding:

*So. What does he do?*

*He's a writer.*

*What kind of writer?*

*Political. Investigative.*

*Okay. And what countries does he write about?*

*China.*

*Not Russia?*

*China. I don't see anything on Russia. I'll search again. . . No, nothing really. But he writes about doctors. And organs. Killing for organs.*

*Oh, for fuck's sake. Who would he see?*

*I don't know. Chinese in Moscow?*

*Well, they are only here for five days. And they will have to drive most of the time just to get to Estonia.*

The back and forth, and the exasperation, went on for another five minutes. Then the unsmiling border agent said, "Here are your passports." It occurred to me much later that their Google search hadn't turned up my Brookings Institution research on the nuclear warfare capabilities of the *Soviet Union* (not "Russia"). We thanked her and walked back with studied ease to the RAV4. Perhaps it had been moved, almost imperceptibly. But if they had installed a tracking device, I didn't care anymore. There would be no Chinese and no Kazakhs in Moscow, just a vast empty hotel and a full day in Red Square for Josephine's entertainment.

The gate lifted, *La Bamba* came on the CD player, and the road was *plowed*. After months in Kazakhstan, it felt like a miracle.

A father and son, ice fishing, wave to us from the Ural River. By Josephine de Haan-Montes.

Five days of beautifully plowed roads later, with Russian convicts shoveling off the bridges, we were at the Estonian border. We waited for four hours while the guards looked for a receipt of entry from the post-Soviet Commonwealth of Independent States (CIS), a final bureaucratic impediment to entering the Schengen Zone. Once we realized that they wanted a piece of paper specifically from the Red Bridge border with Azerbaijan, I dug it up from the RAV4 trash pile, and the Russian border guard and I performed a prisoner exchange: He accepted the receipt, while I disconnected the British consulate from Josephine's phone. We shook hands, the best of friends now, and 60 seconds later, we entered Estonia

First, and only, road trip selfie, Estonia. By Josephine de Haan-Montes.

After five minutes of driving in the zone of freedom, a bad feeling came on. Like an actor who has just completed a long performance, I felt fragile, wrung-dry, and slightly hysterical. Perhaps someone—my beloved uncle, or my father-in-law—had passed away. I couldn't reach my wife on Josephine's iPhone, so I called my son's boarding school and insisted that they drag him out of class, so he could assure me that everyone was fine, proving once again that I did not possess psychic abilities.

I did not have to keep it together anymore. I have no strategy to offer here, other than: *Whether it is Estonia or Aralsk, when you finally make it into relative safety, consider pulling into the first hotel, ordering two stiff drinks, and check in for the night.*

We made our way to Berlin in two days and to the Hook of Holland in one more. Decompression was setting in. It was enhanced when we drove onto the ferry headed for the English coast. Instead of armed guards, we were met by young crew members, riding bicycles, wearing summer shorts, smiling, and telling us to just park anywhere we pleased. My request for a free cabin upgrade, based on nothing at all, was rewarded with a first-class stateroom for two, with a grand porthole facing the bow.

As the ferry pushed back from the dock into the North Sea night, Josephine and I went out to have a smoke on the front deck. No passengers joined us. Yet there were at least twenty truckers to the right of us, having a drink and a smoke, separated from the passenger side by a chain link fence. My friendly nod in their direction was not returned, for we were no longer nomads. Their road stretched out to the horizon of a working man's life. Our road would come to an end with a two-hour drive into London tomorrow morning.

My wife had arranged a small party for us, so after dropping off Josephine's bags in the morning, we simply fell asleep on the couches at my flat and surfed mindlessly for most of the day. When the guests arrived—Enver Tohti, Josephine's sister Gabrielle, and my wife—we pulled out the Russian vodka and mottled tins of caviar that Josephine had purchased in the GUM department store on Red Square (just before we, and everyone else, gawked at the masked Chinese tourists spilling out of GUM, for all the world looking like hunted animals, and I could imagine the world's borders still crashing shut just behind us).

No one in London was thinking about the Coronavirus yet. And no one was all that interested in our story, or perhaps, in the story as we wanted to tell it. There almost seemed to be gentle disappointment that nothing had gone wrong. It wasn't quite: *No car chases? No cigarettes extinguished on Josephine's arm? Just numerical estimates of organ harvesting selection in the camps?*—but, well, it all *seemed* anti-climactic in the telling somehow. Josephine admitted that camp refugees talking about their passport problems had bored her at times, and Gabrielle laid into Josephine's insensitivity. Enver went on a tear about unreliable Uyghur witnesses. My wife wondered when I would shave off that scraggly beard.

But *nobody got arrested or killed,* Josephine and I kept repeating solemnly, like a couple of maudlin drunks.

We behaved badly, or at least, self-indulgently. But then, that night, so did everyone. The party was a premonition—nothing to do with the Land of Make Believe this time—of my new, strange, incompatibility with ordinary life. My strategy for the aftermath had been *build your cover, nurture it. Then ditch it, and the beard, on the side of a Schengen Zone highway.* But I didn't follow my own directive. In less than a year, I'd be leaving on a new tour of duty.

# 7

# THE COUNTRY OF LOST UYGHURS

This chapter serves as a faded remnant of a shelved project to exploit an obscure legal technicality. Perhaps that technicality could have changed the trajectory of Beijing's war on the Uyghurs and Kazakhs, perhaps not. The value of the field research undertaken is for the reader to judge. The project was the brainchild of Rodney Dixon KC of London, who has close connections to the International Criminal Court.

Secluded and double-landlocked, Tajikistan is the poorest nation within the core Central Asian states. To relieve its global isolation, a local Dushanbe activist told me that Tajikistan "likes to join everything." In 1998, Tajikistan, alone among the core Central Asian states, became a signatory to the Rome Statute of the International Criminal Court (ICC).[228] Here's the legal twist: According to Rodney there is ICC precedent to investigate non-signatory countries, such

---

228    I exclude Afghanistan's complex relationship with the ICC because the "core" Central Asian states
       are less defined by geography than by their shared history as former Soviet republics. In the reader's
       interest, to keep the word-count under control and to promote "flow," this is also my final footnote.
       From this point on, my on-the-ground Tajik and Kyrgyz witnesses and my forced labor refugees in
       Turkey represent previously unpublished, original material. The critical organ harvesting references
       have already appeared in Chapters 2 through 5, are directly contained within the text, or, in the case
       of the final chapter, there are references within the PowerPoint presentation images and text which
       readers can easily access.

as China, *if China is operating in an ICC signatory country, such as Tajikistan.* Theoretically then, the ICC could investigate all of Beijing's actions against the Uyghur and Kazakh peoples.

The problem for Rodney was that Tajikistan (and to a lesser extent, Kyrgyzstan), from a field research standpoint, is a blank. Serikzhan Bilash, the head of Kazakhstan's Atajurt group, told me he had plans to investigate Tajikistan on the ground. But year after year, events precluded Atajurt inroads into the circumstances of Uyghur refugees in Tajikistan. What existed were rumors, third-hand accounts of a Chinese-run effort to deport Uyghurs back to Xinjiang.

Rodney called my colleague Adrian Zenz at the Victims of Communism Memorial Foundation looking for someone who could do the field research in Tajikistan. Zenz brought up this potential tour of duty directly with me.

I'm not the sort of bloke who falls asleep thinking the world's okay because the ICC is on the case. Frankly, I don't think Rodney is either. However, living in China did give me some insight into the Party leadership mindset.

The ICC evolved from the Nuremberg trials. I believe that the Chinese leadership, on a visceral level, fears three scenarios: 1) internal purges, 2) a Ceaușescu-style popular revolt and 3) a lost war over Taiwan followed by ICC trials of the CCP leadership.

The status of Uyghurs in Xinjiang, in my view, is one of *deferred genocide*. Uyghur tissue types are mapped after age 12, and the alkaline hydrolysis crematoria are functional. Potent Uyghur activism in the West combined with German anthropologist Adrian Zenz's systematic analysis of leaked CCP documents has creating a sustained Western media narrative: Beijing is accused of mass detention, forced labor, tubal ligation, and rape. The Party plays for stalemate: eventually democracies will run out of genocide declarations, fresh outrages, and sanctions on cotton, tomato paste, and human hair wigs. The ICC venture would be a wild card, a gamble, yet I thought it might keep the game going or even win a critical hand if Uyghur survival was on the line.

Rodney and I are both optimistic by nature and keen for adventure. To ward off my post-Kazakhstan PTSD, I needed a new foray, the wilder the better. But there was also a simple human impulse, which emerged from my travels in Turkey.

"Killer China, killed my sister in the camp!" By the author

We arranged to meet with Kuresh Ibrahim, whose sister was killed in camp and had lost his wife to a "re-education" camp three years ago. His story is more routine than you might think. Half the Uyghur refugees in Turkey live with the fact that some of their extended family back in Xinjiang are incarcerated. For children, it's the orphanage. One death in the family is not unusual. If it's an adult in their late twenties, it's often talked about as a "disappearance."

I also met with a group of Uyghur mothers in exile. Chinese officials had separated their children from them a few minutes before their plane took off for Istanbul, on a technical pretext. *Don't worry. Your children will be on the next plane*, they were told.

There's a broken, distracted look in the women's eyes. They are desperate for information, yet a glimpse of the truth can be shattering. One mother saw her tiny daughter in a Chinese state broadcast about Chinese State care of Uyghur children. She was alive, healthy, growing, yet her hair was shorn in the Han Chinese style, and her face, a mask of submission. Another mother thought she saw her teenage daughter on TikTok digging a ditch in sync to a generic pop song.

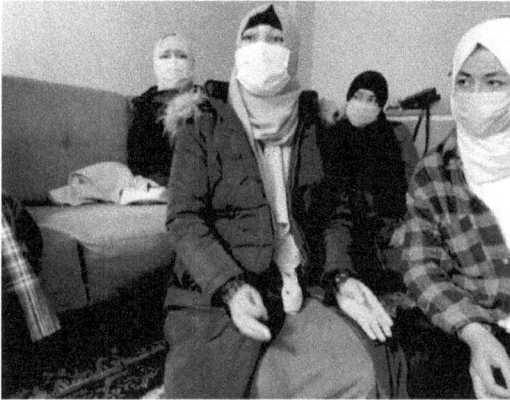

The orphan mothers of Istanbul. By the author.

I can't help them. People give me sheets of information on their wives, their husbands, their kids, all painstakingly translated, but I've given up handing over case files to the State Department. There are too many. Instead, I feel a transactional obligation to listen, to take a photograph of Kuresh's makeshift banner, and to remark on the children's faces. Perhaps I have the power to distract them temporarily from their survivor's guilt. All these witnesses are safe in Turkey, for the moment. President Tayyip Erdogan's agreement with Beijing reportedly to deport approximately 10,000 undocumented Uyghurs to Tajikistan in exchange for Sinovac vaccinations, is said to have stalled in the Grand National Assembly. For now, perhaps, but Beijing doesn't forget a deal.

I'm not an activist, but I must do *something*. Maybe I can get my best fixer, Bavdun "Bavi" Umer to come along. We will be moving through a world of Covid restrictions. I briefly considered purchasing life insurance, but now I've agreed to Rodney's terms.

This partially explains my strange hurry-up dance, urging Bavi to speed through the Kuresh interview, and get to the point: because Kuresh worked in the Tajik bazaars. And we have a plane to catch.

*　*　*

What you will read here was once a confidential account for the ICC only. I suspect preserving that serves little purpose anymore, so let's get those yellowing pages out into the sunlight because the original impetus still matters. If the Chinese Communist Party pursues and entraps people in Tajikistan, based solely on their ethnic and racial identity, to deport them to Chinese concentration camps, what does that tell you about Beijing? Perhaps the Nazi roundup of the Hungarian Jews and Romani speaks to you. It does to me. The US silence in the wake of Beijing's Belt and Road Initiative and China's extraterritorial aggression in Central Asia speaks to me too.

Like all documents of this nature, it leads with an executive summary. What follows has been lightly edited: some descriptions of individual witnesses have been altered or truncated for their protection, and I've added a few personal comments.

## OVERVIEW

This is a mid-point assessment on the status of Uyghurs in Tajikistan.

We left the Chinese border area two days ago and are currently on the banks of the Panj, overlooking an Afghan border town occupied by the Taliban a few weeks back. Over the next couple of days, we will make our way through the Pamirs back to Dushanbe, and, if a local flight becomes available, continue to Tashkent, Uzbekistan, then on to Osh and Bishkek in Kyrgyzstan. Sources tell us that some Uyghurs who formerly worked in Tajikistan may be found in these three locations.

There are many questions remaining. For example, we cannot make an estimate of how many Uyghurs crossed the China-Tajikistan border to escape persecution in Xinjiang over the last two decades. However, we have confidence in the following conclusions:

1. Uyghur entrepreneurs from Xinjiang started the largest bazaars in Tajikistan's three main cities: Dushanbe, Khujand, and Qurgonteppa. These Uyghur merchants and their families constitute the vast majority of Uyghurs in Tajikistan.

2. Ten years ago, well over 1000 Uyghurs worked in Tajikistan's bazaars. Just a little over 100 remain.

3. Every Uyghur in the bazaar may have been associated with one or two others at home (for example, a wife and a child). There were 2500 to 3000 Uyghurs in Tajikistan ten years ago. An 85% to 90% reduction of the Uyghur population over time is generally consistent among our witness accounts.

4. Some of the Uyghurs fled to Tashkent, Bishkek, Osh, and Almaty back in 2015. Most of the Uyghurs who worked in Tajikistan's bazaars went back—or were deported—to Xinjiang between 2017 to 2019.

Beijing used two methods:

5. First, the exploitation of family ties. Chinese authorities threatened family members in Xinjiang with detention based on "foreign contacts." The Uyghur expat in Tajikistan would receive a series of increasingly urgent phone calls from the family, imploring them to come home to East Turkestan, "just to check in," or to "help the family."

6. Second, the use of force or implied force. The local Chinese Consulate would intentionally delay visas and other paperwork. Chinese Public Security Bureau operatives inside Tajikistan and local Tajik police would exploit these irregularities to interrogate Uyghurs at the bazaar (in one case the police locked down an entire bazaar for questioning) and then forcibly deported Uyghurs to Xinjiang, likely through the Kulma Pass. The deportation was carried out in batches of approximately ten people at a time to avoid international attention.

7. Only a handful of the Tajikistan Uyghurs have returned from Xinjiang. The Uyghurs who are allowed to remain in Tajikistan have little or no knowledge of the fate of their former colleagues, and it is considered dangerous to make inquiries.

8. The Chinese Consulate controls the remaining Uyghurs who work in Tajikistan bazaars through a system of rewards, threats (from the Chinese Public Security Bureau and the local Tajik police), and internal Uyghur informers.

9. Our visit to the Kulma Pass checkpoint confirms that Beijing is using Covid-19 as a pretext to tighten control of the border in both directions. While Chinese operators may, in some cases, be allowed to carry cargo into Tajikistan, Tajik truckers, who formerly might spend a couple of days in a "Kashgar turnaround," are presently forbidden to enter Chinese territory. Formerly a working border—it was even used by the occasional Western backpacker—the Kulma Pass is now exclusively a container exchange point.

10. The Chinese have occupied a sizeable amount of former Tajik territory to the north of the Kulma Pass border checkpoint. Photographs taken from our vehicle demonstrate that the Chinese have constructed a formidable three-layered barbed-wire barrier, including elevated 360-degree surveillance cameras at regular intervals, armed patrols, and what appears to be a newly completed and substantial Chinese military base. Our conclusion is that these barriers were not simply constructed to keep Tajiks from allowing their herds to graze in the new Chinese territory. The barriers were also constructed to prevent potential Uyghur refugees from the Kashgar area from entering Tajikistan by foot.

What follows is a detailed, personal, and confidential description of the field research that has led to these conclusions.

## BACKGROUND

Kazakhstan and Kyrgyzstan are like Mars. The air's a little toxic from industrial effluvia, but it's mapped out, and Kazakhstan is target rich.

Even Kyrgyzstan has a government-approved office sympathetic to camp refugees, however toothless its dealings with China. All of that was on the eve of the pandemic; since then, two of Atajurt's founding members have died in medical or Kazakh police custody (author's note 2026: the other founders, are currently under arrest and awaiting sentencing), and Chinese agents, or cut-outs, beat two camp witnesses so badly that they required extended hospitalization. I would revisit Almaty, but with the Covid pandemic as the pretext, Kazakhstan is suddenly requiring elaborate business visas of all foreign visitors.

When it comes to Uyghurs, Tajikistan isn't even Mars. It's Venus: wrapped in clouds and seldom visited. Although Tajikistan shares a significant land border with China, close to the major Uyghur population centers of Kashgar and Artux, it's usually not considered a viable Uyghur escape route because of the forbidding mountains. Empty Uyghur plains stretch nearly to the first range of the Pamirs and the Tajik border. Freedom is a challenging four-day off-road hike from Kashgar, theoretically possible when the snow recedes in the summer months.

A couple of years ago, *Washington Post* reporter Gerry Shih made it out to Murghab in the Pamir mountains. He reported on a Chinese military base built just inside the southern corner of the Tajik border with China and the northern border of Afghanistan's Wakhan Corridor. Chinese troops from a Xinjiang unit came to town in search of snacks and phone data. Shih learned that they have been there for three or four years, partly in response, Shih theorizes, to the suicide bombing at the Chinese embassy in Kyrgyzstan, carried out in 2016 by the Syrian Al-Nusra Front. The *Washington Post* perspective was that, given the international context, a Chinese military base in Tajikistan is not that big a deal. There's some truth to that; if the State Department succeeds in its current diplomatic initiative, Tajikistan will be the only country in the world to simultaneously host Chinese, Russian, and American military assets.

That the Chinese Communist Party have designs in Central Asia is not in question; Tajikistan, awash in Chinese investment and infrastructure, is essentially a Chinese province, with a bit more freedom of religion. China's military base on the previous Tajik side of the border presumably was constructed to guard against militants, to protect China's investment in mineral extraction of the Pamir mountains, and—this is the controversial and unproven part—to assist in seizing Uyghurs fleeing from China to Tajikistan and Afghanistan and transporting them back to the Xinjiang camps.

A Qurgonteppa state building, Tajikistan. By Bavdun Umar.

If Rodney Dixon can show: 1) that Uyghurs have crossed the Chinese border to escape persecution—and they undoubtedly have, however small their numbers, 2) and that Chinese operatives inside Tajik borders are assisting in taking the Uyghurs back to China, 3) then, even though China is not a signatory of the ICC, the ICC can theoretically investigate China for mass detention, organ harvesting, forced labor, sexual violence against Uyghur women, and so on. According to Dixon, even a handful of witnesses can set the train in motion.

## THE LEAD

Back to Kuresh in Istanbul: Kuresh lived and worked mainly in the Korvan Bazaar in Dushanbe, Tajikistan, for over a decade. He fled to Istanbul when Beijing trained serious heat on the Uyghurs. But he reckoned that there were still Uyghurs hiding out, among them an old friend of his, a man named "Abdurishit," an older, cultured man, a thoughtful man: *Here is his phone number. Perhaps you can find him in the Korvan Bazaar, on the outskirts of Dushanbe. But perhaps the Uyghur Quarter of the bazaar has been cleared out.*

Either way, maybe Abdurishit, if we could find him, could shed light on how the Uyghurs were seized. Was it Simon Legree crossing the Ohio river, whip in hand, or maybe it was a quiet deportation: the gentle knock on the door by a Tajik policeman, the bureaucratic excuse about papers not being quite in order, then the bus with black windows to the border, and more paperwork at the Kulma Pass checkpoint with a representative from the Chinese consulate looking on. All quite legal. The idling trucks would be the last sound of relative freedom before the bus reached a camp, prison, or secret detention center somewhere in the Kashgar region, where the deported Uyghurs would be interrogated and then incarcerated or killed, or perhaps, depending on their age and health, exploited for their organs.

I had some additional sketchy leads; a couple of human rights activists on the ground in Dushanbe, informal local US Embassy cooperation, a local investigator, and my translator/fixer Bavi. I'd worked with Bavi in Almaty the previous year and in Turkey this year. He's brave, and he can read strangers extremely well.

I couldn't imagine that any other reporters would be on the ground, or even many tourists on the road in Tajikistan with the world still under quasi-lockdown. I had my anxiety dreams, but I was also excited by the prospect of *terra incognita*, of first tracks, of getting back on the road in Central Asia.

## METHODS

If you are easily found on the Internet (my Wikipedia page said that I was a "human rights defender," for example), how and where you enter an authoritarian state can determine whether you are followed the entire time, sporadically, or not at all. Having lived in China for three years and having worked with Chinese dissidents for two decades (and interviewed a few police investigators from the other side), I like to think I have a feeling for the human element of Chinese security. Start with the idea that life in a totalitarian state is very dull. So provide distractions and bright shiny objects. Develop a fun and pointless cover story and live it. Try to get in when there's a local holiday and the country is in motion. Most of all, operate on the assumption that the security operatives have surrendered to their screens. Once they start relying on electronic intelligence, they feel in control, and they disregard the beat cop. Yet if you are going to a state that relies on informers and only secondarily on electronic spying, it's not clear that any of this will work.

Rory Byrne of Security First provides spy training for nice human rights types. He told me that I needed a drop system. Holding on to witness information in a one-party state like Tajikistan was too great a risk, so I should download witness findings using *Tresorit*, which maintains a secure portion of the cloud accessible by my home base, the Victims of Communism Memorial Foundation in Washington, DC. Then delete everything sensitive on the local device.

The pandemic was a clarifying factor on the entry—no tourists, backpackers or human rights investigators on the plane in—and the only way to enter Tajikistan was with a visa and through Dushanbe airport border control. The border guards were relaxed, the airport was tiny, and the passport readers didn't appear to work. Following a (non-voluntary) Covid test, the last time I would see anyone wearing masks in Tajikistan, my visa was ruled in order. I did not observe an attempt to check my identity on the web. Back in London, I had created a makeshift "vaccine passport," a bound photo mini-album of my doctor jabbing AstraZeneca into my shoulder, displaying the batch number and so on. The pictures brought a faint smile to the border control policewoman, and a stamp on my passport.

## ON THE GROUND

I'll avoid describing Dushanbe in exotic terms: It's full of trees, Tajiks age well, great food, and so on. More pertinently:

1. It's apparently impossible to buy a true burner phone, a legacy of Tajikistan's relatively successful attempt to keep Afghan terrorists from entering the country.

2. Foreigners stand out even if they have used auto-tan and dyed their beard black (in Ankara, Turkish citizens asked me for directions; in Tajikistan, I got stared at constantly).

3. The Great Leader, Emomali Rahmon, adorns every state building and most commercial buildings as well. Islam, in the form of minarets and mosques and fasting, remains a relatively hidden force.

4. Instead of the call to prayer, around 7 am the police begin broadcasting threats to drivers over powerful mobile megaphones. There's a whole *I warned you bitch!* quality to these arrests, like a drunken man working himself up to give his wife a good beating in front of the kids.

5. The entire country is a small town. Everybody watches everybody.

Tajik policeman using mobile megaphone, Dushanbe. By Bavdun Umar.

I felt like I was starting over in Beijing, 1998. In Almaty, we had a system: there were people who desperately wanted to tell their stories, and some of them even felt secure enough to do so, given our Almaty safe house, and our minimalist security protocols. Here, we would have to improvise.

The first day was spent in our target area: Korvan Bazaar, a market initially started by Uyghurs from China. I've explored a couple of the great bazaars in Baku and Almaty, but Korvan was like a small city, easily a mile, end to end.

We approached three potential fixers in the bazaar but made no immediate progress with burner phones, so we couldn't call Abdurishit securely. At least Bavi was able to identify that the Uyghur area of the market "used to be" by Gate 9. This doesn't sound like much progress but just being back among the swarming crowds and that peculiar raw aesthetic quality of Central Asia—the swarm, the discarded tools, the glitter, and the filth, all in swirling motion—made me want to shout from the rooftops. We had made contacts and would check with the phone fixers first thing tomorrow

Korvan Bazaar, Dushanbe. By Bavdun Umar

The next morning, I woke up at 6:30am, turned on my dual secure-core VPN, and was alerted to an opinion piece by a Chinese/Indian author just released in Asia Times: "Why Xinjiang is central to US cold war on China." It was a hit-piece on Adrian Zenz and, inexplicably, on me. I've written some influential pieces on Uyghur organ harvesting over the years and testified in many government hearings, but over the last two years I've intentionally published very sparingly, just a video talk or brief online presentations to let my patrons and colleagues know what I've found. Adrian, on the other hand, has come out with a groundbreaking new research report every two to three months, with dense global media coverage. Yet this article went to great pains to repeatedly use the phrase "Zenz and Gutmann," portraying the two of us as Cold War operatives who systematically spread lies about the Uyghurs (the Uyghurs, of course, simply want to be left alone). The contrived focus on the Gutmann/Zenz machine was particularly apparent in the early edition (for security reasons, I didn't take a screenshot, and the Wayback Machine couldn't find it). The author explicitly stated that Gutmann is finishing a new book based on his travels in Central Asia and interviews with Uyghur refugees.

Fair enough, a researcher could glean all this simply by watching an obscure one-hour lecture that I gave on Kazakhstan for Victims of Communism. So if I had seen this piece in Vermont or London? I would have shrugged it off as any publicity is good publicity, much the way Adrian reacted in Minneapolis: "Too many attacks like this to count," he said to me. Yet sitting in my hotel room drinking instant coffee on my second morning in Dushanbe, the essay read as a command to Tajik authorities: Follow Gutmann. Interrogate. Deport.

I'd been looking forward to the Korvan Bazaar. Now I felt sickened by the prospect of a day of surveillance, and potentially serious consequences for Bavi, all before we had spoken to a single witness. Over breakfast, Bavi coolly suggested that we should move into a short-term flat as soon as possible. He made some calls. Then we blew the day off shopping at the mall.

## FIRST CONTACT

The next day, anxiety was outweighed by restlessness. We couldn't wait for burner phones any longer—all three phone fixers at the Bazaar had come up short—and there appeared to be a significant risk in continuing to search for contraband SIM cards. So we hit the 9th gate of the Korvan Bazaar anyway, starting up little conversations, walking through the alleys that might have Uyghur sellers, looking for the shadows of the people that, according to Kuresh, had once dominated this vast marketplace.

Eventually Bavi, using his usual charm, was able to establish that the Uyghur sellers were definitively in gate two. On the long hike over to the gate, I was attracting too many fixed stares, so we agreed that I would duck into a small worker's café. Bavi continued into gate number two alone.

About 40 minutes in, I received a single word from Bavi on Threema: "bingo." Bavi had not found Abdurishit, but he had found one of his acquaintances: let's call him "Mansur," a Uyghur fabric seller, about 40 years old, soft-spoken and intellectual.

Bavi approached Mansur, asking for Abdurishit, and the conversation quickly veered into human rights. Mansur gestured toward the back of his stall whispering that Bavi was "very lucky, so lucky" to have found him. The other Uyghurs were *informers*. And Bavi's discreet questions in different areas of the Bazaar had apparently been not discreet at all.

"The entire Bazaar is looking for you," Mansur said, gesturing at his phone. "Everybody knows about you. There are two of you right? And you are the one from Kazakhstan. So, where's your white-guy friend?"

Mansur came from Kashgar in 2005. In 2016, the order came: *return*. Beijing used threats to the family as the lure, visa problems as the hook. Calls and text messages from Kashgar and Artux poured in: *Come home, please.*

"Yes. Yes, of course, many of us suspected it was an excuse to throw us into the camps. Anyway, there used to be about 100 Uyghurs in the bazaar. Now there are fewer than 30."

Mansur is one of the survivors; over time, he acquired all the legal papers and even managed to briefly see his family in Kashgar in

2017. Mansur believes, or wants to believe, his family are still okay. He still supports them financially. Mansur did not know how Uyghurs in the rest of Tajikistan are doing, but he explained in a whisper how the Uyghurs are controlled inside the Korvan Bazaar.

Every Friday, the Dushanbe market people get a day off, and the Uyghurs must attend a meeting led by a man. Mansur described him as "the God of the Uyghurs." Anyway, let's call him "Gazi."

Gazi owns most of the Uyghur restaurants in Dushanbe. If you are a Uyghur, you go to Gazi for favors. If you have problems, Gazi can solve them, because a lot of people work for Gazi at the Bazaar. Some of them work as Gazi's informants. "And Gazi works for China," Mansur said.

Mansur did not whine about Gazi. Mansur acknowledged that the local Chinese Consulate in Dushanbe has provided drugs and medicines to Chinese citizens, and even the Uyghurs, too, during the pandemic. Gazi may work for the Chinese consulate, but there's a certain Uyghur warmth there; Gazi provides financial and community stability, and physical protection. He's an anchor, a point of stability in a twilight, stateless world.

Mansur tacitly seemed to support the Uyghur cause; he winced when Bavi referred to the crimes Beijing has inflicted on the Uyghurs in China. Mansur confirmed that many Uyghurs had been escorted back to China using force. He confirmed that he knew our witness, Kuresh, back in Istanbul. Mansur said that he wanted to help stop the crimes, but they had spoken too long, and they might be reported. Mansur said he would be free Friday, and he would see us confidentially. Then he gave Bavi the new number for Abdurishit.

This first contact occurred within the space of twenty minutes and was constantly interrupted by business and market chaos. Sitting in the café, I received a blitz of Threema messages from Bavi:

*I am coming*

*prepare to go . We need to go now*

*can you gi outside*

*I can not find that cafe*

I met Bavi outside a minute later. He whispered "we go," and we began race walking on the edge of stalled traffic in the noonday sun, just to be in motion, and to find a way out. We turned the corner where we had made our first contact in our fruitless quest for burner phones, fled into a dark taxi and raced away. Perhaps Mansur or Abdurishit would come through, but either way, the Korvan Bazaar was dead to us now.

"Bavi" (Bavdun Umar). By the author

## TO THE MATTRESSES

We moved into a large flat a day later. The owner and the real estate agent didn't ask for a contract, and I had brought enough American cash to pay them both. The flat was a massive, romantically decorated government property, one of the perks of our owner working in the "anti-corruption" unit. We were now in the equivalent of an ornate burner apartment.

We wandered around Dushanbe that day, just to complete the tourist pose. In the early evening, we joined a couple of Kazakhs whom we had met sightseeing, to hang out with an old friend of theirs, "The Colonel," a good-humored man who was apparently the number one law enforcement official in Tajikistan and a towering figure to the Dushanbe police. The Colonel had invited us for Iftar, the breaking of the Ramadan fast, at a relatively fancy restaurant that provided a karaoke-style room without the music, the girls, or the booze.

It was a familiar scenario: The American gets all the questions, and if he shows equal parts of humor and backbone—Central Asians hate apologists—he is rewarded with vodka. The BLM riots had been in the news. My statement, *the US is not a racist country, Russia is a racist country*, followed by my downing a large shot, drew smiles and general noises of approval around the table. My tolerance for alcohol—I appear drunk, but I remember everything—is my lone superpower. I drank one bottle and started in on a second one, allowing me to ask the Colonel some slurred questions about Tajik law enforcement.

*Where do you get your information and intelligence?*
*From informers. We have them everywhere throughout the country.*
*How do you keep them loyal?*
*We pay them.*
*What if the bad guys pay them more?*
*We pay them more than the bad guys can afford.*

Even when I asked directly, the Colonel never mentioned electronic surveillance. Probably because they didn't really have it.

After the dinner, the Colonel invited Bavi and me into his capacious black SUV and proceeded to drive us around Dushanbe for several hours. He picked up his brother, his son, a chick, a loaf of fresh bread, all while flaunting all the rules: speeding wildly, passing via the oncoming traffic lane, and deliberately crossing into sensitive areas of the capital, so that we could see the expression on the capital policeman's face, and the stumbling apology, when the beat cop grasped that he was speaking to the wifebeater-in-chief. When the Colonel finally dropped us off near our burner apartment—Bavi made sure it was a couple of blocks from where we lived—he was definitely "going to the Pamirs with us!" Our friendship, or more accurately his assessment of me as a potentially useful American contact, rather than a spy or some sort of do-gooder milquetoast, was sealed.

With the combination of the safe house and the night with the Colonel (both Bavi and I kept his number handy in case we are pulled in by the Tajik police), the surveillance—you can feel it, even when you can't see it—was switched off. But not for the witnesses. The next day, the reversals began. Mansur made excuses and bailed on any further interviews. Abdurishit finally agreed to a meeting, but it was a bad omen when he didn't take his mask off. He resolutely lied and stonewalled: he didn't know about any disappearances. He didn't know Kuresh (they ate together regularly). His wife, back in Xinjiang, was fine. By way of an of apology to us, or perhaps to himself, he offered one pearl of wisdom: *Maybe Allah will take care of the Uyghurs. It's in his hands.*

Neither of these witnesses were likely to be a security threat. We had acquired a makeshift burner phone at this point, the meeting with Abdurishit was in a secure location, and Bavi and I sensed that both Mansur and Abdurishit had enough residual care for the Uyghur people that they wouldn't rat on us for a bit of the Colonel's silver. Yet these two witnesses confirmed that Gazi was real, and he had a lock on them.

We were safe but defeated, and the days were going by.

I had hedged my bets by previously creating a separate team in a different location, but they were getting nowhere. How could it be otherwise when three out of four people that one spoke to were outright informers? Only one of us had scored a real unguarded interview:

Bavi. He did it by ignoring security "best practices" for a minute and presenting who we were honestly. This was a significant personal risk. There was no doubt in my mind, based on Mansur's interview, that Dixon's thesis was basically correct, but how could we prove anything, if no one would talk to us? And a question had emerged: Why had the Chinese allowed any of the Uyghurs to stay? Why hadn't they taken them all? Perhaps the answer was in front of us; perhaps we weren't just dealing with a country of informers. The Uyghurs who remained in Tajikistan were selected by the Chinese for their venality, passivity, small-mindedness, *and their nearly complete disregard for the fate of their people.*

I didn't like to think about them this way. The Uyghurs who remained were damaged, frozen in place with fear. Abdurishit was suffering. So was Mansur. But something would have to change.

I recognized, from the minute that I arrived at the Dushanbe airport, that my white-guy face, and my chronic incompetence with Russian, constituted a security risk, even greater than Bavi's dash through no-man's-land at the Korvan Bazaar. The logical thing to do was to simply outsource the entire operation. Yet I resisted doing this for four reasons.

- First, risk should be shared.

- Second, I had built a reputation of operating from solid evidence. If I weren't present at an interview, for some people, however unfair it might seem, the interview didn't happen.

- Third, for the witness, the presence of an American citizen opens up the idea of potentially escaping Tajikistan, however unlikely.

- Fourth, Bavi had taken a risk, but what was the "safe" option? To target young Uyghur sellers, but pose as businessmen who just happened to like buying Uyghur hats and so on? Then we would attempt to invite the targets to an intimate little Iftar shindig where we could gently turn the conversation to the Uyghur situation. Safe perhaps, but the young Uyghurs would say: *Why can't you just discuss business at the market stall?* Caught in a lie, we would have no choice but to grit our teeth and smile harder.

- No. *Share the risk.* If we expected witnesses to say who they were, we would have to say who we were, and why we came here, and wait for the hammer. But I refused to take chances with nothing to show in return. So, we would bend the rules: Bavi did not record Mansur, but from now on we would record witnesses surreptitiously and download them into our secure outpost of the cloud as quickly as possible.

## SOUTHERN MAN

We headed down to Qurgonteppa, the third largest city in Tajikistan. After an afternoon in its Bazaar, a fraction of the Korvan Bazaar, really, we attracted a group of dedicated watchers as we made our way through the Chinese fabric section, the traditional domain of whatever Uyghurs were left. As we bargained at one stall with a friendly young Tajik couple, they invited us to Iftar at their house. I think the invitation was sincere. They were intrigued by having an American at their house—

yet an hour before we were to arrive, they called and stated that their grandfather had just been admitted to the hospital. Would they be at the market tomorrow? Maybe, maybe not. It all depended on their grandfather's health, you see. Whatever Gazi-equivalent existed in the Qurgonteppa market, he had laid down the hammer.

Qurgonteppa bazaar, entrance to the "Chinese Market." By Bavdun Umar

It was a moment of despair, a new low. But we found a cheap hotel, rose early the next morning, and headed back to the bazaar. We were invited for tea at stall after stall but our attempt to find the one lead that we had generated the day before, a Uyghur seller named Abdul, simply stalled. At this point I noticed a dilapidated stand, apparently closed. Dying for a cigarette, I wandered over and lit up. A man sitting nearby made some motions that smoking was forbidden. He was apparently a security guard for the bazaar, and we engaged in a pleasant conversation while I asked him, in my broken Russian, to forgive me, and he assured me, as if explaining to a child, that *we always forgive the first mistake!*

As he wandered away, a door opened from the inside. It was a wiry middle-aged man, close-cropped hair and wise, slightly mocking, eyes. I said hello. Bavi had just arrived and began a process of pleasantries, revealing that he was a Kazakh citizen but a Uyghur by birth. The man hustled us inside.

We call him "Southern Man." A Uyghur born in Xinjiang, he had a connection who about twenty years ago had opened bazaars in Uzbekistan and Tajikistan and a cargo business, mainly importing from China. Southern Man was a smuggler. Nothing gave him greater pleasure than describing the best way to drive a ton of meat across the Kazakh/Uzbek border using back roads. We interviewed him for four hours, and contraband occupied three of them. Eventually, the connection closed the company, and Southern Man took on managing three stalls.

From the beginning, this was a share-the-risk interview. Southern Man began revealing information about the Uyghur diaspora in the first ten minutes and then asked us why we were so interested. The UFO had landed, and it was time to say that we came in peace. "Human rights" I replied.

This is Southern Man's assessment of what happened to the Uyghurs:

"There were more than a thousand people in the Tajikistan bazaars back in 2017. It was crowded with Uyghurs. From 2017 to the Summer of 2018 the Tajik police came in and started detaining Uyghurs. The local police took the Uyghurs and gave them to the Chinese consulate. Then the Chinese consulate sent them to China."

Bishkek was even worse, Southern Man added. But a softer method was employed with some of the Uyghurs. Family members back in Artux or Kashgar would call in and ask them to return home. "Your mother will be in prison if you don't come back," they were told.

The Uyghurs were cleaned out. According to Southern Man,

there were over 400 Uyghurs in Dushanbe, mostly from Artux, the vast majority working in the market. "Now," he said, "there are 40 to 50 people left in the Korvan Bazaar." (Mansur had estimated 30 Uyghurs remaining in the Korvan Bazaar). In Khujand, it wasn't quite as bad. Southern Man estimated that it had been 300 Uyghurs in the Bazaar, and there were 60 or 70 people now. Qurgonteppa was the worst: over 300 Uyghurs, now 18.

## SOUTHERN MAN'S ESTIMATE OF UYGHURS IN THE TAJIK BAZAARS

| BAZAARS | PRE-2017 | CURRENT | LOSS |
|---|---|---|---|
| Dushanbe | 400 | 40 | -360 |
| Khujand | 300 | 60 | -240 |
| Qurgonteppa | 300 | 18 | -282 |
| **TOTAL** | 1000 | 118 | -882 (88% loss) |

If any single quality characterizes Southern Man, it is that he is not a fantasist. He may be a shark (he tried to set himself up as a fixer for pay at one point, and we had to inform him that he was a primary witness and could not play any such role), and he may almost pathologically mistrust the West and foreigners in general. Yet it is my impression, and Bavi's as well, that he is honest about what he knows and what he does not know. Southern Man was not claiming that he knew the exact figures of Uyghurs in the markets, only in Qurgonteppa. Nor was Southern Man claiming that he knew how many Uyghurs were in Tajikistan at any given time, only those Uyghurs who directly worked in the bazaars.

If we assume that some of these Uyghurs had family members who did not work in the bazaar directly (for example, Uyghur couples tend to have at least two children if not more), we can easily imagine that the bazaar figures could be multiplied two or three times to arrive at a crude estimate of Uyghurs in Tajikistan, both before and after. For example, we could speculate that there were approximately 3000 Uyghurs in the pre-2017 era and approximately 350, or probably far fewer, now.

This is not simply a theoretical point. We ended up interviewing three witnesses, one from each market: Southern Man from Qurgonteppa, Mansur from Dushanbe, and a young man whom I'll call "Nazur" from the Khujand bazaar.

Khujand Bazaar in the North. By Bavdun Umar.

Of these witnesses, I'll spend the least time on Nazur, essentially a somewhat charming drug-user. He did not agree to extensive interviews, in part because he had little confidence in himself or his ability to make good in the West, if that were a possibility. Even the Chinese consulate rejected his recent request to go back to Xinjiang. I suspect Nazur was attempting to flee from his debts.

Nazur's powers of observation are low. While he confirmed what we had already learned, that the Chinese had cleaned the Uyghurs out of the markets, and that the remaining Uyghurs are tightly controlled, he had few details to add. The one exception may have been the numbers. Possibly through an ambiguity in the translation of my question, he said that there "were thousands of Uyghurs" in Khujand in 2017, when he first arrived. He was clearly not referring to workers in the bazaar, but Uyghurs as a whole. He thought the number of Uyghurs in Dushanbe was about the same. Nazur had no information on Qurgonteppa during the same time period.

This is thin ice to build an estimate of Tajikistan's Uyghur population from 2017 to the present, and we may never know the numbers with certainty. Indeed, it bears repeating that the Chinese Consulate may have selected the Uyghurs who remain in the Tajik markets in part because of their disinterest in such sensitive questions.

Tajik witnesses in the markets of Khujand and Dushanbe— we spoke to several—tended to have sympathy for the Uyghurs' mistreatment by China, both in Xinjiang/East Turkestan and in Tajikistan, and they were aware that the number of Uyghurs had drastically diminished from their bazaar over the years, yet they had little in the way of numerical estimates.

## CHINESE CONTROL

This is Southern Man's account of the current systems used to control the remaining Uyghurs in the Qurgonteppa Bazaar:

"The bazaar has a contract with China. China has not listed the Uyghurs officially. They don't pay taxes, for example. Only the Han Chinese pay taxes, not the Uyghurs. The Chinese director of the bazaar contract is in the Chinese consulate. The Chinese Consulate's main instrument of control is that all visas for the Uyghurs must go through them. This allows the deportation process to start, or even stop, at any time. Simultaneously, the Consulate offers benefits, for example, medications for Covid-19, and an exclusive pipeline for Chinese fabrics."

The enforcers of the Consulate, the beat cops, are Chinese Public Security Bureau agents. As Southern Man said, "If there are 18 people, there are 18 agents." These agents share daily meals, often two times a day, with the local Tajik police, including a few police recruits drawn from Artux, where most Uyghurs in the bazaar originate. Drawn on a napkin, it looks something like this:

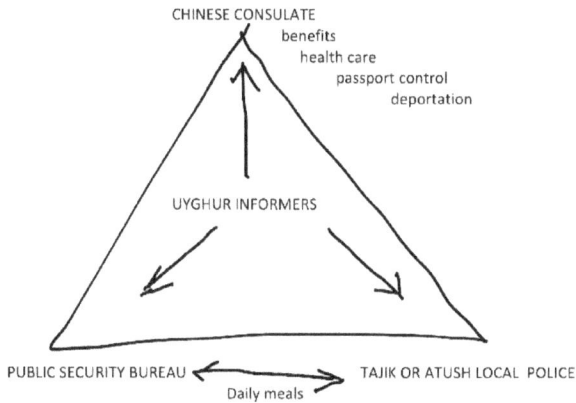

CHINESE CONSULATE
benefits
health care
passport control
deportation

UYGHUR INFORMERS

PUBLIC SECURITY BUREAU ⟷ TAJIK OR ATUSH LOCAL POLICE
Daily meals

We asked Southern Man, is it possible to speak to anyone in the bazaar? In a low voice, Southern Man described a once vibrant Uyghur community that had become isolated, atomized, and adrift:

"People here are living in stress, even after 10 years in Tajikistan. They are afraid to go home, afraid to stay. They are depressed. You can go home, and you can come back. But they cannot. And if you ask them to speak to you? You are teasing them, in a sense. You are free and they are not. They are afraid. They cannot talk to you. Some of them are drunks now. The Chinese Consulate loves this. If there were 100 Uyghurs here, they would all be afraid of each other. Since the crackdown started, there are no more *meshreps* [traditional Uyghur Muslim parties]. People do not talk to each other. They gossip. They report."

Southern Man made a frank assessment of his own chances of survival inside the current system.

"The other Uyghurs are afraid of me. . . . But I'm scared of them too. They watch me. But I'm relaxed. I'm a good-time guy. And they see my friends, my supercool friends The first one, he goes to the prostitutes, so he's a sex maniac. The second one, he drinks. The third one, he smokes. So the [Chinese] Public Security Bureau does not think that they have to watch me that carefully. And I avoid people like you because I do not know if you are good or bad. I look in your eyes and I see 60% good, but 40% bad."

Indeed, this ratio would shift back and forth in the coming weeks. Once Southern Man realized he couldn't get any money out of us, he began to prevaricate. Maybe he would tell these stories to the larger world someday. Maybe not. And he is not altogether wrong about us; we did tape him without his knowledge on two devices, really, just as a way of taking notes. He came up to Dushanbe a week later and clarified some of the points in the original interview (we did not tape him the second time).

Southern Man hasn't sold the clean phone that I loaded with Signal and a VPN, not yet anyway. If he does, he can still be found again. But he has already taken a significant risk to himself and his family, and I respect this too.

## THE TAJIK POLICE

If Southern Man provides one inside view of what happened to the Uyghur community, a local Tajik investigator, "Leo"—I will leave it there—can provide some insight into the Uyghur deportations from the perspective of Tajikistan's police forces. Leo spoke with law enforcement insiders, mostly working professionals, to create a comprehensive picture of the Uyghur deportations. Leo is a sincere man, and he spoke with confidence about his findings.

Leo began by saying that in the North, in Khujand:

"It went down like this. Fifteen years ago, maybe 12 years ago, the Uyghurs opened up a bazaar. It was a majority Uyghur bazaar, dominated by Uyghurs from Artux. They were trading in fabrics, Chinese mostly, and most of the region was buying from them. They had good fabrics and good prices. The owner of the bazaar was a Uyghur man, most likely from Xinjiang. I can give you his name if you need it [Bavi would ultimately interview him in Istanbul]. Anyway, he was set up on some sort of taxation charges–that's the hearsay anyway—and he lost the ownership of the bazaar."

Leo paused.

"I went to that bazaar every year, but I noticed that there were fewer and fewer Uyghurs trading there over time. Then in 2016 to 2017 there was a drastic reduction of numbers of Uyghurs trading in the bazaar, particularly middle-aged Uyghurs, female Uyghurs. There were a couple of hundred Uyghurs selling in the bazaar; now there's a maximum of. . . maybe 15 Uyghurs there? And of the Uyghurs that are left, some say: 'We might be leaving soon.'"

"I asked them: 'Why would you leave?'"

"Because our families have been calling us."

Leo paused to gather his thoughts.

"So yes, the Uyghurs started to recede in 2015, and they would go off to Kyrgyzstan and Uzbekistan, or go home to Xinjiang. But then in 2016 to 2017, there were raids, conducted by the local police force. At one point the police cordoned off the entire bazaar. My friend, a policeman, saw this, and even participated in the sweep. They would take the Uyghurs out. And the Tajik police would say, 'There is a problem with your documents. You must go back to China. No, there is no discussion, you have broken the law, you must go back.'"

"That's the way it was. There's always a problem with the registration. They wouldn't get their documents extended. They also closed many Uyghur restaurants. These were very popular."

According to Leo, a SWAT Team containing mixed forces (Tajik ICE, responsible for customs and enforcement, and the Kommittee for National Security or KMV, responsible for expat control) carried out the forced removal of the Uyghurs.

"My contacts saw this, and they saw them being taken to deportation centers. The centers were near the airport."

Guard post from a distance, Chkalov city SWAT team headquarters. By Bavdun Umar

Leo's account is correct. Bavi was able to establish—it's kind of an open secret among cab drivers—that they took the Uyghurs to Chkalov city SWAT team headquarters, an eight-minute drive from Khujand Airport. Then they would be interrogated, processed, and flown to China. As Leo points out, his contacts did not see the actual deportation, but I suspect the guard tower that Bavi photographed from the taxi was possibly the last sight of Tajikistan for those who entered a bus with no windows. Although, as Leo points out:

"There was a direct flight from Khujand to Urumqi back then. They were taken away in batches."

"Why did they take them away in batches?"

"In part, to avoid people like you finding out about it. To avoid noise."

"Why did they leave any Uyghurs behind?"

"Well, we are fellow Muslims, so it's a little easier for us too this way. And they cannot kill off the business completely. Don't wreck the Silk Road, the goods must continue to roll in from China. The Uyghurs traditionally occupy this role."

"Who controls the Uyghurs now?"

"The KMV [the Tajik successor to the KGB]. Local police will only do what they have been told to do. The KMV has direct contact with the Chinese Consulate. The local police does not have contact with the Chinese Consulate. Because the local police will leak."

Leo said: "For the Chinese it's easy to be in Tajikistan. There are no consequences." And he speculates that five Chinese-owned plants in Tajikistan provide the Party with almost unlimited economic clout. He refers to a road worker incident back in 2014, where Chinese workers were openly permitted to rough up a bunch of local Tajik road workers as a symbol of China's free hand.

"The Chinese know where the money can be made, and they make it."

"Aside from the Uyghurs, were other groups deported?"

"No."

"Were the deportations being done on behalf of Beijing?"

"Only the top people know. It creates deniability."

"What do you think?"

"I asked my friend [a Tajik policeman] that question, and he said: "I don't know. Maybe they [the CCP] fed the Tajik government some information about terrorism. We have orders to deport the Uyghurs. We had a job to do. We did it."

## THE CHINESE BORDER

The entrance to the Kulma Pass. By Bavdun Umar

We had three objectives in the Pamirs.

First, to learn whatever we could about Uyghurs coming over the Tajik border (or being taken back to the Chinese border) in Murghab and to look for signs of Chinese military influence. We made it to Murghab, but I became too friendly with a potential informer quite early on, and, in the interests of safety, I bailed out from questioning others. I suspect that people were telling the truth when they said that few Uyghurs had passed through town.

Second, to see if the Kulma Pass checkpoint was still a possible escape route for Uyghurs coming from either direction and to assess whether it could be used by a human being coming over the border on foot.

Third, to view any Chinese military installations. It's germane that the world's largest uranium deposit is close by in Tajik territory.

The second and third objectives were potentially the most demanding, so we saved them for last. Fortunately, we were joined by an American volunteer.

James Stram in Tajikistan. By Bavdun Umar

A reminder: My daughter Josephine and I became friends with James in Azerbaijan, on our way to Almaty in December 2019. We were coming from Germany, while James had started his trip much further away, in Spain. But the key difference is that we were driving an SUV and staying at trucker motels, while he was riding a bicycle and sleeping in a tent. I was impressed by his easy, stoic attitude, his physical courage, and his blog, "James on a Bike," gave him the perfect eccentric-American cover story for his presence in the Pamir mountains. I've lightly edited his "4x4 ROADTRIP" blog entry.

"The day started like the rest, a change in plans. Instead of heading to Karakul we would spend more time further south and attempt to drive up to the Kulma Pass to see the Chinese border with our own eyes. The road from Murghab to the pass was only slightly less scenic and slightly less maintained than the rest of the Pamir hwy. In other words, it was awe-inspiringly beautiful, and you had to hold on to the door handles with clenched fists. For long stretches it was better to just drive off-road in the desert then avoid the potholes in the road. An hour or so past Murghab there was a large road sign, indicating distances and letting us know who was responsible for the nicer pavement ahead, completed in 2000. Probably an early part of the Belt and Road Initiative. It was the first man-made object we'd seen for a while. Once we passed the last (and only) intersection the road only goes to China. There was a checkpoint and a reasonably strong barbed wire fence extending as far as you can see on either side of the checkpoint. Our driver, and all-around great guy. . . talked to the Tajik soldiers at the checkpoint. After a while a soldier whipped out his old soap bar cell phone and called his superior. Eventually. . . [our driver] got to talk on the phone, and explained that we (Bavi, Ethan and I) are among the first tourists in the country since Covid, and since my round-the-world bike trip got cut short in Almaty I've been dreaming of biking the Pamir hwy, and if possible, crossing at the Kulma Pass to the Karakorum hwy in China. Letting us see the pass would be a great way to welcome tourists back to the Pamirs. He agreed, as long as a soldier rode in the car with us. Done and Done."

"Our new soldier friend was a super nice guy. 24 years old, sporty, and a had a good eye for spotting wildlife. Other than one Kyrgyz yak herder, who had special permission, there were no people on this side of the fence. . . . [Our driver] was taking a pretty big risk by bringing us there. Bavi, our Uyghur translator, fixer, and photographer certainly got some justifiable chills approaching China. If we did get interrogated at some point, Ethan and I had the backing of the American empire, Bavi. . . not so much."

The Chinese border, Kulma Pass, May 2021. By Bavdun Umar

"We got up to the border, and it really sunk in. We were 14,313ft high, surrounded by mountains much higher. It was cold, and windy, and you could clearly see the Chinese flags, and giant Chinese characters on their border station. There was a Chinese style pagoda, with what looked like a soldier in it staring at us. The Tajik side was a little less Orwellian, but still not very inviting. Another soldier came out to meet us. He was also very friendly. We were told not to take any pictures, and our passports were checked again. . ."

"We learned of a couple of Chinese citizens that were denied entry back into China, due to Covid apparently. They attempted to cross illegally in the mountains but were spotted, and then rounded up by Tajik guards and brought to the Chinese border station, where they were quickly admitted into the country, straight to jail. While we talked about border stories. . . Bavi walked to the toilet and covertly snapped some of the best and only pictures of this border station. . . . He was able to take more pictures, and then swap out the SD card with one of just fun tourists pics, in case they asked to see his camera."

"We said goodbye. . . . As we drove away we offered the border guard some candy and he took the whole bag. We headed back down to the checkpoint feeling quite accomplished. After stopping to snap some pics of a couple of dead Yaks we dropped off our soldier, with 100 somoni ($9) in his hand."

The Tajik border fence. By Bavdun Umar

The Chinese had recently taken land from Tajikistan, extending their border down into the valley, taking valuable grazing land from the Tajik herders and bringing their border within spitting distance from the road from Kulma pass to Rangkul. We had to see it.... [Our driver] asked our new soldier friends about the status of the road (think poorly marked jeep path). They said it would probably be passable, so [our driver] took the opening to say we would try, but we might come back if it's too wet. A cover for the possibility that we would get to see the Chinese border fence and then turn around."

"Getting there was quite the drive.... At one point sand dunes had encroached right up to the Tajik fence, and after looking for another way, we figured the only way to continue was to actually cross through an opening in the Tajik fence. I gave it a semi-real chance that as soon as we did there would be sirens and angry voices on loudspeakers, maybe even Chinese voices. But we used some logic and made the decision to continue. It was still Tajik territory, and the only way towards Rangkul, which the soldiers approved us going to."

Chinese military base in newly acquired Chinese territory. Camera in foreground. An FBI analyst believes that the bulk of the base is underground. By James Stram

"As we continued we got some good pictures of a new Chinese base on the border, which was quite a tense moment. . . . The Chinese border was triple barbed wire fences, Chinese flags every 50 ft or so. Also, every 100ft or so was a tall post with a pair of giant cameras, and the cameras were rotating to follow us as we drove by. The feeling of being watched was palpable. We didn't dare slow down or roll the window down. At one point we drove past a man standing outside his truck by one of the cameras, just staring at us. . . . We tried our best to take as many pictures as we could without being too obvious, at one point Bavi handed the fancy camera back to me since the rear windows were a bit tinted. I'm sure the pictures China got of us are way better than the ones we got of them."

Chinese triple wire fence seen from "no-mans-land". By Bavdun Umar

"Finally the road veered away from the border. We stopped at a scenic spot and took pics of some yaks and mountains, we are tourists after all, and talked to a local herder. Ethan couldn't contain his satisfaction, and gathered us for a big group hug, "It doesn't get any better than this. . . ." "I gave it everything I could." Bavi was still quiet, but with a successful grin on his face, this could be the photo that gets him a new life in Hawaii. I felt useful, and got a nice rush from the adrenaline. We then hurried back into the car and drove straight back, on possibly the most beautiful road in the world, to the little trucker canteen in Murghab where we had become regulars."

Turning away from the border (Tajik base on left, 2nd probable Chinese base on right).
By Bavdun Umar

Our discovery, the presence of a Chinese military base north of the Kulma pass was not accidental. Back in London, before I left for Turkey and Tajikistan, I spent a day scanning the Tajik-Chinese border on Google Maps. Not far from the Kulma Pass, there was a small, indescribable nest of blurry brown clouds that appeared to be rendered or at least unnatural. I had no explanation, only that this visual anomaly was hiding the base (it's visible now). It is also relevant that one of the largest global concentrations of uranium in the world, a "yellowcake" mine, lies less than 50 kilometers away. We had driven by the mine a few days before. I suspect that the Party may have already drawn a nine-dash line around it.

## KYRGYZSTAN

Flights out of Dushanbe were prohibitively expensive because of Covid, so we had to exit Tajikistan by crossing the northern border to Uzbekistan on foot. Uzbekistan is considered somewhat protective of its Uyghurs, although the Uyghur language and traditions are gently suppressed in favor of assimilation. Yet in the Kokand bazaar, reportedly established by Uyghurs, we were able to confirm from the local vendors and the security supervisor that the market experienced an exodus of its Uyghur merchants over the last couple of years and is now Uyghur-free.

A few days later, James was turned back from the Kyrgyz border because he had an American passport (in an irrational Covid technicality, typical of that time, US passport holders could only enter Kyrgyzstan through the airport, while, as a dual citizen, my British passport was kosher). James was ultimately able to fly back to the United States four days later.

From an investigative standpoint, every border crossed in Central Asia reduces one's invisibility. We had to cross two borders, on foot, to get into Kyrgyzstan and one of our party was publicly turned back. Our goal was to avoid risking the identity of the Tajik witnesses. Therefore, we decided to keep our time in Kyrgyzstan relatively short, just under ten days. We had to work fast.

What happened to the Uyghurs of Kyrgyzstan? Bavi and I interviewed two Uyghur witnesses, Axman in Osh and Teaman in Bishkek. Their collective testimony was very similar to Southern Man's: The Party implemented a mirror-image deportation process throughout the Kyrgyzstan markets in tandem with the Tajik operation. The key difference is that the Kyrgyz deportations exploited electronic surveillance rather than a human informer system, and the Uyghurs of the Madina market in Bishkek, a key thoroughfare on China's belt and road, are young, wealthy, and well-supplied with Chinese export products. Yet a numerical comparison over the same time period between the Uyghur deportation rate in Kyrgyzstan (87%) and Tajikistan (88%) is essentially identical.

Axman/Teaman estimate of Uyghurs in the Kyrgyz bazaars

| BAZAARS | PRE-2017 | CURRENT | LOSS |
|---|---|---|---|
| Madina | 3000 | 500 | -2500 |
| Kara-Suu | 1000 | 45 | -955 |
| Dordoi | 400 | 35 | -365 |
| "Chameleon" | 300 | 4 | -296 |
| **TOTAL** | 4700 | 584 | -4116 (87% loss) |

Rodney Dixon converted the report that you have just read into evidence for internal use by the ICC and created a short press release, heavily redacted to protect the Tajik and Kyrgyz witnesses. Bavi and I worked on a follow-up ICC report using new Uyghur witnesses in Istanbul that amplified the extent of Chinese PSB activities throughout Tajikistan. Ultimately Rodney Dixon's pitch to the ICC was covered by the *Economist*, the *Independent*, Reuters, AP, Radio Free Europe, and the *Times* of London.

If a Congressional delegation wants to go on a fact-finding mission on the Pamir Highway, I'm available. I know the right driver and I suspect the Colonel, because he's a good sport, might appreciate an invitation too.

## PERSONAL POSTSCRIPT

Let's go behind the curtain. The *New York Times* was supposed to be first with the Tajik story, and the press conference was supposed to take place a week earlier. I received a message from Dixon when Bavi and I were still in Osh, mentioning that the NYT and the *Times* of London stories were imminent. I didn't want to have a fight with Dixon over sub-par communication on both sides, so I told Bavi to leave his phone behind while we went for a midnight walk to Sulaiman-Too Sacred Mountain, a stunning rock formation that towers above Osh. Sitting on a stone ledge, I explained that we had a day, maybe two days, to get out of Central Asia. We would have to catch a plane to Bishkek tomorrow and then fly standby to Istanbul.

*Why, Ethan?*

*Once the* Times *of London and the* New York Times *story comes out, the Colonel will realize what has happened. They'll retrace our steps. They'll make a deal with Kyrgyz security. They'll start looking for us at the airports.*

*No, that won't happen. The State Department will protect us. They know we are here.*

*No Bavi, no! I mean, didn't you ever watch* Mission Impossible *when you were growing up? The State Department will deny any knowledge of us. It's always been like this with spies. And that's what they will say we are. I'm so sorry. I thought you knew this.*

Bavi was silent now, staring into the emptiness of the cliffs below us. Seeing his stricken face in the moonlight was like being physically injected with a guilt serum.

*Okay Bavi, okay. Let's walk back to the hotel. I'll call Dixon now and beg him to hold the story for a week.*

Dixon agreed. Piqued, the NYT dropped the story completely. The *Times* of London agreed to hold the story back for a week.

Five days before Rodney Dixon had scheduled the new press conference on our secret investigation, Bavi and I went to the Madina bazaar. It takes approximately six minutes to walk through the Uyghur section, particularly if one is trying to count the surveillance cameras. They are affixed to the ceiling, eight feet apart, like a sprinkler system, creating an visible gauntlet. There is no corner to hide in, no action unseen, and no one really knows who is watching and listening at any given time. One of our witnesses, a Medina bazaar veteran, related a story about receiving a call from a Chinese authority telling him to replace his shipping container because it was rusty and decrepit and getting on his nerves. About halfway down the hall, you know you have arrived at the Chinese section of the bazaar because the cameras disappear.

Despite the surveillance, Bavi insisted on going back to the Uyghur section and systematically attempting to find a potential witness. After an hour of trying, I suggested we go to the loading dock. I lit a cigarette and told Bavi that he had been incredibly brave, not just in the Madina Bazaar, but throughout all the bazaars of Tajikistan. We came in with no solid leads. Bavi built them purely on the look of a man's face or a movement of their eye.

*I'm grateful, Bavi.*

*Ethan, I do not do these things for you. I do them for my people.*

If that sounds hostile, we both knew it was the opposite. Rather than passing the accountability to me, Bavi was acknowledging his responsibility for the risks he had taken.

Before we left Tajikistan, I bought Bavi an open-ended ticket to Istanbul. Two days before Rodney Dixon had scheduled the new press conference on the investigation, Bavi and I were planning to leave Kyrgyzstan. The night before the flight, I suggested that Bavi should use that ticket tomorrow morning.

*Bavi, let's face it. We're a hot mess right now. Cooked. Finished. Chewed up. I'll get us a couple of rooms in a Turkish hotel with a nice, heated pool. Kazakhstan is dangerous for you now. Trust me here.*

*Ethan, the Kazakh border is an hour away. I need to see my dad. He has a heart problem.*

I flew to Istanbul, and Bavi made his way on foot back into Kazakhstan. It's possible that Tajik or Kyrgyz authorities traced our investigation. Either way, a few weeks after Dixon's press conference, the Kazakh police took Bavi down to the station and asked why he was working with Mr. Ethan Gutmann. The police said Gutmann was a very bad man and that Bavi was now their informant. It all spilled out on a Signal call to Bavi's home. I'd never heard his voice sound like that before.

I reached out for help with my US government and human rights contacts. A rumor campaign started behind my back, that I had somehow "gone native." After my return from Central Asia, I fractured three teeth from grinding at night, an indicator of PTSD. With this betrayal, as if discarding one's foreign team member like a used tissue would somehow demonstrate that I was *a serious man*, my jaw started to work on a fourth tooth, an indicator of rage.

I could already see the writing on the wall. *The ICC would do nothing about Chinese operations in Tajikistan.* It's even worse today, so again, let's break the fourth wall. Given the ICC's grossly overplaying their hand in the Israeli case and the subsequent hardening of US political opposition and contempt for the ICC's already tenuous legitimacy, along with the ICC chief prosecutor who has several sexual harassment cases biting him in the ass, *I would never have put Bavi under risk for such a gang of feckless poseurs.* If that's going native, then yes, I did it. I'm guilty. Take me away.

And yet, *de facto* loyalties had formed. Rodney Dixon and Bob Fu, and a couple of key allies in the State Department and the UK parliament, understood Bavi's value, or maybe they just didn't want to deal with my hairy eye. We arranged for the Kazakh authorities to "accidentally" intercept a message from the UK that Bavi was *a person of interest.*

Maybe that worked. After a month or two, Bavi made his way to Almaty airport on a cheap commuter bus. My State Department contact in Kazakhstan theorized that if Bavi could just make it to passport control without incident, the Kazakh authorities would be glad to see his backside. State was right.

Bavi never did make it to Hawaii. But a few years later, on his own initiative, Bavi ignored the Kazakh military's final attempts to draft him (presumably to the Ukrainian front) and "went native" in Kentucky: Green card, driver's license, outdoor pool, living the dream. So, here's to Bavi publishing his memoirs, and I hope they'll be titled "Pool Party!"

Sometimes things just work out.

# 8

# THE ROAD TO SLAVERY

It's morning in Istanbul, and Joseph is locked into a 50-yard-stare. We have the world's most beautiful view from the top floor of an old-fashioned Istanbul hotel. The Topkapi Palace is up the road, Hagia Sophia's on the left, the Bosporus on the right. But Joseph is reliving what happened in 2018: incarceration, torture, forced labor, "drug therapies," and nearly fatal illness in a Xinjiang concentration camp.

Joseph's birth name is Ovalbek Turdakun. I use his adopted Christian name because I don't want to jinx his run of nearly supernatural luck. His wife, Julie, grimly determined to ingratiate herself with the Xinjiang camp authorities, was able to get Joseph released in just under a year. That was their first miracle.

Making it across the Kyrgyzstan border in 2019 with their 9-year-old son Daniel, perhaps the only such case that anyone is apparently aware of, was miracle #2.

The family settled into a dismal cold-water flat where I first interviewed "Joseph" in Bishkek, Kyrgyzstan, back in 2020. When I returned to Bishkek in June 2021, coming from Southern Kyrgyzstan this time, Joseph asked me for miracle #3.

Chinese agents were openly monitoring him and had passed the word along that on December 17, 2021, Joseph and Daniel, the two members of the family with Chinese passports, would be deported from Kyrgyzstan back to Xinjiang. That would leave Julie, a Kyrgyz citizen, to pine away in the Kyrgyzstan mountains somewhere. After warning them that this would not be easy, I promised to try to help them escape before the deadline, but I knew that Bavi and I had already attracted too much attention in Kyrgyzstan.

When I returned to Europe, I went to my friends, starting with Bob Fu. With the assurance of financial and professional support from China Aid, a Chinese Christian group based in Texas, which quietly runs the world's most experienced dissident rescue operation, I called my friend Conor Healy, a guy in his mid-twenties who had already distinguished himself as a *wunderkind* expert on Chinese surveillance. He boldly volunteered to lead the physical rescue (he admits he was at least one sheet to the wind at the time). I won't say that much about Conor's rescue. It's a good enough story that he ought to tell it himself, except that there are some techniques worth emulating right now—traveling with a crowd, building a plausible cover story, and not losing one's nerve when the lights go out in the apartment, and you are the only apartment with that problem in all of Bishkek, and you think that the next sound will be the door being kicked in by the special police (it was a blown fuse). And some cautionary tales: If you are going to buy a whole bunch of plane tickets in a taxi one hour before the flight, *Argos*-style, make sure you have the best mobile provider that money can buy, or choose a different country. But the bottom line is that Conor is an imposing man, about six and a half feet with an intellect to match the frame. And critically, Conor used every facility, every strength in his possession, to make sure that the Kyrgyz authorities did not break up the group at passport control.

The family was on a plane out of Bishkek on December 15th with 48 hours to spare – technically it was miracle #3, but Conor, Bob and I called it *a Christmas Miracle.*

Merry Christmas from the Turdakuns. Joseph, Julie, and Daniel enroute from Bishkek to Istanbul. By permission of Conor Healy

Now I'm in charge of the Argos part of the story: looking after a very worried family who do not think that I know what I am doing. It's April 2022, but miracle #4 hasn't arrived. The family has been waiting in Istanbul for the Department of Homeland Security to grant approval for them to enter the US. I can't read Julie's thoughts, but I've been here with the Turdakun family for over two months now so I am developing a familial sense of the things she can't say to me, at least politely.

*Why did we leave? At least back in Kyrgyzstan we could speak the language. Maybe we could have hidden somewhere. At least we were in control.*

Julie's right about the control part; Bob Fu tells them to change flats every week. I tell them to avoid buses and metros where the Turkish police occasionally perform spot checks of IDs. A few weeks ago, Julie came down pretty hard with Covid. I haltingly mentioned to Joseph that the family should avoid getting PCR tests or even routine medical treatment. It was an ugly thing to have to say, but Joseph already knew that Turkish authorities might easily report them to the Chinese consulate. We heard reliable rumors that the Chinese authorities were furious that the family had slipped out of Kyrgyzstan. Deportation from Turkey would mean almost certain death for Joseph, and the Chinese orphanage for Daniel. He's a very bright boy, gifted with languages. If he were lucky, the PLA would remake him as a spy for the Chinese Communist Party.

The family has escaped from outright hell, but Istanbul is purgatory, a waiting room filled with treasures of the east, many of them booby-trapped. And whatever degree of heaven that America can provide comes with its own costs:

"Ethan, will there be television cameras filming us in Washington, DC?"

"Could be, Joseph. Look, you are the first Christians to make it out of the Xinjiang camps and into America. The first Kyrgyz family. Maybe even the first intact family."

"You will make sure there is no Chinese media there, right?"

"I can't do that Joseph. The US is a free country."

Julie can't hold back: "Can we cover up our faces then?"

"No."

Joseph smiles in a sad way: "Tell me again. Why do we have to do this?"

I choose to ignore the my-wife-still-has-family-in-Kyrgyzstan subtext and respond:

"You mean, what we are doing today? It's called 'media training.' We are just trying to get you used to the camera. Look Joseph, the press is interested in you. If the press weren't interested, we would be waiting here much longer."

Joseph comes out with it, the memory that haunts him. After the prisoners had sung Communist songs for their breakfast, Chinese concentration camp guards liked to play a video, shot in cinema verité style. It began with Chinese plainclothes agents tackling Uyghurs, cramming them into unmarked cars, and pulling bags over their heads. Then, the camera would pan to a wider shot, revealing, not China, but a foreign street with signs in German, Arabic, or English. Joseph says the film was a tease: *Run away. Please try it. We're everywhere. Even Washington, DC.*

Our conversation is being shared remotely with a British media expert, part of Rodney Dixon's team. Sensing that Joseph is warmed up, she speaks Chinese:

"Joseph, there's one question that any American reporter will ask you: We've all heard from the Chinese Government that the 're-education camps' are over. That you have all been retrained. Now they have shut the camps down. There is no more forced labor. Everyone has gone home."

Joseph is silent for a moment. Then he starts sketching on the notepad in front of him, and his voice drops: "Let me tell you about my camp, about the buildings where I lived."

"The walls were 18 inches thick. Exactly. Reinforced concrete. I believe it has a metal frame inside. The cell doors are thick like that, too, just a few inches less, but they are metal. Like a bank vault, you see? Each door has eight electronic locks: two to each side, top, bottom. When they release that door, you could hear the bolts snapping back."

Joseph drums his fingers on the table: "One after the other. Now, the door can open. But there is a massive steel bar in the middle. This bar holds the door to the concrete frame. So, you really have only a crack in the door, just big enough for a prisoner to duck his head underneath, just wide enough so they can shimmy through. Every prisoner took two minutes to get through that door, nearly an hour to empty the cell on average, you understand. But it didn't matter to the police how long it took. Everything they did was about preventing escape. All the corners were rounded, so we couldn't hit our heads on a sharp corner and then somehow run away from the hospital. Each prisoner had three police assigned to them; if you were big and fat, you got five."

Joseph explained that even if the police magically disappeared during a natural disaster, the robust walls ensured that the camp would become a mass tomb. "Even a 7.0 earthquake could not free us from such a structure."

"Do you think anyone builds something like that to last a year or two?" Joseph asks, his gaze falling on the screen, then on me. "No, of course not. This is for the future. This is permanent."

It was our last media training. Three weeks later, we flew to Dulles. US government officials greeted the Turdakun family at the immigration line with Washington DC baseball caps and freshly baked chocolate chip cookies. Miracle #4: America came through. Yet we hadn't put so much effort into rescuing Joseph because he had Party documents or nuclear secrets. Leaving aside the raw humanitarian pull of a family about to be ripped to shreds, we rescued Joseph because he has a superpower: total recall, a nearly photographic memory of the internal camp layout—the fleeting glimpse of the rape room and the exact location of every Hikvision camera, even the one above the toilet. Every day, Joseph whispered questions to his cellmates about the camp's factory, until one of them hissed, "You are trying to form numerical estimates, aren't you? Stop it. You'll get us all killed."

"*This is for the future.*" Joseph is referring to a conditional future, one where the Uyghur people survive, but are permanently exploited for slave labor.

I swear by witness testimony gathered in the field, but I do not believe in crystal balls. Instead, two observations: First, CCP policy often moves like a steamroller. Once a direction is set, it's difficult to change course. Second, one way to assess Joseph's prediction—it's not the only way, but it's the road less traveled—is to follow the historical trajectory of Uyghur forced labor through the voices of the laborers.

Seeking out Uyghur refugees, with legal status or otherwise, I travelled to Central Asia and to the center of Turkey. Local authorities correctly view this sort of investigation as bad for their countries' relations with China. So, I approached the refugees very quietly. Most had family in China, so I did not demand names. I recorded their testimony, sent it out securely, and deleted it from my mobile device.

I interviewed an elderly Uyghur man with the classic white beard and steady gaze in a southern Kyrgyz village not far from Osh. Since he had grown up in Xinjiang/East Turkestan, local Chinese officials ordered him to work about three days a month back in 1985. When I asked him the nature of his work for China, he grinned at the formality of my question and said, "I shoveled shit for the Party."

A Chinese intellectual or "black class" who had been sent to the countryside during the Cultural Revolution might have talked about such an experience for hours. Even Xi Jinping mentions getting manure splashed on his face as a village party secretary. For elderly Han Chinese, these are rite-of-passage humblebrags. Their children *won't ever have to work in such jobs*. Yet not a single Uyghur or Kazakh told me their story that way. Weren't those stunning economic advances supposed to happen to the Uyghurs and Kazakhs too? Or was a future of shoveling shit baked in? Perhaps. Or perhaps there was a golden age where the world was in balance, then something went horribly wrong.

*Abdurehim Parach in Istanbul. By the author*

As a veteran of "over forty" forced labor gigs, Abdurehim Parach, Uyghur intellectual and poet, embodies Uyghur stoicism; Uyghur forced labor dramatically predates Western journalistic awareness and "it didn't all start with Xi Jinping" he says. Instead, imagine a *slow boil*—with the frog, the Uyghur people, making increasingly futile attempts to jump from the pot. I asked Parach, raised in a village of 3000 Uyghurs in the Kashgar region, if back in 1985, when he was nine, his village controller was Chinese or Uyghur. "Back then?" he said, "It didn't matter."

"From that time in my life, I know we have *hasha*—*hasha* means forced labor—in my village." Parach describes it as a way of paying taxes for those with little money. Every year Uyghur families would pick "a chosen one," usually one of their sons, to go to the fields for a couple of weeks or, alternately, raise the money for a bribe. If the chosen one or the bribe didn't show, officials would hit the family with a fine. "It was a normal thing for the Uyghur population that we have to work for free, for the State. . . just traditional, normalized, *hasha*. And we did not disagree with this. Never."

The *hasha* itself often had little value in total crop yield, but for the local Party members, forced labor created a tradeable currency. "Yasin," a farm boy with crinkly laughing eyes, took me through the flowchart.

### District Controller

- Bio: Party Member, "usually Han Chinese"—appointed by Beijing
- Visibility: Seen once a year
- Function: Keep Beijing investment funding flowing in
- Reward: "Embezzle 20% of investment funding"

### Village Controller

- Bio: Party member, Chinese or "suck-up Uyghur"—position for 10k
- Visibility: Inauguration of new projects (potential manure on face)
- Function: Make District Controller look good
- Reward: Slice of District Controllers embezzlement

### Small Village Controller

- Bio: Uyghur—position "can be bought for a sheep"
- Visibility: Intermittent
- Function: Enforce hasha
- Reward: Perceived prestige and petty control

### Micro Districts Controller

- Bio: Uyghur—appointed by Small Village Controller
- Visibility: Often seen in the fields
- Function: "Watchdog and border collie"
- Reward: Bribes from families to avoid hasha, about $60 per family

### Family Controllers

- Bio: Uyghur—appointed by Micro Districts controller
- Visibility: Seen everywhere
- Function: "Complete loyalty to the Micro Districts Controller"
- Reward: "Avoid really hard labor" for families and cronies

Parach saw this petty bureaucracy as a small price to leave Uyghurs alone: two days of work a month per family. Confiscation of land as a last resort. No armed guards patrolling the cotton fields. No son separated from his family for more than a month. Uyghur women don't do *hasha*.

In January 1994, Parach says, the wind shifted: "A frigid, bitterly cold winter. My friends and I were sliding on the frozen pond on our way to *hasha*." At the assembly point, "Chinese authorities commanded us 'to clear every irrigation gulley of ice.'" The young men thought they were joking: "This might make sense somewhere else. But there was no water coming into the irrigation system at all. In Kashgar, the winter is bone dry. In the spring, fresh rain would melt the ice in a couple of hours." The boys speculated that this was some sort of game "to keep us busy, to keep us from gathering together, or to keep us from plotting against the State?" One boy boldly said, "There is no real reason to clear the ice." The Chinese response was to enlist the entire village. "We spent three days using pickaxes and shovels on four kilometers of ice that had formed on the irrigation channel. . . . Every family had to clear five to ten meters." After that, "*hasha* became endless. The authorities ordered five days of work a month,. . . but now it was make-work: poorly timed cotton harvests, digging soil that was never planted,. . . just making sure your time was never your own." Yasin noticed the shift that summer: Chinese bosses withheld drinking water in the cotton fields just to "break the workers."

On February 5, 1997, the PLA fired on Uyghur protesters in Ghulja. If you include the subsequent mass arrests, Bahtiyar Shemshidin, a former PSB agent in Ghulja, told me that internal police estimated 400 deaths. In the wake of Ghulja, the *hasha* obligation per family doubled to 70 days a year. Yasin watched as Chinese authorities ordered Uyghurs to prepare fields for cotton planting. "Then Han

Chinese entrepreneurs, who had apparently made a deal with the local authorities, came and planted the cotton."

\* \* \*

In Aksu prefecture, "River Boy" grew up in a Uyghur village on the banks of the Muzat River. He spoke in awe of its "intense chill" and its "extremely fast and powerful current, always shifting." In 1998, when River Boy was 17, the village controllers announced that the Muzat would be "diverted." They ordered the Uyghur boys to the riverbank, where metal "tripods" had been delivered by truck. *Lay them across the river*, the boys were told, *this is the easy part.*

Yet the "tripods" were as heavy as tank traps, requiring two boys to lift them, even for a few seconds. The stone-faced boys stood still, while the Uyghur elders drifted down to the river and talked loudly among themselves: "They could use nearly any heavy machinery to dig, or to move foundations into the river, or even dump stones and gravel in the river. But instead, they want to use our boys!" The village controllers listened, huddled, and solemnly declared that the big push would start tomorrow.

The next morning the boys and the elders took their places. On cue, a detachment of police marched in and "a Chinese policeman shot his pistol into the air." The elders went silent as "three policemen pushed a boy into the river." Panicking, the boy eventually found his footing, balancing against the changing current, and boys began moving the tripods to the river's edge and beyond. As two boys made their way a few yards into the Muzat, the tripod sunk deep into the riverbed. Their grip wildly distorted, everyone watched the boys gasp and submerge, gasp and submerge, eyes bulging. Then, like a double barrel, they both shot down the river. "The remaining boys. . . struggled back to shore.

Some were crying, 'We don't want to go back. We're all going to get killed.'"

A Uyghur search party headed down the Muzat. A few hours later they carried the boy's corpses into the village center where a thousand Uyghurs were waiting. Five police cars drove into the center. Again, a single policeman called for order and fired his pistol in the air. This time everyone screamed, "Shoot us, shoot us! Look how many of us are here! How many of us do you think you can kill?"

The police slowly backed away. The Uyghurs swarmed the police detachment, ripping the guns from their hands. The policeman who had fired the first shot of the day was tied to the front of a tractor. The high-water mark of the Muzat Incident was a Uyghur farmer driving the bound policeman into the river and submerging him over and over "until he begged for his life."

Before sundown, 30 PLA armed soldiers marched into the village center and carried out house-to-house raids. "Separatists" were driven away in the cool early hours and sentenced to three years in prison. There was no inquiry into the deaths, the child labor, or the diversion plan. Local *hasha* continued, but the projects were quietly scaled down. On the riverbank, the tripods rusted like a brutalist memorial to the fallen. There was never another attempt to divert the wild Muzat.

\* \* \*

It was a September day, hot and dusty as usual. Meryem Sultan was lined up in front of the school with three classes of Uyghur schoolkids waiting for the buses. Back when she was nine, Meryem hated these school trips to the country. She had to pick caterpillars off the crops because, she was told, Chinese people liked to eat them. Kind of weird. When she was ten, what bugged her was that she was the smartest kid in the class, but now the teachers said they had to pick cotton.

Then they told Meryem off, right in front of everyone: "Meryem, your results at school mean nothing. If you can't pick cotton? You're useless." It was humiliating, but other kids were getting regular beatings for slacking off. Anyway, it was "just part of going to school," so Meryem did it. Turned out, she could pick faster than almost anyone in the class, especially the boys. Once she got going, she was "an addict."

Now she was 13 years old. And Meryem and her friend Hanzokre were kind of excited, standing at the front of the line, when the first bus arrived. But the other buses never came. So the teachers ordered all three classes onto the bus. Everyone jammed in, nearly 45 kids in all, sitting on each other's laps, laughing and shouting. The teachers led the students in a few songs. The open windows helped a little at first, but the road was long, four hours, and as they crept along the old village roads, clouds of red dust filled the cabin. The holiday mood faded. Meryem had been separated from her friend in the crush. She knew that Hanzokre's older brother, a 15-year-old boy named Alimjan, or "Ali," was on the bus somewhere. He had a health problem. Actually, everyone knew it. And now, as if in a dream, she could hear Hanzokre, near the front of the bus, shouting, "My brother has a heart condition. He says he cannot breathe."

The bus drove on. Ali's sister kept begging the driver to stop. The teachers said that Ali was just "playacting." Finally, Ali collapsed and fainted. Even then, the bus drove on. After an hour, a teacher examined Ali's body, and the bus pulled over by the side of the road. The teachers called for an ambulance. After an hour delay, a "prison minibus" drove up, loaded Ali inside, and drove off to a hospital. His sister was told to stay on the bus, everyone was told to shut up, and they arrived at their new home, an abandoned prison from the Tarim Laogai system in Onsu County, Aksu Prefecture, with plastic sheeting rolled over the floor. There were rats around, frogs, too, but the cotton fields were "infinite" and taller than Meryem's head. After a long day's work, she knew she would sleep okay.

That night, Meryem thought that Ali was just resting and getting better at the hospital. But maybe it was the teachers who were playacting all along. Ali was dead. To this day, none of the students know whether he died at the hospital, on the side of the road, or on the bus itself.

Throughout that cotton harvest for two months, year after year, Meryem knew that her fellow Han Chinese students were back in the classroom. And she also knew, although she wouldn't have described it that way back then, that her teachers were getting some sort of kickback from the Uyghur students working out in the fields. Meryem would ultimately find out that Ali's family got some money, probably a thousand dollars, in exchange for silence. There was no school assembly, no counseling, no acknowledgment of the death. The day had started as normal. It was to be remembered as normal.

Meryem was told that another student died in the cotton fields around that time. She heard the rumors that two boys drowned when a Uyghur village was ordered to divert a river. She didn't ask many questions. Instead, she looked to her studies and picked cotton, two months out of every year, until she was 18 years old. Sometimes Meryem saw Ali in her dreams, but that was years ago.

When Meryem enrolled in Peking University, she asked her tutor, "Will we have to carry out any forced labor?" and everyone burst out laughing. It was the beginning of a great shift inside: "It made me rethink why we had to obey all these strict rules from early childhood on. I realized that they wanted to train us to be like machines, to obey without question whatever orders we received from above, to make us listen only to the Party."

Recently Meryem's old middle school (Onsu County No.

1) was converted into a concentration camp, (Onsu No. 1 Labor Union Committee). Meryem believes that the camps are simply an extension of the "machine" principle, as if the Uyghur people had been transformed into an infinite cotton field, so high that no one can see it from the ground.

Meryem Sultan, the "good picker"- by Bavdun Umar

I've never interviewed a woman in a niqab before. The one visual clue that I have to go on—her eyes—are intelligent and expressive.

It was May 2007, graduation time. Rabiya was 17 years old, selected for "special exams" to determine "future arrangements.... Yet before we even learned the exam results, I, along with 25 other young female students, were guided into a large hall." The head teacher announced they had been chosen for "a wonderful opportunity: free training courses, such as Chinese language studies, to prepare you for work in mainland Chinese factories." There was silence. "None of us had agreed to take part in any training courses," Rabiya said, "but now we were locked in the hall. Our teachers surrounded us. Watching us. Even when a girl had to go to the toilet, two teachers would escort her there and back." To avoid conflict with the parents waiting outside the school, the teachers ran out the clock. Twelve hours later, a bus arrived, and the girls were taken to the "Vocational Training High School of Payzawat County" in darkness. Three weeks later, the girls were forced onto a guarded train. In Tianjin, Chinese managers drove them to a large factory compound and said: "You are group #3."

\* \* \*

In the same county, a 16-year-old Uyghur woman, "Graduation Girl," was told to collect her diploma in a "special ceremony." Yet after the students filed into the auditorium, they noticed security guards locking the doors. The head teacher raised his hands and waited patiently until the whispering stopped. Then he said, "'You will be going to inner China. And you will work.'"

Parents gathered around the school entrance, and a representative spoke: "Your daughters must go to the fabrics. But they will be carefully supervised and completely safe." The new *hasha* requirement for each Uyghur family is one year's work, he explained. So, if you *leave and go home right now?* Your family will be free from *hasha* until your daughter returns. Yet if "a girl does not go to the fabrics, . . . *if her parents try to get in the way. . .* the days of *hasha* will increase."

\* \* \*

Rabiya is certain that 210 Uyghur girls sewed male shorts on an assembly line. But she can't read Chinese characters, so the brand of clothes, the factory name, and its location was a mystery. But it didn't matter. They were forbidden to leave the compound. They never even saw the Chinese workers. Rabiya suspects they were on a piece-rate, so they worked normal hours. "The only Chinese working at night" were the managers. "We worked in a big hall, with one camera in the center—it would rotate to watch anyone it liked—and cameras on the ceiling in all four corners." To use the toilet, they had to hold up a metal card. If the surveillance camera didn't see the card, "we were all punished by losing our salary."

The factory administrators told the girls their salary was the equivalent of $50 a month. Two weeks later, they were told, "You all came to Tianjin by train. So now you have to pay your fare." Six months later, they were told, "You have to pay for your return train fare." So, the salary was really $35, assuming they made quota: "Some days we had to finish 800 items, other days 700. . . . We usually worked until 12 pm or even 1 am. You know, we had to be up before 6 am. But they didn't care if we were exhausted. Even when we were sick." Every 15 days, the girls got a day off to wash their clothes. Rabiya said, "We were still very young, and we had never been separated from our family for so long. Every time we called our parents, we ended up weeping." Rabiya's mother would say: "Be patient, the year will pass so quickly. By the grace of God, you will come home soon." But her voice would crack, so Rabiya knew she was crying, too.

*　*　*

In early September, Graduation Girl was put on a "special train with no locals, fully controlled. There were about 150 of us in each car, plus teachers and guards." The girls were taken to a factory compound in Beijing to sew fashion bags for Da Xing, a Chinese clothing company, 10 to 12 hours per day. The meals were sustenance-level to coax the girls into purchasing snacks at the company food stands. "There were no official violations or humiliations of Uyghurs, . . . but there was constant racism. The Chinese workers would always say: 'you stink of sheep's oil.' They treated us in this way."

\* \* \*

Rabiya and her co-workers had a direct Uyghur supervisor. They called him "Uncle," and he was the lightning rod for all their complaints. Yet halfway through the year, at midnight, Uncle confronted the Chinese factory directors, "You're making these children work extremely long hours. Why do you pressure them? Why do you exploit them more than you need to?"

"They have to keep working. They cannot leave the job now."

Uncle made the first move, an arm grab. There was a grapple, a bite, a counter-bite, and then the Chinese beat Uncle "quite severely." That night, a couple of the Uyghur girls made secret plans to escape but discovered they couldn't legally board a train to Urumqi. A truce settled in.

One night at 1 am, Uncle spoke to the factory directors again. "It's too late now. We must stop and let these children go and rest, as they're working tomorrow as well."

"They have to *finish the order!*"

"If you don't allow them to rest, how can they continue working!?"

The shoving began. Then the Chinese directors surrounded Uncle, knocked him down and stomped on him "without mercy." Spontaneously, the Uyghur girls began throwing pieces of machinery at the directors. But the directors seemed distracted—was Uncle dying? While the ambulance was enroute, it all sunk in: Uncle was gone, maybe dead—the girls' only connection to Kashgar, to Payzawat County, the only thing stopping the Chinese from kidnapping them all. The girls came together on the factory floor, holding each other, moaning, fainting, weeping, praying for someone to save their lives. Before this, all Rabiya wanted was her turn to call home. Now, Rabiya was absolutely certain of one thing: *I will never see my family again.*

The next morning, a contingent of the Uyghur administrators

came to the dorm. The girls stood together and declared in solidarity: "We won't work anymore."

"You have a one-year contract. It's not over. You have to work, you must continue. The factory has a huge emergency order right now. You must fulfill it."

With no money, no escape, and Uncle in the hospital, the girls went to work in silence. When the year was done, Rabiya went home on the train. Her parents offered a bribe, it was accepted, and Rabiya never went back to inner China.

Rabiya's niqab was well-pressed. The way Rabiya told me her story tells me that she does not fear local imams, much less the peering eyes of an American Jew. I suspect that Rabiya wore her niqab because she trusts no one.

*　*　*

In the summer of 2008, the Chinese authorities put Graduation Girl and her fellow workers on a train back to Kashgar. To squelch the local rumors that she had somehow been violated in inner China, and to prevent her from being pulled into a second year of forced labor, a farm boy, "Batur," married "Graduation Girl" one year later.

A happy ending was still possible back then. Recall the reassurances—"carefully supervised" and "completely safe"—that the school had given to the parents. Despite Rabiya's terror of kidnapping and never seeing her family again, Uyghur females weren't systematically targeted for sexual trafficking. Both Rabiya and Graduation Girl slept on individual bunks, 12 women or 6 women to a room respectively, rather than spooning with co-workers to keep warm on a cement floor. Both girls ate halal. No one was forced to eat pork. No microphones and cameras in the dormitory or the toilets. Chinese guards didn't rape them. There were no disappearances. A decade later all these paper-thin protections would be gone.

Shortly after the wedding, Graduation Girl's husband, Batur, got in a quarrel with a low-level Chinese official about Uyghur girls being shanghaied at their graduations. Batur's punishment for *stirring up trouble* was to survey agricultural acreage "on the behalf of the Chinese State." Every year, Party officials allocated more farmland for Chinese. And if they needed irrigation, fertilizer, roads, local authorities would provide them, but not for Uyghurs. For a Uyghur farmer, the land is *everything*. Now Batur had to count the Chinese spoils. Batur claims he doesn't remember the numbers. Yet as the Uyghur lands receded, working the new Chinese fields was now *a 100-day annual commitment* to be filled by Uyghur farm families.

\* \* \*

A Uyghur cook, Yusef, ran a mobile food unit in a vast *bingtuan*, Chinese paramilitary installations that promote Han Chinese settlement in Xinjiang. Yusef describes his *bingtuan* as "endless, endless fields. Like an endless sea. You cannot see the border.... It's too far. And the fields are white with cotton, and all of the workers are Uyghurs. Only Uyghurs."

Many were Uyghur college students, ripped out of the classroom, and forced to listen to motivational speeches in the barracks: "'You need to thank the University from your soul for giving you this guidance from the Chinese Communist Party,' shit like that." But Yusef says it all came down to armed Chinese soldiers patrolling the fields. In July 2009, Urumqi exploded briefly into race riots between Uyghurs and Han Chinese. Before July, Yusef said, "The soldiers kept up a professional exterior." After July, the soldier's "racism" was openly liberated. "We don't work with Uyghurs," they would say with contempt.

Beginning in 2015, the Party ordered the camp construction. A mass surveillance structure, employing human checkpoints and electronic readers that can remotely determine a person's race and stress level, became standard. By the end of 2016, one million were detained in the camps. Initially, the camps were indoctrination. Over time, they would become housing for forced labor. And while the Party denies mass incarceration, psychoactive medications, torture, rape, sterilization, shaving of female hair for Chinese wig exports, deportation of Uyghurs from abroad, and organ harvesting, forced labor had already been rebranded as a jobs program.

\* \* \*

Back in Turkey, a man I call "Abraham" caught the full scale of the shift, simply by giving me a clipped rundown on his family. His wife and all of his children are incarcerated and working or confined to orphanages. His three brothers are in prison, one picking cotton, the others producing cement. I asked Abraham if he ever speaks with his family. He replied, "No one is home. Children and old people only. Everyone is in the camps being forced to work. Or in orphanage. Or in prison."

| Abraham's family | Hasha |
|---|---|
| Wife, "educational" facility | Camp factory |
| Disabled son, camp | Forced labor factory |
| Three sons, orphanages | ? |
| Adopted son, prison | Hard labor |
| Brother #1, prison | Cotton |
| Brother #2, prison | Cement factory |
| Brother #3, prison | Cement factory |
| Sister, prison | (Daughter in sewing factory) |

What Abraham is describing has a name: *chattel slavery*. One is born a slave, an asset, with no rights to a family. The auction blocks are electronic these days, but the result is the same: rip up the family, break up the culture, and reduce the individual to a pack mule.

There was nothing inevitable about this. The Party had off-ramps: for example, the "Go West" project, a precursor to the Belt and Road Initiative, promised to build modern infrastructure, elicit foreign funds, and get some money in the Uyghurs' pockets. *They will assimilate.*

We may never know if certain factions of the Party had relatively good intentions, however patronizing, for the Uyghurs and Kazakhs, because the real key date for the Party is not the Ghulja Incident, or the Kunming Train Station attack, or the Urumqi riots, but 9/11. Portrayed as CIA proxies on September 10, the Party re-branded Uyghur separatist groups as Islamic terrorists on September 12. There will always be young men who will pick up a gun—I interviewed one Uyghur who had trained as a rebel soldier—but to concentrate exclusively on action/reaction is to miss the performative aspect of the Party's war on terrorism. The target audience is Han Chinese. The war is not meant to be won, but to create an enduring justification for the Chinese State's assault on the Uyghurs.

Why is the Party doing that? It's hardly definitive, but one can find patterns in refugee testimony, particularly by what's missing: Islamophobia barely comes up. Or the Hui Muslims of China who speak Mandarin, so they don't seem to appear in the camps. Yet nearly half the camp refugees mention Han Chinese racism—not the inflated currency of micro-aggression that we worry about in the West, but genuine "these people are monkeys" racism.

\* \* \*

The question is, what does the future of Uyghur employment really look like? Prison labor is universally overlooked. It's the last stop on the human rights train. Yet while raw numbers of Uyghurs in the camps may decrease over time, many have been transferred to prisons, and the camps are increasingly focused on forced labor outputs.

A man in his early forties, "Ali" has a face that is simultaneously taut and wrinkled, underfed, with all-knowing eyes, exactly what you might expect from a man who lived through what he calls "12 years of slavery. . . . I've never been paid by the Chinese State for any of the work that I've done."

Ali was detained in 1998, interrogated for two years, and then worked continuously until 2012. His initial job was in "First Prison factory," 20 buildings, 5000 workers, all producing cement floor tiles. Ali stacked, loaded, and unloaded. He was careful, but the problem was the sheer weight; half the workers had broken legs, feet or both.

Ali's next job was cutting and polishing novelty stones. Little physical strength was required, just setting stones into metal frames, using "a big pot, filled with liquid glue." They had masks, but the smoke from the glue combined with chemicals to make the stones shiny was "toxic." Ali had chronic dizziness, disorientation, and "my eyes constantly watered if I didn't have the mask on really tight."

His final job was an assembly line of 150 people making trousers for oil company workers. The shift was 12 hours. Ali sewed pockets. The production line created "fine dust," but the deadlines were firm, so the dust piled up in waves, like an abandoned house in the desert. "Nobody cares about health. You just have to work and work. Nobody cares if you wear a mask or eye protection. . . . The dust collects on your body and can create an issue with your lungs if you don't wear a mask, but the dust also blocks your vision while you are sewing. . . . Your eyes become weak. The noise hurts your brain. You feel faint all the time because there's so little food. . . . It's really just about persecution."

In 2005, the UN sent an investigative team to visit Urumqi First Prison. Ali and the other prisoners were told beforehand to simply work, and to keep their expressions neutral–never mind the arbitrary beatings and humiliation. I asked Ali to reflect on any moments that might have been tolerable in some way, and he recalled with pride that, before his death, Nurmuhemmet Yasin, the famous Uyghur author of "The Wild Pigeon," was his cellmate.

After a body search to make sure he wasn't carrying notes, Ali was released in 2012. He fled to Vietnam, Cambodia, Thailand, Malaysia, and finally, Turkey.

Ali was technically charged as a "separatist." His sentence, which was constantly being extended, was purely based on his consistent refusal to inform on his friends. Ali said that the charge itself was "irrelevant and ridiculous." It was never about politics, just personal loyalty:

"Once the Party realized... that they could make money on ordinary Uyghurs, they created these excuses—you are a separatist, you use WeChat—and they turned all of East Turkestan into an assembly line. The Chinese are growing Uyghurs, and Uyghurs have to work in these prisons. For free. For nothing. There are no charges, there is no guilt. My crime, and my friends' crime? *It is to be born on the wrong place on this earth.*"

I didn't have the heart to ask Ali whether he had a wife or a girlfriend. His disappointment and irritation when I brought the interview to a close after three hours, *just when we were getting going,* seemed to answer that. I suspect that Ali's fate is a premonition of the Uyghur future: women working in factories and confined to dormitories until they are past child-bearing age, and isolated, desperately lonely men who will die from cancer and organ failure well before their time.

*　*　*

The Uyghur refugees want a way back to the promised land, but there's no light on the horizon to guide them. Or maybe just a flicker.

In December 2022, students in Chinese universities held candlelight vigils commemorating an apartment building fire in Urumqi. Covid locks prevented entire families from escaping, while a Uyghur mother screamed piteously as her children burned. Obviously, the Chinese students were sick of lockdowns and perhaps the Uyghur mother was merely a useful prop. Yet every undergraduate who held a candle, ostensibly for the Uyghur dead, was knowingly exposed to facial recognition and faced academic ruin.

Let there be light. This is China's antebellum moment—an insecure political elite leading a great nation even further into darkness, into a full-scale revival of humanity's oldest crime. It will take millions of candles to light China's way back.

# 9

# HEARTS AND LUNGS

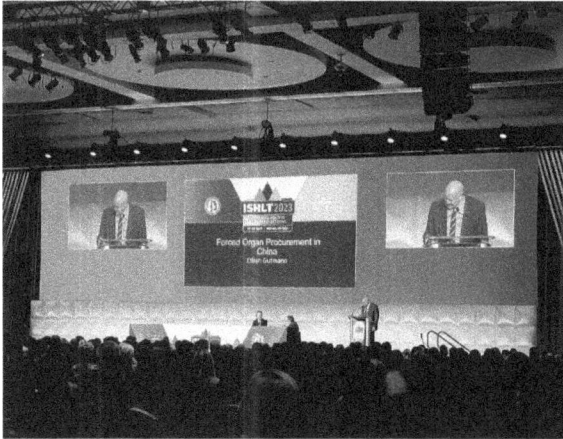

Changing times; the first day of the heart and lung transplantation conference. By ISHLT staff.

I'm old school, so for me this is still the age of PowerPoint, and this chapter is a single presentation. Dr. Jacob Lavee persuaded the International Society of Heart & Lung Transplantation (ISHLT) to give me the keynote address on the first day of the 2023 ISHLT Annual conference in Denver. Arguably the most influential individuals in the transplant world, the audience was comprised of 3600 heart and lung transplant surgeons.

ISHLT set the table in late 2022 by declared an "academic boycott" of China, i.e., no Chinese input within ISHLT medical publications, and no Chinese attendance of ISHLT conferences. Three Chinese surgeons slipped into Denver anyway. ISHLT responded by hiring an experienced bodyguard. Unlike the Mayor Ko press conference, I told the big guy to be as visible as he liked, and I promised to turn into a rag doll if he wanted to throw himself in front of a bullet, a blow-dart, or a cream pie. Two Chinese surgeons left noisily in the middle of my presentation, cursing and slamming the door. The third surgeon may have stayed, possibly to make a bootleg (to promote candor, ISHLT speeches or presentations are not recorded).

This PowerPoint presentation, simultaneously remedial and advanced, resembles CliffsNotes to a textbook. The key takeaway can be summarized in a single word: *continuity*—the historical continuity of China's transplant industry over time, regardless of the targeted victim group.

Some findings are better expressed in visual format. I've held those findings back in previous chapters, so they will be new to you here. At the same time, to avoid repetition, I significantly edited and shortened my recent research contributions, including swapping out some images. Because of conference restrictions on discussing off-label use, I avoided the ECMO issue.

The presentation starts below.

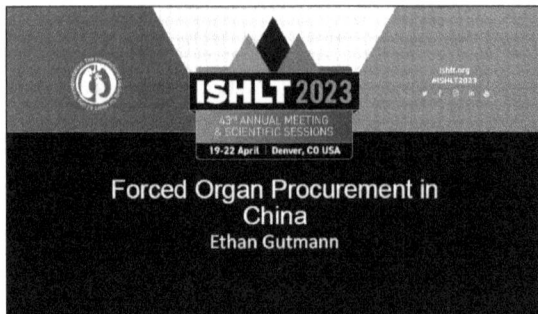

Thank you for your invitation. Special thanks to the Chair of the ISHLT Ethics Committee, Dr. Are Holm. The following relevant financial relationships exist related to this presentation: No relationships to disclose, and I will not discuss off-label use and/ or investigational use of any drugs or devices.

I'll briefly explain what attracts me to human rights field research. It's in my blood. This is my grandfather on my maternal side: Robert Redfield, Anthropologist.

Most of his field research was in Chiapas, Mexico.

This was my father, David Gutmann, a psychologist. His field research was in Mexico, and the Golan Heights. He also did day-care. My interview techniques often mimic what I overheard while playing in the corner of a hut.

In 1999, as a business consultant in Beijing, I watched police shove Falun Gong women into unmarked vehicles. That experience, combined with my family background, led to my overseas interviews with Falun Gong refugees, and more recently, this photo of an interview in Almaty with a Xinjiang camp refugee. In China, if I tried to speak with a Falun Gong or a Uyghur, an "enemy of the Chinese state," multiple arrests, and even deaths could follow.

Confidential field research with refugees outside China is one method to get information while doing no harm.

Yet it's problematic. In China, everyone has an agenda. So do China's victims. I have an agenda, too. To get things right. To cull bad information. I've been known to spend 12 hours with a witness, wearing the subject down, encouraging them to speak about their direct experience, not what they think I need to hear.

Today I'm going to give you a short timeline of the evolution of Chinese organ harvesting of political and religious prisoners, or in human-rights speak, "prisoners of conscience."

Death row prisoners: Late 1980s to mid-1990s

First Uyghur political prisoners: 1995-1998

Majority Falun Gong: 1999-2014

Majority Uyghurs: 2015-2023

Western response

One way to think about that evolution is to look at organ sources. Beijing admits that Chinese transplant surgeons extracted organs from death row prisoners, essentially common criminals sentenced to death under Chinese law, until at least 2015. My focus is on what Beijing won't speak about: political and religious prisoners. These prisoners are seldom officially sentenced to death. But they are exploited as organ sources for the Chinese transplant industry. Over the years organs have been sourced from Tibetans, House Christians, and Turkic ethnicity groups such as Kazakh and Kyrgyz. Today I'll concentrate on the central victim groups—Uyghurs and Falun Gong.

For "Death Row" and "First Uyghur political prisoners," I'll draw on my own field research.

Research on "Majority Falun Gong" harvesting is robust. I'll draw your attention to critical materials.

The current period, "Majority Uyghurs," is a challenge. I'll give you the results of my field research.

Finally, I'll shift to "Western response," particularly ISHLT's new stance, and the Congressional Stop Organ Harvesting Act of 2023. And I'll speculate on a potential challenge for ISHLT.

This is a Chinese Communist Party execution field, the birthplace of Chinese organ harvesting. We don't know the photo's provenance. US intelligence suspects the location is Xinjiang, late 1980s. The man gazing defiantly at us has just shot the prisoners who lie at his feet. He wears a makeshift glove to avoid back-splatter. It's all legal. Each death-row prisoner wears a poster listing their crimes. There may be surgeons present, but we don't see them. Harvesting was opportunistic, not routine.

Same period. This woman murdered her husband in his sleep, so the Party allowed this photo to be widely distributed. The death penalty in this case was not controversial in China.

If we look over the gunman's shoulder, we can just make out several white vehicles. These may be hospital vans.

This former policeman described an execution field in 1992 much like the one in the previous picture. He told me there were medical vans representing different hospitals around the periphery. A medical van finished up with a prisoner. Curious, the policeman looked inside the body bag. The chest was "empty."

I won't show you an image of the next witness: a Uyghur transplant surgeon from Sun Yat-sen Memorial hospital. The year was 1992, the same setting, but the surgeon stayed in the medical van. An executed male was brought in, and while the transplant surgeon extracted the prisoner's kidneys, he noticed a purple line on the man's neck. The police had wrapped a wire around the man's throat to keep him silent in court. The possibility that the man had been a political prisoner haunted the surgeon.

Nijat was the only Uyghur in a special Public Security Bureau unit that performed political prisoner executions in Urumqi. Nijat explained that, in 1994, screams "like, from hell" were heard coming from the medical vans. In 1996, the unit's medical director told Nijat that the bullet was aimed to induce shock, not immediate death.

In 1995, Dr. Enver Tohti, a Uyghur surgeon confessed that he had extracted the kidneys and liver of a wounded convict on a political prisoner execution ground near Urumqi. Tohti says

that the gunshot wound was not fatal and admits "I killed that man."

In 1997, The Party banned Ramadan celebrations in the Uyghur city of Ghulja. Uyghurs protested at the Ghulja town hall. By the end of the day, the Chinese military had killed

400 Uyghurs and continued to execute 10 Uyghurs per day for several months after the "Ghulja Incident"

Bahtiyar, a local Ghulja policeman, reported to me that local hospitals were forbidden to treat Uyghurs. Muslim burials, which involve handling the body, were forbidden. Corpses were wrapped by the hospitals, buried, and the cemeteries were patrolled by armed guards.

A young Uyghur doctor—I won't show you an image of him—confessed that in the same year, 1997, he was ordered to take blood samples from Uyghur political prisoners in an Urumqi prison. When the doctor asked for the reason behind the blood samples, he was explicitly told that it was for transplants. Six high-ranking Chinese Communist Party cadres had just flown in from Beijing to receive the organs. In 1998, six new cadres arrived, and the doctor did a second round of blood tests.

A word about Falun Gong.

The rise of Falun Gong

From 1992 onward Falun Gong rose from an exercise in a park to a spiritual practice numbering 70 million people. Think of it as a

Buddhist Revival movement: less about qigong and health, more about virtue: truth, compassion, and forbearance. Some people here were illiterate. But Falun Gong was attractive to university students and professors too. One thing that bothered the Party: that boy in front with the borrowed uniform.

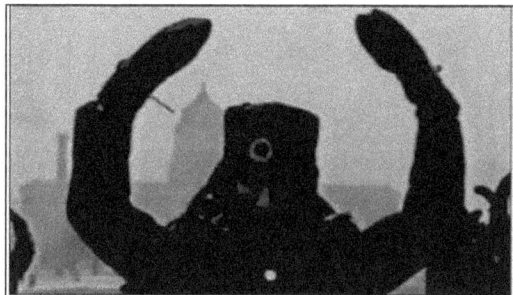

Boys like that were growing up and entering the People's Liberation Army. The Party was also infected at the highest levels. From a Marxist perspective, this is the template for seizing power, a movement which can jump across class lines and rural/urban divides, a movement without affiliation or initiation fees. Falun Gong spiritual values were seen as challenging the vision of a new, muscular, nationalist China.

These were Falun Gong morning exercises in the early Summer

of 1999. On July 20, Chinese State Security launched its largest action of scale since the Cultural Revolution, the eradication of Falun Gong.

2001

By 2001, many practitioners were in "Shenyang Prison City." Approximately one million Falun Gong were incarcerated in labor camps, prisons, detention centers, and "black jails," finally leveling off to 450,000 by 2013.

Prominent human rights lawyers David Matas and David Kilgour wrote the first report on Chinese organ harvesting in 2006.

It remains the Ur-stone of the investigation. It includes:

- A discrepancy between the execution rate in China and reported transplants, about 7000 per year by 2006.

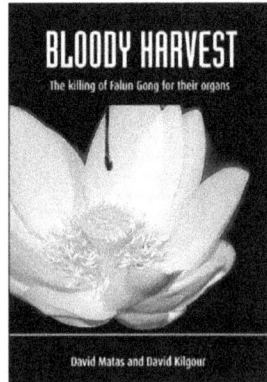

BLOODY HARVEST

The killing of Falun Gong for their organs

David Matas and David Kilgour

> ## Shanghai's Zhongshan Hospital Organ Transplant Clinic, 16 March 2006:
>
> - M: ... So how long do I have to wait [for organ transplant surgery]?
> - Doctor: About a week after you come ...
> - M: Is there the kind of organs that come from Falun Gong? I heard that they are very good.
> - Doctor: All of ours are those types.

- Transcripts of recorded phone calls with Chinese doctors— for example, this call establishes a week waiting time, and the presence of Falun Gong organs.

| item | expense |
|---|---|
| kidney transplant | US$62,000 |
| liver transplant | US$98,000~130,000 |
| liver-kidney transplant | US$160,000~180,000 |
| kindey-pancreas transplant | US$150,000 |
| lung transplant | US$150,000~170,000 |
| heart transplant | US$130,000~160,000 |
| cornea transplant | US$30,000 |

- Chinese ads with transplant prices.

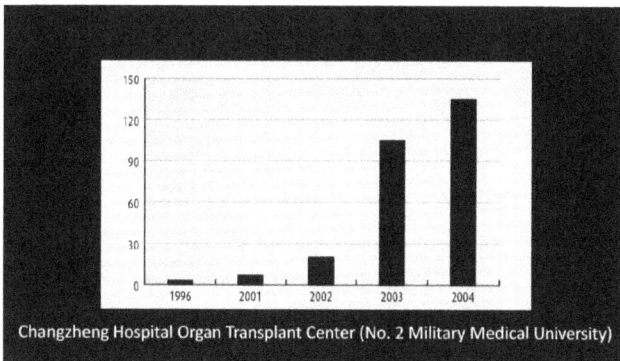

Changzheng Hospital Organ Transplant Center (No. 2 Military Medical University)

- An example of a rise in liver transplants coinciding with the incarceration of Falun Gong.

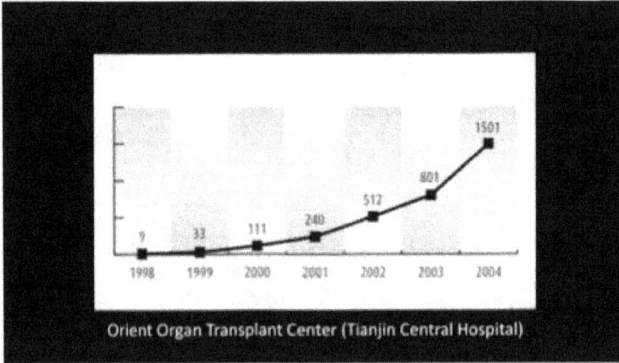

Orient Organ Transplant Center (Tianjin Central Hospital)

- Another example.

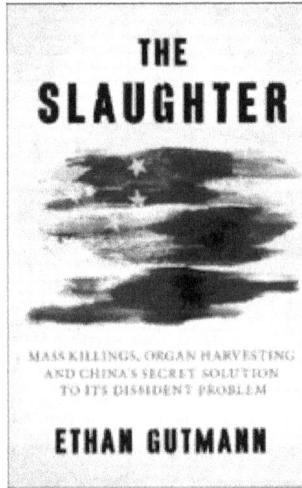

My book was published in 2014. It had five new components.

First, it established that Uyghurs were targeted for harvesting, then Falun Gong, Tibetans, and select House Church Christians.

Second, I interviewed 50 Falun Gong refugees. Here's one of them: In Guangdong Prison, Yu Xinhui described specialized medical examinations for Falun Gong prisoners only—extended blood tests, abdomen examination, EKG, urine test, and close examination of the corneas without any corresponding vision tests. The guards acknowledged the tests were for organ harvesting.

Many Falun Gong were severely damaged from torture. Many of the women had been raped. I'm not showing you those photos. But the prison guards made it clear that the tests weren't about their overall health, just their organs. In detention, one in five Falun Gong was given repeated "retail-organs-only" examinations. Based on disappearances following medical tests, I estimate that from 2001 to 2008, about 65,000 Falun Gong were harvested, approximately 8000 to 9000 per year

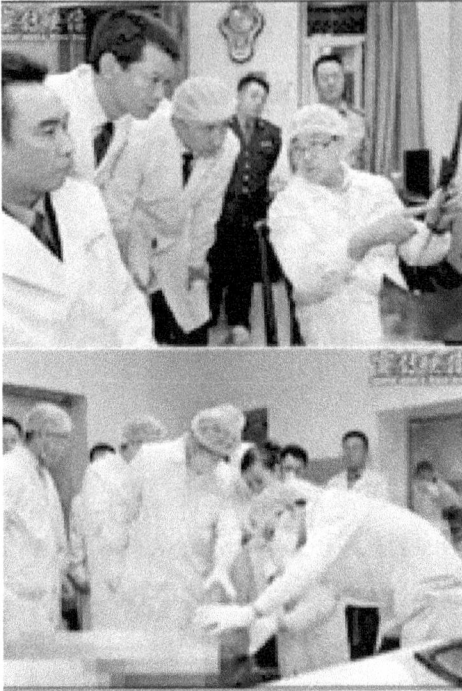

Third, organ harvesting was state-authorized. Wang Lijun (above, with the glasses) was China's most famous policeman and the right hand man to top Party official, Bo Xilai. Wang opened his own organ harvesting center in Jilin City and was given a prestigious award for a new lethal injection method.

Fourth: New witnesses, such as Taiwanese doctor, Ko Wen-je. Chinese transplant doctors said Ko's Taiwanese patients would receive good quality because "all the organs will come from Falun Gong."

One more, not in the book.

I met "Cat" in Tokyo. Cat was once a Yakuza attending to his chieftain in the Armed Police Hospital, Beijing. While waiting for his Chieftain's liver to stabilize, Cat wandered into a room where a man lay, restrained and sedated, his wrist and ankle tendons severed. Cat asked the director of surgery who the man was.

*That's the liver donor.*

*Who is he?*

*A terrorist.*

*What kind of terrorist?*

*Falun Gong.*

Cat didn't really care. But Cat ultimately left the Yakuza and now he has come out with a credible story.

Fifth: It never ended. In 2013, this Falun Gong practitioner was given organ-examinations with 500 others on a single day.

Beijing's answer to these allegations—that's their spokesman, Huang Jiefu—was to employ a semantic trick:

*We will reform. We will end the organ harvesting of prisoners.*

There's some evidence that China lowered the rate of prisoner execution. Yet Beijing's definition of "prisoners" never actually included Falun Gong, Tibetans, House Christians, or Uyghurs. So, in 2015, when the Chinese leadership announced an end to the exploitation of death row prisoner organs, and a tour of Chinese transplant hospitals, one member of the Transplantation Society ethics committee, Dr. Jacob Lavee, an Israeli heart transplant surgeon and a member of the ISHLT Ethics Committee, criticized the decision: *"As a son of a Holocaust survivor, I feel obliged to not repeat the dreadful mistake made by the International Red Cross visit to the Theresienstadt Nazi concentration camp in 1944, in which it was reported to be a pleasant recreation camp."*

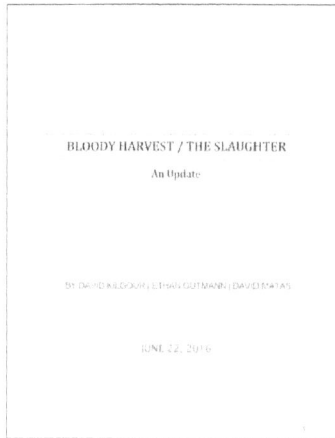

BLOODY HARVEST / THE SLAUGHTER

An Update

BY DAVID KILGOUR, ETHAN GUTMANN, DAVID MATAS

JUNE 22, 2016

One year later, our 2016 report, using individual hospital numbers and specifications, made the case that the annual number of transplanted organs in China was not 10,000 per year, but 60,000, *at a minimum.*

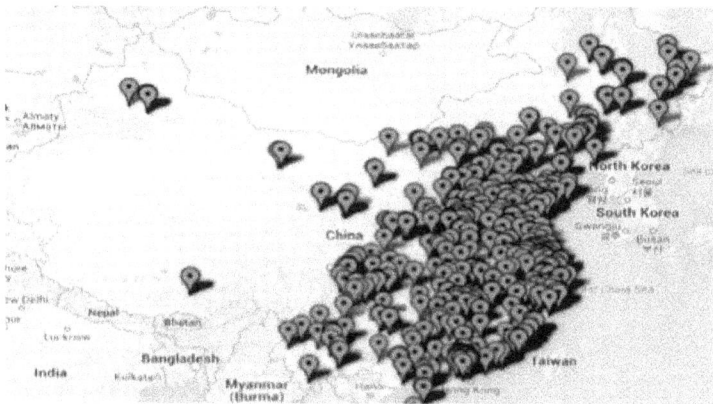

In total, 865 institutions associated with transplantation were identified.

Table 2.3 Classification of 712 hospitals conducting liver/ kidney transplants:

| Type of Transplant Centre | Count |
|---|---|
| National-level military and civilian liver and kidney transplant centres approved by the Ministry of Health in 2007 | 78 |
| Liver and kidney transplant centres designated by the Ministry of Health in 2007 | 68 |
| Subtotal | 146 |
| Unapproved large-scale (mainly 3A) transplant centres | 405 |
| Unapproved medium-size (mainly Class 3C and Class 2) transplant centres | 161 |
| Subtotal | 566 |
| Total liver and kidney transplant centres investigated | 712 |

Here's a sample. The report is 700 pages with over 2000 endnotes, 90% referencing Mainland sources.

BMC Medical Ethics

**Analysis of official deceased organ donation data casts doubt on the credibility of China's organ transplant reform**

**Abstract**

**Background**

Since 2010 the People's Republic of China has been engaged in an effort to reform its system of organ transplantation by developing a voluntary organ donation and allocation infrastructure. This has required a shift in the procurement of organs sourced from China's prison and security apparatus to hospital-based voluntary donors declared dead by neurological and/or circulatory criteria. Chinese officials announced that from January 1, 2015, hospital-based donors would be the sole source of organs. This paper examines the availability, transparency, integrity, and consistency of China's official transplant data.

**Methods**

Forensic statistical methods were used to examine key deceased organ donation datasets from 2010 to 2018. Two central-level datasets — published by the China Organ Transplant Response System (COTRS) and the Red Cross Society of China — are tested for evidence of manipulation, including conformance to simple mathematical formulae, arbitrary internal ratios, the presence of anomalous data artefacts, and cross-consistency. Provincial-level data in five regions are tested for coherence, consistency, and plausibility, and individual hospital data in those provinces are examined for consistency with provincial-level data.

In response, Beijing claimed that any shortfall in transplant volume was being filled by China's new voluntary donation program. Two years later there was a powerful discovery by Dr. Jacob Lavee, Victims of Communism Fellow Matthew Robertson, and statistician Raymond Hinde.

Fig. 18 Chinese official donor registry data fitted to a quadratic model

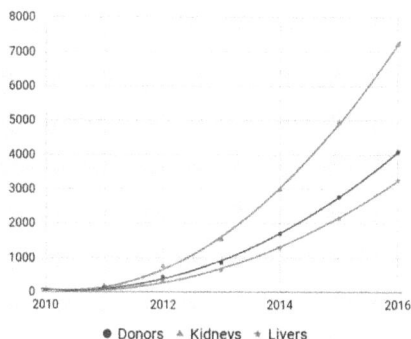

● Donors ▲ Kidneys ✳ Livers

A November 2019 paper in BMC Medical Ethics shows that China's voluntary organ transplant data from the China Organ Transplant Response System (COTRS) conforms extremely closely to a simple quadratic model. This, along with numerous other anomalies, indicate the data may have been falsified. (BMC Medical Ethics)

Beijing's charts showing exponential growth in Chinese citizens offering voluntary organ donations—the new, "reformed" system of organ procurement—was constructed not on accurately reported data, but on a relatively simple equation, created to mimic exponential growth. Beijing's reform was a lie.

Extensive data analysis of the Chinese transplant world by Dr. Jacob Lavee and Matthew Robertson established definitively that in China, death by heart extraction was the normal procedure for the "donor," rather than the exception.

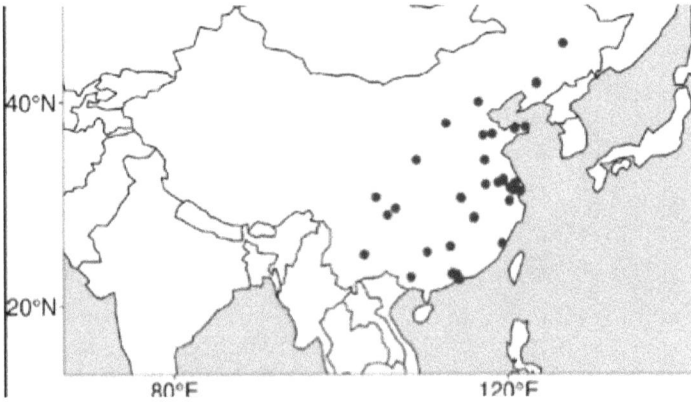

This map identifies a national pattern of problematic brain death declarations.

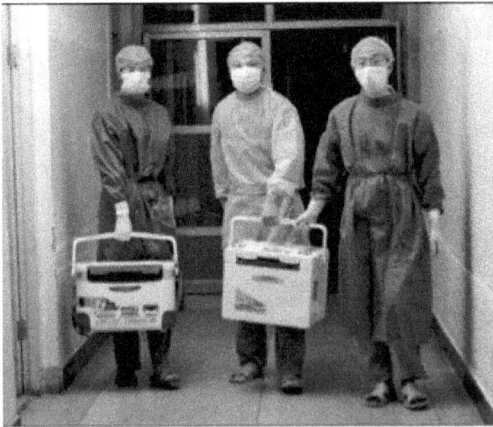

Live organ harvesting had come of age. These were the new executioners.

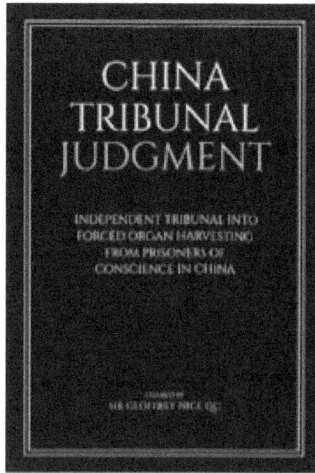

One last book. The result of several years of research, including both Falun Gong and Uyghur witness testimony, the China Tribunal Judgment is the most comprehensive study on Chinese forced organ harvesting at this time.

Now I'll move to the Uyghurs. Scroll back to 2103. In five Chinese provinces, policemen entered Falun Gong homes to administer blood and DNA tests, a clue that the Falun Gong organ supply was running thin.

One year later, the Party ordered approximately ten million Uyghurs to get a blood and DNA test.

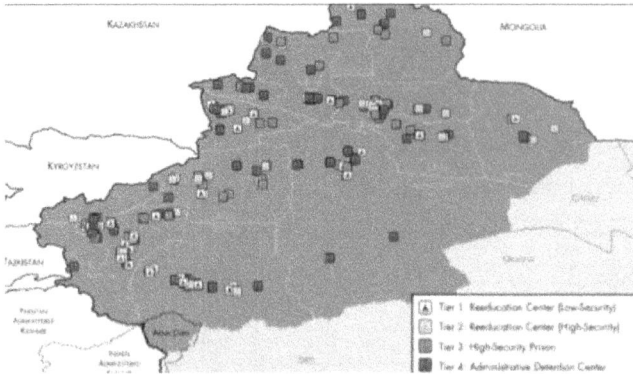

This is an extremely conservative depiction of the internment camps in 2017 by the National Geospatial-Intelligence Agency. By the end of 2016, the incarceration of Uyghurs, Kazakhs, and other Turkic minorities, according to State Department estimates, was 800,000 to three million.

As the camp system matured, we received glimpses of prisoner movements. And we intercepted an order to construct nine major crematoria in Xinjiang.

"Aksu Triangle"

Let's look at one crematorium in Aksu.

Two "re-education" camps, one for 16,000 people and one for 33,000 people, built around a pre-existing hospital (Aksu Infection Hospital), and 900 meters from both camps, a large crematorium.

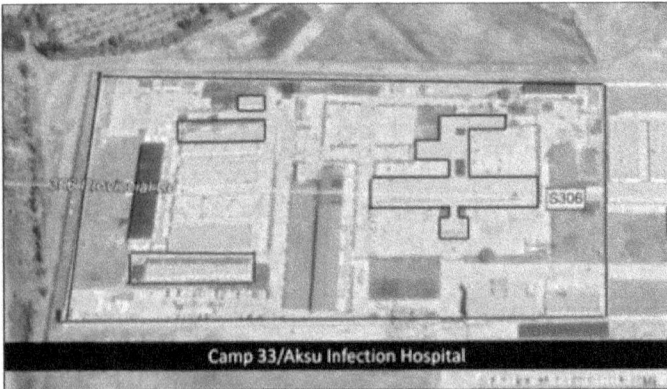

Camp 33/Aksu Infection Hospital

A close-up of the original hospital facility, outlined on the right, the camp constructed around it. A Uyghur veteran of the Aksu prison system told me: "Aksu Infection Hospital was originally used for SARS virus patients." In 2013, the hospital evolved into a treatment center for "religious" or "extreme Muslim" dissidents. Taped phone calls affirm that the hospital performs organ extractions and transplants.

Crematorium

The crematorium was also familiar to the prison witness: "The air smells like scorched bones." Another Uyghur male from the Aksu area drove by the crematorium every day and confirmed a strong noxious odor. The waste pipes leading to the river suggest that the crematorium uses a *burn* method: Intense heat, filtration, and to keep smoke at a minimum, a "re-burner."

Aksu International Airport

Aksu International Airport is less than a 30-minute drive from the hospital.

"Human organ transport channel"

The airport has a "Human Organ Transport Channel," essentially a fast lane supplying transplant hospitals near the Chinese coast. All Xinjiang "Green Passages" are one way, export only.

First Hospital, Zhejiang Province

One probable end user, First Hospital in the Shanghai region, is an official "big brother" to Aksu Infection Hospital. Beginning in 2017, First Hospital's liver transplants increased by 90% while kidney transplants increased by over 200%. First Hospital successfully performed the first double lung transplant on a Covid patient—an advertisement to the world that even during the pandemic, *China was open for business.*

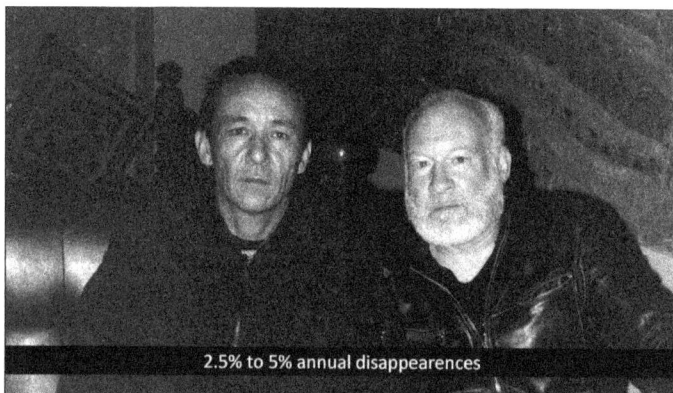

2.5% to 5% annual disappearences

I'll summarize the results of my refugee testimony in Central Asia. My witnesses, from twenty different camps, were surprisingly consistent.

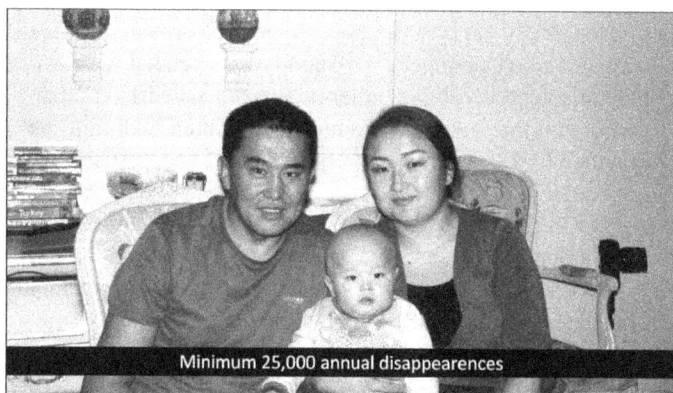

Minimum 25,000 annual disappearences

I estimate that 25,000 to 50,000 Uyghurs are harvested for their organs annually. I'm going to close with policy.

Think back to where we were in 2016 at the Foreign Affairs hearing, ostensibly on the same side, but in a position of stalemate. The Congressional representatives didn't know much about transplants, but they knew something about the Chinese Communist Party. And everyone in the room knew that the Western transplant community's attempt at a "soft reform" of the Chinese transplant industry had stalled. So, they grilled Dr. Francis Delmonico, but Resolution 343, "regarding persistent and credible reports of systematic state-sanctioned organ harvesting," never made it onto the Senate floor. Capitol Hill wanted to operate in tandem with the Western medical consensus, and that consensus was to avoid conflict with China.

Let's move to the present. Some of you may not have been aware of the Uyghur disappearances. But everyone here is aware that Beijing has been doing *something* to the Uyghurs. You may not have made up your mind about the origins of Covid. Yet would anyone say that Beijing never lied about Covid? The Western medical community did not break the "engagement" consensus. Beijing did.

> Given the body of evidence that the government of the People's Republic of China stands alone in continuing to systematically support the procurement of organs or tissue from executed prisoners,[7-10] submissions related to transplantation and involving either organs or tissue from human donors in the People's Republic of China will not be accepted by ISHLT for the purposes listed above. This policy, including whether other countries systematically engage in the use of organs or tissue from non-consenting human donors and should be subject to this restriction, will be reviewed on an annual basis pending independently obtained proof that these practices have ceased.

So when ISHLT banned Chinese transplant publication in 2022, it was a flare in the Capitol Hill night sky. The House recently voted for the Stop Organ Harvesting Act of 2023, 413 to 2. In essence, the act prevents Chinese transplant doctors from entering the US as if everything were normal. It exposes their associates around the world. Finally, the act calls for a major effort to gather information on the Chinese transplant system.

So while the ISHLT is aware of some efforts to reform the

Chinese organ donation system and establish it on legitimate brain-dead consenting donors, I think it's fair to say that until the ISHLT or affiliates gets an unrestricted chance to examine the system independently, on the ground, there is no basis to lift the academic boycott started by ISHLT or the legal actions detailed in the House Stop Organ Harvesting act of 2023.

In short, ISHLT stood up. And now you have the whip hand. Yet I'm going to make a prediction here; in the very near future, you will encounter a solution to the China problem. Not unrestricted access on the ground—the Party can't do that –but "smart health care," a world where AI will connect all medical devices globally from transplant robotics to ECMO in full transparency, a "democratization of data." No statistician necessary; AI will pick up any suspicious anomalies. But can Beijing alter the input data? Can China's AI outsmart our AI? Well, yes, they can. And there's that history problem. Perhaps Beijing should investigate? Offer apologies and compensation? Or does medical history really not matter that much?

And can we trust a repeat offender?

This photo was taken by Josephine, my foster daughter. It's of Rahima Senbai, our Kazakh "nomad witness," and Rahima's eldest daughter, in their small home in the Kazakh countryside. Rahima's bunkmate and best friend in the camps was named Araya. She was 27 years old, healthy, DNA-and-blood-tested. One evening Rahima woke up because the bed had gone cold. Araya had been taken from their shared covers on a winter's night.

For two decades, faced with variations of these cases, the Western transplant community has maintained silence. That's changing now, but the transplant community is not yet a unified force.

Maybe precedent can shed some light. As I said, my father was a psychologist, so even as a little boy, I knew that the World Psychiatric Association denounced Soviet psychiatric hospitals for torturing political dissidents. Soviet psychoanalysts were not welcome at Western conferences. They couldn't publish in our journals. No joint development of psychoactive drugs. That never changed. Not even during the Gorbachev years. Yet the irony is that through Lavee and Robertson's research, we know far more about what takes place in Chinese transplant hospitals than we ever knew about the Soviet psychiatric hospitals.

With the whip hand comes an obligation. Not to the good surgeons of China (of which there are many), not to Beijing's engagement with the world, not to the feelings of the Chinese people. The first obligation is to Rahima and her daughter, to ensure that their shared bed will never go cold again.

In closing, I pledge that I'll always be candid about what we know and what we don't know. And it would be an honor to work with you going forward. That concludes my remarks.

# AFTERWORD

The presidential palace in Dushanbe is a soaring piece of gilded Central Asian architecture. In a vast hall seemingly built for giants, underneath a golden dome and bathed in sunlight, lies the "main conference table," so large that a hundred chairs easily fit around the circumference. Off to one side, there's a normal, unmarked door, and a crowded little room with low clearance, no windows, and a single table, just big enough for a family. The air smells of disinfectant.

It was here, in June 2014, that the deal was done. In what was then still called the "Shanghai Six," the Chinese Communist Party, with Russia by its side, laid out a plan to the Central Asian members of the Shanghai Cooperation Organization, Tajikistan, Kazakhstan, Uzbekistan, and Kyrgyzstan. The subject was the permanent resolution of the Uyghur question.

I suspect that table has rarely seen such glory again. The furnishings look dated, frozen in time. Like a hotel room, unused for legal or superstitious reasons, it may receive a "light turn" once a month, but no cleanser is strong enough to hide the stench of fratricide.

*   *   *

Fourteen years ago, I wrote an essay titled "The Xinjiang Procedure" for a DC political journal, *The Weekly Standard*. That journal is gone now, but my final paragraph is consistent with my views today:

"The implications are clear enough. Nothing but self-determination for the Uighurs can suffice. The Uighurs, numbering 13 million, are few, but they are also desperate. They may fight. War may come. On that day, as diplomats across the globe call for dialogue with Beijing, may every nation look to its origins and its conscience. For my part, if my Jewish-sounding name tells me anything, it is this: The dead may never be fully avenged, but no people can accept being fatally exploited forever."

Few of my non-Uyghur, colleagues will publicly speak in favor of Uyghur self-determination. There are several reasons.

The first reason is that we work directly with Uyghur activists. We respect their views. Many Uyghur activists believe that avoiding the call for Uyghur self-determination is a matter of simple survival. Advocacy for "Uyghur separatism" is exactly what the CCP wants, a justification to hammer the Uyghurs even harder. A little closer to home, Uyghur activist leaders justifiably fear that their loved ones—many are in detention—would be the first to be punished, even executed. They don't want to make a deal with Beijing, but they can't close the door either. For most Uyghur activists, this problem is insoluble.

The second reason we stay silent on Uyghur self-determination is to follow the Washington consensus. Living with the Chinese Communist Party appears nearly inevitable, and the door must always stay open for dialogue.

The third reason is unavoidably tainted by self-interest. Speaking openly about an independent East Turkestan can destroy one's viability as a China analyst. You may not get a Chinese visa. Or a position in a

University with Chinese funding. The US State Department may keep you at arm's length. You may become ineffectual.

Most of my work is based on speaking to witnesses in the field and around the world. It's what I'm good at, I like having a visceral connection to the evidence, and the beauty of it all is that it solves the third problem. Quite spontaneously, the witnesses often speak for me.

My involvement with the Uyghur issue was initially a byproduct of my research into the conflict between the Chinese State and Falun Gong. I stumbled into the first secret cases of state-sponsored forced organ harvesting of prisoners of conscience and created the term "The Xinjiang Procedure" because my interviews indicated that the first blood was drawn in Xinjiang in 1994. When the CCP began running out of Falun Gong practitioners to harvest for their organs or perhaps had been too bloodied by Falun Gong's exposure of China's transplant system, in 2014, the Party began the "health checks" of Uyghurs once again.

In this book, I have compared the Chinese Communist Party to "a dog that returns to his vomit." I stand by that pungent biblical phrase because the Party doesn't even deny it anymore. In December 2024, the Autonomous Region Health Commission in China announced its goal of "six more human organ transplantation medical institutions in the region by 2030." Why is Beijing so brazen? Why would Putin and Xi publicly discuss organ transplants in service of their planned 150-year lifespans, as if they were comparing routine maintenance on their vintage Maseratis? Because they can. Because the West is not paying attention.

The Uyghur cause has been eclipsed: Afghanistan, followed by Russia/Ukraine, followed by Gaza/Israel have depleted the oxygen in the room. Even our rescue of a Christian Kyrgyz family was treated as a distraction by the Department of Homeland Security, only clearing the way when Wall Street Journal reporter Chao Deng threatened to run a story that the Turdakun family was being left to twist in the wind. The International Criminal Court has an acute case of attention deficit disorder, but they are largely following established human rights organizations, and the legacy media. Primary funding for investigative work is lagging. A potential patron asked why I can't just interview camp refugees remotely, as if that was a secure option, as if the tedious, remarkably unproductive meetings that we all experienced during the Covid lockdown taught us nothing about the limitations of technology to elicit honest human responses.

The only bright spot appears to be the campaign against Uyghur forced labor. The initial effort was to monitor Western supply chains, initially meant to administer financial pain in Beijing. That part has worked. Corporations have altered their supply chains, allowing them to feel better about themselves and virtue-signal to their customers. These are not bad things, they are good things, yet we need to be realistic. Western corporate embarrassment and a modicum of restraint may have little effect on Beijing. Perhaps there is no easy way to measure if Uyghur and Kazakh forced labor on the ground is increasing or diminishing. Perhaps we don't want to know. Yet without that basic accounting, the fight against Uyghur forced labor risks becoming an abstraction, a DC cottage industry, a game of edicts and papal dispensations to Western corporations.

Am I suggesting that the whole rotten system, including the US State Department, is corrupt? No. But I am saying that the State Department is not good at tracking moving targets. *None of us are.* How does the Chinese Communist Party respond to embarrassment? By hiding, adapting, altering the production process, and adding new layers of complexity. *Beijing loves games.* And this is equally true for China's transplant industry.

*All we can do is alter the stakes of the game.* I don't have a 20-point plan for that, just an amplification of my one parting thought. Modern humans don't tend to fight for their re-emergence as a nation-state over issues of slavery alone. They rise up—often it's a delayed response to the precedent—when mass murder and wanton neglect have placed their future survival as a people in question. For Ireland, it was the potato famine. Ukraine, Stalin's mass starvation. Israel, the Nazi gas chambers. And for East Turkestan, it should be organ harvesting.

You are entitled to your own views on Israel or the Ukraine—or on Irish independence for that matter. Two of these three states are in bloody, seemingly endless wars over their existence while I write this. And Irish independence cost many lives over many years. So it's not an easy ride, yet all these nations, however improbably, came back from the dead. A Uyghur state is *not* impossible.

But it is improbable that Uyghur autonomy or liberation will come, like a gift, handed down from the Chinese State. Sterilization, forced labor, even rape: from the Chinese perspective, these are normalized techniques of control and exploitation, part of the traditional CCP playbook. Nor can the cause of Uyghur freedom count on assistance from the Chinese masses. In my lifetime, the Chinese people have endured decades of forced sterilization and abortion, periods of mass starvation engineered by state ideology, and systematic dehumanization and humiliation during power struggles such as the Cultural Revolution. Even organ harvesting, in my calculation, has been used on Han Chinese Falun Gong practitioners in numbers similar to the Uyghurs. The Falun Gong tragedy—and believe me, I don't use that word lightly—is that independence from their own people and their own land is only possible in exile. Most Falun Gong practitioners despise the CCP but love China passionately. So they struggle with the Sisyphean task of trying to free China itself.

The mature Han Chinese citizen is calloused but not stupid. They are aware of the enforced re-education of the Uyghurs and other Turkic groups. Without a single leaked document or investigative report, they can easily imagine the excesses: the crowding in the concentration camps, the workers in the cotton fields, the forced marriages of Uyghur women to Chinese males, perhaps even a measure of the sexual exploitation. Many Han Chinese lived through these exact conditions, so these excesses can be justified as simply a delayed stage of development for the Uyghurs.

The single crime that stands out, the ongoing crime that the Chinese Communist Party has perpetuated on the Uyghur people, is organ harvesting by a mile (or more accurately, 57 miles, the length achieved by laying out the corpses shoulder to shoulder). And if China gets away with it, and stumbles into a PLA blockade or even an invasion of Taiwan, the Uyghur stalemate will no longer hold, and the unchallenged harvesting precedent will take over. The Uyghur people won't be a global concern in such a conflagration. They'll be invisible. The Party's imperative to finish the job, to simply eliminate the Uyghur race, would become a serious option.

Nor will Uyghur liberation come from Islam. Faced with extinction, we need to be brutally honest. There have been many successes of Uyghur activism, mostly in the West. Yet it's paper thin: many Americans and Europeans embraced the Uyghurs precisely to reassure themselves that they are not "Islamophobes" after all. Yet the Uyghur attempt to attract the assistance of the Islamic world, no matter how sincere the effort—and meaning no disrespect to those Uyghurs who have tried—has failed. Even Islamist terrorists didn't trust the Uyghurs and ended up exploiting them, while diplomats from Muslim states supplied raw meat to Chinese propagandists with their "fact-finding" missions to Xinjiang.

In fact, Uyghur culture has never fit into the Muslim hard line. Perhaps Uyghur culture will never truly fit into anyone's conception of a hard line because it's not a line at all. Uyghur culture is a tapestry, an achingly beautiful tapestry. And that is the true explanation of why a few of us—we happy few—have dedicated ourselves to the preservation of Uyghur culture.

Resolved then, that Uyghur liberation is improbable, let us turn to the unlikely. Here are three factors in the unlikely column's favor:

## DC

The current US administration is impatient with traditional human rights and suspicious of alliances. The impatience imperative has led to a collapse of Uyghur activist funding and some highly skilled individuals being sidelined. Yet the latter imperative contains potential opportunity. This administration is not interested in preserving the status quo, the central impediment to American action. More explicitly, President Donald Trump does not respect the legacy of the Shanghai Six and their antiseptic little room. So yes, the US could theoretically assist, but, as I have explained to my Taiwanese friends so many times, *America only helps the bold.*

## EVENTS

Because of the Ukraine war, the Russians are absent from Central Asia, creating a temporary power vacuum. Beijing, in a state of low-level economic crisis, cannot afford the Global Belt and Road Initiative, but it can afford to pluck the low-lying fruit. The energy and mineral reserves of the Pamir and the Kyrgyz mountain ranges—these are the South China Sea of China's Western frontier.

Central Asian state leaders cannot continuously sustain authoritarian control if their young men are plucked from the soil to be thrown into a Russian imperial war. Nor can they afford the Chinese seizure of energy, yellowcake, and land. Back in 2014, the Central Asian nations did not protest the Uyghur death warrant. They sold out their Uyghur brothers and sisters on the cheap, for a few Belt and Road expressways. But in doing so, they are finally beginning to realize they signed their own death warrants, merely on a different time frame.

Joseph was sold by his brothers to the Ishmaelites for twenty pieces of silver, but ultimately Joseph brought redemption to the entire family. A free and democratic East Turkestan, however chaotic and imperfectly realized, has the revolutionary potential to act as the engine of liberation for all of Central Asia.

## UYGHURS

I have seen the Uyghurs grow from a panoply of local self-appointed leaders, jockeying for position and occasionally arguing over scraps, into a unified power that, at least for one shining moment, shook the West and renewed the bi-partisan Congressional opposition to Beijing. I also witnessed the stirring of latent democratic impulses and self-governance in the Uyghur psyche—an epic story, deserving its own book.

Many Uyghur leaders can't outright embrace Uyghur self-determination yet, but they could consider embracing the *rationale* for it. Cast aside the idea that organ harvesting is a "Falun Gong issue." Own it. Then attack with fury and resolve. Congressman Chris Smith created a comprehensive organ harvesting bill. It's waiting in the wings. It's up to the Uyghurs and Kazakhs to midwife the process of passing it.

Thermo Fisher Scientific HLA kits were used on an estimated 10 million Uyghurs and Kazakhs in 2014 to 2016 to test their DNA. Thermo Fischer is highly vulnerable to both legal and congressional action. Uyghur and Kazakh doctors and scientists should spearhead the prosecution.

A key battle for the hearts and minds of the Western transplant community has been won. The most important group of surgeons in the West have sustained a full and comprehensive academic boycott of the Chinese transplant industry. The remaining Western surgeons? They fear you. Flood their transplant conferences with Uyghur and Kazakh voices.

*  *  *

That's all I have to say. There can be no Hollywood ending for such a grim investigation. But it's been the privilege of a lifetime to work with such brave individuals. So many of you took the risks. When we were tired, you stayed by our side. When we failed, you came through. Some of you can't be named here, but you know who you are. Keep the faith.

# ACKNOWLEDGEMENTS

I usually start with funding, but this was an unusual investigation that took on a group identity over time. Conor and Bavi described their experiences in identical terms: *The scariest/most exciting thing I've ever done*. Even the consistently cool-headed James reported getting "a nice rush from the adrenaline." In the field, Josephine was brave—only experiencing some blowback, usually a sort of blankness, like the aftermath of a vivid hallucination, when we were safe. It helped that we were not operating alone. We had a second fixer/translator in Kazakhstan and a similar arrangement in Tajikistan. We merged multiple teams—call it *crowd-camouflage*—in the Turdakun family rescue from Kyrgyzstan.

The home team always had infinitely more to lose. Some, like Bekzat Maksutkhan, and other activists of Atajurt, are suffering through detention, threats to their family, and facing 10-year prison sentences while I write this. Others, like Serikzhan Bilash, face a life of permanent exile. All are guilty of a wide-ranging struggle to build a better, more independent, Kazakhstan.

Those who worked directly with us in Tajikistan, Uzbekistan, Turkey, and Kyrgyzstan did not, to my knowledge, receive serious consequences, from our involvement. That's a good thing, yet I find it frustrating that I can't speak about individual contributions. Even the simplest activities—driving across a fenceline, handling a checkpoint, boarding an airplane, confinement in crowded conditions, or simply talking a witness into testifying—involved some level of risk. One family—they will recognize themselves in the next statement—selflessly upended their lives for months for the freedom of another. All of them share in the successes, and they were mostly successes, and all of them took chances that I could not compensate them for. Not even close.

We were not operating in China, merely in the authoritarian states of Central Asia. Yet shortly after we left, the Kazakh police used Covid as pretext for a general political crackdown, and some of our witnesses—we don't know exactly which ones—were apparently deported back to China. I don't believe that our interviews were to blame, yet it troubles me that my voice recordings may be their last testament. And consider what we don't know, even now. In the period where Bavi was being interrogated by the Kazakh police, I was quietly mocked in DC for trying to get a member of our team out of harm's way. Yet my main concern was that I wasn't even sure that Signal.org, my lifeline to Bavi, was still secure in Kazakhstan. When I brought the issue up with my intelligence guru at the time, Rory Byrne, the CEO of Security First, said *if Signal was corrupted it would be on the front page of the* Financial Times. Or would it? To this day no single individual in US or UK intelligence can tell me if using Signal in the Kazakh desert is like lighting a flare in the night sky. Of course, I knew that if I was arrested by the Kazakh, Kyrgyz, or Tajik police, a single cigarette burn on my arm—the pain would fade in a couple days—could be my meal ticket for DC dinner parties for years to come. But Josephine, as an attractive young woman, was a target. Bavi, a Uyghur by birth, could have been subject to extreme torture. Even after Bavi's relatively mild meeting with Kazakh authorities, he was threatened with induction into the military. That group hug on the morning Josephine and I left Bavi and Almaty behind contained an unspoken pledge that there would be no neglect or betrayal. One year ago, the three of us fulfilled that pledge with a new embrace, this time in an Albany, NY bus station.

My motto throughout this investigation was *share the risk*, and there is one person (two if one incudes Brian Wu) who did that for me in Taiwan. My literary agent and publisher, Maryann Karinch represented me in Taipei, where the three of us stood on stage in a press conference that might easily have gone south. I'm profoundly grateful to Maryann for sharing the risk in Taipei, attending my speech to the surgeons of the International Society for Heart and Lung Transplantation, and gently nudging me to finish this book.

I'll touch on failure. I've gone through my version of the rules: pick the right entrance, the right cover story, and maintain discipline without being showy about it. I've also discussed an unnecessary risk, taking evidence across the border, and I want to thank Rory Byrne, and the folks at Tresorit.com for teaching me a better method. But as an amateur, I overlooked the most obvious rule of all: don't ever assume you can use the same method twice. Don't use *the same team* twice. *Build your cover, then discard it.* Of course I liked our team. Of course I didn't want to start over. Tajikistan, just isolated enough from Kazakhstan, seemed to confirm that I didn't have to. While I was home, I published just enough results to convince myself that I had not betrayed the cause or witness security, results that I presented in two Congressional hearings and caught the attention of the Kazakh authorities. To have the maximum policy impact, I needed to hit print on the Kazakh interviews, although I still hoped that I could somehow return to Kazakhstan and gather more data. Or perhaps my underlying urge was just to drive down another road on the dark side of the moon.

Every year, a new tour: Kazakhstan, then Tajikistan, then the Turdakun family rescue, then a plan to go to Pakistan, just one more bet at the table. At the end of the day, I'd be too tired for my teeth to grind. As the plan solidified, I asked intelligence sources for their thoughts on Pakistan and was told: *You will die there.* In lieu of an unmarked grave, old friends in Taiwan raised just enough funding for me to return to Taipei for half a year. It turned out that everyone had moved on from the Ko controversy. So Taipei, formerly full of intrigue, became a pleasant city to get precision dental work done at a discount price, and to start writing again.

I'm grateful to my friends in Taiwan, particularly Brian Wu and his employees, for putting up with me and my wife while I was coming down off my Central Asian high. I also want to thank Abraham Armstrong, formerly of Victims of Communism Memorial Foundation (VOC), for looking over my shoulder on an early draft of the forced labor chapter. He wisely suggested that I stop documenting everything, and get back to what I was good at, telling a story.

I've already mentioned the intellectual contributions of three individuals who played a major role in getting the investigation going: Leeshai Lemish, Enver Tohti, and Rahima Mahmut. Several individuals also contributed to this book at certain critical moments, among them, my colleagues at VOC: Adrian Zenz, Matthew Robertson, Serkan Tas, and Ashlee Davis. For early support of the investigation, Kristina Olney and Dr. Murray Bessette of the Remembrance Society, and Cheryl Yu in Taiwan. From the China Tribunal, Sir Geoffrey Nice, attorney Hamid Sabi, and Professor Arthur Waldron. From the International Coalition to End Transplant Abuse in China (ETAC), my friend and colleague David Matas, Director Susie Hughes, Louisa Greve in DC, Benedict Rogers in London, Becky James in Bristol, Dr. Wendy Rogers and Prof. Maria Fiatarone Singh in Australia, Yukari Werrell in

Japan, Margo MacVicar in New Zealand, and Attorney Clive Ansley in Canada, who represented me in the Mayor Ko case and others. From Doctors Against Forced Organ Harvesting, Dr. Adnan Sharif on ECMO, Gina Sturdza, and Israel's "lion" of medical resistance to Chinese forced organ harvesting, Dr. Jacob Lavee.

Within the Uyghur community a couple of names stand out: Rebiya Kadeer, Dolkun Isa of the World Uyghur Congress, Rushan Abbas of Campaign for Uyghurs, Abdulhakim Idris from the Center for Uyghur Studies, Kaiser ÖzHun, Dr. Maya Mitalipova, Dr. Mamtimin Ala, Dr. Sayragul Sauytbay, and particularly Salih Hudayar of the East Turkistan Government in Exile who, along with Rodney Dixon, conceived the Tajikistan investigation.

In the UK: Benedict Rogers, David Campanale and Matthew Hill. In California: Randolph Quon. In India: Venus Upadhyaya. Everywhere else, there was Anastasia Lin.

In Washington, DC, the organ harvesting investigation has no greater friend than Congressman Christopher Smith, along with Scott Flipse and Piero Tozzi of the Congressional Executive Commission on China (CECC). I'm also grateful to Nina Shea of the Hudson Institute for her efforts to promote the issue in the religious community, Attorney Terri Marsh for her continued support of my research, Toy Reid who promoted my research within the State Department (and a few others whom I can't name, particularly in the intelligence community), and Bob Fu from China Aid, who generously paid for the Turdakun family's flights and the extended expenses necessary to get them out of Istanbul and into a new life in America. Which reminds me that it's time to talk about funding.

The critical "first dollar" came from Peter Recknagel of Recknagel Consulting in Frankfurt and Eastsong Consulting in the US. Peter is a natural leader, an enthusiastic supporter of my research, and he generously provided equipment to my enterprise. The second patron was Jacob Wallenberg of the Peder Wallenberg family. He provided state-of-the-art recording equipment, particularly useful in the European interviews, and a nearly limitless supply of high-quality coffee beans. The third patron was Karl Janjek, the Czech entrepreneur and financial force behind the Czech-language publication of *The Slaughter*, who came up with an early research grant that not only kept the lights on, but paid for my first trip to Turkey with Rahima and the remarkable interviews with Rukiye.

There were two cases where the funding did not yield the expected results.

Heather White, a brilliant investigative film director, was responsible for getting us several grants, including one from a NYC feminist film collective, Women Make Movies (WMM). However, even candid footage of our investigative process in Tajikistan could have created massive problems. Everyone acted in good faith, but we couldn't film the witnesses and the dramatic moments that Heather needed to get things out of the development stage. So the funding became a backstop. I used it to finance a camera for Bavi, which not only served us well in Tajikistan but became a key element in Bavi getting a US green card. The grant also allowed me to print "WMM location scout" name cards for us—very useful at the ubiquitous crossing points in the Pamir mountains and might even have given us a fighting chance at the Chinese border had things gone poorly.

ETAC gave me a modest grant to put out my preliminary results when I returned from Kazakhstan. I wrote the "The Nine-Points Memo" in response, yet I was reluctant to put out details on my Kazakh witnesses while they were being rounded up and deported to China. I'm sorry that the memo didn't work out for ETAC as planned, yet there is no sign of a retraction in China's transplant industry at this time, the conclusions haven't changed, and I hope that the comprehensive accounts in this book will ultimately benefit our shared cause.

A couple of important mentions. On the Hungarian road trips, both Dolkun Isa of the World Uyghur Congress and the Pro Minoritate Foundation generously defrayed extra expenses, granting us the financial freedom to conduct our first background interviews within the Uyghur Diaspora of Germany and Central Europe. My mother-in-law volunteered to pay for gifts for the witness households, an important Central Asian custom. My former associate and beloved friend, the late David Kilgour, kindly gave me a modest no-strings research grant during this period as well. Yet the European research also established that a piecemeal approach wasn't going to cut it. The central problem of this investigation was attracting constant, unwavering financial support.

That presented a problem.

When you strip away the moral gloss, the human rights field basically operates as a media business. Success is measured by counting likes, retweets, and press mentions, in service of awareness of the issue, followed by activism or a policy shift. Permanently solving a human rights problem isn't actually required and ironically may reduce long-term funding. Primary human rights research—fieldwork—adds further complication because it's essentially a gamble. It can't be fully tethered to a policy or an ideological framework. Or a bureaucratic framework, which explains why it's so difficult to operate with state funding. Government research funding is set up to handle business or diplomacy—check into hotel, meet client for dinner, keep receipts—but not field research, which entails buying the services of a barefoot doctor in the Pamir mountains, or black-market burner phones in Georgia, cash only, no trace of the exchange. The US government may not tamper with actual research results, but it can't comfortably authorize research into anything too controversial. Forced labor, yes, mass murder, um, maybe not so much. Field research, like sponsoring a ship to explore the Northwest Passage in the age of exploration, is much less risky for the researcher these days, but, in an age of instant results and expectations, it's murder on the sponsoring organization. There are only a handful of patrons in the world with the long-term vision to support it.

I received my first personal grant from the Earhart Foundation, a small contribution toward my first book, *Losing the New China*, followed by more substantial funding on *The Slaughter* in Earhart's final years.

Not long after Earhart closed (by design), the Sarah Scaife Foundation took an interest in my work. In cooperation with the Victims of Communism Memorial Foundation, where I'm a senior research fellow, Scaife awarded the lion's share of funding for this book, on an annual basis. But it goes a little further than that. The Scaife folks also showed patience, beyond all reasonable expectations at times, not only with the uncertainties of field research, but with my pause in the publication of the results. Perhaps they understood the reasons, perhaps not. But the critical point is that they never tried to influence the results or push my interpretation towards a specific political agenda. Their support for my research was pure and unwavering. This is the ideal model for good fieldwork results, and any failures along the way, and there are many, are my responsibility alone. The bottom line is that the investigations on the ground in Central Asia that form the beating heart of this book were simply impossible without their full support.

Finally, to my wife and my son, who put up with me when I came home crazy from the wars—it never does seem to really get that much easier, does it?—thank you for your sacrifice, and for your editing, but most of all, for your endless humor, and for preserving my place at the hearth.

# ABOUT THE AUTHOR

**Ethan Gutmann,** an award-winning China analyst and human-rights investigator, told the story of Falun Gong organ harvesting with intelligence and heart in his acclaimed book *The Slaughter*. His searing reporting drew death threats—and helped bring down Taipei's mayor, Dr. Ko Wen-Je for complicity in Beijing's organ harvesting operations. As a result of his efforts, he was nominated for the Nobel Peace Prize in 2017. After his success in spotlighting the operations of China's transplant tourism, Gutmann's way forward was clear. Refugees were crossing the Kazakh border, fleeing China in a vivid display of human endurance. But Beijing had changed the rules. Throughout Central Asia, human rights investigators were now considered spies. The Chinese press explicitly identified Gutmann as a new "Cold Warrior." Gutmann mustered a 4×4 with no GPS tracker, his foster daughter, skis, a paper map, and a compass. They drove from Germany to the Kazakh border where they were searched and biometrically photographed. Then, from the standpoint of electronic surveillance, the duo vanished into thin air. The full story is in *The Xinjiang Procedure*. Gutmann's affiliations have included the Victims of Communism Memorial Foundation, the Foundation for Defense of Democracies, the Free Congress Research and Education Foundation, and the Brookings Institution. Gutmann has testified before the U.S. Congress, the European Parliament, and the United Nations.

# INDEX

abortion,
and sterilization, 8-9, 9n1, 21, 35, 259, 407
forced, 259, 407
post-rape, 243, 272
Aksu Triangle
  airport (international), 397-398
  Aksu Infection Hospital, 396
  camp population, 396
  camps, 396
  crematorium, 395, 397
  crematorium security guard salary, 156
  First Hospital Zhejiang, 398
  forced labor, 359
*green lane*, 94, 398
  history (of compound), 396
*smells like scorched bones*, 397
  witness accounts, 396-397
Almaty
Aiman Umarova, 170
Almaty airport (ALA), 163, 346
Atajurt, 283-286, 302
entry, 211-212
  safe house (Almaty flat), 171, 214, 214n192
  US Consulate, 220n204, 294
Ansley, Clive, 74-75
APCO Beijing, 124
Aralsk, 200, 206-208, 217, 298
Atyrau, 202
Bahtiyar Shemshidin, 380
Bavi (Bavdun Umar)
  and ICC, 343-346
and Kazakh police interrogation, 345
  and Madina Bazaar, 344
and US, 340, 346
  as Tajikistan fixer, 314-319, 321-325, 332

  escape to Istanbul, 346
  Kazakh military draft threat, 346
BBC
  and David Campanale, 30n6
  and reportage, 40,
157n166, 229n203
Beijing Anzhen Hospital, 88,
88n68, 90
Belt and Road Initiative, 112, 204, 305,
336, 342, 409-410
Beyneu
  and Christmas cards, 199-200
Bilash, Serikzhan
  and Atajurt, 283-286, 302
  and Bekzat, 284-286, 413
  and Kazakh government, 413
  and witnesses, 229n203, 249-250
  as Uyghur-critic, 285n223
Bishkek ATM, 286
Bishop Sanchez Sorondo,
121, 137, 149
Bloody Harvest/The Slaughter: an Update,
57n30, 127-128, 149, 390
Bo Xilai, 56, 113n111, 386
border crossings and checkpoints
  Commonwealth of Independent States
(CIS), 190, 297
  four standard elements, 179-180
  George and "first impressions"
(Kuryk), 196-198
  Red Bridge, 189-191, 297
  *someone who is on your side*, 183
  Transnistria, 182-184
  truck routes, 176, 186-187, 299
Brooks, David, 131
British Naval Intelligence,
168, 191, 206

Bunin, Gene
    and the Xinjiang Victims Database,
162, 162n172, 163n173
"Buzz,"    194, 292
Caspian Sea Ferry
    Kuryk, 196-198
    Port of Alat, 192-194
"Cat" (and the Yakuza
chieftain), 387
Caucasus Mountains, 187
CECC (Congressional Executive
Commission on China), 117
Chapman, Jeremy, 122-123, 130
Chen Jingyu,
    and Didi Kirsten Tatlow, 133-134
    and Ko Wen-je, 100-101
    Wuxi People's Hospital, 86, 86n62, 94
China-Japan Friendship Hospital
    and Liu Deruo, 85n60
China Tribunal (London)
    China Tribunal Judgement, 52,
58, 144, 393
    Sir Geoffrey Nice, 57, 143
textbook, 57, 57n30, 120, 331
Chinese Communist Party (CCP
or "Party")
    and DNA, 264, 264n215
Cultural Revolution, 6, 353, 382, 407
elusive harvesting strategy, 109n102, 111-
113, 123-127, 148-149
    nuclear weapons testing, 25-27
playbook, 148-149, 487
    racism, 32-35, 363, 366-368
shoveling shit, 353
Camps (Xinjiang)
    associated crematoria, 101, 155-156,
302, 395-397
    construction of camps, 282n221, 367
    dance, 258
    mass executions, 155
    number of detainees, 27-28, 154-155,
281-282, 282n221, 367
    satellite imagery (see Aksu Triangle)
    surveillance 140-141, 156, 247, 367
    this is for the future, 352
    toilets, ratio to prisoners, 256
    Western reporters, 156

Chao Deng (Wall Street
Journal), 406
Chinese Human Rights
Defenders
    and Sophie Richardson, 142
Chinese forced organ harvesting
    basic evidence, 52, 57-62
    basic facts, 52-54
    basic timeline, 52, 55-56, 376-400
    CCP, 60, 108-113, 123-127, 405
    eBay gold rush, 63, 126
    Falun Gong vulnerability, 59-61, 73
    halal organs, 121, 121n126
    human stable, 58-59, 62, 73
    killed-to-order, 125-126, 311
    mass medical testing, 9, 56, 139-142,
141n142, 145, 234, 241, 405
    organ tourism, 51, 53, 53n17, 54, 56,
60, 85n60, 97, 98-99, 125, 130, 133
    prisoner organs (death row), 54-56, 58,
86n62, 108, 108n101, 118-119, 126, 388
    running out of Falun Gong, 108-109,
109n102, 405
    suicides (Chinese surgeons), 127
    the chest was empty, 249, 378
    transplant industry, 51-52, 59, 62, 68,
97, 107-109, 114, 118, 124-131, 138
    transplant prices, 53, 53n17, 53n18,
96-97, 383
    transplant reform, 108, 118-127, 131,
136-145, 388-391, 400-401
    transplant volume, 54, 59n38, 83, 92n81,
104, 108, 127-129, 149, 150n149,
282n221, 390-391
    voluntary donations, 53-54, 53n14,
108, 120-121, 126-134, 144-145, 390-391
CIA
    and Ko Wen-je, 64, 66, 70, 101-
102, 102n90
Color coding (harvesting
selection)
    red mark, 224-225
    bracelets, 227-228
Congress, US
    foreign affairs hearing, 118-121,
129-131, 134, 399-400
Control Yuan (Taiwan), 51n11, 98-99,
99n86, 101

Covid-19
  border troubles, 341
  coronavirus (origins, early days), 117, 122, 125, 125n125, 145, 410
  First Hospital double-lung transplant, 398
  *vaccine passport*, 313
  Chinese switch from ECMO to ventilators, 103, 103n94
  Urumqi fire, 371
  *we could get stuck*, 288-289, 289n224
cross-matching
  blood-sample-plus-cheek-swab, 107
Dalai Lama, 110n105, 113
de Haan-Montez, Josephine
  border crossings, 180-184, 188-190, 196-198, 295-297
  *cat-like satisfaction*, 227
  meaning of "28," 218-219
  PTSD, 207-210
Dead Donor rule, 49
Denyer, Simon, 161n170
Delmonico, Francis
  "the hot seat," 129-130
  and Huang Jiefu, 114-119, 126-146, 149, 388
  and Li Ka-shing, 130-131, 130n129
  and young Chinese transplant surgeons, 120
  Chinese hospitals verification, 130
  Foreign Affairs hearing, 128-131
  open letter, 118
Dixon KC, Rodney
  Adrian Zenz, 312
  Bavi "rescue," 345-346
  delay of publication, 343-344
  ICC, 301-303, 310-311
Doctors Against Forced Organ Harvesting (DAFOH), 89, 153
DNA
  cheek swabs, 106-107, 263-264
  Human Rights Watch, 139-142
  kits (see Thermo Fisher), 140, 140n140, 410
  surveillance, 141n142, 264n215
  testing/tissue typing, 56-59, 73, 97, 101, 106-109, 107n100, 140, 218-220, 263-265, 393-401, 410

Dushanbe
  presidential palace, 403
East Turkistan
  as independent state, 221n197, 403-411
  traditional name, (author's note)
  "East Turkestan" versus "Xinjiang," (Author's note)
ECMO
  and Covid (double lung transplant), 398
  and pediatric diseases, 89n73, 90
  Chen Jingyu, 86n62, 104, 100-101, 133-134,
  clinical application (harvesting), 9, 49-51, 51n11, 82-94
  *First Medtronic ECMO Training Course*, 82-94
  Hemovent, 103-104
  Jiangsu Saiteng Medical Technology, 103-104
  Medtronic, 50-51, 82-94
  MicroPort, 104
  mobile ECMO, 103-104
  organ viability timeframe, 50
  profitability, 53, 94, 97, 136-137, 148-149, 228
Epoch Times, 128, 138
Erdogan, Tayyip
  Sinovac/Uyghur deportation deal, 304-305
execution
  and live harvesting, 53, 61, 85n61, 93, 98, 113-114, 151, 316, 391-392
  bruises, 47, 271-272
  meals, 29
Falun Gong
  and China Tribunal (London), 144-147
  and Dr. Charles Lee, 107n100, 128, 218-219, 218n195
  and Theresa Chu, 72-77
  and trauma, 16
  and US Congress, 117, 410
  *final solution*, 107, 108-109, 109n102
  gang-rape, 34-35
  harvested (live), 53, 61, 85n61, 93, 98, 113-114, 151, 316, 391-392
  harvested (numbers), 59

in Laogai, 56, 109, 282n221
in Taiwan, 72-75
in Xinjiang camps, 251-252, 261-262
Minghui, 105-106
Shen Yun, 144
*tragedy*, 407
vulnerability, 59-61, 73
*water torture*, 37-38
WOIPFG, 83, 107n100, 218n195, 228,
Faraday (STALIN anti-spying
bag), 169-170, 170n179, 174, 196,
214, 214n192
Fraser, Campbell, 122-123
Fujian Medical University Union
Hospital
    and Dr. Chen Liangwen, 87, 87n65
Fuwai Hospital
    and Dr. Song Yunhu, 86, 86n63
Gao, Simone, 106n99
"Gazi," 318, 321, 324
Ghulja massacre, 5, 55, 111, 114, 249, 356,
368, 379-380
Gibson, Jaya, 105n97
Great *Kurultaj*, 158-159
Guangzhou Medical University First
Affiliated Hospital
    and Dr. He Jianxing, 91, 91n79
Gulbahar Jelilova
    camp, 3, 226-228
China Tribunal (London), 187n200
color coding, 226-228
    interrogation/Sexual
humiliation, 33-34
    rape, 227
selection (for organ harvesting), 226-228
Uyghur Tribunal (London), 227
Gutmann, David, 375
hacking, Chinese, 174, 215n194
hacking, Falun Gong, 106, 218
Harbin Medical University
Second Hospital
    and Dr. Han Zhen, 92, 92n80
Harvard University, 146
*hasha* (forced labor)
    "Abraham's family" 367-368
    "Ali" and *12 years of slavery*, 368-370
    "Graduation Girl" (Beijing factory
labor), 362-366

"I shoveled shit for the Party," 353
"River boy" and the wild Muzat, 357-368
    "Yasin" (flowchart), 355, 356-357
    and Abdurehim Parach, 354, 356
    and Meryem Sultan (child
labor), 358-361
    and Rabiya (Tianjin factory
labor), 361-365
    Batur's agricultural survey of stolen
land, 366
    Yusef and the *bingtuan*, 366-367
Hebei Medical University Second Hospital
    and VP Liu Su, 89, 89n73
Hinde, Raymond, 144, 390
Hoja, Gulchehra
    Aksu, 395-398
    Bavi, 170-171
    Radio Free Asia, 139, 170
House Church Christians
    Bob Fu, 109-110, 229n204, 348-350
    Eastern Lightning harvesting, 109-110
    vulnerability, 109-110
Human Rights Watch
    report on "health checks," 139-142
    Sophie Richardson, 139-142
    surveillance (vs. harvesting), 139-142,
141n142, 234, 405
Huang Jiefu
    and Dr. Francis Delmonico, 114-119,
126-146, 149, 388
    and Li Ka-shing, 130-131, 130n129
    and Pope Francis, 138
    *look at the* future, 119
    semantic tricks, 120-121, 398
    Vatican, 105-107, 125n125, 137-138
Ibrahim, Kuresh, 303-317
International Criminal
Court (ICC)
    and Rodney Dixon, 301-303, 310-311
    Nuremberg Trials, 302
    *The ICC would do nothing*, 345
International Coalition to End Transplant
Abuse in China (ETAC)
    China Tribunal (London), 143
    Ko Wen-je, 79
    Susie Hughes, 141n143
International Society of Heart & Lung
Transplantation (ISHLT)

2023 Annual conference in
Denver, 373-374
 ISHLT "academic boycott" of
China, 374, 401
 keynote address, 375-402
Investigative principles
 do no harm, 163, 163n175
 free from intentional lies or
propaganda, 213, 279
 share the risk, 323
Investigative tools
 *a proper joyride*, 165
 Airbnb versus hotels, 175
 an American citizen, 323
 burner phones, 168, 199, 205,
217, 286, 313
 cash, 169
 Dictaphone, 169, 215n194, 295
 false Facebook posts, 174
 film (black and white), 169
 intelligence, 103n93, 168, 191, 206-
207, 286, 377, 414
leave no trace, 163n175
 maps, 169, 182, 186-187
 populate the data sticks, 291
 Reflectacles, 170, 170n179,
197, 286, 291
 Rory Byrne, Security First, 312
 skis, 169, 172, 180-81
 Snow Leopard, 169, 184, 197-198
 Stalinbags, 169-170, 170n179, 174,
196, 214, 214n192
 the "wrong" Kazakh border, 164
 Tresorit.com, 312
 untraceable vehicle (pre-2005), 172
 wetransfer.com slowdown, 290
Investigative goals
 a sense of scale (numeric), 150n149
 witness safety, 215n194
Ireland, 407
Ishmaelites, 410
Islam, 10, 313, 408
*Islamophobia*, 4, 32, 34, 111, 368
Israel, 119, 133-134, 345, 388,
405-407
Japanese organ tourists,
60n39, 85n60

Jiangsu Province
People's Hospital
 and Dr. Wang Ping
(suspected), 90, 90n76
 and Dr. Zhang Shijiang, 90, 90n75
Jiangsu Saiteng Medical Technology
Company, 103-104
Kandyagash, 204-205
Kyrgyzstan
 Axman/Teaman estimate of the
Kyrgyz bazaars, 342
 deportation rate in Kyrgyzstan (87%)
and Tajikistan (88%), 342
 Madina Bazaar, 342-344
 *What happened to the Uyghurs*, 325-330
Kao, Bob, 76
Kazakh security
 and Russia's Foreign Intelligence
Service (SVR), 291
 Atajurt, 284-285
bribe (fine), 210-211, 293-295
 DHL incident, 290
 interrogation, 345
 Taraz (cop city), 211, 293
Khujand, 306, 327-334
Kilgour, David, 106,
114-118, 302
Ko Wen-je
 "4th National Cardiopulmonary
Transplantation," 83
 "accused the DPP," 99n87
 "has no case," 99n86
 "Ke Wenzhe," 89, 89n72
 "something should be done," 66
 "unification with the motherland!" 101
 interview account from The
Slaughter, 62-70
 and campaign contributions, 102
 and Dr. Chen Jingyu, 86n62,
94, 100-101
 and Dr. Vincent Sue (Su Ih-jen, Dr.
Sue), 51n11, 98
 and Falun Gong, 72-77
 and real estate, 102
 and Theresa Chu, 72-77
 and Tung Wen-Hsun, 71
 ankle monitor, 102
 Bob Kao, 76

Brian Wu (Wu Hsiang-hui), 77-81, 94-95
  bringing, teaching ECMO to China, 101
  campaign manager, 67-68, 81-82
  CIA, 67-68
  Clive Ansley, 74-5
  Concentric Patriotism Association, 72, 77
  Control Yuan, 51n11, 98-99, 99n86, 101
  criminal charges, defamation (Gutmann), 99, 99n86
  denial of interview, 72
  ECMO, 9, 49-51, 51n11, 82-94
  emails, 68-70, 74, 76, 81
  Huang Shiwei, 74
  indicted, 102
  Jing Tian, 97
  karaoke, 71
  Ko's army, 80-81, 98
  legacy, 103-104
  Liberty Times, 80
  Maryann Karinch, 80, 94-95
  media self-censorship, 99
medical license, 102
  Medtronic, 50-51, 82-94
  organ broker, 71, 75
  press conference, 94-99
  Taipei Times, 100
  visits to Mainland, 101
  Wuxi People's Hospital, 86, 86n62, 94
Kyzylorda, 208-209
Lemish, Leeshai
  Ko interview, 62-70
  Minghui, 105-106
"Leo"
  2017: "drastic reduction" of Uyghurs, 330-332
  Chinese road crew incident, 333
Chkalov City SWAT team headquarters, 332
  deportation centers, 332
  direct flight from Khujand to Urumqi, 333
  Kommittee for National Security or KMV, 333

Tajik ICE, responsible for customs and enforcement, 333
  Tajik police raids, 331
Uyghur origin of Khujand bazaar, 331
London
  leaving, 169
  welcome back party, 299-300
Lavee, Jacob
  and Didi Kirsten Tatlow, 133-134
  and ISHLT/TTS, 62, 119, 310, 373, 388
  and Matthew Robertson, 144-145, 147, 390-391, 402
  Israeli HMO China ban, 112, 388, 417
  Theresienstadt, 388
Mahmut, Rahima, 2-4, 13-18, 20, 27, 33-47, 40n10
Makat, 200-202
"Mansur," 317-319
Matas, David, 114-118, 124, 128, 130, 134, 136, 143, 382
Meng Xu (Beijing Heart Transplant Center), 87n66, 87-89
Minghui
  cheek swabs, 115-116
  Muslim hard line, 409
Nanjing First Hospital
  and Dr. Chen Xin, 89n69
"Nazur," 327-328
New York Times
  Didi Kirsten Tatlow, 131-139, 144
  Metro Desk (Shen Yun hit piece), 144
"Nijat," 379
nomadic brotherhood
  code of honor, 186
  Silk Road, 112, 158-159
numbers chapter (interviews)
  1 "Fatimah," 212-221
  2 Sayragul, 221-226
  3 Gulbahar, 226-228
  4 Tursunay, 228-233
  5 Baqytali, 233-235
  6 "Mujahit," 235-236
  7 "Arman," 236-238
  8 Omer, 238-240
  9 "Milqa," 240-245
  10 "The Teacher," 245-246

11 "Ear Man," 246-247

12 Tursynbek, 247-250

13 "Aisha," 251-253

14 Rahima, 253-255

15 Nurlan, 255-257

16 Gulzira, 258-260

17 "Bright Morning," 260-262

18 Ovalbek (Joseph), 262-263

19 "Mina," 263-268

20 "Samal," 268-276

charts, 279-280

Muslim burial, 248-250, 261, 276-277

new medical sites in

Xinjiang, 282n221

    summary (Chapter 5), 281-282

    underground clinics, 268-276

    zone of probability, 280

O' Connell, Phillip, 136

Parks, Rosa, 152

Pidgeon, Mark

    *Over the hills and far away*,

177-178, 293

President Orban, Viktor, 159

Pharmaceuticals (Chinese)

    and Covid, 125n125

    and Transplant industry, 93, 124-127

    confidence in, 124-127

    pillar industry, 124

People's Liberation Army (PLA) , 51

PLA 309 military hospital, 129

Press Conference (Taipei)

    and bodyguards, 94

    and Brian Wu, 95, 97-98

    and Jing Tian, 96-97

    and Maryann Karinch, 94-95

    before and after ECMO, 97

PTSD, 208-210, 236, 303, 341

Public Security Bureau (PSB)

book purchase, 113

Putin, Vladimir, 405

Qurgonteppa, 306, 310, 323-330

Quon, Randolph, 130n129

"Ranger," 170-171, 211-

212, 283-292

"reader-first" policy,

    "East Turkestan" versus "Xinjiang,"

(Author's note)

"Western," (Author's note)

Reflectacles, 170, 170n179, 197, 286, 291

Recknagel, Peter, 172-173, 204

Redfield, Robert, 385

Reid, Toy, 117

Robertson, Matthew, 128, 141n143, 144-

147, 390-391, 402

"Rukiye" (Perhat, Rukiye)

    "Amina," 38-39, 40n10

    "Shaheed," 40, 47

    "Water prison," 37-38

    aunt, 38-39, 40n10

    childhood, 1-2, 3-9

    children, 10-13

    condoms, 44-45

    dream, 25-26

    electric shock, 16, 23-24, 28, 31, 35,

36, 44, 47

    familicide, 9, 22, 24-25

    father, 4-9, 26, 43

    fingernail/toenail extraction, 16,

22-23, 28, 35

    gang rape, 20, 30-31, 30n6, 35-36, 42-47

    grandparent familicide, 5-6

    Hadachan (and Imam), 12-13

    homosexual rape, 20, 31, 33, 35, 44

    *Iron Lady*, 18, 40

    interrogation/resistance, 5, 7, 16-20, 28-31,

35-36, 40-41

    kidney extraction, 7-9

    medical testing, 7-9

    mother, 8-9, 22

    *mother's milk*, 17

    nationalism/separatism, 5-7, 9-10, 47

    nuclear testing, 26-27

pedicide, 12-14, 16

pornographic display, 20-21, 35-36

Rahima Mahmut, 2-4, 13-18, 20, 27,

33-47, 40n10

rape room, 20-21, 23, 27-31, 42-45

    sexual femicide, 35-36, 45-47

timeline difficulties, 11-12, 15,

21, 33, 40n10

    underage rape, 20, 29, 31, 40

Urumqi, 4-5, 11

*yalmavus*, 2, 3, 14

Russia

"Transnistria," 182-184
and Kazakh surveillance, 168, 291
and Tajikistan/Central Asia, 309-310, 409-10
border crossings 176, 182-184, 289-291, 295-297
*Shanghai Six*, 403
Second Xiangya Hospital
    and Dr. Yin Bangliang, 90, 90n74
Shandong Provincial Hospital
    and Dr. Meng Long, 91, 91n78
    and Dr. Zhang Lin, 89, 89n70
"Shanghai Six," 403, 409
Shenyang Military Command General Hospital
    and Dr. Wang Huishan, 89, 89n71
Shenyang Prison City, 222, 382
Slaughter, The
    Clive Ansley, 74-75
    Ko demands for rewrite, 74-77, 74n47
    PSB purchase, 113
Taiwan edition, 77-78
Smith, Chris (Congressman)
    "Resolution 343," 57, 143, 400
    Stop Organ Harvesting Act, 143, 377, 400-401
"Southern Man"
    Chinese Consulate control of Uyghurs, 307, 328-330
    estimate of Uyghurs in the Tajik bazaars, 325-327
Soviet Union, 207, 296
sterilization, forced
    and Adrian Zenz, 10n1, 262
    Rukiye's mother, 8-9
    Carceral sterilization, 21, 35, 259, 407
Stram, James
    *4x4 ROADTRIP*, 335-340
James on a Bike, 193
    Kazakhstan, 242-244, 193-199, 289-292
    *two-lane Mad Max* (Route E60), 193, 191-192
    volunteer (Tajikistan), 241n224, 278, 284

Sun Yat-sen Memorial hospital, 379
Taraz, 211, 293
Taiwan
    legal system, 100, 62n41
    mayor's race, 71
    media, 67n43, 72, 75-76, 99
    Ministry of Health, 98-99
organ tourists, 51, 98-99
    social media, 80-81, 100-101
Tajikistan
    Abdurishit, 311-320
and Serikzhan Bilash, 302
    Chinese Communist Party designs, 310, 328-333, 341, 409
    Chinese military base (new), 338-341
delay in Times and NYTs story, 343-344
    ICC postmortem, 344-346
    Kulma Pass, 335-337
    Murghab, 309, 334-5, 340
    Pamir Mountains, 306, 309-343
    Signatory (ICC), 301
within the core Central Asian States, 301n228
Tajik Bazaars
    Khujand, 306, 326-33
    Korvan (Dushanbe), 306, 311-319
    Qurgonteppa, 306, 310, 323-330
Tajik/Chinese border
    Chinese military base (new), 338-341
    Kulma Pass, 335-337
    World's largest uranium deposit, 351
Tatlow, Didi Kirsten
    "not deductive, but inductive," 145
    "organ wastage," 132
    and Dr. Chen Jingyu, 133-134
    and Dr. Jacob Lavee, 133-134
and Dr. Phillip O'Connell, 136
    editors, 134-135, 138
    *Tatlow Effect*, 138
TTS (see also Delmonico, Francis)
    "trust and verify," 140
    China junkets/verification tours, 121-123
    Jeremy Chapman, 122
    reputation, 120
    "The Colonel," 319-321, 343

Theresa Chu, 72-77

Thermo Fisher, 140,
140n140, 410-411

Threema, 171, 317-319

Tianjin First Central Hospital (Oriental
Organ Transplant Center)
    and Matthew Robertson, 60,
92n81, 129

Tiananmen Square,
161, 161n169

Tibetans
    carceral and surveillance
infrastructure, 110, 174
Dalai Lama, 110n105, 113
    harvesting, 56, 60, 97, 110,
376, 385, 388
    Lhasa, 93, 110

Tohti, Enver
    "a fully programmed robot," 152
    and "British intelligence
agent," 153-154
    Chinese nuclear testing, 26
Christian Uyghur advocacy, 154, 159
EU Parliament, 152
    investigative research, 26, 52, 61, 153,
163, 163n174, 379
Irish Parliament, 152
psyche, 153
    road trips, 154-170
    Westminster, 79, 151

Treasure, Tom
    and Wellcome Trust, 114-116

Trump, Donald, 409

TPP (Taiwan People's
Party), 51, 102

Turdakun, Ovalbek (and
family) rescue
    "This is for the future," 352
    and Bob Fu, 348-350
and Conor Healy, 348-349
Julie's thoughts, 349-350
    miracles #1, #2, #3, and #4, 347-352
    permanence of camp structure, 352
    the memory that haunts, 351

Tusvanyos, 159, 159n168

Ukraine    , 156, 176, 182-188,
346, 405-409

Umarova, Aiman, 170, 229, 287

US State Department, 71, 163n173, 304,
309, 343, 346, 394, 405-406

Uyghurs
    activists, 55, 213, 404,
    and East Turkistan, (Author's note), 3,
111n106, 221n197, 158, 370, 404-410
    and Rebiya Kadeer, 111
    and Washington consensus, 404
    as tapestry, 409
    camp refugees, 30n6, 32, 149, 156,
161-162, 368, 406
    Chinese public, 111
    deferred genocide, 302
    Han Chinese machismo, 111-112
    Party view (internal), 111-113
    pronunciation, 110-111, 111n106,
    Uyghurs who remained in
Tajikistan, 332

Uzbekistan (Kokand), 341

Victims of Communism Memorial
Foundation, 141n143, 302,
316, 400

Vincent Sue (Su Ih-jen),
51n11, 98

Wang Lijun, 113n111, 386

Weekly Standard, 404

Wiesel, Elie, 152

WOIPFG
    "28" versus "29," 218, 218n195, 219
    and Dr. Charles Lee, 107n100, 128

Wu, Harry, 114

Wuhan Tongji Hospital
    and Dr. Chen Zhonghua, 85, 85n61

Wuxi People's Hospital,
    "one lung transplant every three
days," 86n62
    2008 Conference, 82, 85-86, 85n59,
88, 91-93, 112
    and Dr. Chen Jingyu, 86n62,
88, 94, 133

Xinjiang (select terms)
    "Autonomous Region Health
Commission," 405
    bingtuan, 112
    pronunciation, 111n106
    secret laboratory, 113

valuation, 112-113
Zenz, Adrian, 9n1, 302, 315-316
Zhejiang Children's Hospital
    and Dr. Lin Ru, 89n73
      ECMO, pediatric diseases, 89n73, 90
Zhongshan Hospital (Shanghai)
and Dr. Wang Chunsheng, 98, 98n67
and volume, 86n63, 139
Zhongshan People's Hospital (People's
Hospital of Zhongshan City)
    and extractions, 101, 101n77

www.ingramcontent.com/pod-product-compliance
Lightning Source LLC
Chambersburg PA
CBHW020450270326
41926CB00008B/556